The Lost Secret of Speaking Perfect English

The Moving Mouth Dictionary

Peter F. Bulmer

Strategic Book Publishing and Rights Co.

Strategic Book Publishing and Rights Co.
12620 FM 1960, Suite A4-507
Houston, TX 77065
www.sbpra.com

ISBN: 978-1-60976-003-8

Design: Dedicated Book Services (www.netdbs.com)

Dedication

A book based on creating a new aid and approach to speaking and understanding the English language, written by a mother tongue speaker who was born and bred in England, has to be dedicated to one's parents and to one's family, which of course one gladly does. Though, in my case, one should also go at least one paw further and include a dedication to Tara, a beautiful, black Labrador with big, white, and expressive pointing eyes who took me by the hand and introduced me to the world of animals.

I remain convinced that Labradors would make the best English teachers if they could speak English, and it may well be that they do—only we just do not know it yet. They are already the best communicators in any language with their universal sensory awareness. They certainly licked my jowls and vowels into shape with their howling and growling.

I would also like to dedicate this book to all teachers of any subject who are trying to make the world a better place for children, and have not lost sight of the fact that children will spend a much greater portion of their lives living as adults than as children. This is where they are potentially at far greater risk from more damage in the future. Though we should seek to protect children, we should not put them in cotton wool. This will not prepare them for the world, and we should not use their childhood experiences as an excuse and a down payment to take away their rights when they grow into adults.

Acknowledgements

These must go to all the Italian students and business people who have inspired me with their enthusiasm for wanting to speak English very well, something Italians are most ideally suited to do. I would also like to recognise the language schools that have allowed me a lot of flexibly with my teaching methods.

Of the companies and business schools, I would like to mention Eni and Chemic in Rome, and in Milan, the Bocconi Business School, Uni Credit, and the many wonderful people I have met at BNP and at Marsh Insurance. In addition, my thanks go to consulting companies like Accenture and particularly The Boston Consulting Group, Teleroute, Wings Jet Air Sarl, and Square Post Productions in Milan, Italy.

Of the language schools, I would like to thank the Derby School in Rome and Berlitz in Milan, Paola Forni and her team, and particularly the I.L.S. International Language School (via Disciplini) in Milan, Nicoletta Basile, Peter Luntz, and their very supportive team.

A special mention must go to Guido Guidi, who has been a good friend throughout the development of this dictionary. I am appreciative of his family's passion for aviation and his dedication to learning and speaking English well, which has been an inspiration to me. Margherita Iallonardo has been an exceptional friend who has also prodded me to continue with what has been a very challenging but interesting and absorbing project. Marilena Agentiero's enquiring mind has raised many questions, and her brilliance with Excel has saved me a lot of time in quantifying mouth movement patterns and helped me tidy up this dictionary for publishing. I could not have done this without her help.

I would also like to acknowledge the many students who suspended their disbelief and kept an open mind, which is so important in learning and teaching English, because every student is different. In doing so, I owe them a great debt, not because of what I taught them but for what I have learned from them.

Many students have inspired me by their opened minded enthusiasm. Those mentioned below are just a few I would like to acknowledge, as they represent the many who have inspired me more than they can know. I apologise for not mentioning every single one!

Lorenzo Barbagli	Paola Rotteli	Laura Bergamaschi
Emanuele Greco	Marco Stucchi	Cristian Jezdic
Giuliana Carbone	Giulio Leporatti	Giuseppe Todisco
Corrado Ceri	Marco Locatello	Alexandra Cerulla
Francesco Malvezzi	Marco Valentino	Franzosi Claudia
Domenico Martelli	Generoso Cogliano	Gabriele Monzini
Andrea Villa	Antonella Fanuzzi	Alberto Mendolia
Emanuele Patrini	Alberto Meloni	Giuseppe Seller

Table of Contents

Preface

Originally, the main purpose of the dictionary was to use it as a tool to help my Italian students speak English, but it also improved my own knowledge of English. Having checked over 11,000 words ten times, I cannot help but learn something. This has certainly given me the opportunity to fumble around within the mechanics of the language with a torchlight so to speak, which has allowed me to improve my English teaching methods.

There is very little material available to give students a technique for mastering the physical mechanics of speaking English. Without one, teaching and learning English can sometimes seem an inadequate and almost surreal activity for teachers and students.

One should not have to be a Buddhist to learn English, though one can be forgiven for thinking that it might well help. Among many students there is an awful, resigned, sinking feeling that all the work they are doing is not for this lifetime, and that hopefully they will come back speaking English in the next life. That seems to be all that keeps them going, particularly those who have reached an invisible learning ceiling, and who do not see how they can climb through that ceiling.

From these equal amounts of hope and despair came the idea of using the concept of howling and growling. The premise that English is a howling and growling language goes back to the very roots of the language. It is not a new idea that the English language is full of onomatopoeia, moving mouth movements and patterns, and repeating sounds and consistent rhythms that are closely related to animalistic howling and growling behaviour.

These mysterious and comforting sounds, rhythms, and movements exist in many English nursery rhymes. This has long been apparent to those who are fascinated by the English language. However, this is perhaps one of the few occasions in recent times where these powerful and primitive sounds and movements have been adapted and quantified as the basis for a more precise notation to help people speak English clearly and well. This seems to be overdue but a natural and inevitable development to help students break through that ceiling.

Many people could be forgiven for thinking that good pronunciation and clear speaking are something that they should perfect only after they have spent a lifetime learning English, but this mentality is rather like the final reward or the final treat of dessert after the main meal of spaghetti mixed with alphabet grammar. On the contrary, speaking English clearly should be at the very heart of learning English, and the result of learning English in a properly structured way right from the beginning. There is an added benefit of speeding up that learning and retention process.

The English rhythm combined with using vertical mouth movements is a very important part of that process. Rhythm is closely connected with English grammar. Rhythm may well be the mother of the English language, and grammar may well be described as her child and invention. Using horizontal mouth movements in lieu of vertical ones can seriously cut corners on rhythm, and can therefore restrict breathing, which can then alter rhythm. This can lead to the inability to breathe, which can also then affect grammar and reduce the ability to autocorrect. This leads to the slow strangulation of the flow of words, followed no doubt by a coma and then perhaps by the painful and often embarrassing sudden death of one's English!

Vertical mouth movements are therefore essential for speaking English well. Luckily, these are not so difficult to identify if one has an enquiring mind and, just as important, if some help is at hand.

Once we identified the main simplified vertical mouth movements, it was easy to be sceptical that they would apply to all of the permutations of different words, but it has been surprising to learn how versatile these notations are and how generic and inherent they are to the English language.

Even some of the notations themselves, particularly **GAR** and *HOO,* run happily through many English words as a combination of letters, such as *garb, garbage, garbled, garden, gargantuan,* or *hood, hoot,* or *hooray.* These are just at the beginning of many English words; there are many running through the middle, such as *regarding*, and at the end, like *sugar*!

The mirror effect of these mouth movements and the sequential symmetry that combines both the emotional meaning and the sound of a word can often be changed simply by putting them in either the forward or the reverse position. For example, ironically, in the sport rowing, rowing is a forward mouth position, but when diametrically reversed, the whole meaning is changed where this is then more about sticking one's oar in, as with rowing in an argument or quarrel, as many couples like to do! Take note of the effect, for example, of the jaw dropping in these movements, which emphasises certain individual letters. This is literally a jaw dropping and stunning event and phenomena, particularly the way it reduces stress on certain letters and increases it on others. This gives these movements a surprising amount of extraordinary precision, fluidity, and clarity that was not apparent at first, and it will be a great surprise to many students learning English that this is even possible.

Originally, I thought that phonetics would not play a role in this dictionary. In fact, I thought the world would be a happier place without phonetics, which seems sometimes to force people into mimicking and memorizing sounds associated with letter combinations. But clearly these key mouth movements do have strong sound associations, and it is impossible to ignore this. It can be very helpful to use both approaches. Doing so combines the very best of phonetics with the very best of fluid vertical mouth movements, which makes the dictionary much more helpful as an aid for speaking English clearly.

This dictionary has in fact turned out to contain two families of the key vertical mouth movements: *howling* and **growling**. These family groups are associated with certain key simplified phonetic sounds and notations that run through the words in the dictionary consistently. It does seem that combining mouth movements with phonetics is a very powerful tool, though not necessarily the other way 'round!

In this dictionary, the emotion of mouth movements tends to override phonetics, so some compromises have been made regarding the emotional meanings of words and mouth movements and phonetics to allow simple phonetic sounds to come through. This is particularly so with the small reversed *a* and the big *A ay* sound, which does not always follow the emotion of the word because the benefit of keeping these two sounds in mirror opposite mouth movements is so beneficial, and the gains are so great for pronunciation and fluency. It is also more helpful to follow this rule consistently and persistently throughout the dictionary. However, there is no doubt that the simple phonetic connections of these mouth movements have tended to reinforce the existing patterns of mouth movements. But following phonetic sounds unquestioningly can be very unwise, and emotion and the body language of the mouth are just as important for company and social communication.

It is important to remember that certain phonetic sounds are produced by both forward and reverse movements, particularly the very empathizing **GAR** and *HAO* movements. This is useful because *HAO* produces a slightly softer sound than **GAR** and is less emotional. This is helpful for words that contain the *ou* and the *air* sound, which, depending on meaning, need to be stressed differently: less stressed with forward positions and more stressed with reversed movements. So these notations and movements are not set in stone; should the reader like to reduce emotion on less emotional words, *HAO* can be substituted for **GAR** or even *HOO* for **GRR**. There is no question that the problem of homophones and homographs can be solved primarily by using different mouth movements based on the emotional meaning of the word.

From the mouth movements and notations used, and those that *The Moving Mouth Dictionary* goes on to suggest, one can even develop the ability to see, quantify, and, just as important, discuss the repeat patterns of English words—something that is rarely done. It was not expected to see them so clearly emphasised and defined to the extent that they are. Though it is logical that if speaking is to be an automatic process for mother tongue speakers, the word patterns and the combinations of mouth movements within those word patterns will be very consistent and simplified, and likely will be focused on key repeating patterns. English, when we get right down to it, does seem to be a very **GAR/GAR** and *HOO/HOO* language. Another aspect that we did not expect to see was that in addition to simple key phonetic variation sounds for certain letters, the notations themselves could be used in other ways and could have supporting roles to mouth movements in helping to give guidance for breathing in or out and for indicating low, medium, and high stress words.

The importance and power of all these patterns, whether mouth movements for words or internal letter patterns, physical or phonetic, opens up very interesting avenues for studying and teaching English, particularly for the absorption and retention of the English language. This allows learners of the language to use all their faculties—their memories and their ears, in combination with the muscle memory of their jaws—to reflex and access vocabulary and grammar from their brains, particularly verbs, and to help students do this instantaneously and automatically. Bear in mind that often one of the major challenges for learning English is the ability to access what one has just learnt rather than accessing what one is learning or hopes to learn or remember in the future.

Understanding English mouth movements and word patterns can put students much more in control of the language, which can give them more confidence for anticipating and dealing with the challenges ahead in what can be for many a very hairy ride to mastering the spoken English language!

If one needs any proof that English is a very versatile and rhythmic language with its roots lying deep within the earliest beginnings of howling and growling of Neanderthals and Homo sapiens, this dictionary might help to add to that discussion. Interestingly, the phrase *Who are you? (HOO/ HAO/HOO)* seems to be spoken daily by primates to unwelcome strangers in many of the forests of the world!

These notations could at the very least help to form a useful basis and a reference point for a more down to earth, universal, and simple discussion on improving on how to say English words clearly, which seems almost impossible to do at the moment, and is an important conversation that is continually being ignored in the teaching of English. In some cases, this has become regarded as almost a taboo subject, an extension of 'We are English, and therefore we do not discuss in public religion and sex, and under no circumstances whatsoever do we ever discuss English pronunciation, and certainly not in a bar in the East End of London!'

As this dictionary was developed, another area that was so unexpected to see was the potential to use this system to help people who have impaired hearing or who have had their education interrupted . These notations could also be used in the same way that musical notes are used. As long as one can read and understand the notation, whether using Braille or sight-reading, combined with the use of the mouth as a simple recorder, one could continue to improve one's English. Even if one cannot hear what one is saying, there is no reason why someone with no sight and no hearing cannot gain confidence that he or she can make the same sounds as students who are sighted and have perfect hearing. One can learn to speak English extremely well by focusing on mouth movements since one is not dependent on hearing or mimicking sounds. This method also has the potential to help students who suffer from dysphonetic dyslexia (rather than dyseidetic dyslexia) by making the process of connecting phonetics with letters and symbols a simpler one.

The hope of *The Moving Mouth Dictionary* is that it will take some of the pain and torture out of learning English for those who would like to speak English clearly. The hope above all is that it does not add to the interminable drudgery and misery that many students have gone through in learning the English language.

The title *The Lost Secret of Speaking Perfect English* refers to the idea that it seems convenient to sanitize and rewrite the history of our origins. Perhaps this is one of the prime situations where it does help to be reminded that we are all primates, and thus we have an innate connection with animals, whether as primates swinging from branch to branch, as prehistoric fish in an early aquatic soup, or as reptilian creatures slithering around on our tummies. We have a lot to learn from these animal connections, especially because we do seem to have lost contact with them. This can strike an interesting chord with both children and adults in the process of learning and retaining English as they unlock many of the lost sounds, threads, and secrets that are contained in the never-ending, beautiful mystery of the English language.

Introduction

The dictionary is designed to be used as an aid for speaking very clear, understandable English, and to do this in the most comfortable and natural way. This ability is perhaps the greatest challenge facing speakers of the English language for our generation. The challenge for many people is not to write but actually to speak English clearly. Never have there been so many people speaking English and so few people understanding all that is being said!

Some of the concepts mentioned in the introduction to this dictionary will hopefully be expanded in two succeeding books that will go into much greater detail and will offer additional support to the dictionary. For the best results, the reader should use *The Moving Mouth Dictionary* in conjunction with *The Lost Secret of Speaking Perfect English, Part One and Part Two*, when they become available. Though this is not entirely necessary, these books will go into greater depth on some of the areas highlighted here. There will also be a website under the name www.breathingenglish.org, which will provide additional assistance, support, and updates.

The total words in this dictionary currently are in excess of 11,000, but the concept involves a working and expanding dictionary that will be updated as required. The projection is to increase the available words significantly every twelve to eighteen months or so, bearing in mind that it is estimated that there are over one million words in the English language.

The dictionary also teaches the differences between some of the most confusing words in the English language, including some homographs and homophones, which hopefully will provide relief to the many who are struggling to learn these. There are also many words in the English language that have only one letter differences between them, and if not pronounced correctly, can completely alter the meaning of the sentence, such as *plague/ plaque, beard/heard, aisles/exiles, friend/fiend, hallowed/allowed*, and *senate/sedate*. Also, certain word spellings have very little connection to how that word is pronounced, such *people, leopard, cough, hiccough*, or *gunwale*.

The dictionary uses a system of simple vertical and natural mouth movements that are a guide to producing phonetic sounds, how best to speak them clearly, and, very importantly, how to do so automatically and fluently without putting too much stress on the mouth. The dictionary is designed to give students a simple technique and a simple system of notation for speaking English very clearly and effectively. These mouth movements are not set in concrete. Speaking English well does seem to be more of an art than a science, though sometimes it also seems more of a sport than an art, as it has a lot in common with the basic principles of rowing, skiing, or golfing.

One should also avoid using extreme forward and/or heavily reversed mouth movements in English, as these will create the very affected voice associated with certain parts of the south of England, which may be more Germanic in origin than English. Extreme forward movements can create strange, overstressed, ethnic and Celtic sounds that can transport one up to the North as far as the Glens of Scotland!

All the recommended vertical mouth movements are natural and thus should not be forced. You should also avoid speaking English with too few mouth movements and substituting too many tongue movements, as this will create pressure and encourage horizontal mouth movements. It is recognised that the phonetic system has made a major contribution to helping people all over the world to achieve the correct sounds, and certainly, it has helped ears to flap in the right direction for making those word sounds, but unfortunately, the mouth is often left in limbo, wondering which road to take and how to get there.

The current standard phonetic dictionary does not offer a technique for how to make those sounds. There is a tendency to rely too heavily on phonetics and sounds in the teaching of English, and in doing so, students are bound to reproduce and imitate those sounds in an unstructured way. In addition, some of the sounds in the standard phonetic dictionary have a tendency to be a little too reversed and too extreme. These certainly do encourage slightly affected and even old-fashioned and archaic sounds, particularly in words that change little *o* sounds to little *a* sounds.

There is even an unkind suggestion, perhaps a little unfair, that the English phonetic dictionary is fostering and encouraging accents and even could be one of the prime causes of accents. This could certainly be true if the average student actually spent time using the phonetic dictionary, but there seems to be some serious doubt about that, though many teachers clearly do. The phonetic pronunciation of the word *education*, for example, as taken from the phonetic dictionary, is *déjà kaysh'n*, which seems to have been lifted straight out of a Pink Floyd song. Though great in its own way, it would equally encourage both an East End of London accent and a very affected South London accent. It also becomes clear from the phonetic dictionary that how the current Queen pronounces a small *a* in a word could phonetically be the same as how someone from the East End of London,

America, or Australia would pronounce it. Ironically, all are equally correct in the eyes of the phonetic dictionary. Even if all of them could end up pronouncing an incomprehensible pronunciation of the final word, all would be phonetically correct according to the phonetic dictionary!

The current phonetic dictionary seems unnaturally biased to converting nearly every small *o*, *u*, or *a* into a very reversed *a* as a matter of principle and phonetic dogma. *The Moving Mouth Dictionary* takes a more relaxed and modern approach. One can replace a small *a* on occasion with a forward small *o* as in *orange* if the sound is much more natural. This is preferable to being obsessively driven to produce the small *a*. This is often more in keeping with the emotional meaning of the word, and is often more in keeping, very surprisingly, with how the English alphabet is actually used rather than how it is drilled in schools. This method is also more in keeping with its connection to the Latin origin alphabets, both of which seem much closer than is generally thought or accepted.

To new learners, the English language seems unable to lend itself to speaking very fast and clearly, though this is a misconception. With the right technique, very few languages can keep up with it, and very few can be clearer! English does tend to involve more mouth movements than many other languages. So it is not surprising that this can be overwhelming, and in the effort to reduce this effect, many national and ethnic voices have been created, partly to reduce stress on the mouth while speaking. Accents have also been used in an almost desperate way to increase fluency and belonging, but, unfortunately, not with any clarity in many cases.

The repetitive nature of two similar repeating mouth movements at the beginning of many words and the use of two directly opposite mouth movements in many words add enormously to this challenge. Together these may seem to be an insurmountable obstacle, but in fact, they are an area of great advantage if the words are broken down correctly as we say them. These repetitive mouth movement combinations are also essential for breathing and for reducing pressure on the mouth.

The use of the phonetic system has proved to be very limiting and often struggles to convey the sounds of an emotion and intonation, such as the sounds of empathy, concern, sadness, apprehension, anger, happiness, and fear. The combined effects of vertical mouth movements are much better equipped to form these sounds.

In many cases, the phonetic system does not allow for different pronunciations of similar spellings of words. Even when it does, it does not advise on how to make those sounds based on the actual emotional meaning of the words, as seen with the verb *to tear* paper and the noun to cry *a tear*, nor does it differentiate between differently stressed verbs and nouns, such as *to light a light, light*. It does not show how to finish the key letters within words and at the ends of words, which is essential if the words are to be heard clearly.

The connection between facial expressions and body language and words and mouth movements was so important in the primate world that existed long before humans could speak, yet it seems also to have been completely lost and forgotten, and along with it the beauty of the English language and our ability to communicate emotionally and clearly. Other primates do not communicate out of the sides of their mouths, as this would reduce their audience, diminish their ability to get their point across, and reduce their life expectancy!

As previously mentioned, the dictionary does follow, in addition to vertical mouth movements, a few simple but very important phonetic associations with each mouth movement. This is a useful guide, particularly with the main challenge of when to use, for example, a big *A* or a small *a*, except when the meaning of the word and the emotion of the word mean the mouth movement is more predominant than the sound of the word.

The dictionary, as far as phonetics is concerned, takes a very simplified approach; it is more helpful to associate certain key phonetic sounds with certain key mouth movements than it is to have no sounds associated with those movements. This is true even if there is more than one phonetic sound and letter to each mouth movement, as is the case with **GAR** and *HAO*.

The system uses two main family mouth movements with an additional three of each type, which are three variations that are, in turn, the direct opposites of these main movements. These very importantly advise which direction of the mouth's compass we need to take as we are speaking, and on which road we need to travel to get there.

The student is encouraged to use the tongue vertically, and rarely horizontally, if ever, in this strategy. This is not unlike other primates, who do not howl, growl, bark, or woof out of the sides of their mouths. If they did, I know a Labrador named Tara who would disagree and would woof at them in the most questioning way!

The Tongue

Generally, for primates the tongue is used for licking and tasting, swallowing, and other emotional activities, but its use in speaking English has been and can be exaggerated, and it has tongue tied and doomed clear English in the process. The number of positions for the tongue has been reduced to two in this dictionary: one goes up behind the upper set of teeth mainly for *t* and *d* sounds, and one darts between the two sets of teeth only for most of the words containing the *th* sound.

The rest of the time, the tongue snoozes away quietly and happily in its lair at the bottom of the lower jaw, waiting to pounce and to encourage reflexive breathing. The *th* in the English language is a very underrated feature, and there is a danger that it will die out, particularly if we do not fully understand the whole physiological point of it. If we do allow it to disappear, the English language will be much harder to speak well.

It seems to be a rare example of where the body has teamed up with the brain to produce this amazing *th* breathing combination to induce reflex breathing and to increase the oxygen flow into the brain and body to aid speaking. Breathing is essential for speaking English well, and it is no less than quite amazing when we ponder it for a moment.

To Speak or Not to Speak Clear English

The aim of this dictionary is to put within the reach of all students the ability to speak clear and understandable English in an easy and affordable way, and to converge mother tongue national and regional ethnic voices. If they do get in the way of speaking clear English, then the language will often fail the basic criteria of a language, which is to create simple, clear, and understandable communication.

There is definitely a connection between singing and using one's mouth vertically. Singing naturally converges disparate accents because it focuses on the universal standard diaphragm that we all possess. Therefore, this reduces the effect of the very egocentric, idiosyncratic, overbearing and dominating mouth.

We should never forget that confused and unclear voices can be socially divisive in that they can restrict social interaction, create confusion, cause accidents such as air crashes, shorten one's career, and seriously hamper one's work, social progress, and job mobility, both locally and internationally. Speaking unclear English is very limiting and restricting in a way that is socially unfair, unnecessary, and frustrating to people who wish to progress professionally and personally.

A *laissez-faire* approach to unclear voices in our schools and universities means that we are taking a *laissez-faire* approach to clear English communication. These traditional homes of the English language could and should aspire to be the very centre of global excellence instead of being the leaders of spreading global English confusion!

In the world of high-speed Internet communication and converging cultures, spoken language, particularly the English language, is perhaps the last main barrier standing in the way of clear world communication. By focusing on a universal, easy to understand system of notation that is similar to music notation, people who are hard of hearing or who have a tendency to be dyslexic will be able to take part in this development, to everyone's benefit.

How to Use the Moving Mouth Dictionary

Each word is broken down into units as it changes mouth-movement direction to show the continued direction or progression of those movements. These are described as **mouthables**, which is perhaps not the nicest of words, but it is very descriptive. It also provides a clear distinction between its meaning and that of the term *syllable*. How we break down a word is the key to saying that word effectively. In the phonetic dictionary, we have to search out the syllables and their breakdowns then completely ignore them, and then check the phonetics of how to say them, which will then give us a very different breakdown. In the approach that we have here, we only have to glance at mouthables to have a good chance of saying and spelling the word correctly. It is a three-in-one approach!

Mouthable units also tend to be very consistent because they create repetitive mouth movement sequences that hold far fewer surprises for the student than the traditional syllables. This helps the development of predictable English patterns for learning, which is important for retention and has the effect of building confidence naturally.

The basic unit of the notation is a **mouth movement** rather than a syllable; the two often coincide in the dictionary, but not always. The vertical mouth movements of each word are notated for speaking very clearly and deliberately at the optimum and more deliberate speed that is used for presentations and explanations. These are structured in a way that can, where the same two families of howling and growling coincide, be merged, blended, and concertinaed through a form of high-speed, supercharged breathing into multiple word phrases or multiple mouthable words.

From these notations, we can see that there are very distinct patterns in English phrases and even patterns within the words themselves that follow similar mirror patterns. These patterns encourage ear, muscle, and mouth movement memories in a mother tongue speaker of clear English. This coordination helps to make the speaking of English more of the automatic process that is natural for mother tongue speakers of good, clear English.

One of the aims of the dictionary is to teach this technique to secondary language speakers and to make them aware not only of mouth movements for combinations of letters, but of words and phrases that follow very similar patterns. This will aid retention and make spelling and pronunciation more predictable.

The other purpose is to help mother tongue speakers of English to speak clearly so that when secondary language learners have learnt to speak English, they will find it easier to understand what mother tongue speakers are saying. Both are important aims that seem to have been largely ignored or disregarded as being unrealistic or unattainable objectives.

Howling and Growling Strategy

In this strategy, there is a simple notation for each movement based on different combinations of the two main types of movements of *Forward Howling* (*H*) and **Reversed Growling** (**G**), which are opposite movements. This is important because moving the mouth directly backwards and directly forward into the opposite position naturally reduces stress on individual mouth movements and encourages more automatic and reflexive moments. Very simply, the notation *H* pushes the mouth forward, and **G** moves the mouth into a reverse position, not unlike the manual gears of a car.

There are three additional movements of each family type, and these indicate how and when to open the mouth wider and by how much, which is a way of reducing stress on the mouth. Most importantly, these movements increase empathy and soften the voice. (A) denotes **Aquatic Mouth Movements**, which tend to create low stressed words and which also reduce stress on certain key letters. (D) denotes **Downward Jaw Dropping Mouth Movements**, which are used when medium stress is required on certain key letters, particularly the final letters of a word or certain individual letters contained within those words. Finally, there is the action of moving the tongue between the teeth for typical **TH** words, which are shown with a single (T) notation for **TH Upward Tongue Mouth Movements** and additional higherstressed, upward movements and reflexive breathing words. This is the basic principle.

These mouth movement notations naturally tend to create the right stress on the letters in a word and are all part of the two main families of mouth movements. The key stressed groups have a *HOO* notation with a double *OO* and are forward, higher stressed movements, and **GRR** notation with a double **RR** and are doubly higher stressed movements. When compared to the three other movements, though, these must not be stressed too heavily.

An **added** (**A**) means the mouth should be open more, and an **added** (**D**) means the lower jaw should be dropped to reduce pressure. An **added** (**T**) means the tongue should be sharply tapped between the two sets of teeth, directly behind the top set of front teeth.

Many words have the same mouth movements and patterns. Where their directions and families coincide, mouth movements can be dramatically reduced, as they are ideal for concertinaing, blending, and merging into each other sequentially. This is why, when speaking English, it is essential to have a solid feel for the compass direction of each combination of letters, single letters, or mouthables that the combination of letters takes and leads the mouth naturally into.

This effect, once understood, means it is much easier to speak English well and clearly by using vertical mouth movements. These vertical mouth movements are the keys to the process, and they are extremely efficient and much more logical because they obviously combine very well with breathing through the mouth. It is much more natural to work with the flow and direction of mouth patterns and mouth movements rather than try to work against the natural flow of mouth movements. Doing so will inevitably contort and twist the mouth or result in squashing the very life and breath out of the words being spoken, flattening and squeezing them into horizontal movements that will constrict the flow of breath, obstruct clear sound, confuse rhythm, and obstruct breathing.

The simplification of the effect of vertical mouth movements is dramatically increased through the expansion of breathing in and out through the mouth and nose, though largely through the mouth in English. This is only effectively possible through vertical movements.

Trying to speak English well and clearly with horizontal mouth movements is like trying to win a one-hundred-metre race while wearing high-heeled shoes. It is counterproductive for communication and dangerous for language health, and it can be a little undignified as well. This merging concertina effect is particularly important for many English words that contain the repetition of two or more movements of the same type or the same family.

Words that begin with a repetition of mouth movements such as **GAR/GAR** and *HAO/HAO* are difficult to say in a fluid way unless the first mouth movement is retained without closing the mouth for the next mouth movement. This simple but important technique is lost on many speakers of English, but if it were universally appreciated, it would take a lot of stress out of speaking the language. English repetitive mouth movements are far from being a hindrance; they are an aid and a big advantage to speaking the English language, but only if the mouth is operated vertically.

It is important for some words to be breathed, as in the case of the amazing word *unbelievable*. Multiple units or multi-mouth movement words aid this process as long as they are going in the right direction, and they even help if they are not! This supercharged breathing technique is the same as those used in common, everyday greetings and phrases, such as, *How are you*? They all have the same requirement and use a similar technique, just like being able to say *unbelievable*, *administration*, or *management*. These phrases and words can, by using **the English breathing technique**, build around vertical mouth movements and reduce even further to at least a minimum of the main two mouth movements: one at the beginning and one at the end of the word. Focus on the first key mouth movement at the beginning of the word, and the last mouth movement at end of the word. When only the first movement and the last mouth movement of the words and phrases are the main focus, the words and phrases can be said extremely quickly and heard very clearly indeed when using the English breathing technique.

It is very important to appreciate that vertical mouth movements are much more precise than horizontal movements. The latter seem to have been singlehandedly responsible for creating the extraordinary phenomenon in the English language of the homophone and the homograph, which account for over two thousand words in the English language that people have largely given up on differentiating. Other than through the very comforting context of the sentence, these should not be attempted under any circumstances with horizontal mouth movements. This is an enormous admission of defeat for the English language, and we should not put up the white flag of surrender and give up on using these words correctly. Many are covered in *The Moving Mouth Dictionary* using different vertical mouth notations, and they can be spoken clearly using vertical mouth movements. Furthermore, by using vertical mouth movements that have more or less stress and emotion, and that are more in keeping with the meaning of the word and its type, the words homophone and homograph could become largely obsolete.

When supercharged breathing is required and kicks in, it can allow speaking at a very rapid speed with increased and impressive rounded onomatopoeia, which is a key feature of the power of the English language. This can be done much faster than with horizontal mouth movements, with much mouth comfort, and yet can be heard so clearly that it leaves many other speakers standing on the starting line of English, particularly in many low-level 'kick-off' company presentations!

The Moving Mouth Strategy

The system is composed of two main categories of mouth movements, each containing three further vertical mouth movements. These are either open or partially open, but they are never completely closed when speaking. They are not excessively reversed but are not excessively forward moving, either; rather, they are very natural and relaxed movements. These key sequential mouth movements are split into two main opposite positions of *howling* and **growling**.

To further emphasise these two simple main concepts, howling (*HOO*) drives the mouth gently forward and north, and is more external and away from the body. It is naturally more physical, and tends to be more active and pushes the mouth forward. It is often used for active verbs like *caught* or comforting for nouns like *home* or *moon*.

Growling (GRR) drives the mouth gently into reverse and south, and pushes the mouth gently in the opposite position back closer into the body and is therefore more internal, but less physically active. Therefore, it is much more emotional and much more about the feelings and sensations of certain actions, such as *dream/dreamt, creep/crept*, and more emotional nouns and adjectives.

The very nature of growling means that it tends to stress words and letters more naturally and sharply than howling. In choosing the direction of mouth movements and the stress of the words, it is impossible to ignore the emotional meanings of words, something that the dry world of the often complicated and sonic screeching of pure phonetics does not take into account.

Rhythm

Vertical mouth movements allow us to use our mouths vertically, combined with the use of the diaphragm and of course with the very vital support of the English rhythm. Rhythm seems to be the invisible skeleton of the English language onto which grammar and words are firmly placed. Without rhythm, there would be very little structure holding the English language together. Students would enter a Bermuda Triangle where they would, and often do, become irretrievably lost, drifting without a compass in a morass of confusing rhythms of different national grammars and vocabulary.

The English rhythm can be defined simply as ***one word equally up in sound followed by one word equally down in sound, however short or long the numbers of the letters in the word.***

The importance of rhythm in providing support and structure to the English language and its use as an invisible framework for autocorrecting and regulating the speed of speaking and breathing cannot be over emphasised. Learning to breathe with a vertical mouth movement technique and using

English rhythm should be as important as learning grammar in English, as all three support one another.

Breathing through the Mouth and Bert

It is important here to define types of breathing. Breathing through the nose tends to trigger a conservation of air that is slowly released, which is not optimal for speaking English well. Breathing through the mouth encourages the expelling of air that words can surf out on quickly and naturally, and it is vital for adding power and stress to words in English.

As a rough guide, the **Higher Stressed Mouth Movements** such as *HOO* and **GRR** tend to be used for breathing out and exhaling through the mouth. **Medium Stressed Movements** such as *HTO* and *HDO* and **GTR** and **GDR** tend to be used for taking air in through the mouth either through upward tongue movements or downward jaw movements. **Low Stressed Aquatic Movements** such as *HAO* and **GAR** are used for inhaling and exhaling, and are important for empathy.

These mouth movements and their number can be described and suggested as approximately the closest positions for speaking perfect English, and, if required, with shorter abbreviations of **VS-MM-BERT**, which stands for Vertical Sequential Mouth Movements, Breathing English, Rhythm Technique, which is still quite a mouthful, though personally I do not describe it this way. Perhaps **BERT** works as an acronym, which is also an old English Christian name, which brings English back to where it should be. I hope Bert does not mind being associated with this; certainly, it would not be possible to have made any progress without him!

Phonetics

To move on to this tricky subject, each mouth movement has been given a consistent and repeatable notation that is associated with simple and phonetic connections in the same way that a musical note is shown on a sheet of music. This is not of course Beethoven or Mozart, but could include some tiny bits of Elgar, the famous English composer. As you read on, it is possible to see the connection!

The concept is to provide another much simpler alternative and a much more comprehensive method to the phonetic system. As a point of discussion that seems to have lost contact with much of the emotion and empathy of words, phonetics has tended to encourage the mimicking of sound in an unstructured way by encouraging horizontal mouth movements.

That reduces the optimum number of mouth movements, which inhibits breathing and speaking clearly.

The above could be a controversial statement for lovers of phonetics, but it is perhaps long overdue. Now, as millions of new secondary English speakers appear each year, it is evident that the focus should come back to speaking English more clearly and developing ways of doing it more naturally, which is the whole aim of *The Moving Mouth Dictionary*.

Howling and Growling: Notations and Abbreviations

Howling

The following four forward movements are based on early humankind's natural animalistic mouth movement of howling. Howling mouth movements tend be more external and active, use less emotion, and are used on their own; they seem more comforting and soothing for familiar and secure situations, and are more external and environmental.

The HOO: Forward Wolf Mouth Movement

This is the extreme howling wolf movement and the direct opposite of **GRR**. This creates naturally higher stressed words and letters as shown in the sentence *You howled too soon!*

This is a fully extended and partially open howl designated by the gentle funnelling of the mouth. It can be represented symbolically or pictorially by the phrase *the wolf howling at the moon*.

The mouth width opening between the teeth is no less than the thin nail tip end of the index finger, but it produces a soft, flexible mouth as used when softly blowing candles out on a birthday cake. The two forward double *OO*s are there to emphasise the importance and the extra stress of this position as used in words such as *moon, food, good, woof, zoo, woo, loo, moo,* or even in the actual word *hoo*. There are strong Anglo Saxon connections in England with the Hoo Peninsula in Kent, a river spur separating the two rivers of the Thames and Medway. Also, there is an actual word and place of the ancient burial ground and final resting place of Sutton-*Hoo*, high up on the hill. There is even a crater named on the far side of the moon called Wan-Hoo named after the first attempted Chinese astronaut of the Ming dynasty. Perhaps, after all, this is why the wolf likes to howl at the moon. The word *hoo* is also found in the Japanese language and even in the Kannada language in India. In addition to double *OO* that is part of *hoo,* this position also includes words with just one *O* such as the words *you, who*, or *home*, which tend to make similar sounds.

The movement is also largely associated with the much more stressed endings of verbs, such as the *t* and the *d* sound that we find mainly in the past tense of verbs. It is actually much easier to stress *t* and *d* in this *HOO* forward movement because doing so gently pushes the mouth forward. The tip of the tongue automatically follows and taps behind the top set of teeth, as shown by *booked*, *caught*, or *put*. This movement is also used for the *all* sound that one finds in words such as *fall*, *call*, *tall*, or *shawl*.

This applies to the big *O* sound at the beginnings of words such as *over* and *open*, but not for the little *o* sound that one finds with *orange*, which is a different sound—see *HAO*.

The movement is used for the big *U* as in *use*, *uniform,* and *union* at the beginning of words (but not for the small *u* as in *utter*—see **GAR**). All the other three howling positions start from this gentle forward position and use the *HOO* mouth width position as its base shape and form.

Additional HOO Notes

Less emotional words ending in *d* and *t* tend to imply *HOO* mouth positions, which are stressed and are often strong in onomatopoeia. Also, after the heavily stressed *t* and *d* sounds, this often encourages the intake of breath afterwards, because verbs are stressed. After stressing a verb, it is important to breathe; furthermore, since *HOO* is more stressed, it is ideal for the heightening of onomatopoeia.

The direction of the *HOO* mouth: forward

The vertical width of the *HOO* mouth: tip of the index finger

The phonetic *HOO* connection: This is associated with the forward *HOO* sound, the big *O* and the big *U*, *t* and *d* sounds, the *all, aw, au,* and *tor* sounds, and the *–tion* sound, as in *administration*. It is also associated with words ending in *ble*, *ckle*, and *tle*, such as *able, tickle, twinkle*, and *little*.

The *HOO* position is commonly found at the ends of words or on its own but also at the beginning and in the middle of words.

Breathing *HOO* type: exhale directly outward. The tendency is for this position to be used for breathing out rather than for breathing in as one would expect with higher stressed words.

Level of *HOO* stress: high stress on groups of letters with the inability to put stress on individual letters, except at the end of the words where there are *t* and *d* sounds, which are heard very distinctly.

The HTO-Forward Reptilian Mouth Movement

This is represented by the following image: **a sleepy, slothful python.** The reptilian howling movement is the direct opposite of **GTR** and creates naturally higher stressed words and letters, as in the associated phrase, *Arthur's Thursday's Earth.*

This is still a fully extended, partially open funnelling of the mouth in a pagan animalistic howl (mouth opening width is the thin tip end of the index finger) but with an extended forward mouth. A slow reptilian or python tongue touches briefly between the tops of the front set of teeth. The *t* is for tongue, and in this howling position, it emphasizes the *TH* English pagan mouth used in words such as *north, thor, those, Thursday, Earth, author, through, sooth, sloth, throw, threw,* and *thou* (but not thee, which is **GTR**).

The movement is largely associated with the nouns and adjectives *those* and *Thursday, authority, authorisation,* and the *soothing* sound. There are not so many verbs using a forward *TH* such as *thought* or *authorise.*

Additional HTO Notes

TH words create a pagan reverence as is shown with the ancient god of *Thor* and the national and legendry English hero *Arthur*—or was it *Arthor*? This seems a combination of *Earth* and *Thor*, and not least, the word *authorisation* seems to be asking for the approval of Thor. This position encourages quick intakes of breath through the mouth and encourages the neck to reflex backwards and the mouth and head to move upwards. This in turn stimulates reflexive breathing through the mouth, for English *TH* words require a high intake of oxygen for breathing, which therefore can just as quickly be expelled with great power if required. (Inhaling through the nose makes it much more difficult to exhale quickly.) *HTO* is actually an anachronism for *happy to oblige*—presumably, happy to oblige to breathe— something everyone speaking English should be prepared do if they want to make progress!

The direction of the *HTO* mouth: forward and upward

The vertical width of the *HTO* mouth: the tip of the index finger

The *HTO* position is commonly found at the end of words.

The phonetic *HTO* connection is exclusively the *TH* forward sound.

Breathing type for *HTO*: inhale upwards and inwards. This creates the intake of a reflexive breath through the mouth by tapping the tongue upwards between the top set of teeth.

Level of stress for the *HTO* mouth: high to medium. High stress is on the two *TH* letters, but there is a tendency for medium stress on the others.

The HAO-Forward Aquatic Mouth Movement

This is represented by the image *the solitary goldfish*. The aquatic howling movement is the mirror opposite of **GAR** and creates naturally lower stressed words. As found in this very well-known English nursery rhyme phrase, but rarely understood, *how now brown cow*, where the final letters of each word are hardly touched or stressed. It is also the traditional mouth position that is requested by British dentists and doctors when they ask one to say, *'Ah'* (or do they mean *are*?) and creates, naturally, a very open mouth for the dentist or doctor to peer down. *HAO* actually rhymes with *cow*, and it is also found in the Chinese language. There is even an atoll called Hao. How to get to *HAO* and Hao is described below!

This is where the vertical mouth opening is wider than it is for the first two positions (*HOO* and *HTO*), but it is still in the same forward position. However, this is a much more open position that stretches to the width of the thick end joint of the index finger (the opposite end of the thin index finger). This is approximately twice the mouth width of the *HOO* position, thus causing the mouth to open wider, which creates a funnelling effect in a forward mouth movement similar to that which an aquatic fish would make. This is very similar to watching the mouth of a goldfish in its bowl, endlessly coming up for air or feeding, and can be found in words such as *what*, *where*, *how*, *are*, *far*, *car*, *how*, *now*, *brown*, *cow*, and *her*. There is very little pressure on the final letters of these words. This is often used specifically to take pressure off the letter *r* in words such as *where* and *are*, and the letter *a* in words such as *air*, *pass*, and *star*. This also creates lots of empathy (there used to be ten Haos in a dong, the Vietnamese currency). The atoll Hao is found in the Tuamotu Archipelago in French Polynesia, also known as the Island of Harp (the *r* is not stressed but the *p* is!) and is no doubt a favourite place for goldfish!

Additional HAO Notes

The tongue remains in the bottom section of the mouth. The wider mouth movement naturally creates empathy, which softens the voice and helps to encourage breathing in and out through the mouth in the same way that singing does. (*HAO* can be used in some cases as a substitute for **GAR** because it is a softer and less stressed movement, and the two mouth positions are often interchangeable.)

The direction of the *HAO* mouth: forward

Vertical width of the *HAO* mouth: the thick joint end of the index finger

The *HAO* phonetic connection: Apart from the *r* sound, this movement is also strongly associated with the very important big *A* (*ay*) sound as in *way* and *day*. In the alphabet, the *ay* sound can be heard in the background of the alphabet letters *j, k,* and *h*. The *ay* sound often appears when one least expects to hear it and is often more prevalent in *ai* combinations in words such as *paint, saint, straight,* or *train*, but also as the *A* sound in *cave, brave,* and *save*. This movement is used for the lower stressed *ou* sound in the word *noun* and the lower stressed *ow* sound in *how*.

The movement is used also in the very distinct small *o* sound as in *object, optic, orange,* and *otter* rather than the big *O* sound in *over*, which is used in *HOO*. The small *o* in this moving mouth dictionary has been used sometimes as a substitute for the small *a* sound. The standard phonetic dictionary tends to use too many old fashioned small *a* sounds and in very reversed movements. This tendency to rely too much on small *a* sounds, which rely on using too many **GAR** mouth movements, often makes the English language sound too harsh and artificial as well as superciliously and outrageously posh. The *HAO* small *o* is an ideal substitute for reducing the small *a* sound and for softening and modernising the sound of the English language, which can, if movements are over reversed, be a little too harsh and aggravating to the ear. The *HAO* movement is also used for the *er* sound in the middle of words, as it is a quicker movement than *HDO*, though they both create similar sounds. It is also strongly associated with the *ARE* sound and is often used to reduce the stress of the final letter *r* of a word. It also converts the small *a* in words such as *pass, grass,* and *class* into the *ARE* sound. It is also ideal for helping to say less stressed words in a more delicate way as in *air* or *fair*.

The *HAO* mouth position is normally found at the beginning of words, sometimes in repetitive movements, and often on its own. It can be found in the middle of words, but it is not so common at the end of words.

Breathing type for the *HAO* mouth position: exhaling directly outward, though it is used for both inward and outward breathing as it can access air very quickly in great quantities. Probably the natural position for breathing in a large gulp of air before one takes the plunge before speaking English or diving underwater, which produce the same feeling!

Level of stress for *HAO:* low stress, particularly on groups of letters, and the inability to put any stress on individual letters

The HDO-Forward Jaw Dropping Mouth Movement

The stunning human English vertical jaw drop of the lower jowl or jaw, known as the human howling movement is the opposite of **GDR** and creates naturally medium stressed words such as those in the phrase *super pony over water*. Strangely enough, *HDO* is also an anachronism for the Human Development Organisation, which seems very appropriate. One likes to think this is exclusively a human mouth movement, as it does seem slightly more sophisticated than the other movements, and humans have to feel superior! Though that might be a myth, as it seems to be the same movement a wolf or dog would make when releasing a big bone that has been stuck in its mouth! Certainly, this is a very versatile movement and seems more sophisticated than the other movements.

This movement is very closely connected to the *HAO* in that it does reach the same vertical mouth width and creates a similar effect in sound, but it tends to be a slower movement and is much more flexible in that it can add pressure on the final letters of words, something the *HAO* position cannot do. In addition, it can also do the opposite and add slightly more stress on individual letters in the middle of words by dropping down to any letter it likes, including the letters at the ends of words. This is something that the *HAO* cannot do, so it is much more versatile. Often it starts like the *HOO* sound as an extended, open funnelling of the mouth in an extreme animal howl, but with the bottom jaw dropping at the end to allow a subtransitional extension movement to an *HAO* howl. (It tends to move from *HOO* to *HAO*.)

This is a very important movement for enabling the mouth to remain vertical when used in howling words such as *pony*, *sugar*, *okay*, *hungry*, and *water*. This has almost the same effect in sound as aquatic movements have, as it doubles the mouth opening on the final movement, but this actually involves two movements and allows us to put a little more pressure on the final letters and *r* and *t* in nouns and adjectives that use the *HDO* position, such as *water*. The *HAO* movement is a slightly different and much quicker single movement.

HAO can often act as a substitute for *HDO* because they are very similar sounds, as in the words *okay* or *Tuesday*. *HDO* is a slower movement from *HOO* to *HAO* and tends to involve two more movements than *HAO*, which is a single and faster movement that creates a similar sound effect.

It often allows some contact or touch of the lips, tongue, or on the roof of the upper mouth. This is found with the single letters *f* and *m*, and *HDO* tends to push the head down, as in the words *daughter* or *water*.

Additional HDO Notes

HDO is also a transitional position, in that it often moves from a howl to what would tend to be an uncomfortable howling position, and it does reduce stress. Whether howling or growling words ending in *ing*, *y*, *day*, *ter*, or *ry*, multiple syllable words with *ra* or *at* in the middle tend to require jaw dropping or a more open aquatic movement, such as the word *administ(ra) tion*. These movements are very useful for finishing off the final letters of nouns to improve clarity. It is very important for taking pressure off the mouth and is one of the keys to speaking English and maintaining a vertical mouth position. Also, on *HDO*-forward, jaw dropping often occurs and tends to be associated with words that end in *ch*, *ge*, *e*, *se* and *te*.

After a drop of the lower jaw, there is the added advantage of encouraging reflexive intakes of breath at the end of a word through the lower jaw as if the jaw is a simple hand pump. When writing songs, being aware of and using words that tend to require jaw dropping can be very helpful for singers. Jaw dropping is one of the secret and lost weapons of speaking English clearly and precisely and maintaining a vertical mouth position. *HDO* is also an acronym for *heavy water*, which is just another stunning, jaw-dropping fact!

The direction of the *HDO* mouth: forward

The vertical width of the *HDO* mouth: tends to move from the thin end tip of the index finger to the thick joint end of the index finger, from *HOO* to *HAO*.

The *HDO* position usually is found at the ends of words.

The phonetic *HDO* connection is very similar to the *HAO*, though the *HDO* is used more at the end of words for *te* and *ter* sounds.

Breathing *HDO* connection: downward and inward

This is used largely for breathing in through the lower jaw, which acts as a very efficient intake pump for inhaling air before breathing out the next word.

Level of stress for *HDO*: medium stress on individual letters and higher stress on groups of letters

To remember the four howling positions, associate them with the following phrase: *Run Arthur's pony now! (HOO/HTO/HDO/HAO)*

Growling Mouth Movements

The following four reverse movements are based on early humankind's animalistic mouth movements of growling—**G is for the growling g force!** **Growling** is much more internal than *Howling*. **Growling** seems more egocentric, personal, passionate, and emotional. Often, it is used when talking about oneself or one's close relations, and it is more emotional and internal, and implies deeper feelings and sensations. For this reason, words using growling sounds, with the exception of growling verbs, tend to use higher-pitched, shorter, and sharper movements than words using howling sounds.

The **GRR**-*Reverse Cat Mouth Movement*

The growling cat movement is the direct opposite of *HOO*. It creates naturally higher stressed letters and words, as shown in the phrase *I feel very angry*, though not angry about having to learn English of course! Coincidentally, the **GRR** notation is the onomatopoeic shorthand for **Growling** and for text messages, but it is not a clenched teeth growl.

The shape of the mouth when making this sound is similar to when a human being smiles or when an animal is angry and growling, snarling, or snapping. It can be an offensive or defensive position and thus it is protective, and it can show pleasure, pain, fear, or even ecstasy.

These are all very extreme and opposite emotions, but all are conveyed with the same mouth movement: the mouth is a partially open growling mouth, not quite closed, about the width of the thin end of the index finger. This minimum gap is very important, as this is not a clenched teeth movement. It is not possible to speak clear English through clenched teeth, because this makes the movement unnecessarily angry and harsh, inhibits sound and breathing, and seriously reduces the flexibility of the mouth. This movement is more emotional than the *HOO* howling family movements. It is a much more internal sound, such as the big *I* and the big *E* in *me*.

The double **RR** emphasises the more stressed and reversed nature of this key animalistic mouth movement and is used in words such as *I*, *we*, *me*, *my*, *eye*, *dry*, and *die*.

Additional **GRR** *Notes*

These are used for verbs, where the actions are often combined with sensations and feelings, particularly the present tense of irregular verbs such as *eat*, *dream*, *weep*, *creep*, and *sleep*, creating an onomatopoeic effect when stressed. Like the *HOO* movement, and after a reversed and stressed growling *t* or *d*, this also encourages a sharp intake of breath. It is particularly used with the heavily stressed spelling of *ted* at the end of the simple past tense of regular verbs that start with a *t* or *d* in the present tense, and is pronounced in the *sid/tid* sound after endings of regular verbs (we can use GRR here specifically in case of verbs, because the difference between a small i when heavily stressed regular verb ending is not so different from a big E in normal conversation).

The direction of The **GRR** Mouth: reversed

The vertical width of the **GRR** mouth: thin end of the tip of the index finger

The **GRR** position is usually at the beginning of words or on its own, but it is also used for the ends of words.

The phonetic **GRR** connections: largely associated in this case with the big letter *I* sound, as in *I am, light, flight, night,* and *sight,* but not the little *i* sound in *ink.* The regular verb past tense *ted/tid* is a sole and notable exception verb ending, and as such, it is heavily stressed. This position is also used for the big letter *E* in *see, tea, free* or *re* for the beginning of words as in *rethink* (but not the little *e* sound in *entity*).

Breathing type for **GRR**: exhale outward. This is largely for breathing directly out, but it is also used for the repetitive inward and outward breathing associated with words that are more emotional.

Level of stress for **GRR**: high stress on groups of letters but not on individual letters, except with the letters *t* or *d* at the ends of words

GTR-*Reverse Reptilian Mouth Movement*

The **quick busy** reptilian movement (the opposite of *HTO*) naturally creates higher stressed words and letters; remember the phrase, *breathe think teeth!* **GTR** is ironically associated with fast cars. This certainly is the **GTR** of **TH** tongue movements, and it is much quicker and faster than the sleepy old and slow python (*HDO*). Similarly, it can overtake the slow, sleepy python any time on the road, which tends to drive a slower, old banger! This is a much younger and a more active, pushy, get-ahead snake!

Like **GRR**, this growling is done with a partially open mouth —about the width of the thin tip nail end of the index finger—which allows just enough space for the tongue to briefly protrude between the teeth and then hit the backs of the top front teeth very rapidly, neatly, and quickly.

This **GTR** movement is largely associated with the indefinite article *the*, with adjectives, and with the words *this* or *that.* The *t* in this **growling** notation emphasises the **TH** tongue movement. If instead of the very reversed **TH** sound one hears the very deadly dull thud of the **D** sound, then unfortunately, one's tongue is not in the right position between the teeth—it is behind them. The **TH** is also contained in words such as *that, then, this, three, breathe, think, panther, threaten,* and *thanks.* The **TH** sound creates great reverence and is used in words denoting important people such as *mother, brother,* and *father.* This is about the mouth heading south and not going north and forward, as one finds in howling, but going back in reverse, perhaps a little like a Michael Jackson moonwalk!

Additional **GTR** *Notes*

This tends to actually create reflexive physiological breathing activity and can and should create sharp intakes of breath through the mouth, as there is a tendency to push the head back with this movement so that the air can be expelled through the mouth in the next word or phrase (not expelled through the nose). This is the whole point of *the*, which should always be separated from the noun for the best impression. Even words such as *think* and *breathe* have a **TH** sound that actually makes one pause for thought and breath. Oxygen is a great source for feeding the brain! Most **TH** words are **GTR** connected rather than howling connected like *HTO*. **TH** words do have a tendency to be growling, because this sound is naturally much easier to cope with as the tongue moves closer to the teeth in this reversed position. In the old days of English language instruction, one would have included *thy* and *thee*, which are now largely obsolete, but not the forward movement of *thou*, which is also rarely used. This illustrates how important the **TH** has been to the English language. In fact, we discard **TH**s at our peril. If we try to do this, it will be because we do not fully understand how important the **TH** sound is for breathing and adding power and emotion to our words. Furthermore, in eliminating the **TH** sound, we have not understood the foundational semantics of the English language.

The direction of the **GTR** mouth position: reverse

The **GTR** mouth position is usually at the beginning of words, though it is also sometimes at the end of words.

The phonetic **GTR** connection: the exclusive reversed **TH** sound

The breathing type for **GTR**: inward and upward

This is a reflexive type of breathing through the tongue tapping between the upper front teeth.

Level of stress for **GTR**: high stress on the two letters **TH**, but medium stress on the others

GAR-*Reverse Aquatic Mouth Movement*

The sad shark movement, or the sad gar movement, is actually not a very nice looking freshwater fish found in the US, though it is probably misunderstood and has a heart of gold. (The gar fish seems more of a cross between a Dolphin and Alligator, although it is a fish. It has a different mouth structure from a shark, but when it opens its mouth in reverse position to attack, it is very GAR, and its wide mouth reveals many sharp teeth!) The reverse aquatic movement, which is opposite of the forward *HAO*, naturally creates low stressed words and letters; remember the phrase *sad, bad gar*!

This mouth movement is a very prolific phonetic movement. It is often used repetitively, and is largely associated with two of perhaps the most commonly used letters and sounds in the English language: the little happy *i* sound in *initial* (but not the big *I* sound in *I am*) and the little *a* sound in *apple* (but not the big *A* sound in *able*). This reversed movement can change *O* into *a*, as in *opinion*; it can change *O* into *wun*, as in *one*; it can change *O* into little *u*, as in the word *onion*. The list continues with **GAR**, even turning a big *U* into a tiny *u*, as in *under*. Once one appreciates that this is a prolific movement and covers many repeating phonetic sounds and movements, English becomes less complicated and more fluid. Knowing how to handle this mouth movement is one of the keys to speaking English well. It is important to realise that when faced with repeating **GAR** movements, such as in the word *insensitivity*, you should not panic!

Pronouncing the word *in-sen-si-ti-vi-ty* involves largely **GAR** movements. The key is not to close the mouth for each individual movement but to breathe through one mouth movement. However, the limitation of this movement is that it cannot stress individual letters or finish letters, just as its cousin the *HAO* movement cannot do.

The mouth is held fairly wide and open, and the growling movement is twice the width of **GRR**, approximately the thick joint end of the index finger. The **A** emphasises the aquatic nature of this mouth position as in the poor misunderstood *shark* that not everyone appreciates. The movement can also be used to put more stress on the *ou* and *ow* words, where the *ar* sound is similar but more stressed than the *HAO* sound.

Additional **GAR** Notes

This produces a very onomatopoeic empathic effect, and is more Elgar than Beethoven (remember the phrase *Are you feeling sad?*). It is similar to the effect of *HAO*, and is often used where **C, D, P, N**, and **L** do not want to be stressed. **GAR** encourages exhaling at the end of a word. One of the key repetitive movements and secrets of the English language is that it very conveniently covers many secondary phonetic sounds of many letters of the alphabet.

However, holding the sound for too long, and making it sound too reversed, can cause a very affected **GAR** type of voice because it does not allow one to finish letters at the ends of words, such as the final *d* sound in the word *sad*. People who think they are very posh often use this mouth movement; some do not always have very clear voices, and this movement was probably partly responsible for creating the stutter in Edward VI's voice when he tried to pronounce the word *king* (Kin-g **GAR**/*HDO*). In the word *king*, **GAR** is the first mouthable and is used for not putting stress on the *n*, which is hardly heard. Then, if the mouth is not moved forward in the *HDO* movement for the final *g* in *king*, and unless the mouth is quickly pushed forward on the *g*, there will be enormous stress on the mouth. This can create a stutter under certain emotional conditions.

This problem illustrates that it is impossible, even unwise, to try to speak clear English using only the reversed **GAR** position, as some of the current British family do; you are unable to finish the final letters of words just as many people listening to these types of voices often find. To get the best effect of this mouth movement, it should be much more open than **GRR**. This is important for softening the voice, creating empathy, and reducing further stress on the mouth.

The direction of the **GAR** mouth: reverse

The phonetic **GAR** connection is one of the most incredibly versatile movements of the English language because it covers a variety of sounds that are often found at the beginning of words, such as the *a* in *apple*, the *i* in the word *in*, the *e* in *eternal*, the u in *utterly*, and the more stressed *ou* in *shout*. It can be used for a more stressed *air* sound in the word *stairs*, and sometimes the *oi* sound in the word *oil*. It is very useful for blending and merging many sounds, but it is not good for finishing the final letters of words, though it is used exceptionally in *ty* combinations (insensitivity), where it is pronounced as *ti*. This is a very versatile movement, much more versatile than its opposite *HAO*, but like the *HAO* aquatic position, **GAR** has the same limitation in that it cannot be used for finishing letters at the ends of words, as King Edward VI of England painfully discovered.

The **GAR** position is in repetitive movements at the beginnings of words, and very occasionally at the ends of certain words.

Breathing **GAR** type: The **GAR** movement is used primarily for outward breathing, though it can be used for inward breathing as well.

Level of **GAR** stress: low stress on groups of letters and on individual letters

GDR-*Reverse Jaw Dropping Mouth Movement*

This movement is the direct opposite of *HDO* and naturally creates medium stressed words and letters, such as *never here is better*! Though there are some strong connections between the German language and English, there is no suggestion that this position has evolved directly from the old German Democratic Republic!

The **GDR** is connected very closely by sound with the **GAR** position, just like the aquatic position in the *HDO* and *HAO* howling sounds. But it also is based on two movements: wide partially open growling as in the **GRR** movement (moving from the thin end of the index finger to the thick joint end in two movements as in **GAR**) with a subtransitional extension to lower jaw drops. The **D** emphasizes the dropping of the lower jaw, as demonstrated when pronouncing the words *he, here, in, as, she, never,* and *better.*

Additional **GDR** *Notes*

GDR is a transitional mouth movement that is used for quickly moving out of inflexible growls and for reducing pressure. It is also used for suddenly stopping the sound or for shorter-sounding pronouns and prepositions such as *in, he,* and *she,* and for less important people than the **GRR** (*I* or *me*) in the same way that *HDO* does, but to a greater extent. The lower jaw drop, which tends to also drop the head down at the same time, creates, along with the **GTR** movement, the up and down head movement that is found in British parliament; boardrooms of better English speakers use this for emphasis in public speaking. It is a similar substitute for Italian hands and tends to make English a nodding type of language, which probably causes many MPs to nod off during question time in the houses of parliament! The **GDR** also encourages reflexive inhaling through the lower jaw, particularly on short words such as *in, at, his,* and *he.* The growling jaw drop seems more prevalent than in howling because growling itself tends to create more stress on the mouth than howling. The verb *is* can be spoken much better using a jaw drop on the *s* rather than the usually higher-stressed **GRR** position for some verbs. This is important exception for verbs if one is to avoid sounding like an overheated bumblebee.

This sound is also associated with reverse -*ce* at the ends of words, or for combinations of *nce and nt,* or for putting more downward pressure on *n, l, c, s,* and *p* in the middle of words.

This vertical reverse movement can completely stop the sound of a word by opening the mouth. This is the opposite of many languages, wherein the action of closing the mouth seems to stop the sound, which is more logical, but the English cannot do this; they have to be different, of course! This effect is obvious with the two short words *he* and *here*. If the word *he* is reverse jaw dropped too slowly, it becomes *here*; try it! This often involves short pronouns and prepositions. See the previous explanation for the *HDO* sound, as many of the same endings apply, and jaw dropping is used to reduce the growling effect and the passion or emotion of a word; it also encourages intakes of breath at the end of a word. It is often used to put more stress on the last mouth movement of a letter for nouns, but also reduces the strong and sometimes deafening American *r* in phrases such as *How is the weather?* Also, it is important for reducing the sound of the *t* on what can create an embarrassing word otherwise, such with the words *bed sheet* and *sheet of paper*.

Direction of **GDR** mouth movement: reversed and downward

The **GDR** mouth position is formed at the ends of words for reducing pressure and softening the final *t* sound. It is also formed in the middle of words, and when stressing individual letters.

The phonetic **GDR** connection: similar to the **GAR** position, though it is slower

Associated **GDR** breathing type: downward and inward, with the lower jaw acting as an inward inhaling pump.

Level of **GDR** stress: medium stress on groups of letters with the ability to create medium stress on individual letters

One phrase for remembering all four individual growling movements: *They feel sad here* (**GTR GRR GAR GDR**).

Vertical mouth movements naturally increase fluency by reducing pressure on the mouth.

Reducing pressure on the mouth in English when using your mouth in vertical movements is often done by not holding a mouth position for too long. This is why opposite movements are ideal and helpful in reducing stress on the mouth, particularly when it becomes uncomfortable with the much reversed and emotional **GRR** family of words.

The pressure is also reduced by fluid movement either into opposite movements or by increasing the distance between the roof of the mouth. This also increases flexibility, as English cannot be spoken clearly through clenched teeth. Because the mouth is moving and not static, these movements reduce pressure—another important effect. A moving mouth reduces pressure; a static mouth that is trying to speak tends to create pressure. At the same, a moving mouth produces patterns that are often repetitive of the same and similar movements but that create phrases with very different letters, words, and meanings. Repetitive mouth movements in themselves can reduce pressure on the mouth, but this is not always appreciated or understood.

The secret is to retain one mouth position in order to make the next two or three repetitive movements for different or similar phonetic sounds of the same mouth movement, as we have seen with **GAR/GAR**. Repetitive mouth movements also enable the concertina and breathing technique to kick in and dramatically increase breathing power, intonation, and fluency. This simple method of repetitive forward and reverse movements, particularly for **GAR/GAR** and *HAO/HAO*, naturally reduces pressure on the mouth without having to resort to extreme measures such as collapsing the mouth into horizontal mouth movements.

In addition to the above methods of taking the pressure off the mouth by movements, the jaw dropping downward *HDO* and **GDR** movements have the classic effect of opening the mouth wider. These are the classic key movements for reducing pressure because the bring a full stop to sounds, which naturally creates a much more relaxed mouth than attempting to halt sounds with clenched teeth. This then encourages the overuse of the tongue to reduce pressure and therefore tends to increase decibels on certain letters when they actually should be reduced. When in doubt, if the speaker feels that mouth pressure is building, he or she can use these jaw dropping mouth positions to reduce that pressure automatically, which causes the speaker to pause and take a breath, which is always a good strategy when speaking English.

These movements naturally reduce the pressure on the mouth and encourage the fluent vertical movements that help us to stress individual letters as needed, either in the middle of a word or at the end of a word. This helps rhythm, and therefore helps grammar and autocorrecting, retention, and breathing. All of this helps the student to speak very clear and perfect English in a number of impressive ways.

Further Basic Details to Help You Get into the Moving Mouth Dictionary

Where it is possible, the most dominate, single-mouth movement is notated along with its direction.

On the left side of the dictionary is the word itself in English, and for the best results, use this dictionary alongside another translation dictionary of your choice.

The breaks in the words in the middle column of the dictionary are called mouthables. These show how best to say the word slowly, and sometimes these do follow syllables, but largely they are written the way the word would be said only if the syllables follow the change in mouth movements.

The third column on the right shows the recommended notation and the pattern of the notation, which gives options either to say the word slowly for presentations or more quickly through breathing and focussing the first mouth notation and sometimes the last.

Please note that verbs are consistently stressed and are therefore very important for rhythm. These mouth movements tend to be simplified for that reason and tend to be largely *HOO* or **GRR** positions; these come first in order in the dictionary, and the nouns and adjectives come after.

Simplified mouth movements for verbs are also helpful for triggering, retaining, and accessing verbs quickly. The same verbs used as nouns or adjectives would be pronounced differently and with more variations, which are often more aquatic.

The Moving Mouth Dictionary largely follows the phonetic dictionary as a basis, though not to every letter, and this dictionary tends to encourage the speaker to use fewer reverse mouth movements, particularly **GAR** movements that tend to emphasise the small *a* (*at*) and *u* (*utter*) sounds. This dictionary encourages the use on of a softer *HAO* small *o* as a substitute for the small *a*. This creates a more natural, fluid sound where required and develops a more modern and up-to-date international English sound that is socially more inclusive and helps to create a very clear voice.

The Moving Mouth Dictionary emphasises and extends the sound, power, and emotion to combine more effectively with the meanings of words and the body language of words. This creates excellent, clear, and modern English as well as classless socially mobile voices that can compete at the very highest level internationally.

The combination of these mouth movements with more predictable basic phonetic sounds consistently associated with certain letters means that the guessing of how to pronounce a word is largely removed through mouth muscle memory and repetitive jaw movements, which leads to greater confidence and efficiency in speaking English.

In this dictionary, the first two letters of a mouth movement are the predominant phonetic sound. However, sometimes in English you might come across a few odd words where it would be unwise to stress the first letter of key mouth movements. A few examples are the words *leuk(a) emia* and *hy(a)enas*, where the *a* is not stressed; *i(s)land*, where the *s* is not stressed; *h(e)ight*, where the *e* is not stressed; and in determining the difference in pronunciation between *height* and the variations of *e(i)ther* or *(e)ither*. Where the letter is not stressed, it is encircled by two brackets ( ) or otherwise, as in this case, a normal and standard aquatic *a* position is used, but there are surprisingly few of these very challenging spelling aberrations.

English Alphabet in Mouth Positions

These are recommended positions close to how the alphabet letters are used rather than how they are usually taught in schools.

Letter	Mouthable	Nearest Phonetic Group
A	*HAO*	*ay*
B	**GRR**	**BE**
C	**GRR**	**CE**
D	**GRR**	**DE**
E	**GRR**	**EE**
F	**GAR**/*HDO*	*e/f*
G	*HOO*	*GE*
H	*HAO/HDO*	*ay/ch*
I	**GRR**	**I**
J	*HAO*	*J/ay*
K	*HAO*	*K/ay*
L	**GAR/GDR**	*e/l*
M	**GAR**/*HDO*	*e/m*
N	**GAR/GDR**	*e/n*
O	*HOO*	*O*
P	**GRR**	**PE**
Q	*HOO*	*Q U*
R	*HAO*	*AR*
S	**GAR/GDR**	*e/s*
T	**GRR**	**TE**
U	*HOO*	*U*
V	**GRR**	**VE**
W	*HOO/HOO*	*UU*
X	**GAR/GDR**	*e/x*
Y	**GRR**	**WI**
Z	**GAR**/*HOO*	**Ze**/*d*

Guide to the Pronunciation of English Cardinal Numbers

1	one	o-ne	**GAR/GDR**
2	two	two	*HOO*
3	three	th-ree	**GTR/GRR**
4	four	four	*HOO*
5	five	fi-ve	**GRR**/*HDO*
6	six	si-x	**GAR/GDR**
7	seven	se-ven	**GAR**/*HDO*
8	eight	eigh-t	*HAO/HOO*
9	nine	ni-ne	**GRR/GDR**
10	ten	te-n	**GAR/GDR**
11	eleven	e-le-ven	**GAR/GAR**/*HDO*
12	twelve	twe-lve	**GAR**/*HDO*
13	thirteen	thir-tee-n	**GTR/GRR/GDR**
14	fourteen	four-tee-n	*HOO*/**GRR/GDR**
15	fifteen	fi-f-tee-n	**GAR/GDR/GRR/GDR**
16	sixteen	si-x-tee-n	**GAR/GDR/GRR/GDR**
17	seventeen	se-ven-tee-n	**GAR**/*HDO*/**GRR/GDR**
18	eighteen	eigh-tee-n	*HAO*/**GRR/GDR**
19	nineteen	ni-ne-tee-n	**GRR/GDR/GRR/GDR**
20	twenty	twe-n-ty	**GAR/GDR/GAR**
21	twenty-one	twe-n-ty-o-ne	**GAR/GDR/GAR/GAR/GDR**
30	thirty	thir-ty	**GTR/GAR**
40	forty	four-ty	*HOO*/**GAR**
50	fifty	fi-f-ty	**GAR/GDR/GAR**
60	sixty	si-x-ty	**GAR/GDR/GAR**
70	seventy	se-ve-n-ty	**GAR/GAR/GDR/GAR**
80	eighty	eigh-ty	*HAO*/**GAR**
90	ninety	ni-ne-ty	**GRR/GDR/GAR**

100	one hundred	o-ne-hu-n-dre-d	**GAR/GDR/GAR/GDR/GAR/** *HOO*
200	two hundred	two-hu-n-dre-d	*HOO*/**GAR/GDR/GAR/***HOO*
1000	one thousand	o-ne-th-ou-sa-nd	**GAR/GDR/GTR/GAR/GAR/** **GDR**
2000	two thousand	two-thou-sa-nd	*HOO*/**GTR/GAR/GAR/GDR**
1000000	One million	o-ne-mi-lli-o-n	**GAR/GDR/GAR/GAR/***HAO*/ *HDO*
	One billion	o-ne-bi-lli-o-n	**GAR/GDR/GAR/GAR/***HAO*/ *HDO*
	One trillion	o-ne-tri-lli-o-n	**GAR/GDR/GAR/GAR/***HAO*/ *HDO*
	One quadtrillion	o-ne-qua-d-tri-lli-o-n	**GAR/GDR/***HAO*/*HDO*/**GAR/** **GAR/***HAO*/*HDO*

Guide to the Pronunciation
of Ordinal Numbers

1st	The-fir-st	**GTR-***HOO*/*HDO*
2nd	The-se-co-nd	**GTR-GAR/***HAO*/**GDR**
3rd	The-thir-d	**GTR-GTR/***HOO*
4th	The-four-th	**GTR-***HOO*/*HTO*
5th	The-fi-fth	**GTR-GAR/GTR**
6th	The- si-x-th	**GTR- GAR/GDR/GTR**
7th	The-se-ve-nth	**GTR-GAR/GAR/GTR**
8th	The-eigh-th	**GTR-***HAO*/**GTR**
9th	The-ni-nth	**GTR-GRR/GTR**
10th	The-te-n-th	**GTR-GAR/GDR/***HTO*
11th	The-e-le-ve-nth	**GTR-GAR/GAR/GAR/GTR**
12th	The-twe-l-fth	**GTR-GAR/GDR/GDR**
13th	The-thir-tee-nth	**GTR-GTR/GRR/GTR**
20th	The-twe-n-ti-e-th	**GTR- GAR/GDR/GAR/GAR/GTR**
21st	The-twe-n-ty-fir-st	**GTR-GAR/GDR/GAR/***HOO*/*HOO*
50th	The-fi-f-ti-e-th	**GTR-GAR/GDR/GAR/GAR/GTR**
100th	The-hu-n-dre-d-th	**GTR-GAR/GDR/GAR/***HDO*/**GTR**
1000th	The-th-ou-san-dth	**GTR-***HTO*/*HAO*/**GAR/GTR**

Guide to the Pronunciation
of the Days of the Week

Monday	Mo-n-day	**GAR/GDR**/*HAO*
Tuesday	Tues-day	*HOO/HAO*
Wednesday	We(dne)-s-day	**GAR/GDR**/*HAO*
Thursday	Thur-s-day	*HTO/HDO/HAO*
Friday	Fri-day	**GRR**/*HAO*
Saturday	Sa-tur-day	**GAR**/*HAO/HAO*
Sunday	Su-n-day	**GAR/GDR**/*HAO*

Guide to the Pronunciation
of the Months of the Year

January	Ja-n-u-ar-y	**GAR/GDR**/*HOO*/*HAO*/**GAR**
February	Fe-bru-ar-y	**GAR**/*HDO*/*HAO*/**GAR**
March	Mar-ch	*HAO*/*HDO*
April	A-pri-l	*HAO*/**GAR/GDR**
May	May	*HAO*
June	Ju-ne	*HOO*/*HDO*
July	Ju-ly	*HOO*/**GDR**
August	Au-gu-st	*HOO*/**GAR**/*HOO*
September	Se-p-te-m-ber	**GAR/GDR/GAR**/*HDO*/*HDO*
October	O-c-to-ber	*HAO*/*HDO*/*HOO*/*HDO*
November	No-ve-m-ber	*HOO*/**GAR**/*HDO*/*HDO*
December	De-ce-m-ber	**GRR/GAR**/*HDO*/*HDO*

English Telephone Alphabet

A	Andrew	A-n-drew	**GAR/GDR**/*HOO*
B	Bravo	Bra-vo	**GAR**/*HOO*
C	Charlie	Char-lie	*HAO*/**GAR**
D	David	Da-vi-d	*HAO*/**GAR/GDR**
E	Edward	E-d-war-d	**GAR**/*HDO*/*HAO*/*HDO*
F	Fox	Fo-x	*HAO*/*HDO*
G	George	Geor-ge	*HOO*/*HDO*
H	Harry	Ha-rry	**GAR/GAR**
I	Isabel	I-sa-be-l	**GAR/GAR/GAR/GDR**
J	Jack	Jac-k	**GAR**/*HDO*
K	King	Kin-g	**GAR**/*HDO*
L	Lucy	Lu-cy	*HOO*/**GAR**
M	Mike	Mi-ke	**GRR**/*HDO*
N	Nellie	Ne-llie	**GAR/GAR**
O	Oliver	O-li-ver	*HAO*/**GAR**/*HDO*
P	Peter	Pe-ter	**GRR**/*HDO*
Q	Queen	Quee-n	**GRR/GDR**
R	Robert	Ro-ber-t	*HAO*/*HAO*/*HOO*
S	Sugar	Su-gar	*HOO*/*HDO*
T	Tommy	To-mmy	*HAO*/**GAR**
U	Uniform	U-ni-for-m	*HOO*/**GAR**/*HOO*/*HDO*
V	Victory	Vi-c-to-ry	**GAR/GDR**/*HOO*/**GAR**
W	William	Wi-lli-a-m	**GAR/GAR/GAR**/*HDO*
X	Xmas	X-MA-S	**GAR/GDR/GAR**/*HDO*
Y	Yellow	Ye-llo-w	**GAR**/*HOO*/*HDO*
Z	Zebra	Ze-bra	**GRR/GDR**

Simplification of English Verb Tenses

It helps to remember that English verbs are stressed much more than other types of nouns and adjectives, and are important for rhythm and speaking; clearly, verbs need to be clear. This means that there is little time to think. It is important, therefore, to simplify tenses. We can do this by using trigger words that are associated with the tenses.

Verb Tense	Key Mouth Movement
1) Present tense (tends to go up in sound)	Today, I *speak* (**GRR**) English. (Also, *I am speaking English.*)
2) Present continuous tense (tends to be monotone)	Every day I *speak* (**GRR**) English.
3) Future (tends to go up in sound)	Tomorrow, I will *speak* (**GRR**) English. (Also, *I am going to speak English.*)
4) Simple past two forms Negative (tends to go down in sound in the past) Positive (tends to go down in sound in the past)	Yesterday, I didn't *speak* (**GRR**) English. Yesterday, I *spoke* (*HOO*) English.
5) Conditional past (tends to go down in sound)	A long time ago, I used to *speak* (**GRR**) English.

By using *I didn't* for the past and *I used to* for a long time ago, we can be more consistent in using the infinitive form, which means we only have to react with a change or extension of the mouth movement in the past. This can naturally simplify tenses.

The Past in Regular Verbs

Remember the basic regular verb rule if the present tense ends in a *d* or *t*. If it is followed by a silent *e*, then it will be pronounced *id* in the past:

Today, I *accept* (*HOO*)
Yesterday, I *accepted* (**GRR**)

If there is no *t* or *d*, then the *e* in *ed* is not sounded:

Today, I book (*HOO*)
Yesterday, I booked (*HOO*)

The *t* or *d* sounds are very important for triggering *HOO* or **GRR** mouth movements in regular verbs, just as they are with irregular verbs.

Simple and Consistent Mouth Movements to Trigger Irregular Verbs

Using simple mouth movements for irregular verbs that need to be stressed in English rhythm and aiding the reflex mouth movements can be done by observing a basic phenomenon: irregular verbs tend to **GRR** in the present tense with a few exceptions, and either go the opposite position *HOO* in the simple past or retain the **GRR** position and go down in sound. Also, associating them with common sound groups can help even more. Here are a few examples to illustrate this point.

GRR / *HOO*	**GRR / GRR**
CATCH/*CAUGHT*	**SLEEP/SLEPT**
TEACH/*TAUGHT*	**CREEP/CREPT**
BUY/*BOUGHT*	**DREAM/DREAMT**
BRING/*BROUGHT*	**BEGIN/BEGAN**
DRIVE/*DROVE*	**RING/RANG**
STRIDE/*STROVE*	**SING/SANG**
WEAVE/*WOVE*	**SWIM/SWAM**
BREAK/*BROKE*	**BREED/BRED**
SPEAK/*SPOKE*	**BLEED/BLED**
WRITE/*WROTE*	**FEED/FED**
RIDE/*RODE*	**LEAD/LED**
RISE/*ROSE*	**FEEL/FELT**
FREEZE/*FROZE*	**SPELL/SPELT**

The verbs listed above are a few examples of irregular verb patterns that have been deliberately shown here in more simplified mouth movements than you will find in the dictionary. This is to highlight the two main mouth movements of irregular verbs, which have a connection to regular verbs, and to show how they can be categorised to aid learning and retention.

Simple Guide to Key Phonetic Sound Bites for the Main Mouth Movements

In addition to a guide to the direction of mouth movements, there are distinct phonetic sounds running through these mouth movements, and often more than one can be associated with each notation. The key phonetic sounds are coming from **GRR** and **GAR** and *HOO* and *HAO* movements.

GRR is associated with the long stressed letter *I* as in *I am* and includes *sky* and *night*. But **GRR** is also connected with the long stressed *e* in *free* and *ease*.

GAR is the most prolific of mouth movements and is used for the largest number of letters, which is very convenient for fluency such as one finds at the beginning of many English words: *a* in *accept, i* in *initial, e* in *except, u* in *utterly, o* where it is converted into an *a* such as in *opinion*, and o where it is pronounced *wu* as in *one*.

GAR is sometimes used in the middle of the word, and where *ou* or *ow* is heavily stressed, and in *oi* where it is heavily stressed as in *avoid*.

GAR also can be used for the heavily stressed *air* sound in *stairs*.

GAR can be used at the end of a word such as the *ty* in at the end of the word *sensitivity*.

HOO is important for pronouncing the *t* and *d* at the ends of words; often this is the case for verbs or where the *e* is not sounded in regular verbs.

The main sound here is the *HOO* sound in *moon*, but also the *O* in *you* and *who*, the *O* in *over, oh,* or *rode,* and the *U* in *uniform* or *unite.*

HOO is used for the *aw* sound that includes or, au, or aw in words such as *call, all, awful,* or *caught*; for words ending in *ble, dle, kle,* or *tle* such as *able, candle, tickle,* or *little*; for words ending in *tion* or *sion* such as *administration* or *aversion.*

HAO is another key position where the sound is generally associated with the sound of the letter *a* as in the *ay* sound; it is a very important sound in the alphabet, as heard in the words *able, acorn,* or *ate*, and also *day, cave, brave* or *ray*; it is also heard in the middle of many words ending with *tion*, such as *administration.*

Also associated with the *ahh* sound in the *are* words in this dictionary, the *aar* sound is normally associated with three letters, and the *ay* sound is either single or two letters.

The *ou* sound as in *about* is softer than **GAR**.

The *HAO* movement is also used to form the *o* sound in *orange* and the *er* sound in the middle of words such as *aversion.*

Typical Mouth Movement Patterns

Having a system of notation for mouth movements allows us to study word patterns and be much more aware of them. If we are having a problem pronouncing a particular word, then it is likely we will have the same problem with other words of the same letter patterns. By taking a particular word and looking it up in a Word document or Excel program, we can look at all the other words that have the same patterns and quickly become an expert on that particular word pattern.

It soon becomes very clear that the English language is a very **GAR/GAR** *HOO/HOO* language. One can see clearly the repetitive nature of English mouth movements and the need for a strategy to handle them. The following are all examples of patterns that can be found at the beginning of English words, but the same combinations can also be found in the middle and at the ends of words.

GAR/GAR/*HDO*	**GRR/GRR**/*HDO*	*HAO/HAO/HDO*	*HOO/HOO/HDO*
a-ba-ck	be-si-de	ar-ca-de	clo-su-re
Bri-ti-sh	Chi-ne-se	blo-sso-m	Eu-ro-pe
ca-li-bre	de-pri-ve	car-to-n	fu-tu-re

The Moving Mouth Dictionary

Where there is the same word mentioned twice in the dictionary, the first is the verb, and the second is a noun or another meaning of the word. Verbs tend to be more extreme and therefore stressed more heavily, and nouns are more aquatic and therefore less stressed.

Ten key recap notes to remember and to aid you before using the dictionary:

1. **Understand the simplifying effect of vertical mouth movements.**
   Get the feel of these four vertical forward positions and four vertical reverse movements. Simply learn to drive your mouth the way you a car: G for reverse, H for forward, four gears for reverse, and four for forward! Very detailed explanations of all the mouth movements are found in the chapter titled Howling and Growling: Notations and Abbreviations. It is also very important to understand the key phonetic associations that these movements have with certain key letters of the English language, such as the phonetic sounds of the small *a* and big *A*, and the different phonetic sounds of the small *e* and big *E*, the two different sounds of *I* and *U* and *O*, and so on. It also is vital to understand that these mouth movements aid in breathing in and out through the mouth.

2. **Understand the simplifying effect of reduced vertical tongue movements.**
   Simply, there are only two main vertical tongue movements used here: one goes behind the upper front teeth, often used for *HOO* movements, and the other goes between the front teeth then taps the upper front teeth. This is used for **GTR** movements. The rest of the time, the tongue sleeps down in the base of jaw. Overuse of the tongue creates horizontal mouth movements, which cause uneven breathing and rhythm, which results in inconsistent grammar and affects the ability to autocorrect.

3. **Understand the simplifying effect of vertical mouthables and their patterns.**
   The repetitive, sequential effect on speaking English clearly, particularly holding the same mouth movement for a number of repetitive movements, such as **GAR**, is a very helpful phenomenon

and an enormous aid for speaking English fluently, such as when pronouncing in the word *sensitivity*. Understanding predictable pattern breakdowns of words will also improve your spelling.

4. **Understand the simplifying effect of increased breathing in and out through the mouth (not the nose!) on multiple vertical mouth movements.**

Vertical mouth movements combined with easy, mouthable, and breakable bite patterns of the word show very clearly the direction of the mouth movements and the patterns. This is very helpful in building confidence, in addition to saying words more consistently and clearly. Also, try to breathe the whole word out, which is very useful for longer words with many multiple mouth movements and helps the jaw and mouth memory. This breathing supercharged effect radically reduces the number of mouth movements required to say a word, which can be further reduced and simplified to a further two: one at the beginning of the word and one at the end. This dramatically increases speed, yet the word can be heard very clearly nonetheless, even with words such as *administration* and *unbelievable*.

5. **Sometimes in the dictionary, a word is mentioned more than once with the same spelling.**

In these cases, the first word is a verb and the second is either a noun or an adjective. Remember, verbs are stressed very heavily, use a partially closed mouth movement, and are very simplified, such as *HOO* and **GRR**. Therefore, verbs have fewer mouth movements than nouns and adjectives have, which tend to have open movements and are more complicated.

6. **Where there is a completely different meaning of a word, but it has the same spelling, this will be notated in the dictionary, such as the words *rowing* and *rowing*.**

The word will and can often be differentiated by its emotional meaning, which can be determined by using a combination of opposite mouth movements. Reverse G mouth movements tend to be more emotional and internal; forward mouth movements are more environmental and external and therefore are less emotional. This allows us to differentiate how we say the words so that they can be spoken with a clear difference in meaning.

7. **Where one letter is not relevant to the pronunciation, it is completely neutralized by fewer stressed mouth movements.**

   This often is found in mouthables of, say, groups of letters of three near the beginning of the word, where the last letter of the three is not stressed, but the first one or two are the key stressed letters. Generally, these will be shown as open movements and can often be found at the beginning of words. Aquatic open movements are ideal for doing this, which is why they are often used with **GAR** and HAO, as in *leo-par-d* for the little *e* sound, though in *peo-ple*, **GRR** is used for a big *E* sound.

8. **Sometimes one or more letters are clearly not relevant but cannot be ignored through a less stressed mouth movement, and, if stressed, would make the word incomprehensible.**

   In these cases, brackets ( ) are put around the letter or letters. There are very few of these, and they are often found near the ends of words such as *recei(p)t* and *gun(wa)le*.

9. **Understand the amazing effect of jaw dropping on the ability to speak clear English and reduce pressure on the mouth.**

   Stress individual letters, particularly in the middle and endings of words, using the **GDR** and *HDO* positions, and notice the effect on speaking very clear English.

10. **Understand the importance of English rhythm in speaking English clearly.**

    This can be defined as *one word up in sound* and *one word down in sound; however small or large, the distance is equal and the same*. This helps autocorrecting the music that English grammar creates and aids in the stressing of verbs. Also, and this is very important, regulating speed helps in the absorption of what is being said, thus aiding both the speaker and the listener. Breathing intonation without vertical mouth movements is just not possible.

You are now ready to go! How about starting by looking up the word *management* or *unbelievable*?

Word	Mouthables	Mouth Movements Notations
A		
A	A	*HAO*
a	a	**GAR**
aback	a-ba-ck	**GAR/GAR**/*HDO*
abandon	a-ban-do-n	**GAR/GAR**/*HAO*/*HDO*
abandoned	a-ban-do-ne-d	**GAR/GAR**/*HAO*/**GDR**/*HOO*
abashed	a-ba-she-d	**GAR/GAR**/*HOO*/*HOO*
abate	a-ba-te	**GAR**/*HAO*/*HDO*
abated	a-ba-ted	**GAR**/*HAO*/**GRR**
abbey	a-bbey	**GAR/GRR**
abbot	a-bbo-t	**GAR**/*HAO*/*HDO*
abbreviation	a-bbre-vi-a-tion	**GAR/GRR/GAR**/*HAO*/*HOO*
abdicate	a-b-di-ca-te	**GAR/GDR/GAR**/*HAO*/*HDO*
abduct	a-b-duc-t	**GAR/GDR/GAR**/*HOO*
abduction	a-b-duc-tion	**GAR/GDR/GAR**/*HOO*
aberration	a-ber-ra-tion	**GAR**/*HAO*/*HAO*/*HOO*
abeyance	a-bey-a-nce	**GAR**/*HAO*/**GAR/GDR**
abide	a-bi-de	**GAR/GRR**/*HDO*
ability	a-bi-li-ty	**GAR/GAR/GAR/GAR**
abject	a-b-jec-t	**GAR/GDR/GAR**/*HOO*
ablaze	a-bla-ze	**GAR**/*HAO*/*HDO*
able	a-ble	*HAO*/*HOO*
abnormal	a-b-nor-ma-l	**GAR/GDR**/*HOO*/**GAR/GDR**
aboard	a-boar-d	**GAR**/*HOO*/*HOO*
abode	a-bo-de	**GAR**/*HOO*/*HDO*
abolish	a-bo-li-sh	**GAR**/*HAO*/**GAR**/*HDO*
abominable	a-bo-mi-na-ble	**GAR**/*HAO*/**GAR/GAR**/*HOO*
aboriginal	a-bo-ri-gi-nal	**GAR/GAR/GAR/GAR/GDR**

Word	Mouthables	Mouth Movements Notations
aborigine	a-bo-ri-gi-ne	GAR/GAR/GAR/GAR/GDR
abort	a-bor-t	GAR/*HOO*/*HOO*
abortion	a-bor-tion	GAR/*HOO*/*HOO*
abound	a-bou-nd	GAR/GAR/GDR
about	a-bou-t	GAR/*HAO*/*HOO*
above	a-bo-ve	GAR/GAR/*HDO*
abrasive	a-bra-si-ve	GAR/*HAO*/GAR/*HDO*
abreast	a-brea-st	GAR/GAR/*HOO*
abridge	a-bri-dge	GAR/GAR/*HDO*
abroad	a-broa-d	GAR/*HOO*/*HDO*
abrupt	a-bru-pt	GAR/GAR/*HOO*
abscond	a-b-sco-nd	GAR/GDR/*HAO*/GDR
absence	a-b-se-nce	GAR/GDR/GAR/GDR
absent	a-b-se-nt	GAR/GDR/GAR/GDR
absentee	a-b-se-n-tee	GAR/GDR/GAR/GDR/GRR
absolute	a-b-so-lu-te	GAR/GDR/*HOO*/*HOO*/*HDO*
absolutely	a-b-so-lu-te-ly	GAR/*HOO*/*HOO*/*HDO*/GDR
absolution	a-b-so-lu-tion	GAR/GDR/*HOO*/*HOO*/*HOO*
absorb	a-b-sor-b	GAR/GDR/*HOO*/*HDO*
absorption	a-b-sor-p-tion	GAR/GDR/*HOO*/*HDO*/*HOO*
abstain	a-b-stai-n	GAR/GDR/*HAO*/GDR
abstemious	a-b-ste-mi-ous	GAR/GDR/GRR/GAR/GAR
abstract	a-b-strac-t	GAR/GDR/GAR/*HOO*
abstracted	a-b-strac-ted	GAR/GDR/GAR/GRR
abuse	a-bu-se	GAR/*HOO*/*HDO*
abusive	a-bu-si-ve	GAR/*HOO*/GAR/GDR
abysmal	a-by-smal	GAR/GAR/*HDO*
abyss	a-by-ss	GAR/GAR/GDR
academic	a-ca-de-mi-c	GAR/GAR/GAR/GAR/GDR
academy	a-ca-de-my	GAR/GAR/GAR/GAR
accelerate	a-cce-le-ra-te	GAR/GAR/*HAO*/*HAO*/*HDO*

Word	Mouthables	Mouth Movements Notations
accelerator	a-cce-le-ra-tor	**GAR/GAR**/*HAO*/*HAOHDO*
accent	a-cce-nt	**GAR/GAR/GDR**
accept	a-cce-pt	**GAR/GAR**/*HOO*
acceptance	a-cce-p-ta-nce	**GAR/GAR**/*HDO*/**GAR/GDR**
access	a-cce-ss	**GAR/GAR**/*HOO*
accessary	a-cce-ssa-ry	**GAR/GAR/GAR**/*HDO*
accessories	a-cce-ssor-ies	**GAR/GAR**/*HOO*/**GDR**
accessory	a-cce-sso-ry	**GAR/GAR**/*HOO*/*HDO*
accident	a-cci-de-nt	**GAR/GAR/GAR/GDR**
acclaim	a-cclai-m	**GAR**/*HAO*/*HDO*
accommodate	a-cco-mmo-da-te	**GAR**/*HAO*/*HOO*/*HAO*/*HDO*
accommodating	a-cco-mmo-da-ting	**GAR**/*HAO*/*HOO*/*HAO*/**GDR**
accommodation	a-cco-mmo-da-tion	**GAR**/*HAO*/*HOO*/*HAO*/*HOO*
accompany	a-cco m-pa-ny	**GAR/GAR**/*HDO*/**GAR/GDR**
accomplice	a-cco-m-pli-ce	**GAR/GAR**/*HDO*/**GAR/GDR**
accomplish	a-cco-m-pli-sh	**GAR/GAR**/*HDO*/**GAR**/*HDO*
accomplished	a-cco-m-pli-she-d	**GAR/GAR**/*HDO*/**GAR**/*HDO*/*HOO*
accomplishment	a-cco-m-pli-sh-ment	**GAR/GAR**/*HDO*/**GAR**/*HDO*/**GRR**
accord	a-ccor-d	**GAR**/*HOO*/*HOO*
accordance	a-ccor-da-nce	**GAR**/*HOO*/**GAR/GDR**
according	a-ccor-ding	**GAR**/*HOO*/**GDR**
accordion	a-ccor-di-o-n	**GAR**/*HOO*/**GAR**/*HAO*/*HDO*
accost	a-cco-st	**GAR**/*HAO*/*HOO*
account	a-ccou-nt	**GAR/GAR/GDR**
accountable	a-ccou-nt-a-ble	**GAR/GAR/GDR/GAR**/*HOO*
accountant	a-ccou-n-ta-nt	**GAR/GAR/GDR/GAR/GDR**
accounting	a-ccou-n-ting	**GAR/GAR/GDR/GDR**
accrual	a-ccru-al	**GAR**/*HOO*/**GDR**
accrued	a-ccrue-d	**GAR**/*HOO*/*HOO*
accumulate	a-ccu-mu-la-te	**GAR**/*HOO*/*HOO*/*HAO*/*HDO*
accurate	a-ccu-ra-te	**GAR**/*HOO*/*HAO*/*HDO*

Word	Mouthables	Mouth Movements Notations
accuse	a-ccu-se	GAR/*HOO*/*HDO*
accustomed	a-ccu-sto-me-d	GAR/GAR/*HAO*/*HOO*/*HOO*
ace	a-ce	*HAO*/GDR
ache	a-che	*HAO*/*HDO*
achieve	a-chie-ve	GAR/GAR/*HDO*
achievement	a-chie-ve-me-nt	GAR/GAR/*HDO*/GAR/GDR
acid	a-ci-d	GAR/GAR/*HOO*
acknowledge	a-c-know-led-ge	GAR/GDR/*HAO*/GAR/*HDO*
acknowledgement	a-c-know-led-ge-me-nt	GAR/GDR/*HAO*/GAR/*HDO*/GAR/ GDR
acorn	a-cor-n	*HAO*/*HOO*/*HDO*
acoustic	a-cou-sti-c	GAR/*HOO*/GAR/GDR
acquaint	a-cquai-nt	GAR/*HAO*/GDR
acquaintance	a-cquai-n-ta-nce	GAR/*HAO*/GDR/GAR/GDR
acquire	a-cqui-re	GAR/GRR/*HDO*
acquit	a-cqui-t	GAR/GAR/*HOO*
acquittal	a-cqui-ttal	GAR/GAR/*HDO*
acre	a-cre	*HAO*/*HDO*
acrimonious	a-cri-mo-ni-ous	GAR/GAR/*HOO*/GAR/*HAO*
acrobat	a-cro-ba-t	GAR/*HOO*/GAR/*HOO*
across	a-cro-ss	GAR/*HAO*/*HDO*
acrylic	a-cry-li-c	GAR/GAR/GAR/GDR
act	a-ct	GAR/*HOO*
acting	a-c-ti-ng	GAR/GDR/GAR/GDR
action	a-c-tion	GAR/GDR/*HOO*
actionable	a-ction-a-ble	GAR/*HOO*/GAR/*HOO*
activate	a-c-ti-va-te	GAR/GDR/GAR/*HAO*/*HDO*
active	a-c-ti-ve	GAR/GDR/GAR/*HDO*
actor	a-c-tor	GAR/GDR/*HOO*
actress	a-c-tre-ss	GAR/GDR/GAR/*HDO*
actual	a-c-tu-al	GAR/GDR/*HOO*/GDR

Word	Mouthables	Mouth Movements Notations
actually	a-c-tu-a-lly	**GAR/GDR/**_HDO_**/GAR/GDR**
actuate	a-c-tu-a-te	**GAR/GDR/**_HOO/HAO/HDO_
acupuncture	a-cu-pun-c-tu-re	**GAR/**_HOO_**/GAR/GDR/**_HOO/HDO_
acute	a-cu-te	**GAR/**_HOO/HDO_
ad	a-d	**GAR/**_HDO_
adlib	a-d-li-b	**GAR/GDR/GAR/**_HDO_
adapt	a-da-p-t	**GAR/GAR/GDR/**_HOO_
adaptable	a-da-p-ta-ble	**GAR/GAR/GDR/GAR/**_HOO_
adapter	a-da-p-ter	**GAR/GAR/**_HDO/HDO_
adaption	a-da-p-ta-tion	**GAR/GAR/GDR/**_HAO/HOO_
add	a-dd	**GAR/**_HOO_
Adder	A-d-der	**GAR/**_HDO/HDO_
addict	a-ddi-c-t	**GAR/GAR/GDR/**_HOO_
addicted	a-ddi-c-ted	**GAR/GAR/GDR/GRR**
addictive	a-ddi-c-ti-ve	**GAR/GAR/GDR/GAR/**_HDO_
addition	a-ddi-tion	**GAR/GAR/**_HOO_
additional	a-ddi-tion-al	**GAR/GAR/**_HOO/HDO_
additive	a-d-di-ti-ve	**GAR/GDR/GAR/GAR/**_HDO_
address	a-d-dre-ss	**GAR/GDR/GAR/**_HDO_
addresses	a-d-dre-sses	**GAR/GDR/GAR/GDR**
adept	a-de-pt	**GAR/GAR/**_HOO_
adequate	a-de-qua-te	**GAR/GAR/**_HAO/HDO_
adhere	a-d-here	**GAR/GDR/GDR**
adhesion	a-d-he-sion	**GAR/GDR/GRR/**_HOO_
adhesive	a-d-he-si-ve	**GAR/GDR/GRR/GAR/GDR**
adjacent	a-d-ja-cen-t	**GAR/GDR/**_HAO_**/GAR/**_HOO_
adjective	a-d-jec-ti-ve	**GAR/GDR/GAR/GAR/**_HDO_
adjoin	a-d-joi-n	**GAR/GDR/**_HAO_**/GDR**
adjourn	a-d-jour-n	**GAR/GDR/GAR/**_HDO_
adjudicate	a-d-ju-di-ca-te	**GAR/GDR/**_HOO_**/GAR/**_HAO/HDO_
adjust	a-d-ju-st	**GAR/GDR/GAR/**_HDO_

Word	Mouthables	Mouth Movements Notations
adjustable	a-d-ju-sta-ble	GAR/GDR/GAR/GAR/*HOO*
adjustment	a-d-ju-st-me-nt	GAR/GDR/GAR/*HOO*/GAR/GDR
adman	a-d-ma-n	GAR/GDR/GAR/GDR
admin	a-d-mi-n	GAR/GDR/GAR/GDR
administer	a-d-mi-ni-ster	GAR/GDR/GAR/GAR/*HDO*
administration	a-d-mi-ni-stra-tion	GAR/GDR/GAR/GAR/*HAO*/*HOO*
admiral	a-d-mi-ral	GAR/GDR/GAR/*HDO*
admire	a-d-mi-re	GAR/GDR/GRR/*HDO*
admission	a-d-mi-ssion	GAR/GDR/GAR/*HOO*
admit	a-d-mi-t	GAR/GDR/GAR/GDR
admittance	a-d-mi-ta-nce	GAR/GDR/GAR/GAR/GDR
admittedly	a-d-mi-tted-ly	GAR/GDR/GAR/GRR/GDR
admonish	a-d-mo-ni-sh	GAR/GDR/*HAO*/GAR/*HDO*
adolescent	a-do-les-cen-t	GAR/*HOO*/GAR/GAR/GRR
adopt	a-do-pt	GAR/*HAO*/*HDO*
adoption	a-do-p-tion	GAR/*HAO*/*HDO*/*HOO*
adore	a-do-re	GAR/*HOO*/*HDO*
Adriatic	A-dri-a-ti-c	*HAO*/GAR/GAR/GAR/GDR
adult	a-dul-t	GAR/GAR/*HDO*
adulterate	a-dul-te-ra-te	GAR/GAR/*HAO*/*HAO*/*HDO*
advance	a-d-va-nce	GAR/GDR/GAR/GDR
advanced	a-d-van-ce-d	GAR/GDR/GAR/GDR/*HOO*
advantage	a-d-van-ta-ge	GAR/GDR/GAR/*HAO*/*HDO*
advent	a-d-ven-t	GAR/GDR/GAR/*HOO*
adventitious	a-d-ven-ti-ti-ous	GAR/GDR/GAR/*HDO*/*HAO*
adventure	a-d-ven-tu-re	GAR/GDR/GAR/*HOO*/*HDO*
adventurous	a-d-ven-tur-ous	GAR/GDR/GAR/*HOO*/*HAO*
adverb	a-d-ver-b	GAR/GDR/*HAO*/*HDO*
adversary	a d ver sa ry	GAR/GDR/*HAO*/GAR/GDR
adverse	a-d-ver-se	GAR/GDR/*HAO*/*HDO*
adversity	a-d-ver-si-ty	GAR/GDR/*HAO*/GAR/GAR

Word	Mouthables	Mouth Movements Notations
advert	a-d-ver-t	**GAR/GDR/**_HAO_/_HDO_
advertise	a-d-ver-ti-se	**GAR/GDR/**_HAO_/**GRR/**_HDO_
advertisement	a-d-ver-ti-se-ment	**GAR/GDR/**_HAO_/**GAR/GDR/GRR**
advertiser	a-d-ver-ti-ser	**GAR/GDR/**_HAO_/**GRR/**_HDO_
advertising	a-d-ver-ti-si-ng	**GDR/**_HAO_/**GRR/GAR/GDR**
advice	a-d-vi-ce	**GAR/GDR/GRR/GDR**
advisable	a-d-vi-sa-ble	**GAR/GDR/GRR/GAR/**_HOO_
advise	a-d-vi-se	**GAR/GDR/GRR/**_HDO_
adviser	a-d-vi-ser	**GAR/GDR/GRR/**_HDO_
advocate	a-d-vo-ca-te	**GAR/GDR/**_HOO_/_HAO_/_HDO_
Aegean	Ae-ge-an	_HAO_/**GRR/GDR**
aerial	ae-ri-al	_HAO_/**GAR/GDR**
aerobics	ae-ro-bi-cs	_HAO_/_HOO_/**GAR/GDR**
aeroplane	ae-ro-pla-ne	_HAO_/_HOO_/_HAO_/**GDR**
afar	a-far	**GAR/**_HAO_
affair	a-ffair	**GAR/**_HAO_
affect	a-ffe-ct	**GAR/GAR/**_HOO_
affection	a-ffec-tion	**GAR/GAR/**_HOO_
affectionate	a-ffec-tion-a-te	**GAR/GAR/**_HOO_/_HAO_/_HDO_
affirm	a-ffir-m	**GAR/**_HOO_/_HDO_
affirmative	a-ffir-ma-ti-ve	**GAR/**_HOO_/**GAR/GAR/**_HDO_
afflict	a-ffli-ct	**GAR/GAR/**_HOO_
affluence	a-fflu-e-nce	**GAR/**_HOO_/**GAR/GDR**
afford	a-ffor-d	**GAR/**_HOO_/_HOO_
afforest	a-fo-re-st	**GAR/**_HAO_/**GAR/**_HOO_
affray	a-ff-ray	**GAR/**_HDO_/_HAO_
affront	a-ffro-nt	**GAR/GAR/GDR**
afield	a-fie-l-d	**GAR/GAR/GDR/**_HOO_
aflame	a-fla-me	**GAR/**_HAO_/_HDO_
afloat	a-floa-t	**GAR/**_HOO_/_HOO_
afoot	a-foo-t	**GAR/**_HOO_/_HOO_

Word	Mouthables	Mouth Movements Notations
aforesaid	a-fore-sai-d	GAR/*HOO*/GAR/GRR
afraid	a-frai-d	GAR/*HAO*/*HOO*
afresh	a-fre-sh	GAR/GAR/*HDO*
African	A-fri-ca-n	GAR/GAR/GAR/GDR
aft	af-t	*HDO*/*HOO*
after	af-ter	*HDO*/*HDO*
afterwards	af-ter-war-ds	*HDO*/*HDO*/*HAO*/*HDO*
again	a-gai-n	GAR/*HAO*/GDR
against	a-gai-nst	GAR/*HAO*/GRR
agape	a-ga-pe	GAR/*HAO*/GDR
age	a-ge	*HAO*/*HDO*
aged	a-ge-d	*HAO*/*HOO*/*HOO*
agency	a-gen-cy	*HAO*/GAR/GAR
agenda	a-ge-n-da	GAR/GAR/GDR/GAR
agent	a-ge-nt	*HAO*/GAR/GDR
aggravate	a-gg-ra-va-te	GAR/GDR/GAR/*HAO*/*HDO*
aggregate	a-gg-re-ga-te	GAR/GDR/GAR/*HAO*/*HDO*
aggression	a-gg-re-sion	GAR/GDR/GAR/*HOO*
aggressive	a-gg-res-si-ve	GAR/GDR/GAR/GAR/*HDO*
aggrieved	a-gg-rie-ve-d	GAR/GDR/GAR/*HOO*/*HOO*
agro	a-gg-ro	GAR/GDR/*HOO*
aghast	a-gha-st	GAR/*HAO*/*HOO*
Agiers	A-gi-ers	GAR/GAR/*HDO*
agile	a-gi-le	GAR/GRR/GDR
agility	a-gi-li-ty	GAR/GAR/GAR/GAR
agitate	a-gi-ta-te	GAR/GAR/*HAO*/*HDO*
ago	a-go	GAR/*HOO*
agog	a-go-g	GAR/*HAO*/*HDO*
agonize	a-go-ni-ze	GAR/*HAO*/GRR/GDR
agony	a-go-ny	GAR/*HAO*/GAR
agree	a-gree	GAR/GRR

Word	Mouthables	Mouth Movements Notations
agreeable	a-gree-a-ble	**GAR/GRR/GAR/***HOO*
agreed	a-gree-d	**GAR/GRR/***HOO*
agreement	a-gree-men-t	**GAR/GRR/GAR/***HOO*
agriculture	a-gri-cu-l-tu-re	**GAR/GAR/GAR/GDR/***HOO/HDO*
aground	a-grou-nd	**GAR/GAR/GDR**
ague	a-gue	*HAO/HOO*
ahead	a-hea-d	**GAR/GAR/***HOO*
aid	ai-d	*HAO/HOO*
ail	ai-l	*HAO/***GDR**
ailed	ai-le-d	*HAO/***GDR***/HOO*
aim	ai-m	*HAO/HDO*
air	air	*HAO*
aircraft	air-craf-t	*HAO/HAO/HOO*
aircrew	air-crew	*HAO/HOO*
airfield	air-fie-l-d	*HAO/***GAR/GDR***/HOO*
airlift	air-li-ft	*HAO/***GAR***/HDO*
airline	air-li-ne	*HAO/***GRR/GDR**
airliner	air-li-ner	*HAO/***GRR***/HDO*
airmail	air-mai-l	*HAO/HAO/***GDR**
airplane	air-pla-ne	*HAO/HAO/***GDR**
airport	air-por-t	*HAO/HOO/HOO*
airsickness	air-si-ck-ness	*HAO/***GAR***/HDO/***GDR**
airstrip	air-stri-p	*HAO/***GAR/GDR**
airtight	air-tigh-t	*HAO/***GRR***/HOO*
airy	ai-ry	*HAO/HDO*
aisle	(a)i(s)-le	**GRR/GDR**
ajar	a-jar	**GAR/***HAO*
akin	a-ki-n	**GAR/GAR/GDR**
alacrity	a-la-cri-ty	**GAR/GAR/GAR/GAR**
ale	a-le	*HAO/HDO*
alias	a-li-a-s	*HAO/***GAR/GAR/GDR**

Word	Mouthables	Mouth Movements Notations
alarm	a-lar-m	GAR/*HAO*/GDR
alas	a-la-s	GAR/GAR/GDR
Albanian	A-l-ba-ni-an	GAR/GDR/*HAO*/GDR/GDR
alcohol	a-l-co-ho-l	GAR/GDR/*HOO*/*HAO*/GDR
alcoholic	al-co-ho-li-c	GAR/GDR/*HOO*/*HAO*/GAR/GDR
alert	a-ler-t	GAR/*HAO*/*HOO*
algebra	a-l-ge-bra	GAR/GDR/GAR/*HDO*
Algerian	A-l-ge-ri-an	GAR/GDR/GRR/GAR/GDR
alibi	a-li-bi	GAR/GAR/GRR
alien	a-li-e-n	*HAO*/GAR/GAR/GDR
alienate	a-li-e-na-te	*HAO*/GAR/GAR/*HAO*/*HDO*
alight	a-ligh-t	GAR/GRR/*HOO*
align	a-li-gn	GAR/GRR/GDR
alike	a-li-ke	GAR/GRR/*HDO*
alive	a-li-ve	GAR/GRR/*HDO*
aloud	a-lou-d	GAR/GAR/GRR
all	al-l	*HOO*/*HDO*
allay	a-llay	GAR/*HAO*
alleged	a-lle-ge-d	GAR/GAR/*HOO*/*HOO*
allegorical	a-lle-go-ri-cal	GAR/GAR/*HAO*/GAR/*HDO*
allegory	a-lle-go-ry	GAR/GAR/*HAO*/GDR
allergic	a-ller-gi-c	GAR/*HOO*/GAR/GDR
allergy	a-ller-gy	GAR/*HOO*/GDR
alleviate	a-lle-vi-a-te	GAR/GRR/GAR/*HAO*/*HDO*
alley	al-ley	GAR/GRR
alliance	a-lli-a-nce	GAR/GRR/GAR/GDR
allied	a-llie-d	GAR/GRR/*HOO*
alligator	a-lli-ga-tor	GAR/GAR/*HAO*/*HOO*
allocate	a-llo-ca-te	GAR/*HOO*/*HAO*/*HDO*
allot	a-llo-t	GAR/*HAO*/*HOO*
allotment	a-llo-t-men-t	GAR/*HAO*/*HDO*/GAR/*HOO*

Word	Mouthables	Mouth Movements Notations
allow	a-llo-w	**GAR/GAR**/*HDO*
allow	a-llo-we-d	**GAR/GAR**/*HOO/HOO*
allowance	a-llo-wa-nce	**GAR/GAR/GAR/GDR**
alloy	a-lloy	**GAR**/*HAO*
allude	a-llu-de	**GAR**/*HOO/HDO*
allure	a-llu-re	**GAR**/*HAO/HDO*
allusion	a-llu-sion	**GAR**/*HOO/HOO*
ally	a-lly	**GAR/GRR**
almanac	al-ma-na-c	*HOO*/**GAR/GAR/GDR**
almighty	al-migh-ty	*HOO*/**GRR/GAR**
almost	al-mo-st	*HOO/HOO/HOO*
alms	al-ms	*HDO/HDO*
aloud	a-lou-d	**GAR/GAR**/*HOO*
altar	al-tar	*HAO*/**GAR**
alter	al-ter	*HOO/HDO*
altered	al-tere-d	*HOO/HOO/HOO*
amalgamate	a-ma-l-ga-ma-te	**GAR/GAR/GDR/GAR**/*HAO/HDO*
amass	a-ma-ss	**GAR/GAR**/*HDO*
amateur	a-ma-teur	**GAR/GAR**/*HDO*
amateurish	a-ma-teur-i-sh	**GAR/GAR**/*HDO*/**GAR/GDR**
amaze	a-ma-ze	**GAR**/*HAO*/**GRR**
amazement	a-ma-ze-men-t	**GAR**/*HAO*/**GDR/GAR**/*HOO*
amazing	a-ma-zi-ng	**GAR**/*HAO*/**GAR/GDR**
ambassador	a-m-bas-sa-dor	**GAR**/*HDO*/**GAR/GAR**/*HOO*
amber	a-m-ber	**GAR/GDR**/*HDO*
ambiance	am-bi-a-nce	*HDO*/**GAR/GAR/GDR**
ambiguity	a-m-bi-gu-i-ty	**GAR/GDR/GAR**/*HOO*/**GAR/GAR**
ambiguous	a-m-bi-gu-ous	**GAR/GDR/GAR**/*HOO/HAO*
ambition	a-m-bi-ti-ous	**GAR/GDR/GAR**/*HDO/HAO*
ambush	a-m-bu-sh	**GAR/GDR**/*HOO/HDO*
amenable	a-me-na-ble	**GAR/GRR/GAR**/*HOO*

Word	Mouthables	Mouth Movements Notations
amendment	a-me-nd-men-t	GAR/GAR/GDR/GAR/GRR
amends	a-me-nds	GAR/GAR/GDR
amenities	a-me-ni-ti-es	GAR/GAR/GAR/GAR/GDR
American	A-me-ri-ca-n	GAR/GAR/GAR/GAR/GDR
amethyst	a-me-th-y-st	GAR/GAR/GTR/GAR/*HDO*
amiable	a-mi-a-ble	*HAO*/GAR/GAR/*HOO*
amicable	a-mi-ca-ble	GAR/GAR/GAR/*HOO*
amid	a-mi-d	GAR/GAR/*HOO*
amidst	a-mi-d-st	GAR/GAR/GRR/*HDO*
amiss	a-mi-ss	GAR/GAR/*HDO*
ammonia	a-mmo-ni-a	GAR/*HOO*/GAR/GAR
ammunition	a-mmu-ni-tion	GAR/*HOO*/GAR/*HOO*
amnesty	a-m-ne-sty	GAR/GDR/GAR/GAR
among	a-mon-g	GAR/GAR/*HDO*
amongst	a-mon-gst	GAR/GAR/*HDO*
amoral	a-mo-ral	*HAO*/*HAO*/GDR
amorous	a-mo-rous	GAR/*HAO*/*HAO*
amorphous	a-mor-phou-s	GAR/*HOO*/GAR/*HDO*
amortize	a-mor-ti-ze	GAR/*HOO*/GRR/*HDO*
amount	a-mou-nt	GAR/GAR/GDR
amphibian	a-m-phi-bi-a-n	GAR/GDR/GAR/GAR/GAR/GDR
amphibious	a-m-phi-bi-ous	GAR/GDR/GAR/GAR/*HAO*
ample	a-m-ple	GAR/*HDO*/*HOO*
amplify	a-m-pli-fy	GAR/*HDO*/GAR/GRR
ampoule	a-m-pou-le	GAR/*HDO*/*HOO*/*HDO*
amputate	a-m-pu-ta-te	GAR/GDR/*HOO*/*HAO*/*HDO*
amputation	a-m-pu-ta-tion	GAR/GDR/*HOO*/*HAO*/*HOO*
amuse	a-mu-se	GAR/*HOO*/*HDO*
amusement	a-mu-se-men-t	GAR/*HOO*/*HDO*/GAR/*HOO*
anachronism	a-na-chro-ni-sm	GAR/GAR/*HOO*/GAR/GDR
anaemia	a-nae-mi-a	GAR/GRR/GAR/GAR

Word	Mouthables	Mouth Movements Notations
anaesthesia	a-na-es-the-si-a	GAR/GAR/GRR/GTR/GAR/GAR
anaesthetize	a-naes-the-ti-ze	GAR/GRR/GTR/GRR/GDR
anagram	a-na-gra-m	GAR/GAR/GAR/*HDO*
analgesic	a-na-l-ge-si-c	GAR/GAR/GDR/GRR/GAR/GDR
analog	a-na-lo-g	GAR/GAR/*HAO*/*HDO*
analogy	a-na-lo-gy	GAR/GAR/GAR/GDR
analyze	a-na-ly-se	GAR/GAR/GRR/*HDO*
analysis	a-na-ly-si-s	GAR/GAR/GAR/GAR/GDR
analytical	a-na-ly-ti-cal	GAR/GAR/GAR/GAR/*HDO*
anarchic	a-nar-chi-c	GAR/*HAO*/GAR/GDR
anarchy	a-nar-chy	GAR/*HAO*/GAR
anathema	a-na-the-ma	GAR/GAR/GTR/GAR
anatomy	a-na-to-my	GAR/GAR/*HAO*/GAR
ancestor	a-n-ce-ster	GAR/GDR/GAR/*HDO*
ancestral	a-n-ce-stral	GAR/GDR/GAR/*HDO*
ancestry	a-n-ces-try	GAR/GDR/GAR/GDR
anchor	an-cho-r	GAR/*HAO*/*HDO*
anchovy	a-n-cho-vy	GAR/GDR/*HOO*/GAR
ancient	an-ci-e-nt	*HAO*/*HDO*/GAR/GDR
ancillary	a-n-ci-lla-ry	GAR/GDR/GAR/GAR/*HDO*
and	a-n-d	GAR/GDR/*HDO*
anecdote	a-ne-c-do-te	GAR/GAR/GDR/*HOO*/*HDO*
anaemia	a-ne-mi-a	GAR/GRR/GAR/GAR
anaesthetist	a-ne-s-the-ti-st	GAR/GAR/GDR/GTR/GAR/GDR
anew	a-new	*HAO*/*HOO*
angel	an-ge-l	*HAO*/GAR/GDR
anger	a-n-ger	GAR/GDR/*HDO*
angle	an-gle	GAR/*HOO*
angler	an-g-ler	GAR/*HDO*/*HDO*
Anglican	An-gli-ca-n	GAR/GAR/GAR/GDR
Anglo-Saxon	An-glo-Sa-xo-n	GAR/*HOO*/GAR/*HAO*/*HDO*

Word	Mouthables	Mouth Movements Notations
angry	an-gry	GAR/GRR
anguish	an-gui-sh	GAR/GAR/*HDO*
animal	a-ni-ma-l	GAR/GAR/GAR/GDR
animate	a-ni-ma-te	GAR/GAR/*HAO*/*HOO*
animosity	a-ni-mo-si-ty	GAR/GAR/*HAO*/GAR/GAR
anise	a-ni-se	GAR/GAR/GDR
aniseed	a-ni-see-d	GAR/GAR/GRR/*HDO*
ankle	a-n-kle	GAR/GDR/*HOO*
anklet	a-n-kle-t	GAR/GDR/GAR/*HDO*
annex	a-nne-x	GAR/GAR/GDR
annihilate	a-nni-hi-la-te	GAR/GRR/GAR/*HAO*/*HOO*
anniversary	a-nni-ver-sa-ry	GAR/GAR/*HAO*/GAR/*HDO*
annotate	a-nno-ta-te	GAR/*HOO*/*HAO*/*HDO*
annotation	a-nno-ta-tion	GAR/*HOO*/*HAO*/*HOO*
announce	a-nnou-nce	GAR/GAR/GDR
announcement	a-nnou-nce-men-t	GAR/GAR/GDR/GAR/*HDO*
announcer	a-nnou-n-cer	GAR/GAR/GDR/*HDO*
annoy	a-nnoy	GAR/GAR
annoyance	a-nnoy-a-nce	GAR/GAR/GAR/GDR
annul	a-nnu-l	GAR/GAR/GDR
annulment	a-nnu-l-men-t	GAR/GAR/GDR/GAR/*HOO*
anonymous	a-no-ny-mou-s	GAR/*HAO*/GAR/*HAO*/*HDO*
anorak	a-no-ra-k	GAR/GAR/GAR/GDR
another	a-no-th-er	GAR/GAR/*HTO*/*HDO*
answer	an-swer	*HAO*/*HDO*
answerable	an-swer-a-ble	*HAO*/*HDO*/GAR/*HOO*
ant	a-n-t	GAR/GDR/*HOO*
antagonism	a-n-ta-go-ni-sm	GAR/GDR/GAR/*HAO*/GAR/*HDO*
Antarctic	A-n-tar-c-ti-c	GAR/GDR/*HAO*/GDR/GAR/GDR
antelope	a-n-te-lo-pe	GAR/GDR/GAR/*HOO*/*HDO*
antenatal	a-n-te-na-tal	GAR/GDR/GAR/*HAO*/*HDO*

Word	Mouthables	Mouth Movements Notations
antenna	a-n-te-nna	**GAR/GDR/GAR/GAR**
anthology	a-n-th-o-lo-gy	**GAR/GDR**/*HTO*/*HAO*/*HOO*/**GDR**
anthropology	a-n-thro-po-lo-gy	**GAR/GDR**/*HTO*/*HAO*/*HOO*/**GDR**
antiaircraft	a-n-ti-air-cra-ft	**GAR/GDR/GAR**/*HAO*/**GAR**/*HDO*
antibiotic	a-n-ti-bi-o-ti-c	**GAR/GDR/GAR/GRR**/*HAO*/**GAR**/**GDR**
antibody	a-n-ti-bo-dy	**GAR/GDR/GAR**/*HAO*/**GAR**
anticipate	a-n-ti-ci-pa-te	**GAR/GDR/GAR/GAR**/*HAO*/*HDO*
anticlockwise	a-n-ti-clo-ck-wi-se	**GAR/GDR/GAR**/*HAO*/*HDO*/**GRR**/*HDO*
antics	a-n-ti-cs	**GAR/GDR/GAR/GDR**
antidote	a-n-ti-do-te	**GAR/GDR/GAR**/*HOO*/*HDO*
antipathy	a-n-ti-pa-thy	**GAR/GDR/GAR/GAR/GTR**
antiquarian	a-n-ti-quar-ian	**GAR/GDR/GAR**/*HAO*/**GDR**
antiquated	a-n-ti-qua-ted	**GAR/GDR/GAR**/*HAO*/**GRR**
antique	a-n-ti-que	**GAR/GDR/GAR**/*HDO*
antiquity	a-n-ti-qui-ty	**GAR/GDR/GAR/GAR/GAR**
antiseptic	a-n-ti-se-p-ti-c	**GAR/GDR/GAR/GAR**/*HDO*/**GAR**/**GDR**
anvil	a-n-vi-l	**GAR/GDR/GAR/GDR**
anxiety	a-n-xi-e-ty	**GAR/GDR/GRR/GAR/GAR**
anxious	a-n-xi-ous	**GAR/GDR/GDR**/*HAO*
any	a-n-y	**GAR/GDR/GAR**
anybody	a-n-y-bo-dy	**GAR/GDR/GAR**/*HAO*/**GAR**
apart	a-par-t	**GAR**/*HAO*/*HOO*
apathetic	a-pa-the-ti-c	**GAR/GAR/GTR/GAR/GDR**
apathy	a-pa-th-y	**GAR/GAR/GTR/GAR**
ape	a-pe	*HAO*/*HDO*
aperitif	a-pe-ri-ti-f	**GAR/GAR/GAR/GAR**/*HDO*
apex	a-pe-x	*HAO*/**GAR/GDR**
apologetic	a-po-lo-ge-ti-c	**GAR**/*HAO*/*HAO*/**GAR/GAR/GDR**
apologize	a-po-lo-gi-ze	**GAR**/*HAO*/*HAO*/**GRR/GDR**

Word	Mouthables	Mouth Movements Notations
apology	a-po-lo-gy	GAR/*HAO*/*HAO*/GAR
apostle	a-po-stle	GAR/*HAO*/*HOO*
apostrophe	a-po-stro-phe	GAR/*HAO*/*HDO*/GAR
appall	a-ppal-l	GAR/*HOO*/*HDO*
appalled	a-ppalle-d	GAR/*HOO*/*HOO*
apparatus	a-ppa-ra-tu-s	GAR/GAR/*HAO*/GAR/*HDO*
apparent	a-ppa-re-nt	GAR/GAR/GAR/GDR
apparition	a-ppa-ri-tion	GAR/GAR/GAR/*HOO*
appeal	a-ppea-l	GAR/GRR/GDR
appealing	a-ppea-ling	GAR/GRR/GDR
appear	a-ppe-ar	GAR/GRR/*HDO*
appearance	a-ppea-ra-nce	GAR/GRR/GAR/GDR
appease	a-ppea-se	GAR/GRR/GDR
appendix	a-ppe-n-di-x	GAR/GAR/GDR/GAR/GDR
appetite	a-ppe-ti-te	GAR/GAR/GRR/*HDO*
appetizer	a-ppe-ti-zer	GAR/GAR/GRR/*HDO*
appetizing	a-ppe-ti-zing	GAR/GAR/GRR/GDR
applaud	a-pplau-d	GAR/*HOO*/*HOO*
applause	a-pplau-se	GAR/*HOO*/*HDO*
apple	a-pple	GAR/*HOO*
appliance	a-ppli-a-nce	GAR/GRR/GAR/GDR
applicable	a-ppli-ca-ble	GAR/GAR/GAR/*HOO*
applicant	a-ppli-ca-nt	GAR/GAR/GAR/GDR
application	a-ppli-ca-tion	GAR/GAR/*HAO*/*HOO*
apply	a-pply	GAR/GRR
appoint	a-ppoi-nt	GAR/GAR/GDR
appointment	a-ppoi-nt-men-t	GAR/GAR/GAR/GAR/*HOO*
apportion	a-ppor-tion	GAR/*HOO*/*HOO*
appraisal	a-pprai-sal	GAR/*HAO*/*HDO*
appraise	a-pprai-se	GAR/*HAO*/GDR
appreciable	a-ppre-ci-a-ble	GAR/GRR/GDR/GAR/*HOO*

Word	Mouthables	Mouth Movements Notations
appreciate	a-ppre-ci-a-te	**GAR/GRR/GDR/***HAO***/***HDO*
appreciation	a-ppre-ci-a-tion	**GAR/GRR/GDR/***HAO***/***HOO*
appreciative	a-ppre-ci-a-ti-ve	**GAR/GRR/GDR/***HAO***/GAR/***HDO*
apprehensive	a-ppre-he-n-si-ve	**GAR/GRR/GAR/GDR/GAR/***HDO*
apprentice	a-ppre-n-ti-ce	**GAR/GAR/GDR/GAR/GDR**
apprenticeship	a-ppre-n-ti-ce-shi-p	**GAR/GAR/GDR/GAR/GDR/GAR/ GDR**
approach	a-pp-roa-ch	**GAR/***HDO***/***HOO***/***HDO*
approachable	a-pp-roa-cha-ble	**GAR/***HDO***/***HOO***/GAR/***HOO*
approaching	a-pp-roa-chi-ng	**GAR/***HDO***/***HOO***/GAR/GDR**
appropriate	a-ppro-pri-a-te	**GAR/***HOO***/GAR/***HAO***/***HDO*
approval	a-ppro-val	**GAR/***HOO***/***HDO*
approve	a-ppro-ve	**GAR/***HOO***/***HDO*
approximate	a-ppro-xi-ma-te	**GAR/***HAO***/GAR/***HAO***/***HDO*
approximation	a-ppro-xi-ma-tion	**GAR/***HAO***/GAR/***HAO***/***HOO*
apricot	a-pri-co-t	*HAO***/GAR/***HAO***/***HOO*
April	A-pri-l	*HAO***/GAR/GDR**
apron	a-pro-n	*HAO***/***HAO***/***HDO*
apropos	a-pro-pos	**GAR/***HOO***/***HOO*
apse	a-pse	**GAR/GDR**
apt	a-pt	**GAR/***HOO*
aptitude	a-p-ti-tu-de	**GAR/GDR/GAR/***HOO***/***HDO*
aquaplane	a-qua-pla-ne	**GAR/GAR/***HAO***/GDR**
aquarium	a-quar-i-um	**GAR/***HAO***/GAR/***HDO*
aqueduct	a-que-du-ct	**GAR/GAR/GAR/***HDO*
Arab	A-ra-b	**GAR/GAR/***HDO*
Arabian	A-ra-bi-an	**GAR/***HAO***/GAR/GDR**
Arabic	A-ra-bi-c	**GAR/GAR/GAR/GDR**
arbiter	ar-bi-ter	*HAO***/GAR/***HDO*
arbitrate	ar-bi-tra-te	*HAO***/GAR/***HAO***/***HDO*
arbitration	ar-bi-tra-tion	*HAO***/GAR/***HAO***/***HOO*

Word	Mouthables	Mouth Movements Notations
arbour	ar-bour	*HAO/HAO*
arc	ar-c	**GAR/GDR**
arcade	ar-ca-de	*HAO/HAO/HDO*
arch	ar-ch	*HAO/HDO*
archaeology	ar-chae-o-lo-gy	*HAO/***GRR***/HAO/HOO/***GDR**
archaic	ar-cha-i-c	*HAO/HAO/***GAR/GDR**
archbishop	ar-ch-bi-sh-o-p	*HAO/HDO/***GAR***/HOO/HAO/HDO*
archer	ar-cher	*HAO/HDO*
archery	ar-che-ry	*HAO/***GAR/GDR**
archetype	ar-che-ty-pe	*HAO/***GAR/GRR***/HDO*
archipelago	ar-chi-pe-la-go	*HAO/***GAR/GAR/GAR***/HOO*
architect	ar-chi-te-c-t	*HAO/***GAR/GAR/GDR***/HOO*
architecture	ar-chi-te-c-tu-re	*HAO/***GAR/GAR/GDR***/HOO/HDO*
archives	ar-chi-ves	*HAO/***GRR***/HDO*
archway	ar-ch-way	*HAO/HDO/HAO*
arctic	ar-c-ti-c	*HAO/***GDR/GAR/GDR**
ardour	ar-dour	*HAO/HAO*
arduous	ar-du-ous	*HAO/HOO/HAO*
ark	ar-k	*HAO/HDO*
are	are	*HAO*
area	a-re-a	*HAO/***GRR/GAR**
aren't	are-n't	*HAO/***GDR**
argue	ar-gue	*HAO/HOO*
argument	ar-gu-me-nt	*HAO/HOO/***GAR/GDR**
argumentative	ar-gu-me-n-ta-ti-ve	*HAO/HOO/***GAR/GDR/GAR/GAR/***HDO*
arid	a-ri-d	**GAR/GAR/***HOO*
arise	a-ri-se	**GAR/***GRR***/HDO*
aristocrat	a-ri-sto-cra-t	**GAR/GAR/***HOO***/GAR/***HOO*
arithmetic	a-ri-th-me-ti-c	**GAR/GAR/GTR/GAR/GAR/GDR**
arithmetical	a-ri-th-me-ti-cal	**GAR/GAR/GTR/GAR/GAR/***HDO*

Word	Mouthables	Mouth Movements Notations
ark	ar-k	*HAO/HDO*
arm	ar-m	**GAR/GDR**
armed	arme-d	**GAR/GDR**/*HOO*
arm	ar-m	*HAO/HDO*
armchair	ar-m-chair	*HAO/HDO/HAO*
armhole	ar-m-ho-le	*HAO/HDO/HOO/HDO*
armistice	ar-mi-sti-ce	*HAO*/**GAR/GAR/GDR**
armoured	ar-mou-re-d	*HAO*/**GAR**/*HOO/HOO*
armpit	ar-m-pi-t	*HAO/HDO*/**GAR**/*HOO*
arms	ar-ms	**GAR/GDR**
army	ar-my	**GAR/GAR**
arose	a-ro-se	**GAR**/*HOO/HDO*
around	a-rou-nd	**GAR/GAR/GDR**
arouse	a-rou-se	**GAR/GAR**/*HDO*
arrange	a-rra-nge	**GAR**/*HAO*/**GDR**
arrangement	a-arran-ge-men-t	**GAR**/*HAO/HDO*/**GAR**/*HDO*
arras	ar-ra-s	*HAO*/**GAR***HDO*
array	a-rray	**GAR**/*HAO*
arrears	a-rre-ars	**GAR/GRR**/*HDO*
arrest	a-rre-st	**GAR/GAR**/*HOO*
arrival	a-rri-val	**GAR/GRR**/*HDO*
arrive	a-rri-ve	**GAR/GRR**/*HDO*
arrogant	a-rro-ga-nt	**GAR**/*HOO*/**GAR/GDR**
arrow	a-rro-w	**GAR**/*HOO/HDO*
arse	ar-se	*HAO/HDO*
arsenal	ar-se-nal	*HAO*/**GAR**/*HDO*
arsenic	ar-se-ni-c	*HAO*/**GAR/GAR/GDR**
arson	ar-so-n	*HAO/HAO/HDO*
art	ar-t	*HAO/HOO*
artefact	ar-te-fa-ct	*HAO*/**GRR/GAR**/*HOO*
artery	ar-ter-y	*HAO/HAO*/**GAR**

Word	Mouthables	Mouth Movements Notations
artful	ar-t-ful	*HAO/HOO/HOO*
artichoke	ar-ti-cho-ke	*HAO*/**GAR**/*HOO/HDO*
article	ar-ti-cle	*HAO*/**GAR**/*HOO*
articulate	ar-ti-cu-la-te	*HAO*/**GAR**/*HOO/HAO/HDO*
artefact	ar-ti-fac-t	*HAO*/**GAR/GAR**/*HDO*
artificial	ar-ti-fi-cial	*HAO*/**GAR/GAR**/*HDO*
artillery	ar-ti-lle-ry	*HAO*/**GAR/GAR**/*HDO*
artisan	ar-ti-sa-n	*HAO*/**GAR/GAR/GDR**
artist	ar-ti-st	*HAO*/**GAR**/*HOO*
artless	ar-t-le-ss	*HAO/HOO*/**GAR/GDR**
arty-crafty	ar-ty-cra-f-ty	*HAO*/**GAR/GAR**/*HDO*/**GAR**
as	a-s	**GAR/GDR**
ascend	a-sce-nd	**GAR/GAR/GDR**
ascendancy	a-scen-dan-cy	**GAR/GDR/GDR/GAR**
ascendant	a-sce-n-da-nt	**GAR/GAR/GDR/GDR**
ascent	a-sce-nt	**GAR/GAR/GRR**
ascertain	a-scer-tai-n	**GAR**/*HAO/HAO*/**GDR**
ascetic	a-sce-ti-c	**GAR/GAR/GAR/GDR**
ascribe	a-scri-be	**GAR/GRR**/*HDO*
aseptic	a-se-p-ti-c	*HAO*/**GAR/GDR/GAR/GDR**
ash	a-sh	**GAR/GDR**
Ash	A-sh	**GAR**/*HDO*
ashamed	a-sha-me-d	**GAR**/*HAO*/**GDR**/*HOO*
ashore	a-sho-re	**GAR**/*HAO/HDO*
Asian	A-si-an	*HAO*/**GAR/GDR**
Asiatic	A-si-a-ti-c	*HAO*/**GAR/GAR/GAR/GDR**
aside	a-si-de	**GAR/GRR**/*HDO*
ask	as-k	*HAO/HDO*
askance	as-ka-nce	*HAO*/**GAR/GDR**
asleep	a-slee-p	**GAR/GRR/GDR**
asparagus	a-spa-ra-gu-s	**GAR/GAR/GAR/GAR/GDR**

Word	Mouthables	Mouth Movements Notations
aspect	a-spe-ct	**GAR/GAR**/*HOO*
asphalt	a-sphal-t	**GAR**/*HOO*/*HDO*
asphyxiate	a-sphy-xi-a-te	**GAR/GAR/GAR**/*HAO*/*HDO*
aspire	a-spi-re	**GAR/GRR**/*HDO*
aspirin	a-spi-ri-n	**GAR/GAR/GAR/GDR**
ass	a-ss	**GAR**/*HDO*
assail	a-ssai-l	**GAR**/*HAO*/**GDR**
assassin	a-ssa-ssi-n	**GAR/GAR/GAR/GDR**
assassinate	a-ssa-ssi-na-te	**GAR/GAR/GAR**/*HAO*/*HDO*
assault	a-ssau-lt	**GAR**/*HOO*/*HOO*
assemblage	a-sse-m-bla-ge	**GAR/GAR/GDR**/*HAO*/*HDO*
assemble	a-sse-m-ble	**GAR/GAR/GDR**/*HOO*
assembly	a-sse-m-bly	**GAR/GAR/GDR/GDR**
assert	a-sser-t	**GAR**/*HOO*/*HOO*
assertive	a-sser-ti-ve	**GAR**/*HOO*/**GAR**/*HDO*
assess	a-sse-ss	**GAR/GAR**/*HDO*
asset	a-sse-t	**GAR/GAR**/*HOO*
assiduous	a-ssi-du-ous	**GAR/GAR**/*HOO*/*HAO*
assign	a-ssi-gn	**GAR/GRR/GDR**
assimilate	a-ssi-mi-la-te	**GAR/GAR/GAR**/*HAO*/*HDO*
assist	a-ssi-st	**GAR/GAR**/*HOO*
assistance	a-ssi-sta-nce	**GAR/GAR/GAR/GDR**
associate	a-sso-ci-a-te	**GAR**/*HOO*/**GDR**/*HAO*/*HDO*
association	a-sso-ci-a-tion	**GAR**/*HOO*/**GDR**/*HAO*/*HOO*
assorted	a-ssor-ted	**GAR**/*HOO*/**GRR**
assortment	a-ssort-men-t	**GAR**/*HOO*/**GAR**/*HOO*
assume	a-ssu-me	**GAR**/*HOO*/*HDO*
assumption	a-ssu-mp-tion	**GAR/GAR**/*HDO*/*HOO*
assurance	a-ssu-ra-nce	**GAR**/*HOO*/**GAR/GDR**
assure	a-ssu-re	**GAR**/*HOO*/*HOO*
assured	a-ssu-re-d	**GAR**/*HOO*/*HOO*/*HOO*

Word	Mouthables	Mouth Movements Notations
asterisk	a-ster-i-sk	GAR/*HDO*/GAR/GDR
astern	a-ster-n	GAR/*HOO*/GDR
astonished	a-sto-ni-sh	GAR/*HAO*/GAR/*HDO*
astonishment	a-sto-ni-sh-men-t	GAR/*HAO*/GAR/*HDO*/GAR/*HOO*
astound	a-stou-nd	GAR/GAR/GDR
astray	a-stray	GAR/*HAO*
astride	a-stri-de	GAR/GRR/*HDO*
astrology	a-stro-lo-gy	GAR/*HAO*/*HOO*/GAR
astronaut	a-stro-nau-t	GAR/*HOO*/*HOO*/*HOO*
astronomer	a-stro-no-mer	GAR/*HAO*/GAR/*HDO*
astronomical	a-stro-no-mi-cal	GAR/*HAO*/*HAO*/GAR/*HDO*
astronomy	a-stro-no-my	GAR/*HAO*/*HAO*/GAR
astute	a-stu-te	GAR/*HOO*/*HDO*
at	a-t	GAR/GDR
ate	a-te	*HAO*/GRR
atheist	a-the-i-st	*HAO*/GTR/GAR/GRR
atheistic	a-the-i-sti-c	*HAO*/GTR/GAR/GAR/GDR
Athenian	A-th-e-ni-an	GAR/GTR/GRR/GAR/GDR
Athens	A-th-e-ns	GAR/GTR/GAR/GDR
athlete	a-th-le-te	GTR/GRR/*HDO*
athletic	ath-le-ti-c	GTR/GAR/GAR/GDR
athletics	ath-le-ti-cs	GTR/GAR/GAR/GDR
Atlantic	A-t-la-n-ti-c	GAR/GDR/GAR/GDR/GAR/GDR
atlas	a-t-la-s	GAR/GDR/GAR/GDR
atmosphere	a-t-mo-sphe-re	GAR/GDR/GAR/GRR/*HDO*
atom	a-to-m	GAR/*HAO*/*HDO*
atomic	a-to-mi-c	GAR/*HAO*/GAR/GDR
atomize	a-to-mi-ze	GAR/*HAO*/GRR/GDR
atop	a-to-p	GAR/*HAO*/*HDO*
atrocious	a-tro-ci-ous	GAR/*HOO*/GDR/*HAO*
attach	a-tta-ch	GAR/GAR/*HDO*

Word	Mouthables	Mouth Movements Notations
attachment	a-tta-ch-men-t	**GAR/GAR/***HDO***/GAR/***HOO*
attack	a-tta-ck	**GAR/GAR/***HDO*
attain	a-ttai-n	**GAR/***HAO***/GDR**
attainment	a-ttai-n-me-nt	**GAR/***HAO***/GDR/GAR/GDR**
attempt	a-ttem-pt	**GAR/GAR/***HOO*
attend	a-tte-nd	**GAR/GAR/GDR**
attendance	a-tte-n-da-nce	**GAR/GAR/GDR/GAR/GDR**
attendant	a-tte-n-da-nt	**GAR/GAR/GDR/GAR/GDR**
attention	a-tte-n-tion	**GAR/GAR/GDR/***HOO*
attentive	a-tte-n-ti-ve	**GAR/GAR/GDR/GAR/***HDO*
attenuate	a-tte-nu-a-te	**GAR/GAR/***HOO*/*HAOHDO*
attic	a-tti-c	**GAR/GAR/GDR**
attitude	a-tti-tu-de	**GAR/GAR/***HOO*/*HDO*
attorney	a-ttor-ney	**GAR/***HAO***/GDR**
attract	a-ttra-ct	**GAR/GAR/***HOO*
attraction	a-ttrac-tion	**GAR/GAR/***HOO*
attribute	a-ttri-bu-te	**GAR/GAR/***HOO*/*HDO*
aubergine	au-ber-gi-ne	*HOO*/*HAO*/**GAR/GDR**
auction	au-c-tion	*HOO*/*HDO*/*HOO*
audible	au-di-ble	*HOO*/**GAR/***HOO*
audience	au-di-e-nce	*HOO*/**GAR/GAR/GDR**
audit	au-di-t	*HOO*/**GAR/***HOO*
audition	au-di-tion	*HOO*/**GAR/***HOO*
auger	au-ger	*HOO*/*HAO*
augment	au-g-me-nt	*HOO*/*HDO*/ **GAR/GRR**
augur	au-gur	*HOO*/*HDO*
August	Au-gu-st	*HOO*/**GAR/***HOO*
auk	au-k	*HOO*/*HDO*
aunt	aun-t	*HAO*/*HOO*
aural	au-ral	*HOO*/*HDO*
aurally	au-ral-ly	*HOO*/*HDO*/**GDR**

Word	Mouthables	Mouth Movements Notations
Aussie	Au-ssie	*HAO*/**GDR**
austere	au-ste-re	*HOO*/**GAR**/*HDO*
austerity	au-ste-ri-ty	*HAO*/**GAR/GAR/GAR**
Australia	Au-stra-li-a	*HAO/HAO*/**GAR/GAR**
Austria	Au-stri-a	*HAO*/**GAR/GAR**
Austrian	Au-stri-an	*HOO*/**GDR/GDR**
authentic	au-the-n-ti-c	*HOO*/**GTR/GDR/GAR/GDR**
authenticate	au-the-n-ti-ca-te	*HOO*/**GTR/GDR/GAR**/*HAO/HDO*
author	au-thor-e-ss	*HOO/HTO*/**GAR**/*HDO*
author	au-thor	*HOO/HTO*
authoritative	au-thor-i-ta-ti-ve	*HOO/HTO*/**GAR**/*HAO*/**GAR**/*HDO*
authority	au-thor-i-ty	*HOO/HTO*/**GAR/GAR**
authorization	au-thor-i-za-tion	*HOO/HTO*/**GRR**/*HAO/HOO*
authorize	au-thor-i-ze	*HOO/HTO*/**GRR/GDR**
auto	au-to	*HOO/HOO*
autograph	au-to-gra-ph	*HOO/HOO/HAO/HDO*
automated	au-to-ma-ted	*HOO/HOO/HAO*/**GRR**
automatic	au-to-ma-ti-c	*HOO/HOO*/**GAR/GAR/GDR**
automobile	au-to-mo-bi-le	*HOO/HOO/HOO*/**GAR/GDR**
autonomes	au-to-no-mou-s	*HOO/HAO/HOO/HAO/HDO*
autonomy	au-to-no-my	*HOO/HAO/HOO*/**GAR**
autopsy	au-to-p-sy	*HOO/HAO*/**GDR/GAR**
autumn	au-tu-mn	*HOO*/**GAR**/*HDO*
autumnal	au-tu-m-nal	*HOO*/**GAR**/*HDO/HOO*
auxiliary	au-xi-lia-ry	*HOO*/**GAR/GDR**/*HDO*
avail	a-vai-l	**GAR**/*HAO*/**GDR**
available	a-vai-la-ble	**GAR**/*HAO*/**GAR**/*HOO*
avalanche	a-va-lan-che	**GAR/GAR/GAR/GDR**
avaricious	a-va-ri-ci-ous	**GAR/GAR/GAR/GDR**/*HAO*
avenge	a-ve-n-ge	**GAR/GAR/GDR/GDR**
avenue	a-ve-n-ue	**GAR/GAR/GDR**/*HOO*

Word	Mouthables	Mouth Movements Notations
aver	a-ver	GAR/*HDO*
average	a-ve-ra-ge	GAR/*HAO/HAO/HDO*
averse	a-ver-se	GAR/*HAO/HDO*
aversion	a-ver-sion	GAR/*HAO/HOO*
avert	a-ver-t	GAR/*HAO/HOO*
aviation	a-vi-a-tion	*HAO*/GAR/*HAO/HOO*
aviator	a-vi-a-tor	*HAO*/GAR/*HAO/HDO*
avid	a-vi-d	GAR/GAR/*HDO*
avoid	a-voi-d	GAR/GAR*HOO*
avoidable	a-voi-da-ble	GAR/GAR/GAR/*HOO*
await	a-wai-t	GAR/*HAO/HOO*
awake	a-wa-ke	GAR/*HAO/HDO*
award	a-war-d	GAR/*HAO/HOO*
aware	a-ware	GAR/GAR
awash	a-wash	GAR/*HDO*
away	a-way	GAR/*HAO*
awe	awe	*HOO*
aweigh	a-wei-gh	GAR/*HAO/HDO*
awesome	awe-so-me	*HOO/HAO/HDO*
awful	aw-ful	*HOO/HOO*
awhile	a-whi-le	GAR/GRR/GDR
awkward	aw-k-war-d	*HOO/HDO/HAO/HOO*
awl	aw-l	*HOO/HDO*
awning	aw-ni-ng	*HOO*/GAR/GDR
awoke	a-wo-ke	GAR/*HOO/HDO*
awoken	a-wo-ke-n	GAR/*HOO*/GAR/GDR
awry	a-wry	GAR/GRR
axe	a-xe	GAR/GDR
axel	a-x-e-l	GAR/GDR/GAR/GDR
axis	a-xi-s	GAR/GAR/GDR
axle	a-xle	GAR/*HOO*
azure	a-zu-re	GAR/*HOO/HDO*

Word	Mouthables	Mouth Movements Notations
B		
B	B	**GRR**
babble	ba-bble	**GAR**/*HOO*
baboon	ba-boo-n	**GAR**/*HOO*/**GDR**
baby	ba-by	*HAO*/**GAR**
babyish	ba-by-i-sh	*HAO*/**GAR**/**GAR**/*HDO*
bachelor	ba-che-lor	**GAR**/**GAR**/*HDO*
back	bac-k	**GAR**/*HDO*
bad	ba-d	**GAR**/*HOO*
badge	bad-ge	**GAR**/*HDO*
badly	ba-d-ly	**GAR**/*HDO*/**GDR**
baffle	ba-ffle	**GAR**/*HOO*
bag	ba-g	**GAR**/*HDO*
baggage	ba-g-ga-ge	**GAR**/*HDO*/*HAO*/*HDO*
baggy	ba-ggy	**GAR**/**GAR**
bail	bai-l	*HAO*/**GDR**
bailiff	bai-li-ff	*HAO*/**GAR**/*HDO*
bait	bai-t	*HAO*/**GRR**
baited	bai-ted	*HAO*/**GRR**
bait	bai-t	*HAO*/**GDR**
baize	bai-ze	*HAO*/**GDR**
bake	ba-ke	*HAO*/*HOO*
baker	ba-ker	*HAO*/*HDO*
bakery	ba-ke-ry	*HAO*/*HDO*/*HDO*
balaclava	ba-la-clava	**GAR**/**GAR**/**GDR**
balance	ba-la-n-ce	**GAR**/**GAR**/**GDR**/**GDR**
balcony	ba-l-co-ny	**GAR**/**GDR**/*HAO*/**GAR**
bald	bal-d	*HOO*/*HDO*
balderdash	bal-der-da-sh	*HOO*/*HAO*/**GAR**/*HDO*
baldness	bal-d-ne-ss	*HOO*/*HDO*/**GAR**/**GDR**
bale	ba-le	*HAO*/*HDO*

Word	Mouthables	Mouth Movements Notations
balk	bal-k	*HOO/HDO*
ball	bal-l	*HOO/HDO*
ballast	ba-lla-st	**GAR/GAR/***HOO*
ballet	ba-llet	**GAR/***HAO*
balloon	bal-loo-n	**GAR/***HOO/HDO*
ballot	ba-llo-t	**GAR/***HAO/HOO*
ballyhoo	ba-lly-hoo	**GAR/GAR/***HOO*
balm	bal-m	*HAO/HDO*
balmy	bal-my	*HAO/***GAR**
balsam	bal-sa-m	*HOO/***GAR/GDR**
Baltic	Bal-ti-c	*HDO/***GAR/GDR**
bamboo	ba-m-boo	**GAR/GDR/***HOO*
ban	ba-n	**GAR/GDR**
banana	ba-na-na	**GAR/GAR/GAR**
band	ban-d	**GAR/***HDO*
bandage	ba-n-da-ge	**GAR/GDR/***HAO/HDO*
bandit	ba-n-di-t	**GDR/GDR/GAR/GDR**
bandwagon	ba-nd-wa-go-n	**GAR/GDR/GAR/GAR/GDR**
bandy	ba-n-dy	**GAR/GDR/GAR**
bang	ban-g	**GAR/***HOO*
banger	ban-ger	**GAR/***HDO*
banish	ba-ni-sh	**GAR/GAR/***HDO*
banisters	ba-ni-sters	**GAR/GAR/***HDO*
bank	ban-k	**GAR/***HDO*
banker	ban-ker	**GAR/***HDO*
bankrupt	ban-kru-pt	**GAR/GAR/***HOO*
bankruptcy	ban-kru-pt-cy	**GAR/GAR/GDR/GAR**
ban	ba-n	**GAR/GDR**
banned	ba-nne-d	**GAR/GDR/***HOO*
banner	ban-ner	**GAR/***HDO*
banns	ba-nns	**GAR/GDR**

Word	Mouthables	Mouth Movements Notations
banquet	ba-n-que-t	GAR/GDR/GAR/*HOO*
banter	ban-ter	GAR/*HDO*
baptism	ba-p-ti-sm	GAR/GDR/GAR/*HDO*
baptize	ba-p-ti-ze	GAR/GDR/GRR/GDR
barbaric	bar-ba-ri-c	*HAO*/GAR/GAR/GDR
barber	bar-ber	*HAO*/*HDO*
barbiturate	bar-bi-tu-ra-te	*HAO*/GAR/*HOO*/*HAO*/*HDO*
bard	bar-d	*HAO*/*HDO*
bare	bare	GAR
barely	bare-ly	GAR/GDR
bargain	bar-gai-n	*HAO*/*HAO*/GDR
barge	bar-ge	*HAO*/*HDO*
baring	bar-ing	GAR/GDR
bark	bar-k	GAR/*HDO*
barley	bar-ley	*HAO*/*HDO*
barmaid	bar-mai-d	*HAO*/*HAO*/*HOO*
barman	bar-ma-n	*HAO*/GAR/GDR
barn	bar-n	*HAO*/GDR
barometer	ba-ro-me-ter	GAR/*HAO*/GAR/*HDO*
baron	ba-ro-n	GAR/*HAO*/*HDO*
baronet	ba-ro-ne-t	GAR/*HAO*/GAR/GDR
baroque	ba-ro-que	GAR/*HOO*/*HDO*
barque	bar-que	*HAO*/*HDO*
barracks	ba-rra-cks	GAR/GAR/GDR
barrage	ba-rra-ge	GAR/*HAO*/*HDO*
barred	bar-re-d	*HAO*/*HOO*/*HOO*
barrel	ba-rrel	GAR/*HDO*
barren	ba-rre-n	GAR/GAR/GDR
barricade	ba-rri-ca-de	GAR/GAR/*HAO*/*HDO*
barrier	ba-rri-er	GAR/GAR/*HDO*
barrister	bar-ri-ster	GAR/GAR/*HDO*

Word	Mouthables	Mouth Movements Notations
barrow	ba-rro-w	**GAR**/*HOO*/*HDO*
barter	bar-ter	*HAO*/*HDO*
base	ba-se	*HAO*/**GDR**
based	ba-se-d	*HAO*/**GDR**/*HOO*
basement	ba-se-men-t	*HAO*/*HDO*/**GAR**/*HDO*
bash	ba-sh	**GAR**/*HDO*
bashful	ba-sh-ful	**GAR**/*HDO*/*HOO*
basic	ba-si-c	*HAO*/**GAR**/**GDR**
basil	ba-si-l	**GAR/GAR/GDR**
basin	ba-si-n	*HAO*/**GAR**/**GDR**
basis	ba-si-s	*HAO*/**GAR**/**GDR**
bask	bas-k	*HAO*/*HDO*
basket	bas-ke-t	*HAO*/**GAR**/*HOO*
basketball	bas-ke-t-bal-l	*HAO*/**GAR**/*HOO*/*HOO*/*HDO*
bass	ba-ss	*HAO*/*HDO*
bassoon	ba-ssoo-n	**GAR**/*HOO*/*HDO*
bastard	bas-tar-d	*HAO*/*HAO*/*HOO*
bastardize	ba-star-di-ze	*HAO*/*HAO*/**GRR**/**GDR**
baste	ba-ste	*HAO*/*HDO*
bat	ba-t	**GAR**/*HOO*
bat	ba-t	**GAR/GRR**
batch	ba-tch	**GAR**/*HDO*
bate	ba-te	*HAO*/*HDO*
bated	ba-ted	*HAO*/**GRR**
bath	bath	*HTO*
bathe	ba-the	*HAO*/**GTR**
bather	ba-ther	*HAO*/**GTR**
bathing	ba-thing	*HAO*/**GTR**
baton	ba-to-n	**GAR**/*HAO*/*HDO*
bats	ba-ts	**GAR/GDR**
batter	bat-ter	**GAR**/*HDO*

Word	Mouthables	Mouth Movements Notations
battered	bat-tere-d	**GAR**/*HDO*/*HOO*
battery	ba-tte-ry	**GAR**/*HAO*/**GDR**
battle	bat-tle	**GAR**/*HOO*
battlements	bat-tle-men-ts	**GAR**/*HOO*/**GAR**/*HDO*
battleship	bat-tle-shi-p	**GAR**/*HOO*/**GAR**/*HDO*
batty	bat-ty	**GAR/GAR**
baulk	bau-lk	*HOO*/*HDO*
bawdy	baw-dy	*HOO*/**GAR**
bawl	baw-l	*HOO*/**GDR**
bawled	baw-le-d	*HOO*/**GDR**/*HOO*
bay	bay	*HAO*
bazaar	ba-zaar	**GAR**/*HAO*
be	be	**GRR**
beach	bea-ch	**GRR/GDR**
beacon	bea-co-n	**GRR**/*HAO*/*HDO*
bead	bea-d	**GRR**/*HDO*
beagle	bea-gle	**GRR**/*HOO*
beak	bea-k	**GRR/GDR**
beam	bea-m	**GRR**/*HDO*
bean	bea-n	**GRR/GDR**
bear	be-ar	**GAR/GRR**
bear	bea-r	*HAO*/*HDO*
beard	be-ar-d	**GRR**/*HAO*/*HOO*
bearing	bear-ing	**GAR/GDR**
beast	bea-st	**GRR**/*HOO*
beat	bea-t	**GRR/GRR**
beater	bea-ter	**GRR**/*HDO*
beating	bea-ting	**GRR/GDR**
beatitude	be-a-ti-tu-de	**GRR/GAR/GAR**/*HOO*/*HDO*
beau	beau	*HOO*
beautician	beau-ti-ci-an	*HOO*/**GAR/GAR/GDR**

Word	Mouthables	Mouth Movements Notations
beautiful	beau-ti-ful	*HOO*/**GAR**/*HOO*
beautify	beau-ti-fy	*HOO*/**GAR/GRR**
beauty	beau-ty	*HOO*/**GAR**
beaver	bea-ver	**GRR**/*HDO*
became	be-ca-me	**GRR**/*HAO*/**GDR**
because	be-cau-se	**GRR**/*HOO*/*HDO*
beckon	bec-ko-n	**GAR**/*HAO*/**GDR**
become	be-co-me	**GRR**/*HAO*/*HDO*
bed	be-d	**GAR**/*HOO*
bedraggled	be-dra-ggle-d	**GRR/GDR**/*HOO*/*HOO*
bee	bee	**GDR**
beech	bee-ch	**GRR**/*HDO*
beef	bee-f	**GRR**/*HDO*
beefy	bee-fy	**GRR/GAR**
been	bee-n	**GRR/GRR**
beer	be-er	**GRR**/*HDO*
beet	bee-t	**GRR**/*HDO*
beetle	bee-tle	**GRR**/*HOO*
before	be-fo-re	**GRR**/*HAO*/*HDO*
beg	be-g	**GAR**/*HDO*
began	be-ga-n	**GRR/GAR/GDR**
beggar	be-gga-r	**GAR/GAR**/*HDO*
beginning	be-gi-nni-ng	**GRR/GAR/GAR/GDR**
begun	be-gu-n	**GRR/GAR/GDR**
behalf	be-hal-f	**GRR**/*HAO*/*HDO*
behave	be-ha-ve	**GRR**/*HAO*/*HDO*
behaviour	be-ha-vi-our	**GRR**/*HAOGAR*/*HAO*
behind	be-hi-n-d	**GRR/GRR/GDR**/*HOO*
being	be-ing	**GRR/GDR**
belated	be-la-ted	**GRR**/*HAO*/**GRR**
belfry	be-l-fry	**GAR/GDR**/*HDO*

Word	Mouthables	Mouth Movements Notations
Belgian	Be-l-gi-an	**GAR/GDR/GAR/GDR**
Belgium	Be-l-gi-um	**GAR/GDR/GAR/GDR**
belie	be-lie	**GRR/GRR**
belief	be-lie-f	**GRR/GAR**/*HDO*
believe	be-lie-ve	**GRR/GAR**/*HDO*
bell	be-ll	**GAR/GDR**
belle	bel-le	*HAO/HDO*
belligerent	be-lli-ge-re-nt	**GAR/GAR/GAR/GAR/GDR**
bellow	be-llo-w	**GAR**/*HOO/HDO*
belly	be-lly	**GAR/GDR**
belong	be-lon-g	**GRR**/*HAO/HDO*
belongings	be-lon-gi-ngs	**GRR**/*HAO*/**GAR/GDR**
beloved	be-lo-ve-d	**GRR/GAR**/*HDO/HOO*
below	be-lo-w	**GRR**/*HOO/HDO*
bels	be-ls	**GAR/GDR**
belt	be-lt	**GAR**/*HDO*
bemused	be-mu-se-d	**GRR**/*HOO/HOO/HOO*
bench	be-n-ch	**GAR/GDR**/*HDO*
bend	be-n-d	**GAR/GDR**/*HOO*
beneath	be-nea-th	**GRR/GRR/GTR**
benefit	be-ne-fi-t	**GAR/GAR/GAR**/*HOO*
benevolent	be-ne-vo-le-nt	**GAR/GAR/GAR/GAR/GDR**
benign	be-ni-gn	**GRR/GRR/GDR**
bent	be-nt	**GAR/GRR**
bequeath	be-quea-th	**GRR/GRR/GDR**
bequest	be-que-st	**GAR/GAR**/*HOO*
Bermudas	Ber-mu-da-s	*HAO/HOO*/**GAR/GDR**
berries	be-rri-es	**GAR/GAR/GDR**
berry	be-rry	**GAR**/*HDO*
berth	ber-th	*HAO/HTO*
beseech	be-see-ch	**GRR/GRR**/*HDO*

Word	Mouthables	Mouth Movements Notations
beset	be-se-t	**GRR/GAR/GRR**
beside	be-si-de	**GRR/GRR/***HDO*
besiege	be-sie-ge	**GRR/GRR/***HDO*
besought	be-sough-t	**GAR/***HOO/HOO*
best	be-st	**GAR/***HDO*
bestow	be-sto-w	**GRR/***HOO/HDO*
bet	be-t	**GAR/***HOO*
betray	be-tray	**GRR/***HAO*
betrayal	be-tray-al	**GRR/***HAO/**GDR**
better	be-tter	**GAR/GDR**
between	be-twee-n	**GRR/GRR/GDR**
beverage	be-ver-a-ge	**GAR/***HAO/HAO/HDO*
bewail	be-wai-l	**GRR/***HAO/**GDR**
beware	be-ware	**GRR/GAR**
bewilder	be-wi-l-der	**GRR/GAR/GDR/***HDO*
bewilderment	be-wi-l-der-me-nt	**GRR/GAR/GDR/***HAO/**GAR/GDR**
bewitch	be-wi-t-ch	**GRR/GAR/***HOO/HDO*
beyond	be-yon-d	**GAR/***HAO/HOO*
bias	bi-a-s	**GRR/GAR/***HDO*
biased	bi-a-se-d	**GRR/GAR/***HDO/HOO*
bizarre	bi-za-rre	**GAR/GAR/GDR**
hib	hi-b	**GAR/GDR**
Bible	Bi-ble	**GRR/***HOO*
biblical	bi-b-li-cal	**GAR/GDR/GAR/***HDO*
bicycle	bi-cy-cle	**GRR/GAR/***HDO*
bid	bi-d	**GAR/***HOO*
bid	bi-d	**GAR/***HDO*
bier	b(i)e-r	**GAR/***HDO*
biff	bi-ff	**GAR/***HDO*
big	bi-g	**GAR/***HDO*
bigamist	bi-ga-mi-st	**GAR/GAR/GAR/***HOO*

Word	Mouthables	Mouth Movements Notations
bigamous	bi-ga-mou-s	GAR/GAR/GAR/*HDO*
bigheaded	bi-g-hea-ded	GAR/*HDO*/GAR/GRR
bigot	bi-go-t	GAR/*HAO*/*HOO*
bigoted	bi-go-ted	GAR/*HAO*/GRR
bike	bi-ke	GRR/*HDO*
bilberry	bi-l-ber-ry	GAR/GDR/*HAO*/GDR
bill	bi-ll	GAR/GDR
billed	bil-le-d	GAR/GDR/*HOO*
billet	bi-lle-t	GAR/GAR/*HOO*
billiards	bi-lli-ar-ds	GAR/GAR/*HAO*/*HDO*
billion	bi-lli-o-n	GAR/GAR/*HAO*/*HDO*
bin	bi-n	GAR/GDR
bind	bi-nd	GRR/GRR
bingo	bi-n-go	GAR/GDR/*HOO*
binoculars	bi-no-cu-lar-s	GAR/*HAO*/*HOO*/*HAO*/*HDO*
biography	bi-o-gra-phy	GRR/*HOO*/GAR/*HDO*
biological	bi-o-lo-gi-cal	GRR/*HOO*/*HAO*/GAR/*HDO*
biology	bi-o-lo-gy	GRR/*HAO*/*HOO*/GDR
birch	bir-ch	*HAO*/*HDO*
bird	bir-d	*HAO*/*HDO*
biro	bi-ro	GRR/*HOO*
birth	bir-th	GAR/GTR
birthday	bir-th-day	GAR/GTR/*HAO*
biscuit	bi-scui-t	GAR/GAR/*HDO*
bishop	bi-sho-p	GAR/*HAO*/*HDO*
bison	bi-so-n	GRR/*HAO*/*HDO*
bit	bi-t	GAR/GDR
bitch	bi-tch	GAR/*HDO*
bitchy	bi-tch-y	GRR/*HDO*/GAR
bite	bi-te	GRR/GDR
bitten	bi-tte-n	GAR/GAR/GRR

Word	Mouthables	Mouth Movements Notations
bitter	bi-tter	**GAR**/*HDO*
bitterly	bi-tter-ly	**GAR**/*HDO*/**GDR**
bivouac	bi-vou-a-c	**GAR**/*HOO*/**GAR/GDR**
bizarre	bi-zz-are	**GAR/GDR**/*HAO*
black	bla-ck	**GAR**/*HDO*
blacken	bla-cken	**GAR/GDR**
blacking	bla-cki-ng	**GAR/GAR/GDR**
blackmail	bla-ck-mai-l	**GAR/GDR**/*HAO*/**GDR**
blackout	bla-ck-ou-t	**GAR/GDR/GAR**/*HOO*
bladder	bla-dder	**GAR**/*HDO*
blade	bla-de	*HAO*/*HDO*
blame	bla-me	*HAO*/*HDO*
bland	bla-n-d	**GAR/GDR**/*HDO*
blank	bla-n-k	**GAR/GDR**/*HDO*
blanket	blan-ke-t	**GAR/GAR/GDR**
blasphemy	blas-phe-my	*HAO*/**GAR/GAR**
blasted	bla-sted	**GAR/GRR**
blastoff	bla-st-o-ff	**GAR/GRR**/*HAO*/*HDO*
blatant	bla-ta-nt	*HAO*/**GAR/GDR**
blaze	bla-ze	*HAO*/**GDR**
bleach	blea-ch	**GRR**/*HDO*
bleak	blea-k	**GRR**/*HDO*
bleary	blea-ry	**GRR/GDR**
bleat	blea-t	**GRR**/*HOO*
bled	ble-d	**GAR/GRR**
bleed	blee-d	**GRR/GRR**
bleep	blee-p	**GRR**/*HDO*
bleeper	blee-per	**GRR**/*HDO*
blemish	ble-mi-sh	**GAR/GAR**/*HDO*
blend	ble-n-d	**GAR/GDR**/*HOO*
blender	ble-n-der	**GAR/GDR**/*HDO*

Word	Mouthables	Mouth Movements Notations
bless	ble-ss	**GAR**/*HDO*
blessing	ble-ssing	**GAR/GDR**
blew	blew	*HOO*
blighter	bligh-ter	**GRR**/*HDO*
blind	bli-nd	**GRR/GDR**
blindfold	bli-nd-fo-ld	**GRR/GDR**/*HOO*/*HDO*
blindness	bli-nd-ne-ss	**GRR/GDR/GAR/GDR**
blink	blin-k	**GAR/GDR**
blinker	blin-ker	**GAR**/*HDO*
bliss	bli-ss	**GAR**/*HDO*
blissful	bli-ss-ful	**GRR**/*HDO*/*HDO*
blister	bli-ster	**GRR**/*HDO*
blizzard	bli-z-zar-d	**GAR/GDR**/*HAO*/*HOO*
bloat	bloa-t	*HOO*/*HOO*
bloated	bloa-ted	*HOO*/**GRR**
blob	blo-b	*HAO*/*HDO*
bloc	blo-c	*HAO*/*HDO*
block	blo-ck	*HAO*/*HDO*
blockade	blo-c-ka-de	*HAO*/*HDO*/*HAO*/*HDO*
blockhead	blo-ck-hea-d	*HAO*/*HDO*/**GAR**/*HOO*
bloke	blo-ke	*HOO*/*HDO*
blond	blo-nd	*HAO*/*HDO*
blood	bloo-d	**GAR**/*HOO*
bloody	bloo-dy	**GAR/GAR**
bloom	bloo-m	*HOO*/*HDO*
blossom	blo-sso-m	*HAO*/*HAO*/*HDO*
blot	blo-t	*HAO*/*HOO*
blotch	blo-tch	*HAO*/*HDO*
blouse	blou-se	**GAR**/*HDO*
blow	blo-w	*HOO*/*HDO*
blown	blow-n	*HOO*/**GDR**

Word	Mouthables	Mouth Movements Notations
blue	blue	*HDO*
bluff	blu-ff	**GAR**/*HDO*
bluish	blu-i-sh	*HOO*/**GAR**/*HDO*
blunder	blu-n-der	**GAR/GDR**/*HDO*
blunt	blu-nt	**GAR/GDR**
blur	blur	*HAO*
blurb	blur-b	*HAO/HDO*
blush	blu-sh	**GAR**/*HDO*
bluster	blu-ster	**GAR**/*HDO*
boar	bo-ar	*HOO/HAO*
board	boar-d	*HOO/HOO*
boarder	boar-der	*HOO/HDO*
boarding	boar-ding	*HOO*/**GDR**
boast	boa-st	*HOO/HOO*
boat	boa-t	*HOO/HOO*
bobby	bo-bby	*HAO*/**GAR**
bodice	bo-di-ce	*HAO*/**GAR/GDR**
bodily	bo-di-ly	*HAO*/**GAR/GDR**
body	bo-dy	*HAO*/**GAR**
boffin	bof-fi-n	*HAO*/**GAR/GDR**
bog	bo-g	*HAO/HDO*
bogey	bo-gey	*HOO*/**GAR**
bogus	bo-gu-s	*HOO*/**GAR**/*HDO*
boil	boi-l	**GAR/GDR**
boiler	boi-ler	**GAR**/*HDO*
boister	boi-ster	**GAR**/*HDO*
boisterous	boi-ster-ous	**GAR**/*HAO/HDO*
bold	bo-ld	*HOO/HDO*
bollard	bol-lar-d	*HAO/HAO/HOO*
bolt	bo-lt	*HOO/HDO*
bomb	bo-mb	*HAO/HDO*

Word	Mouthables	Mouth Movements Notations
bombard	bo-m-bar-d	*HAO/HDO/HAO/HOO*
bombastic	bo-m-ba-sti-c	*HAO/HDO/***GAR/GAR/GDR**
bomber	bo-m-ber	*HAO/HDO/HDO*
bonanza	bo-na-n-za	**GAR/GAR/GDR/GAR**
bondage	bo-n-da-ge	*HAO/***GDR***/HAO/HDO*
bone	bo-ne	*HOO/***GDR**
bonkers	bo-n-kers	*HAO/HDO/HDO*
bonnet	bo-nne-t	*HAO/***GAR/GDR**
bonus	bo-nu-s	*HOO/***GAR***/HDO*
bony	bo-ny	*HOO/***GAR**
book	boo-k	*HOO/HOO*
book	boo-k	*HAO/HDO*
boom	boo-m	*HOO/HDO*
boon	boo-n	*HOO/***GDR**
boos	boo-s	*HOO/HDO*
boost	boo-st	*HOO/HOO*
booster	boo-ster	*HOO/HDO*
boot	boo-t	*HOO/HOO*
booth	boo-th	*HOO/***GTR**
booty	boo-ty	*HOO/***GAR**
booze	boo-ze	*HOO/***GDR**
border	bor-der	*HOO/HDO*
bore	bore	*HOO*
bore	bo-re	*HAO/HDO*
boredom	bore-do-m	*HOO/HAO/HDO*
boring	bo-ring	*HOO/***GDR**
boring	bo-ring	**GAR/GDR**
born	bor-n	*HOO/***GDR**
borne	bor-ne	*HAO/HDO*
borough	bo-rough	**GAR***/HDO*
borrow	bo-rro-w	*HAO/HOO/HDO*

Word	Mouthables	Mouth Movements Notations
borstal	bor-stal	*HOO*/*HDO*
bosh	bo-sh	*HAO*/*HDO*
bosom	bos-o-m	*HOO*/*HAO*/*HDO*
boss	bo-ss	*HAO*/*HDO*
bossy	bo-ssy	*HAO*/**GAR**
botanist	bo-ta-ni-st	*HAO*/**GAR**/**GAR**/*HOO*
botch	bo-tch	*HAO*/*HDO*
both	bo-th	*HOO*/*HTO*
bother	bo-th-er	*HAO*/*HTO*/*HDO*
bottle	bot-tle	*HAO*/*HDO*
bottom	bot-to-m	*HAO*/*HAO*/*HRDO*
bough	bou-gh	*HAO*/*HDO*
bought	bough-t	*HOO*/*HOO*
boulder	bou-l-der	*HOO*/*HDO*/*HDO*
bounce	bou-nce	*HAO*/**GDR**
bound	bou-nd	*HAO*/*HOO*
boundary	bou-n-da-ry	*HAO*/*HDO*/**GAR**/**GDR**
bouquet	bou-quet	*HOO*/*HAO*
bout	bou-t	*HAO*/*HOO*
bow	bow	**GAR**
bowed	bo-we-d	**GAR**/*HOO*/*HOO*
bow	bo-w	**GAR**/*HDO*
bow	bo-w	*HOO*/*HDO*
bowel	bow-e-l	**GAR**/**GAR**/**GDR**
bowl	bow-l	*HOO*/*HOO*
bowl	bo-wl	*HOO*/*HDO*
bowled	bo-wle-d	*HOO*/*HDO*/*HOO*
bowler	bo-wler	*HOO*/*HDO*
box	bo-x	*HAO*/**GDR**
box	bo-x	*HAO*/*HDO*
boxing	bo-xing	*HOO*/**GDR**

Word	Mouthables	Mouth Movements Notations
boy	boy	*HAO*
boycott	boy-cot-t	*HAO/HAO/HOO*
boyfriend	boy-fri-e-nd	*HAO*/**GAR/GAR/GDR**
bra	bra	**GAR**
brace	bra-ce	*HAO*/**GDR**
bracelet	bra-ce-le-t	*HAO*/**GAR/GAR/GDR**
bracken	bra-cken	**GAR/GDR**
bracket	bra-cke-t	**GAR/GAR**/*HDO*
brag	bra-g	**GAR**/*HDO*
braid	brai-d	*HAO/HDO*
brain	brai-n	*HAO*/**GDR**
brainy	brai-ny	*HAO*/**GAR**
braise	brai-se	*HAO/HDO*
brake	bra-ke	*HAO*/**GDR**
brake	bra-ke	*HAO/HDO*
braked	bra-ke-d	*HAO*/**GDR**/*HOO*
bramble	bra-m-ble	**GAR/GDR**/*HOO*
branch	bran-ch	*HAO/HDO*
brand	bra-n-d	**GAR/GDR**/*HOO*
brandish	bra-n-di-sh	**GAR/GDR/GAR**/*HDO*
brash	bra-sh	**GAR**/*HDO*
brass	bras-s	*HAO/HDO*
brassy	bras-sy	*HAO*/**GAR**
brat	bra-t	**GAR**/*HOO*
bravado	bra-vad-o	**GAR**/*HAO/HOO*
brave	bra-ve	*HAO/HDO*
bravery	bra-ve-ry	*HAO/HDO*/**GDR**
bravo	bra-vo	**GAR**/*HOO*
brawl	braw-l	*HOO/HDO*
brawny	braw-ny	*HOO*/**GAR**
bray	bray	*HAO*

Word	Mouthables	Mouth Movements Notations
brayed	braye-d	*HAO*/*HOO*
brays	bray-s	*HAO*/*HDO*
braze	bra-ze	*HAO*/**GRR**
brazed	bra-ze-d	*HAO*/**GDR**/*HOO*
brazen	bra-zen	*HAO*/**GDR**
Brazil	Bra-zi-l	**GAR/GAR/GDR**
Brazilian	Bra-zi-li-a-n	**GAR/GAR/GAR/GAR/GDR**
breach	brea-ch	**GRR**/*HDO*
bread	brea-d	**GAR**/*HOO*
breadth	brea-dth	**GAR/GTR**
break	brea-k	*HAO*/**GRR**
break	brea-k	*HAO*/*HDO*
breakage	brea-ka-ge	*HAO*/*HAO*/*HDO*
breast	brea-st	**GAR**/*HOO*
breath	brea-th	**GAR**/*HTO*
breathe	brea-the	**GRR/GTR**
breather	brea-ther	**GRR**/*HDO*
bred	bre-d	**GAR/GRR**
breeches	bree-ches	**GRR**/*HDO*
breed	bree-d	**GRR/GRR**
breeze	bree-ze	**GRR/GRR**
breezy	bree-zy	**GRR/GAR**
brew	brew	*HOO*
brew	bre-w	*HOO*/*HDO*
brewed	brewe-d	*HOO*/*HOO*
brewery	bre-w-ery	*HOO*/*HDO*/*HDO*
brews	brew-s	*HOO*/*HDO*
bribe	bri-be	**GRR**/*HDO*
bribery	bri-be-ry	**GRR**/*HDO*/**GDR**
brick	bri-ck	**GAR**/*HDO*
bridal	bri-dal	**GRR**/*HDO*

Word	Mouthables	Mouth Movements Notations
bride	bri-de	**GRR**/*HDO*
bridge	bri-d-ge	**GAR**/*HOO*/*HDO*
bridle	bri-dle	**GRR**/*HOO*
brief	brie-f	**GAR/GDR**
brief	brie-f	**GAR**/*HDO*
briefing	brie-fing	**GAR/GDR**
briefs	brie-fs	**GAR/GDR**
bright	brigh-t	**GRR**/*HOO*
brighten	brigh-ten	**GRR**/*HDO*
brigade	bri-ga-de	**GAR**/*HAO*/*HDO*
brilliant	bri-lli-a-nt	**GAR/GAR/GAR/GDR**
brim	bri-m	**GAR**/*HDO*
brimful	bri-m-ful	**GAR**/*HDO*/*HOO*
brine	bri-ne	**GRR/GDR**
bring	bri-ng	**GAR/GRR**
brink	bri-nk	**GAR/GDR**
brisk	bri-sk	**GAR**/*HDO*
bristle	bri-stle	**GAR**/*HOO*
bristly	bri-st-ly	**GAR**/*HOO*/**GDR**
Britain	Bri-tai-n	**GAR**/*HAO*/*HDO*
British	Bri-ti-sh	**GAR/GAR**/*HDO*
Britisher	Bri-ti-sher	**GAR/GAR**/*HDO*
brittle	bri-ttle	**GAR**/*HOO*
broach	broa-ch	*HOO*/*HDO*
broached	broa-chc-d	*HOO*/*HDO*/*HOO*
broad	broa-d	*HOO*/*HOO*
broke	bro-ke	*HOO*/*HOO*
broke	bro-ke	*HOO*/*HDO*
broken	bro-ken	*HOO*/**GDR**
brooch	broo-ch	*HOO*/*HDO*
brother	bro-ther	**GAR**/*HTO*

Word	Mouthables	Mouth Movements Notations
bruise	brui-se	*HOO/HDO*
brunch	brun-ch	**GAR**/*HDO*
brunette	bru-net-te	*HOO/***GAR**/*HDO*
brush	bru-sh	**GAR**/*HOO*
brush	bru-sh	**GAR**/*HDO*
Brussels	Bru-ssel-s	**GAR**/*HDO/HDO*
brute	bru-te	*HOO/HDO*
brutish	bru-ti-sh	*HOO/***GAR**/*HDO*
bubble	bu-bb-le	**GAR**/*HOO/HDO*
buck	bu-ck	**GAR/GRR**
buck	bu-ck	**GAR/GDR**
bucket	bu-cke-t	**GAR/GAR/GDR**
buckle	bu-ckle	**GAR**/*HOO*
bud	bu-d	**GAR**/*HOO*
buddy	bu-ddy	**GAR/GAR**
budge	bu-dge	**GAR**/*HDO*
budget	bu-d-ge-t	**GAR**/*HDO*/**GAR/GDR**
buff	bu-ff	**GAR**/*HDO*
bug	bu-g	**GAR**/*HDO*
bugle	bu-gle	*HOO/HOO*
build	b(u)i-ld	**GAR/GRR**
building	b(u)i-l-ding	**GAR/GDR/GDR**
built	b(u)i-lt	**GAR/GRR**
bulb	bu-l-b	**GAR/GDR**/*HOO*
bulge	bu-l-ge	**GAR/GDR**/*HDO*
bulk	bul-k	**GAR**/*HDO*
bulky	bul-ky	**GAR/GAR**
bull	bu-ll	*HOO/HDO*
bullet	bu-lle-t	*HOO/***GAR**/*HOO*
bulletin	bu-lle-ti-n	*HOO/***GAR/GAR/GDR**
bully	bu-lly	*HOO/***GAR**

Word	Mouthables	Mouth Movements Notations
bum	bu-m	**GAR**/*HDO*
bump	bum-p	**GAR**/*HDO*
bumper	bum-per	**GAR**/*HDO*
bumptious	bum-p-ti-ous	**GAR**/*HDO*/*HOO*/*HAO*
bun	bu-n	**GAR/GDR**
bunch	bu-nch	**GAR/GDR**
bundle	bu-n-dle	**GAR/GDR**/*HOO*
bungle	bu-n-gle	**GAR/GDR**/*HOO*
bunny	bu-nny	**GAR/GAR**
buoy	buoy	*HAO*
buoyant	buoy-a-nt	*HAO*/**GAR/GDR**
burden	bur-den	**GAR**/*HDO*
bureaucracy	bu-reau-cra-cy	*HOO*/*HAO*/**GAR/GAR**
bureaucrat	bu-reau-cra-t	*HOO*/*HOO*/**GAR**/*HOO*
burglar	bur-g-lar	*HAO*/*HDO*/*HDO*
burglarize	bur-g-la-ri-ze	*HAO*/*HDO*/**GAR/GRR/GDR**
burglary	bur-g-la-ry	*HAO*/*HDO*/**GAR/GDR**
burgle	bur-gle	*HAO*/*HOO*
burial	bu-ri-al	**GAR/GAR**/*HDO*
burn	bur-n	**GAR/GRR**
burner	bur-ner	**GAR/GDR**
burnt	bur-nt	**GAR/GRR**
burr	bur	**GAR**
burr	bur-r	**GAR/GDR**
burred	bur-re-d	**GAR/GDR**/*HOO*
burrow	bur-ro-w	**GAR**/*HOO*/*HDO*
bursar	bur-sar	**GAR**/*HDO*
bursary	bur-sa-ry	**GAR/GAR**/*HDO*
burst	bur-st	**GAR**/*HOO*
burst	bur-st	**GAR**/*HDO*
bury	bu-ry	**GAR/GDR**

Word	Mouthables	Mouth Movements Notations
bus	bu-s	**GAR**/*HDO*
bush	bu-sh	*HOO*/*HDO*
bushy	bu-shy	*HOO*/**GAR**
business	bu-si-ne-ss	**GRR/GAR/GAR**/*HDO*
bust	bu-st	**GAR**/*HOO*
busted	bu-sted	**GAR/GRR**
bust	bu-st	**GAR**/*HDO*
busy	bu-sy	**GRR/GAR**
but	bu-t	**GAR**/*HDO*
butcher	but-cher	*HOO*/*HDO*
butler	bu-t-ler	**GAR**/*HOO*/*HDO*
buton	bu-to-n	**GAR**/*HAO*/*HDO*
butt	bu-tt	**GAR**/*HOO*
butt	bu-tt	**GAR**/*HDO*
butted	bu-t-ted	**GAR**/*HOO*/**GRR**
butterfly	bu-tter-fly	**GAR**/*HDO*/**GRR**
buttock	bu-tto-ck	**GAR**/*HAO*/*HDO*
buy	buy	**GRR**
buyer	buy-er	**GRR**/*HDO*
buzz	bu-zz	**GAR/GDR**
buzzer	bu-zz-er	**GAR/GDR**/*HDO*
by	by	**GRR**
bye	bye	**GRR**
byre	by-re	**GRR**/*HDO*
bytes	by-tes	**GRR**/*HDO*

Word	Mouthables	Mouth Movements Notations
C		
C	C	**GRR**
cab	ca-b	**GAR**/*HDO*
cabbage	ca-bb-age	**GAR**/*HDO*/*HDO*
cabin	ca-bi-n	**GAR/GAR/GDR**
cabinet	ca-bi-ne-t	**GAR/GAR/GAR**/*HDO*
cable	ca-ble	*HAO*/*HOO*
cackle	ca-ckle	**GAR**/*HOO*
cackle	cra-c-kle	**GAR/GDR**/*HOO*
cadger	ca-d-ger	**GAR**/*HDO*/*HDO*
cafe	ca-fé	**GAR**/*HAO*
cafeteria	ca-fe-te-ri-a	**GAR/GAR/GAR/GAR/GAR**
cage	ca-ge	*HAO*/*HDO*
cagey	ca-ge-y	*HAO*/*HDO*/**GAR**
cajole	ca-jo-le	**GAR**/*HOO*/*HDO*
cake	ca-ke	*HAO*/*HDO*
calamitous	ca-la-mi-tous	**GAR/GAR/GAR**/*HAO*
calamity	ca-la-mi-ty	**GAR/GAR/GAR/GAR**
calculate	cal-cu-la-te	**GAR**/*HOO*/*HAO*/*HDO*
calculation	cal-cu-la-tion	**GAR**/*HOO*/*HAO*/*HOO*
calculus	cal-cu-lu-s	**GAR**/*HOO*/**GAR**/*HDO*
calendar	ca-le-n-dar	**GAR/GAR/GDR**/*HAO*
calender	ca-len-der	**GAR**/*HAO*/*HDO*
calendered	ca-len-dere-d	**GAR**/*HAO*/*HOO*/*HOO*
calenders	ca-len-ders	**GAR**/*HAO*/*HDO*/*HDO*
calf	cal-f	*HAO*/*HDO*
calibre	ca-li-bre	**GAR/GAR**/*HDO*
call	call	*HOO*
call	cal-l	*HOO*/*HDO*
called	cal-le-d	*HOO*/*HOO*/*HOO*
caller	cal-ler	*HOO*/*HDO*

Word	Mouthables	Mouth Movements Notations
calm	cal-m	*HAO*/*HDO*
calorie	ca-lo-rie	**GAR**/*HOO*/**GAR**
came	ca-me	*HAO*/**GRR**
camel	ca-me-l	**GAR/GAR/GDR**
camelia	ca-me-li-a	**GAR/GRR/GAR/GAR**
camera	ca-mer-a	**GAR**/*HDO*/**GAR**
camomile	ca-mo-mi-le	**GAR**/*HOO*/**GRR/GDR**
camouflage	ca-mou-flage	**GAR/GAR**/*HDO*
camp	ca-mp	**GAR/GRR**
camp	cam-p	**GAR/GDR**
campaign	ca-m-pai-gn	**GAR/GDR**/*HAO*/**GDR**
camphor	ca-m-phor	**GAR/GDR/GAR**
can	ca-n	**GAR/GRR**
can	ca-n	**GAR/GDR**
can't	ca-n't	**GAR/GDR**
Canadian	Ca-na-di-a-n	**GAR**/*HAO*/**GAR/GAR/GDR**
canal	ca-na-l	**GAR/GAR/GDR**
canary	ca-na-ry	**GAR**/*HAO*/**GDR**
cancel	ca-n-ce-l	**GAR/GDR/GAR/GDR**
cancellation	ca-n-ce-lla-tion	**GAR/GDR/GAR**/*HAO*/*HOO*
cancer	ca-n-cer	**GAR/GDR**/*HDO*
candelabra	ca-n-de-lab-ra	**GAR/GDR/GAR**/*HAO*/*HDO*
candid	ca-n-di-d	**GAR/GDR/GAR**/*HDO*
candidacy	ca-n-di-da-cy	**GAR/GDR/GAR/GAR/GAR**
candidate	ca-n-di-da-te	**GAR/GDR/GAR**/*HAO*/*HDO*
candidature	ca-n-di-da-tu-re	**GAR/GDR/GAR**/*HAO*/*HOO*/*HDO*
candied	ca-n-die-d	**GAR/GDR/GAR**/*HOO*
candle	ca-n-dle	**GAR/GDR**/*HOO*
candour	ca-n-dour	**GAR/GDR**/*HAO*
candy	ca-n-dy	**GAR/GDR/GAR**
cane	ca-ne	*HAO*/**GDR**

Word	Mouthables	Mouth Movements Notations
canine	ca-ni-ne	*HAO*/**GRR/GDR**
canister	ca-ni-ster	**GAR/GAR**/*HDO*
cannabis	ca-nna-bi-s	**GAR/GAR/GAR**/*HDO*
cannibal	ca-nni-bal	**GAR/GAR**/*HOO*
cannon	ca-nno-n	**GAR**/*HAO*/*HDO*
cannot	ca-nno-t	**GAR**/*HAO*/*HOO*
canny	ca-nny	**GAR/GAR**
canoe	ca-noe	**GAR**/*HOO*
canopy	ca-no-py	**GAR**/*HOO*/**GAR**
cantankerous	ca-n-tan-ke-rous	**GAR/GDR/GAR/GAR**/*HAO*
canteen	ca-n-tee-n	**GAR/GDR/GRR/GDR**
canvass	ca-n-va-ss	**GAR/GDR/GAR/GRR**
canvassed	ca-n-va-sse-d	**GAR/GDR/GAR/GRR**/*HOO*
canvass	ca-n-va-ss	**GAR/GDR/GAR**/*HDO*
canvassing	ca-n-va-ssing	**GAR/GDR/GAR/GDR**
cap	ca-p	**GAR**/*HDO*
capability	ca-pa-bi-li-ty	*HAO*/**GAR/GAR/GAR/GAR**
capable	ca-pa-ble	*HAO*/**GAR**/*HOO*
capacious	ca-pa-ci-ous	**GAR**/*HAO*/*HDO*/*HAO*
capacity	ca-pa-ci-ty	**GAR/GAR/GAR/GAR**
cape	ca-pe	*HAO*/*HDO*
caper	ca-per	*HAO*/*HDO*
capered	ca-pere-d	*HAO*/*HDO*/*HOO*
caper	ca-per	*HAO*/**GAR**
capital	ca-pi-ta-l	**GAR/GAR/GAR/GDR**
capitalist	ca-pi-ta-li-st	**GAR/GAR/GAR/GAR**/*HDO*
capitulate	ca-pi-tu-la-te	**GAR/GAR**/*HOO*/*HAO*/*HDO*
caprice	ca-pri-ce	**GAR/GAR/GDR**
capsize	ca-p-si-ze	**GAR/GDR/GRR**/*HDO*
capsule	ca-p-su-le	**GAR/GDR**/*HOO*/*HDO*
captain	ca-p-tai-n	**GAR/GDR**/*HAO*/**GDR**

Word	Mouthables	Mouth Movements Notations
caption	ca-p-tion	**GAR/GDR/***HOO*
captivate	ca-p-ti-va-te	**GAR/GDR/GAR/***HAO/HDO*
captive	ca-p-ti-ve	**GAR/GDR/GAR/***HDO*
capture	ca-p-tu-re	**GAR/GDR/***HOO/HDO*
car	car	*HAO*
carafe	ca-rafe	**GAR/***HDO*
carat	ca-ra-t	**GAR/GAR/***HDO*
caravan	ca-ra-va-n	**GAR/GAR/GAR/GDR**
carbohydrate	car-bo-hy-dra-te	*HAO/HOO/***GRR/***HAO/HDO*
carbon	car-bo-n	*HAO/HAO/***GDR**
carbonated	car-bo-na-ted	*HAO/HAO/HAO/***GRR**
carburettor	car-bu-ret-tor	*HAO/***GAR/***HAO/HDO*
carcass	car-ca-ss	*HAO/***GAR/***HDO*
carcinogenic	car-ci-no-ge-ni-c	*HAO/***GAR/GAR/GAR/GAR/GDR**
card	car-d	*HAO/HDO*
cardinal	car-di-nal	*HAO/***GAR/GDR**
cardiologist	car-di-o-lo-gi-st	*HAO/***GAR/***HOO/***GAR/GAR/***HDO*
care	care	*HDO*
career	ca-re-er	*HAO/HAO/HDO*
careful	ca-re-fu-l	*HAO/HDO/HOO/HDO*
careless	ca-re-le-ss	*HAO/HDO/***GAR/GDR**
caress	ca-re-ss	**GAR/GAR/***HDO*
cargo	car-go	*HAO/HOO*
Caribbean	Ca-ri-bbe-an	**GAR/GAR/GRR/GDR**
caricature	ca-ri-ca-tu-re	**GAR/GAR/GAR/***HOO/HDO*
carnage	car-na-ge	*HAO/HAO/HDO*
carnation	car-na-tion	*HAO/HAO/HOO*
carnival	car-ni-va-l	*HAO/***GAR/GAR/GDR**
carouse	ca-rou-se	**GAR/GAR/***HDO*
carousel	ca-rou-se-l	**GAR/***HDO/***GAR/GDR**
carp	car-p	*HAO/***GRR**

Word	Mouthables	Mouth Movements Notations
carped	car-pe-d	*HAO*/*HOO*/*HOO*
carp	car-p	*HAO*/*HDO*
carpenter	car-pe-n-ter	*HAO*/**GAR**/**GDR**/*HDO*
carpet	car-pe-t	*HAO*/**GAR**/*HDO*
carpeting	car-pe-ting	*HAO*/**GAR**/**GDR**
carriage	ca-rria-ge	**GAR**/*HAO*/*HDO*
carrier	ca-rri-er	**GAR**/**GAR**/*HDO*
carrot	ca-rro-t	**GAR**/*HAO*/*HDO*
carry	ca-rry	**GAR**/*HDO*
cartel	car-te-l	*HAO*/**GAR**/**GDR**
Carthusian	Car-thu-si-a-n	*HAO*/*HTO*/**GAR**/**GAR**/**GDR**
carton	car-to-n	*HAO*/*HAO*/*HDO*
cartoon	car-too-n	*HAO*/*HOO*/*HDO*
cartoonist	car-too-ni-st	*HAO*/*HOO*/**GAR**/*HDO*
cartridge	car-trid-ge	*HAO*/**GAR**/*HDO*
carve	car-ve	*HAO*/*HDO*
case	ca-se	*HAO*/*HDO*
cash	ca-sh	**GAR**/*HDO*
cashier	ca-shi-er	**GAR**/*HDO*/*HDO*
cask	cas-k	*HAO*/*HDO*
casket	cas-ke-t	*HAO*/**GAR**/*HOO*
cassette	cas-se-tte	**GAR**/**GAR**/*HDO*
cast	cas-t	*HAO*/*HOO*
casted	cas-ted	*HAO*/**GRR**
cast	cas-t	*HAO*/*HDO*
castanets	cas-ta-ne-ts	*HAO*/**GAR**/**GAR**/*HDO*
castaway	cas-ta-way	*HAO*/**GAR**/*HAO*
caste	cas-te	*HAO*/*HDO*
caster	cas-ter	*HAO*/*HDO*
casting	cas-ting	*HAO*/**GDR**
castle	cas-tle	*HAO*/*HOO*

Word	Mouthables	Mouth Movements Notations
castor	cas-tor	*HAO/HDO*
casual	ca-su-al	**GAR**/*HOO/HDO*
casualty	ca-su-al-ty	**GAR**/*HOO*/**GDR/GAR**
cat	ca-t	**GAR/GRR**
catalogue	ca-ta-lo-gue	**GAR/GAR**/*HAO/HDO*
catastrophe	ca-ta-stro-phe	**GAR/GAR**/*HAO/HDO*
catch	ca-tch	**GAR/GRR**
catching	cat-ching	**GAR/GDR**
catchy	cat-chy	**GAR/GAR**
categorical	ca-te-go-ri-cal	**GAR/GAR**/*HAO*/**GAR**/*HDO*
category	ca-te-go-ry	**GAR/GAR**/*HAO*/**GDR**
cater	ca-ter	*HAO/HDO*
catering	ca-te-ring	*HAO/HDO*/**GDR**
caterpillar	ca-ter-pi-llar	**GAR**/*HAO*/**GAR**/*HDO*
cathedral	ca-the-dral	**GAR/GTR**/*HDO*
catholic	ca-tho-li-c	**GAR**/*HTO*/**GAR/GDR**
cattarrh	ca-ttar-rh	**GAR**/*HAO/HDO*
cattle	ca-ttle	**GAR**/*HOO*
catty	ca-tty	**GAR/GAR**
caught	cau-ght	*HOO/HOO*
cause	cau-se	*HOO/HOO*
caused	cau-se-d	*HOO/HOO/HOO*
cause	cau-se	*HOO/HDO*
caustic	cau-sti-c	*HOO*/**GAR/GAR**
caution	cau-tion	*HOO/HOO*
cautionary	cau-tion-ary	*HOO/HOO/HDO*
cautious	cau-ti-ous	*HOO/HDO/HAO*
cavalier	ca-va-li-er	**GAR/GAR/GAR**/*HDO*
cavalry	ca-va-l-ry	**GAR/GAR**/*HDO/HDO*
cave	ca-ve	*HAO/HDO*
cavern	ca-ver-n	**GAR**/*HOO/HDO*

Word	Mouthables	Mouth Movements Notations
caviar	ca-vi-ar	**GAR/GAR**/*HAO*
cavity	ca-vi-ty	**GAR/GAR/GAR**
cavort	ca-vor-t	**GAR**/*HOO*/*HOO*
caw	caw	*HOO*
cawed	cawe-d	*HOO/HOO*
Cayman	Cay-ma-n	*HAO*/**GAR/GDR**
cease	cea-se	**GRR**/*HDO*
cedar	ce-dar	**GRR**/*HAO*
cede	ce-de	**GRR/GDR**
cede	ce-ded	**GRR/GRR**
ceiling	cei-ling	**GRR/GDR**
celebrate	ce-le-bra-te	**GAR/GAR**/*HAO*/*HOO*
celebrated	ce-le-bra-ted	**GAR/GAR**/*HAO*/**GRR**
celebration	ce-le-bra-tion	**GAR/GAR**/*HAO*/*HOO*
celebrity	ce-le-bri-ty	**GAR/GAR/GAR/GAR**
celery	ce-le-ry	**GAR/GAR**/*HDO*
cell	ce-ll	**GAR/GDR**
cellar	ce-llar	**GAR**/*HAO*
cello	ce-llo	*HDO/HOO*
cellular	ce-llu-lar	**GAR**/*HOO*/*HAO*
cellulose	ce-llu-lo-se	**GAR**/*HOO*/*HOO*/*HDO*
Celtic	Ce-l-ti-c	**GAR/GDR/GAR/GDR**
cement	ce-me-nt	**GAR/GAR/GRR**
cemented	ce-me-nted	**GAR/GAR/GRR**
cement	ce-me-nt	**GAR/GAR**/*HOO*
cemetery	ce-me-te-ry	**GAR/GAR**/*HAO*/**GDR**
censer	ce-n-ser	**GAR/GDR**/*HAO*
censor	ce-n-sor	**GAR/GDR**/*HOO*
censored	ce-n-sore-d	**GAR/GDR**/*HDO*/*HOO*
censorship	ce-n-sor-shi-p	**GAR/GDR**/*HDO*/*HOO*/*HDO*
censure	ce-n-su-re	**GAR/GDR**/*HOO*/*HDO*

Word	Mouthables	Mouth Movements Notations
censured	ce-n-su-re-d	**GAR/GDR/***HOO/HDO/HOO*
census	ce-n-su-s	**GAR/GDR/GAR/***HDO*
cent	ce-nt	**GAR/GDR**
centenarian	ce-n-te-n-ar-i-an	**GAR/GDR/GAR/GDR/***HAO/***GAR/ GDR**
centenary	ce-n-te-n-ar-y	**GAR/GDR/GAR/GDR/***HAO/***GDR**
centennial	ce-n-te-nni-al	**GAR/GDR/GDR/GAR/GDR**
center	ce-n-ter	**GAR/GDR/***HDO*
centigrade	ce-n-ti-gra-de	**GAR/GDR/GAR/***HAO/HDO*
centimetre	ce-n-ti-me-ter	**GAR/GDR/GAR/GAR/***HDO*
centimetre	ce-n-ti-me-tre	**GAR/GDR/GAR/GAR/***HDO*
centipede	ce-n-ti-pe-de	**GAR/GDR/GAR/GRR/***HDO*
central	ce-n-tral	**GAR/GDR/***HDO*
centralize	ce-n-tra-li-ze	**GAR/GDR/***HDO/***GRR/GDR**
centre	ce-n-tre	**GAR/GDR/***HDO*
centrifugal	ce-n-tri-fu-gal	**GAR/GDR/GAR/***HOO/HDO*
centrifuge	ce-n-tri-fu-ge	**GAR/GDR/GAR/***HOO/HDO*
century	cen-tury	**GAR/***HDO*
ceramic	ce-ra-mi-c	**GAR/GAR/GAR/GDR**
cereal	ce-re-al	**GRR/GAR/***HDO*
cerebral	ce-re-bral	**GAR/GRR/GDR**
chaise	chai-se	*HAO/HDO*
chalet	cha-let	**GAR/***HAO*
chalice	cha-li-ce	**GAR/GAR/GDR**
champion	cha-m-pi-on	**GAR/GDR/GAR/***HDO*
championship	cha-m-pi-on-ship	**GAR/GDR/GAR/***HDO/HDO*
chance	chan-ce	*HAO/***GDR**
chancellor	chan-ce-llor	*HAO/***GAR/***HDO*
chancy	chan-cy	*HAO/***GAR**
change	chan-ge	*HAO/HDO*
changeable	chan-ge-a-ble	*HAO/***GAR/GAR/***HOO*

Word	Mouthables	Mouth Movements Notations
channel	cha-nne-l	**GAR/GAR/GDR**
chaos	cha-o-s	*HAO/HAO/HDO*
chaotic	cha-o-ti-c	*HAO/HAO/***GAR/GDR**
chap	cha-p	**GAR/GDR**
chapel	cha-pe-l	**GAR/GAR/GDR**
chapter	cha-p-ter	**GAR/***HDO/HDO*
character	cha-ra-c-ter	**GAR/GAR/GDR/***HDO*
characteristic	cha-ra-c-ter-i-stic	**GAR/GAR/GDR/***HDO/***GAR/GDR**
characterize	cha-ra-c-ter-i-ze	**GAR/GAR/GDR/***HDO/***GRR/GDR**
charcoal	char-coa-l	*HAO/HOO/HDO*
charge	char-ge	*HAO/HOO*
charged	char-ge-d	*HAO/HDO/HOO*
charge	char-ge	*HAO/HDO*
chargeable	char-ge-ble	*HAO/***GAR/***HOO*
charitable	cha-ri-ta-ble	**GAR/GAR/GAR/***HOO*
charity	cha-ri-ty	**GAR/GAR/GAR**
charm	char-m	*HAO/HDO*
chart	char-t	*HAO/HOO*
charter	char-ter	*HAO/HDO*
chase	cha-se	*HAO/***GRR**
chased	cha-se-d	*HAO/***GDR/***HOO*
chase	cha-se	*HAO/HDO*
chasm	cha-sm	**GAR/GDR**
chaste	cha-ste	*HAO/HDO*
chastity	cha sti ty	**GAR/GAR/GAR**
chat	cha-t	**GAR/***HOO*
chatter	chat-ter	**GAR/***HDO*
chatty	chat-ty	**GAR/GAR**
cheap	chea-p	**GRR/***HDO*
cheapen	chea-pen	**GRR/GDR**
cheat	chea-t	**GRR/***HOO*

Word	Mouthables	Mouth Movements Notations
check	che-ck	**GAR**/*HDO*
check	che-cke-d	**GAR**/*HOO*/*HOO*
checkers	che-cker-s	**GAR**/*HDO*/*HDO*
cheek	chee-k	**GRR/GDR**
cheeky	chee-ky	**GRR/GAR**
cheep	chee-p	**GRR/GDR**
cheer	che-er	**GAR**/*HDO*
cheerful	che-er-ful	**GAR**/*HDO*/*HOO*
cheerio	chee-ri-o	**GAR/GAR**/*HOO*
cheery	chee-ry	**GAR/GDR**
cheese	chee-se	**GRR/GDR**
cheetah	chee-tah	**GRR/GAR**
chemical	che-mi-cal	**GAR/GAR**/*HDO*
chemist	che-mi-st	**GAR/GAR**/*HDO*
chemistry	che-mi-st-ry	**GAR/GAR/GAR/GDR**
cheque	che-que	**GAR**/*HDO*
chequered	che-quere-d	**GAR**/*HOO*/*HOO*
cherish	che-ri-sh	**GAR/GAR**/*HDO*
cherry	che-rry	**GAR**/*HDO*
chess	che-ss	**GAR**/*HDO*
chest	che-st	**GAR**/*HOO*
chew	chew	*HOO*
Chicago	Chi-cag-o	*HOO*/*HAO*/*HOO*
Chic	ch-i-c	*HOO*/**GAR/GDR**
chick	chi-ck	**GAR**/*HDO*
chicken	chi-cken	**GAR/GDR**
chicory	chi-co-ry	**GAR**/*HOO*/*HDO*
chide	chi-de	**GRR/GRR**
chief	chie-f	**GRR**/*HDO*
chiefly	chie-fly	**GRR/GDR**
child	chi-l-d	**GRR/GDR**/*HDO*

Word	Mouthables	Mouth Movements Notations
childish	chi-l-di-sh	GRR/GDR/GAR/*HDO*
childlike	chi-ld-li-ke	GRR/GDR/GRR/*HDO*
children	chi-l-dre-n	GAR/GDR/GAR/GDR
Chile	Chi-le	GAR/GAR
Chilean	Chi-le-an	GAR/GRR/GDR
chill	chi-ll	GAR/*HDO*
chilli	chi-lli	GAR/GAR
chilly	chi-lly	GAR/GDR
chime	chi-me	GRR/*HDO*
chimney	chi-m-ney	GAR/GDR/GAR
chimpanzee	chi-m-pa-n-zee	GAR/GDR/GAR/GDR/GRR
China	Chi-na	GRR/GAR
Chinese	Chi-ne-se	GRR/GRR/*HDO*
chink	chin-k	GAR/GDR
chip	chi-p	GAR/GDR
chiropodist	chi-ro-po-di-st	GDR/*HAO*/*HOO*/GAR/GDR
chiropractor	chi-ro-pra-c-tor	GRR/*HOO*/GAR/GDR/*HDO*
chisel	chi-sel	GAR/GDR
chivalrous	chi-val-rous	GDR/*HDO*/*HAO*
chivalry	chi-val-ry	GDR/*HDO*/GDR
chives	chi-ves	GRR/*HDO*
chlorophyll	chlo-ro-phy-ll	*HAO*/*HOO*/GAR/GDR
chocolate	cho-co-la-te	*HAO*/*HOO*/*HAO*/*HDO*
choice	choi-ce	GAR/GDR
choir	choi-r	*HAO*/*HDO*
choke	cho-ke	*HOO*/*HDO*
cholera	cho-le-ra	*HAO*/GAR/GAR
choose	choo-se	*HOO*/*HDO*
choosy	choo-sy	*HOO*/GAR
chop	cho-p	*HAO*/*HOO*
chopped	cho-ppe-d	*HAO*/*HOO*/*HOO*

Word	Mouthables	Mouth Movements Notations
chop	cho-p	*HAO*/*HDO*
chopper	cho-p-per	*HAO*/*HDO*/*HDO*
chord	chor-d	*HOO*/*HOO*
chore	cho-re	*HAO*/*HDO*
choreographer	cho-re-o-gra-pher	*HAO*/**GRR**/*HAO*/**GAR**/*HDO*
chorister	chor-i-ster	*HAO*/**GAR**/*HDO*
chortle	chor-tle	*HOO*/*HOO*
chorus	cho-ru-s	*HAO*/**GAR**/*HDO*
chose	cho-se	*HOO*/*HDO*
chosen	cho-sen	*HOO*/**GDR**
Christ	Chri-st	**GRR**/*HOO*
christen	chri-sten	**GAR/GDR**
christening	chri-sten-i-ng	**GAR/GAR/GAR/GDR**
Christian	Chri-sti-an	**GAR/GAR/GDR**
Christmas	Chri-st-ma-s	**GAR**/*HOO*/**GAR**/*HDO*
chronic	chro-ni-c	*HAO*/**GAR/GDR**
chronological	chro-no-lo-gi-cal	*HAO*/*HOO*/*HAO*/**GAR**/*HDO*
chronometer	chro-no-me-ter	*HAO*/*HOO*/**GRR**/*HDO*
chubby	chu-bby	**GAR/GAR**
chuckle	chuc-kle	**GAR**/*HOO*
chuffed	chu-ffe-d	**GAR**/*HOO*/*HOO*
chum	chu-m	**GAR**/*HDO*
chummy	chu-m-my	**GAR**/*HDO*/**GAR**
chump	chu-mp	**GAR**/*HDO*
chunk	chun-k	**GAR**/*HDO*
chunky	chun-ky	**GAR/GAR**
church	chur-ch	*HOO*/*HDO*
churlish	chur-li-sh	**GAR/GAR**/*HDO*
chute	chu-te	*HOO*/*HDO*
cider	ci-der	**GRR**/*HDO*
cigar	ci-gar	**GAR**/*HAO*

Word	Mouthables	Mouth Movements Notations
cigarette	ci-ga-re-tte	GAR/GAR/GAR/*HDO*
cinema	ci-ne-ma	GAR/GAR/GAR
cinnamon	ci-nna-mo-n	GAR/GAR/*HAO*/*HDO*
cipher	ci-pher	GRR/*HDO*
circle	cir-cle	*HOO*/*HOO*
circuit	cir-cui-t	*HAO*/GAR/*HDO*
circular	cir-cu-lar	*HAO*/*HOO*/*HDO*
circulate	cir-cu-la-te	*HAO*/*HOO*/*HAO*/*HDO*
circulation	cir-cu-la-tion	*HAO*/*HOO*/*HAO*/*HOO*
circumstance	cir-cu-m-sta-nce	*HAO*/GAR/GDR/GAR/GDR
circus	cir-cu-s	*HAO*/GAR/*HDO*
cistern	ci-ster-n	GAR/*HAO*/GDR
citadel	ci-ta-de-l	GAR/GAR/GAR/GDR
citation	ci-ta-tion	GRR/*HAO*/*HOO*
cite	ci-te	GRR/*HDO*
cited	ci-ted	GRR/GRR
citizen	ci-ti-ze-n	GAR/GAR/GAR/GDR
citizenship	ci-ti-ze-n-shi-p	GAR/GAR/GAR/GDR/GDR/*HDO*
citron	ci-tro-n	GAR/*HAO*/GDR
citrus	cit-ru-s	GAR/GAR/*HDO*
city	ci-ty	GAR/GAR
civic	ci-vi-c	GAR/GAR/GDR
civil	ci-vi-l	GAR/GAR/GDR
civilian	ci-vi-li-an	GAR/GRR/GAR/GDR
civilization	ci-vi-li-za-tion	GAR/GAR/GRR/*HAO*/*HOO*
civilize	ci-vi-li-ze	GAR/GAR/GRR/GDR
civvies	ci-vvie-s	GAR/GAR/GDR
claim	clai-m	*HAO*/*HDO*
claimant	clai-ma-nt	*HAO*/GAR/GDR
clairvoyant	clair-voy-a-nt	*HAO*/*HAO*/GAR/GDR
clam	cla-m	GAR/*HDO*

Word	Mouthables	Mouth Movements Notations
clamber	cla-m-ber	**GAR/GDR/**_HDO_
clammy	cla-mmy	**GAR/GAR**
clamour	cla-mour	**GAR/GAR**
clamp	cla-mp	**GAR/**_HDO_
clandestine	cla-n-de-sti-ne	**GAR/GDR/GAR/GRR/GDR**
clang	clan-g	**GAR/GDR**
clanger	clan-ger	**GAR/**_HDO_
clangour	clan-gour	**GAR/GAR**
clannish	cla-nni-sh	**GAR/GAR/**_HDO_
clap	cla-p	**GAR/**_HDO_
claret	clar-e-t	_HAO/_**GAR/GDR**
clarification	cla-ri-fi-ca-tion	**GAR/GAR/GAR/**_HAO/HOO_
clarify	cla-ri-fy	**GAR/GAR/GRR**
clarinet	cla-ri-ne-t	**GAR/GAR/GAR/**_HOO_
clarity	cla-ri-ty	**GAR/GAR/GAR**
clash	cla-sh	**GAR/**_HDO_
clasp	clas-p	_HAO/HDO_
class	clas-s	_HAO/HDO_
classic	cla-ssi-c	**GAR/GAR/GDR**
classical	cla-ssi-cal	**GAR/GAR/**_HDO_
classification	cla-ssi-fi-ca-tion	**GAR/GAR/GAR/**_HAOHOO_
classify	cla-ssi-fy	**GAR/GAR/GRR**
classy	clas-sy	_HAO/_**GAR**
clatter	cla-tter	**GAR/**_HDO_
clause	clau-se	_HOO/HDO_
clavicle	cla-vi-cle	**GAR/GAR/**_HOO_
claw	claw	_HOO_
clay	clay	_HAO_
clean	clea-n	**GRR/GRR**
clean	clea-n	**GRR/GDR**
cleaner	clea-ner	**GRR/**_HDO_

Word	Mouthables	Mouth Movements Notations
cleaning	clea-ning	**GRR/GDR**
cleanliness	clea-n-li-ne-ss	**GAR/GDR/GAR/GAR**/*HDO*
cleanse	clea-nse	**GAR/GDR**
cleanser	clea-n-ser	**GAR/GDR**/*HDO*
clear	cle-ar	**GRR**/*HAO*
clearance	cle-ar-a-nce	**GRR**/*HAO*/**GAR/GDR**
clearing	clea-ring	**GRR/GDR**
clearness	cle-ar-ne-ss	**GRR**/*HAO*/**GAR/GDR**
cleave	clea-ve	**GRR/GDR**
cleft	cle-ft	**GAR**/*HDO*
clement	cle-men-t	**GAR/GAR**/*HOO*
clench	cle-n-ch	**GAR/GDR**/*HDO*
clergy	cler-gy	*HOO/HDO*
cleric	cle-ri-c	**GAR/GAR/GDR**
clerical	cle-ri-cal	**GAR/GAR**/*HDO*
clerk	cler-k	*HAO/HDO*
clever	cle-ver	**GAR**/*HDO*
clew	cle-w	*HOO/HDO*
clewed	cle-we-d	*HOO/HOO/HOO*
clewing	cle-wing	*HOO*/**GDR**
click	cli-ck	**GAR/GRR**
click	cli-ck	**GAR/GDR**
click	cli-cke-d	**GAR/GRR**/*HOO*
client	cli-e-nt	**GRR/GAR/GDR**
cliff	cli-ff	**GAR**/*IIDO*
climactic	cli-ma-ti-c	**GRR/GAR/GAR/GDR**
climate	cli-ma-te	**GRR/GAR**/*HDO*
climax	cli-ma-x	**GRR/GAR/GRR**
climb	cli mb	**GRR**/*HOO*
climbed	cli-mbe-d	**GRR**/*HOO/HOO*
climb	cli-mb	**GRR**/*HDO*

Word	Mouthables	Mouth Movements Notations
climber	cli-mb-er	**GRR**/*HOO*/*HDO*
climbing	cli-mb-i-ng	**GRR**/*HOO*/**GAR/GDR**
clime	cli-me	**GRR/GDR**
clinch	cli-n-ch	**GAR/GDR**/*HDO*
clincher	cli-n-ch-er	**GAR/GDR**/*HDO*/*HDO*
cling	clin-g	**GAR/GRR**
clinged	clin-ge-d	**GAR/GRR**/*HOO*
clinic	cli-ni-c	**GAR/GAR/GDR**
clinical	cli-ni-cal	**GAR/GAR**/*HDO*
clink	clin-k	**GAR**/*HDO*
clinked	clin-ke-d	**GAR**/*HOO*/*HOO*
clink	clin-k	**GAR/GDR**
clip	cli-p	**GAR**/*HOO*
clipped	cli-ppe-d	**GAR**/*HDO*/*HOO*
clip	cli-p	**GAR**/*HDO*
clique	cli-que	**GAR**/*HDO*
clique	cli-que-y	**GAR**/*HDO*/**GAR**
cloak	cloa-k	*HOO*/*HDO*
clobber	clo-bb-er	*HAO*/*HDO*/*HDO*
clock	clo-ck	*HAO*/*HDO*
clod	clo-d	*HAO*/*HDO*
clog	clo-g	*HAO*/*HDO*
cloister	cloi-ster	**GAR**/*HDO*
chlorine	chlor-i-ne	*HOO*/**GAR/GDR**
close	clo-se	*HOO*/*HDO*
closet	clo-se-t	*HAO*/**GAR**/*HDO*
closure	clo-su-re	*HOO*/*HOO*/*HDO*
clot	clo-t	*HAO*/*HOO*
cloth	clo-th	*HAO*/*HTO*
clothes	clo-th-es	*HOO*/*HTO*/*HDO*
clothing	clo-thi-ng	*HOO*/**GTR/GDR**

Word	Mouthables	Mouth Movements Notations
cloudy	clou-dy	GAR/GAR
clout	clou-t	GAR/*HOO*
clove	clo-ve	*HOO/HOO*
clove	clo-ve	*HOO/HDO*
cloven	clo-ven	*HOO/HDO*
clover	clo-ver	*HOO/HDO*
clown	clow-n	GAR/GDR
cloze	clo-ze	*HAO*/GDR
club	clu-b	GAR/*HOO*
clue	clue	*HOO*
clued	clue-d	*HOO/HOO*
clump	clu-mp	GAR/*HDO*
clumsy	clu-m-sy	GAR/*HDO*/GAR
clung	clun-g	GAR/*HDO*
cluster	clu-ster	GAR/*HDO*
clutch	clu-tch	GAR/*HOO*
clutched	clu-tche-d	GAR/*HOO/HOO*
clutch	clu-tch	GAR/*HDO*
cluter	clu-ter	GAR/*HDO*
coach	coa-ch	*HOO/HOO*
coached	coa-che-d	*HOO/HOO/HOO*
coach	coa-ch	*HOO/HDO*
coagulate	co-a-gu-la-te	*HOO*/GAR/*HOO*/*HAOHDO*
coal	co-al	*HOO/HDO*
coalition	co-a-li-tion	*HOO*/GAR/GAR/*HOO*
coarse	coar-se	*HOO/HDO*
coast	coa-st	*HOO/HDO*
coastal	coa-stal	*HOO/HDO*
coaster	coa-ster	*HOO/HDO*
coat	coa-t	*HOO/HOO*
coated	coa-ted	*HOO*/GRR

Word	Mouthables	Mouth Movements Notations
coat	coa-t	*HOO*/**HDO**
coating	coa-ting	*HOO*/**GDR**
coax	coa-x	*HOO*/**GRR**
cob	co-b	*HAO*/*HDO*
cobble	co-bble	*HAO*/*HOO*
cobbler	co-bb-ler	*HAO*/*HDO*/*HDO*
cocaine	co-cai-ne	*HOO*/*HAO*/**GDR**
cock	coc-k	*HAO*/*HDO*
cockerel	coc-ke-re-l	*HAO*/**GAR/GAR/GDR**
cockney	co-ck-ney	*HAO*/**GDR/GRR**
cocky	coc-ky	*HAO*/**GAR**
cocoa	co-coa	*HOO*/*HOO*
cocoon	co-coo-n	*HAO*/*HOO*/*HDO*
cod	co-d	*HAO*/*HOO*
code	co-de	*HOO*/*HDO*
codify	co-di-fy	*HOO*/**GAR/GRR**
coding	co-ding	*HOO*/**GDR**
coeducational	co-e-du-ca-tion-al	*HOO*/**GAR**/*HOO*/*HAO*/*HOO*/**GDR**
coerce	co-er-ce	*HOO*/*HAO*/**GDR**
coercive	co-er-ci-ve	*HOO*/*HAO*/**GAR/GDR**
coffee	cof-fee	*HAO*/**GRR**
coffer	cof-fer	*HAO*/*HDO*
coffin	co-ffi-n	*HAO*/**GAR/GDR**
cog	co-g	*HAO*/*HDO*
cogent	co-ge-nt	*HOO*/**GAR/GDR**
coherent	co-he-re-nt	*HOO*/**GRR/GAR/GDR**
coin	coi-n	**GAR/GDR**
coincide	co-i-n-ci-de	*HOO*/**GAR/GDR/GRR**/*HDO*
coincidental	co-i-n-ci-den-tal	*HOO*/**GAR/GDR/GAR**/*HDO*
coke	co-ke	*HOO*/*HDO*
colander	co-la-n-der	*HAO*/**GAR/GDR**/*HDO*

Word	Mouthables	Mouth Movements Notations
cold	co-ld	*HOO/HOO*
colic	co-li-c	*HAO*/**GAR**/**GDR**
collaborate	co-lla-bor-a-te	*HOO*/**GAR**/*HOO*/*HAO*/*HDO*
collaboration	co-lla-bo-ra-tion	*HOO*/**GAR**/*HOO*/*HAO*/*HOO*
collaborative	co-lla-bo-ra-ti-ve	*HOO*/**GAR**/*HOO*/*HAO*/**GAR**/**GDR**
collaborator	co-lla-bor-a-tor	*HOO*/**GAR**/*HOO*/*HAO*/*HOO*
collapse	co-lla-pse	*HAO*/**GAR**/**GDR**
collapsible	co-lla-psi-ble	*HAO*/**GAR**/**GDR**/*HOO*
collar	co-llar	*HAO*/*HAO*
collarbone	co-llar-bo-ne	*HAO*/*HAO*/*HOO*/**GDR**
colleague	co-llea-gue	*HAO*/**GRR**/*HDO*
collect	co-lle-ct	*HOO*/**GAR**/*HOO*
collection	co-lle-c-tion	*HAO*/**GAR**/**GDR**/*HOO*
collective	co-lle-c-ti-ve	*HAO*/**GAR**/**GDR**/**GAR**/**GDR**
collector	co-lle-c-tor	*HAO*/**GAR**/**GDR**/*HOO*
college	co-lle-ge	*HAO*/**GAR**/*HDO*
collide	co-lli-de	*HAO*/**GRR**/*HDO*
colliery	co-lliery	*HOO*/*HDO*
collision	co-lli-sion	*HOO*/**GRR**/*HOO*
colloquial	co-llo-qui-al	*HOO*/*HOO*/**GAR**/**GDR**
colon	co-lo-n	*HOO*/*HAO*/*HDO*
colonel	colo-nel	**GAR**/*HOO*
colonize	co-lo-ni-ze	*HAO*/**GAR**/**GRR**/**GDR**
colony	co-lo-ny	*HOO*/**GAR**/**GDR**
colour	co-lour	*HAO*/*HAO*
colt	co-lt	*HOO*/*HDO*
column	co-lu-mn	*HAO*/**GAR**/*HDO*
comb	co-mb	*HOO*/*HOO*
combed	co-mbe-d	*HOO*/*HDO*/*HOO*
comb	co-mb	*HDO*/*HDO*
combat	co-m-ba-t	*HAO*/**GDR**/**GAR**/*HOO*

Word	Mouthables	Mouth Movements Notations
combination	co-m-bi-na-tion	*HAO*/*HDO*/**GAR**/*HAO*/*HOO*
combine	co-m-bi-ne	*HAO*/*HDO*/**GRR**/**GDR**
combing	co-mb-i-ng	*HOO*/*HDO*/**GAR**/**GDR**
combustion	co-m-bu-stion	*HAO*/*HDO*/**GAR**/*HOO*
come	co-me	**GAR**/*HDO*
comedian	co-me-di-an	*HAO*/**GRR**/**GAR**/**GDR**
comedy	co-me-dy	*HAO*/**GAR**/**GAR**
comet	co-me-t	*HAO*/**GAR**/*HOO*
comfort	co-m-for-t	**GAR**/**GDR**/*HOO*/*HDO*
comfortable	co-m-for-ta-ble	**GAR**/**GDR**/*HOO*/**GAR**/*HOO*
comfy	co-m-fy	**GAR**/**GDR**/**GAR**
comic	co-mi-c	*HAO*/**GAR**/**GDR**
comical	co-mi-cal	*HAO*/**GAR**/*HOO*
coming	co-mi-ng	**GAR**/**GAR**/**GDR**
comma	co-mma	*HOO*/**GAR**
command	co-mma-n-d	*HAO*/**GAR**/**GDR**/*HOO*
commanding	co-mma-n-ding	*HAO*/**GAR**/**GDR**/**GDR**
commemorate	co-mme-mo-ra-te	*HAO*/**GAR**/*HOO*/*HAO*/*HDO*
commend	co-mme-n-d	*HAO*/**GAR**/**GDR**/*HOO*
commended	co-mme-n-ded	*HOO*/**GAR**/**GDR**/**GRR**
commendation	co-mme-n-da-tion	*HAO*/**GAR**/**GDR**/*HAO*/*HOO*
commensurate	co-mme-n-su-ra-te	*HAO*/**GAR**/**GDR**/*HOO*/*HAO*/*HDO*
comment	co-mme-n-t	*HAO*/**GAR**/**GDR**/*HOO*
commentary	co-mme-n-ta-ry	*HAO*/**GAR**/**GDR**/**GAR**/*HDO*
commentate	co-mme-n-ta-te	*HAO*/**GAR**/**GDR**/*HAO*/*HDO*
commerce	co-mmer-ce	*HAO*/*HAO*/**GDR**
commercial	co-mmer-cial	*HAO*/*HAO*/*HDO*
commiserate	co-mmi-ser-a-te	*HAO*/**GAR**/*HAO*/*HAO*/*HDO*
commission	co-mmi-ssion	*HAO*/**GAR**/*HOO*
commissioner	co-mmi-ssion-er	*HAO*/**GAR**/*HOO*/*HDO*
commitment	co-mmi-t-men-t	*HAO*/**GAR**/**GDR**/**GAR**/*HOO*

Word	Mouthables	Mouth Movements Notations
committee	co-mmi-ttee	*HAO*/**GAR/GRR**
commodity	co-mmo-di-ty	*HAO/HAO*/**GAR/GDR**
common	co-mmo-n	*HAO/HAO/HDO*
commotion	co-mmo-tion	*HAO/HOO/HOO*
communal	co-mmu-nal	*HAO/HOO/HDO*
communicate	co-mmu-ni-ca-te	*HAO/HOO*/**GAR**/*HAO/HDO*
communication	co-mmu-ni-ca-tion	*HAO/HOO*/**GAR**/*HAO/HOO*
communion	co-mmu-ni-on	*HAO/HOO*/**GAR**/*HDO*
communism	co-mmu-ni-sm	*HAO/HOO*/**GAR**/*HDO*
communist	co-mmu-ni-st	*HAO/HOO*/**GAR**/*HDO*
community	co-mmu-ni-ty	*HAO/HOO*/**GAR/GAR**
commutator	co-mmu-ta-tor	*HAO/HOO/HAO/HDO*
commute	co-mmu-te	*HAO/HOO/HDO*
commuter	co-mmu-ter	*HAO/HOO/HDO*
compact	co-m-pac-t	*HAO/HDO*/**GAR**/*HOO*
companion	co-m-pa-ni-on	*HAO/HDO*/**GAR/GAR**/*HDO*
company	co-m-pa-ny	**GAR**/*HDO*/**GAR/GDR**
comparative	co-m-pa-ra-ti-ve	*HAO/HDO*/**GAR/GAR/GAR**/*HDO*
compare	co-m-pare	*HAO/HDO/HAO*
comparision	co-m-par-i-sion	*HAO/HDO/HAO*/**GAR**/*HOO*
compassionate	co-m-pa-ssion-a-te	*HAO/HDO*/**GAR**/*HOO/HAO/HDO*
compatible	co-m-pa-ti-ble	*HAO/HDO*/**GAR/GAR**/*HOO*
compel	co-m-pe-l	*HAO/HDO*/**GAR/GDR**
compelled	co-m-pe-lle-d	*HAO/HDO*/**GAR/GDR**/*HOO*
compelling	co-m-pc-lling	*IIAO/IIDO*/**GAR/GDR**
compensate	co-m-pe-n-sa-te	*HAO/HDO*/**GAR/GDR**/*HAO/HDO*
compete	co-m-pe-te	*HAO/HDO*/**GRR**/*HDO*
competent	co-m-pe-te-nt	*HAO/HDO*/**GAR/GAR/GDR**
competition	co-m-pe-ti-tion	*HAO/HDO*/**GAR/GAR**/*HOO*
competitor	co-m-pe-ti-tor	*HAO/HDO*/**GAR/GAR**/*HOO*
compile	co-m-pi-le	*HAO/HDO*/**GRR/GDR**

Word	Mouthables	Mouth Movements Notations
complacent	co-m-pla-ce-nt	*HAO*/*HDO*/*HAO*/**GAR**/**GDR**
complain	co-m-plai-n	*HAO*/*HDO*/*HAO*/**GRR**
complained	co-m-plai-ne-d	*HAO*/*HDO*/*HAO*/**GRR**/*HOO*
complaint	co-m-plai-nt	*HAO*/*HDO*/*HAO*/**GDR**
complement	co-m-ple-me-nt	*HAO*/*HDO*/**GAR**/**GAR**/**GDR**
complementary	co-m-ple-men-tar-y	*HAO*/*HDO*/**GAR**/**GAR**/*HAO*/*HDO*
complete	co-m-ple-te	*HAO*/*HDO*/**GRR**/*HDO*
complex	co-m-ple-x	*HAO*/*HDO*/**GAR**/**GRR**
complexion	co-m-ple-xion	*HAO*/*HDO*/**GAR**/*HOO*
comply	co-m-ply	*HAO*/*HDO*/**GRR**
component	co-m-po-nen-t	*HAO*/*HDO*/*HOO*/**GAR**/*HOO*
compose	co-m-po-se	*HAO*/*HDO*/*HOO*/*HDO*
composition	co-m-po-si-tion	*HAO*/*HDO*/*HOO*/**GAR**/*HOO*
compost	co-m-po-st	*HAO*/*HDO*/*HAO*/*HDO*
composure	co-m-po-su-re	*HAO*/*HDO*/*HOO*/*HOO*/*HDO*
compound	co-m-pou-nd	*HAO*/*HDO*/**GAR**/**GDR**
compounded	co-m-pou-nded	*HAO*/*HDO*/**GAR**/**GRR**
comprehend	co-m-pre-he-nd	*HAO*/*HDO*/**GRR**/**GAR**/**GDR**
comprehensible	co-m-pre-he-n-si-ble	*HAO*/*HDO*/**GRR**/**GAR**/**GDR**/**GAR**/*HOO*
comprehensive	co-m-pre-he-n-si-ve	*HAO*/*HDO*/**GRR**/**GAR**/**GDR**/**GAR**/*HDO*
compress	co-m-pre-ss	*HAO*/*HDO*/**GAR**/*HDO*
compressor	co-m-pre-ssor	*HAO*/*HDO*/**GAR**/*HOO*
compromise	co-m-pro-mi-se	*HAO*/*HDO*/*HOO*/**GRR**/*HDO*
compulsion	co-m-pu-l-sion	*HAO*/*HDO*/**GAR**/**GDR**/*HOO*
compulsive	co-m-pu-l-si-ve	*HAO*/*HDO*/**GAR**/**GDR**/**GAR**/*HDO*
compunction	co-m-pun-c-tion	*HAO*/*HDO*/**GAR**/**GDR**/*HOO*
computerize	co-m-pu-ter-i-ze	*HAO*/*HDO*/*HOO*/*HAO*/**GRR**/**GDR**
con	co-n	*HAO*/*HDO*
concave	co-n-ca-ve	*HAO*/**GDR**/*HAO*/*HDO*
conceal	co-n-cea-l	*HAO*/**GDR**/**GRR**/**GDR**

Word	Mouthables	Mouth Movements Notations
concealment	co-n-cea-l-men-t	*HAO*/**GDR**/**GRR**/**GDR**/**GAR**/*HOO*
concede	co-n-ce-de	*HAO*/**GDR**/**GRR**/*HDO*
conceit	co-n-cie-t	*HAO*/**GDR**/**GAR**/*HDO*
conceive	co-n-cei-ve	*HAO*/**GDR**/**GRR**/*HDO*
concentrate	co-n-cen-tra-te	*HAO*/**GDR**/**GAR**/*HAO*/*HDO*
concept	co-n-ce-pt	*HAO*/**GDR**/**GAR**/*HOO*
concern	co-n-cer-n	*HAO*/**GDR**/*HAO*/**GDR**
concerned	co-n-cerne-d	*HAO*/**GDR**/*HAO*/*HOO*
concert	co-n-cer-t	*HAO*/**GDR**/*HAO*/*HOO*
concession	co-n-ces-sion	*HAO*/**GDR**/**GAR**/*HOO*
conciliation	co-n-ci-li-a-tion	*HAO*/**GDR**/**GAR**/**GAR**/*HAO*/*HOO*
concise	co-n-ci-se	*HAO*/**GDR**/**GRR**/*HDO*
conclude	co-n-clu-de	*HAO*/**GDR**/*HOO*/*HDO*
concluding	co-n-clu-ding	*HAO*/**GDR**/*HOO*/**GDR**
conclusion	co-n-clu-sion	*HAO*/**GDR**/*HOO*/*HOO*
conclusive	co-n-clu-si-ve	*HAO*/**GDR**/*HOO*/**GAR**/*HDO*
concoct	co-n-co-c-t	*HAO*/**GDR**/*HAO*/*HDO*/*HOO*
concoction	co-n-co-c-tion	*HAO*/**GDR**/*HAO*/*HDO*/*HOO*
concourse	con-cour-se	*HAO*/*HOO*/*HDO*
concrete	co-n-cre-te	*HAO*/**GDR**/**GRR**/*HDO*
concur	con-cur	*HAO*/*HAO*
concussion	con-cus-sion	*HAO*/**GAR**/*HOO*
condemn	co-n-de-mn	*HAO*/**GDR**/**GAR**/**GDR**
condemnation	co-n-de-m-na-tion	*HAO*/**GDR**/**GAR**/*HDO*/*HAO*/*HOO*
condense	co-n-de-n-se	*HAO*/**GDR**/**GAR**/**GDR**/*HDO*
condescend	co-n-de-sce-n-d	*HAO*/**GDR**/**GAR**/**GAR**/**GDR**/*HOO*
condition	co-n-di-tion	*HAO*/**GDR**/**GAR**/*HOO*
conditional	co-n-di-tion-al	*HAO*/**GDR**/**GAR**/*HOO*/*HDO*
conditioner	co-n-di-tion-er	*HAO*/**GDR**/**GAR**/*HOO*/*HDO*
condolence	co-n-do-le-nce	*HAO*/**GDR**/*HOO*/**GAR**/**GDR**
condom	co-n-do-m	*HAO*/**GDR**/*HAO*/*HDO*

Word	Mouthables	Mouth Movements Notations
condominium	co-n-do-mi-ni-u-m	*HAO*/**GDR**/*HOO*/**GAR/GAR/GAR**/*HDO*
condone	co-n-do-ne	*HAO*/**GDR**/*HOO*/*HDO*
conducive	co-n-du-ci-ve	*HAO*/**GDR**/*HOO*/**GAR**/*HDO*
conduct	co-n-du-c-t	*HAO*/**GDR/GAR/GDR**/*HOO*
conductor	co-n-du-c-tor	*HAO*/**GDR/GAR/GDR**/*HOO*
cone	co-ne	*HOO*/**GDR**
confabulation	co-n-fa-bu-la-tion	*HAO*/**GDR/GAR**/*HOO*/*HAO*/*HOO*
confectioner	co-n-fec-tion-er	*HAO*/**GDR/GAR**/*HOO*/*HDO*
confederate	co-n-fe-der-a-te	*HAO*/**GDR/GAR**/*HAO*/*HAO*/*HDO*
confer	co-n-fer	*HAO*/**GDR**/*HDO*
conferred	co-n-ferre-d	*HAO*/**GDR**/*HDO*/*HOO*
conference	co-n-fer-e-nce	*HAO*/**GDR**/*HAO*/**GAR/GDR**
confess	co-n-fe-ss	*HAO*/**GDR/GAR**/*HDO*
confession	co-n-fe-ssion	*HAO*/**GDR/GAR**/*HOO*
confetti	con-fet-ti	*HAO*/**GAR/GAR**
confide	co-n-fi-de	*HAO*/**GDR/GRR**/*HOO*
confidence	co-n-fi-de-nce	*HAO*/**GDR/GAR/GAR/GDR**
confident	co-n-fi-de-nt	*HAO*/**GDR/GAR/GAR/GDR**
confine	co-n-fi-ne	*HAO*/**GDR/GRR/GDR**
confirm	co-n-fir-m	*HAO*/**GDR**/*HOO*/*HDO*
confirmed	co-n-fir-me-d	*HAO*/**GDR**/*HOO*/*HDO*/*HOO*
confiscate	co-n-fi-sca-te	*HAO*/**GDR/GAR**/*HAO*/*HDO*
conflict	co-n-fli-ct	*HAO*/**GDR/GAR/GRR**
conform	co-n-for-m	*HAO*/**GDR**/*HOO*/*HDO*
conformist	co-n-for-mi-st	*HAO*/**GDR**/*HOO*/**GAR**/*HDO*
confound	co-n-foun-d	*HAO*/**GDR/GAR**/*HOO*
confront	co-n-fro-nt	*HAO*/**GDR/GAR/GDR**
confuse	co-n-fu-se	*HAO*/**GDR**/*HOO*/*HDO*
confusion	co-n-fu-sion	*HAO*/**GDR**/*HOO*/*HOO*
congenital	co-n-ge-ni-tal	*HAO*/**GDR/GAR/GAR**/*HDO*

Word	Mouthables	Mouth Movements Notations
congested	co-n-ge-sted	*HAO*/**GDR**/**GAR**/**GRR**
congratulate	co-n-gra-tu-la-te	*HAO*/**GDR**/**GAR**/*HOO*/*HAO*/*HDO*
congregate	con-gre-ga-te	*HAO*/**GAR**/*HAO*/*HDO*
congress	co-n-gre-ss	*HAO*/**GDR**/**GAR**/*HDO*
congressman	co-n-gre-ss-ma-n	*HAO*/**GDR**/**GAR**/*HDO*/**GAR**/**GDR**
conjecture	co-n-je-c-tu-re	*HAO*/**GDR**/**GAR**/**GDR**/*HOO*/*HDO*
conjugal	con-ju-gal	*HAO*/*HOO*/*HOO*
conjurer	con-ju-rer	*HAO*/**GAR**/*HDO*
conman	con-ma-n	*HAO*/**GAR**/**GDR**
connect	con-ne-ct	*HAO*/**GAR**/*HOO*
connection	con-ne-c-tion	*HAO*/**GAR**/**GDR**/*HOO*
connive	co-nni-ve	*HAO*/**GRR**/*HDO*
connoisseur	co-n-noi-sseur	*HAO*/**GDR**/*HAO*/*HOO*
conquer	con-quer	*HAO*/*HAO*
conquest	co-n-que-st	*HAO*/**GDR**/**GAR**/*HOO*
conscience	co-n-sci-e-nce	*HAO*/**GDR**/**GAR**/**GDR**
conscious	con-sci-ous	*HAO*/**GAR**/*HAO*
consciousness	con-sci-ous-ne-ss	*HAO*/**GAR**/*HAO*/**GAR**/*HDO*
conscription	co-n-scri-p-tion	*HAO*/**GDR**/**GAR**/**GDR**/*HOO*
consecrate	co-n-se-cra-te	*HAO*/**GDR**/**GAR**/*HAOHDO*
consecutive	co-n-se-cu-ti-ve	*HAO*/**GDR**/**GAR**/*HOO*/**GAR**/*HDO*
consent	co-n-sen-t	*HAO*/**GDR**/**GAR**/*HOO*
consequence	co-n-se-que-nce	*HAO*/**GDR**/**GAR**/**GAR**/**GDR**
consequent	co-n-se-que-nt	*HAO*/**GDR**/**GAR**/**GDR**
consequential	co-n-se-que-n-tial	*HAO*/**GDR**/**GAR**/**GAR**/**GDR**/*HDO*
conservation	co-n-ser-va-tion	*HAO*/**GDR**/*HOO*/*HAO*/*HOO*
conservative	co-n-ser-va-ti-ve	*HAO*/**GDR**/*HOO*/*HAO*/**GAR**/*HDO*
conserve	co-n-ser-ve	*HAO*/**GDR**/*HOO*/*HDO*
consider	co-n-si-der	*HAO*/**GDR**/**GAR**/*HDO*
considerable	co-n-si-der-a-ble	*HAO*/**GDR**/*HAO*/**GAR**/*HOO*
consideration	co-n-si-der-a-tion	*HAO*/**GDR**/**GAR**/*HAO*/*HAO*/*HOO*

Word	Mouthables	Mouth Movements Notations
consign	co-n-si-gn	*HAO*/**GDR**/**GRR**/**GDR**
consist	co-n-si-st	*HAO*/**GDR**/**GAR**/*HDO*
consistent	co-n-si-ste-nt	*HAO*/**GDR**/**GAR**/**GAR**/**GDR**
console	co-n-so-le	*HAO*/**GDR**/ *HOO*/**GRR**
consoled	co-n-so-le-d	*HAO*/**GDR**/*HOO*/**GRR**/*HOO*
console	con-so-le	*HAO*/*HOO*/*HDO*
consolidate	co-n-so-li-da-te	*HAO*/**GDR**/*HAO*/**GAR**/*HAO*/*HDO*
consonant	con-so-na-nt	*HAO*/**GAR**/**GAR**/**GDR**
consort	co-n-sor-t	*HAO*/**GDR**/*HOO*/*HOO*
consorted	co-n-sor-ted	*HAO*/**GDR**/*HOO*/**GRR**
consort	co-n-sor-t	*HAO*/**GDR**/*HOO*/*HDO*
conspicuous	co-n-spi-cu-ous	*HAO*/**GDR**/**GAR**/*HOO*/*HAO*
conspire	co-n-spi-re	*HAO*/**GDR**/**GRR**/*HDO*
constable	con-sta-ble	*HAO*/**GAR**/*HOO*
constant	co-n-sta-nt	*HAO*/**GDR**/**GAR**/**GDR**
constellation	co-n-ste-lla-tion	*HAO*/**GDR**/**GAR**/*HAO*/*HOO*
constipated	co-n-sti-pa-ted	*HAO*/**GDR**/**GAR**/*HAO*/**GRR**
constituency	co-n-sti-tu-e-ncy	*HAO*/**GDR**/**GAR**/*HOO*/**GAR**/**GDR**
constitute	co-n-sti-tu-te	*HAO*/**GDR**/**GAR**/*HOO*/*HDO*
constitution	co-n-sti-tu-tion	*HAO*/**GDR**/**GAR**/*HOO*/*HOO*
constrain	co-n-strai-n	*HAO*/**GDR**/*HAO*/**GRR**
constraint	co-n-strai-nt	*HAO*/**GDR**/*HAO*/**GDR**
constrict	co-n-stri-ct	*HDO*/**GDR**/**GAR**/**GDR**
construct	co-n-stru-c-t	*HAO*/**GDR**/**GAR**/**GDR**/*HOO*
construe	co-n-strue	*HAO*/**GDR**/*HOO*
consul	co-n-su-l	*HAO*/**GDR**/*HOO*/*HDO*
consulate	co-n-su-la-te	*HAO*/**GDR**/*HOO*/*HAO*/*HDO*
consult	co-n-su-lt	*HAO*/**GDR**/**GAR**/**GDR**
consultant	co-n-su-l-tan-t	*HAO*/**GDR**/**GAR**/**GDR**/**GAR**/*HOO*
consume	co-n-su-me	*HAO*/**GDR**/*HOO*/*HDO*
consumer	co-n-su-mer	*HAO*/**GDR**/*HOO*/*HDO*

Word	Mouthables	Mouth Movements Notations
consumption	co-n-su-mp-tion	*HAO*/**GDR**/**GAR**/*HDO*/*HOO*
contact	co-n-tac-t	*HAO*/**GDR**/**GAR**/*HOO*
contacted	co-n-tac-ted	*HAO*/**GDR**/**GAR**/**GRR**
contagion	co-n-ta-gi-on	*HAO*/**GDR**/*HAO*/**GAR**/**GDR**
contain	con-tai-n	*HAO*/*HAO*/**GDR**
containment	con-tai-n-men-t	*HAO*/*HAO*/**GDR**/**GAR**/*HDO*
contaminate	co-n-ta-mi-na-te	*HAO*/**GDR**/**GAR**/**GAR**/*HAOHDO*
contemplate	con-te-m-pla-te	*HAO*/**GAR**/**GDR**/*HAO*/*HDO*
contempory	con-tem-po-ry	*HAO*/**GAR**/*HOO*/*HDO*
contempt	co-n-tem-pt	*HAO*/**GDR**/**GAR**/**GDR**
contend	con-te-n-d	*HAO*/**GAR**/**GDR**/*HOO*
content	con-ten-t	*HAO*/**GAR**/*HDO*
contest	co-n-tes-t	*HAO*/**GDR**/**GAR**/*HOO*
contestant	co-n-tes-ta-nt	*HAO*/**GDR**/**GAR**/**GAR**/**GDR**
context	con-te-x-t	*HAO*/**GAR**/**GDR**/*HOO*
continent	co-n-ti-nen-t	*HAO*/**GDR**/**GAR**/*HOO*
contingent	co-n-ti-n-ge-nt	*HAO*/**GDR**/**GAR**/**GDR**/**GAR**/**GDR**
continuation	co-n-ti-nu-a-tion	*HAO*/**GDR**/**GAR**/*HOO*/*HAO*/*HOO*
continue	con-ti-n-ue	*HAO*/**GDR**/**GAR**/**GDR**/*HOO*
contour	co-n-tour	*HAO*/**GDR**/*HOO*
contraband	co-n-tra-ba-nd	*HAO*/**GDR**/**GAR**/**GAR**/**GDR**
contraceptive	co-n-tra-ce-p-ti-ve	*HAO*/**GDR**/**GAR**/**GAR**/**GDR**/**GAR**/ **GDR**
contract	co-n-trac-t	*HAO*/**GDR**/**GAR**/*HOO*
contractor	co-n-trac-tor	*HAO*/**GDR**/**GAR**/*HOO*
contradict	co-n-tra-dic-t	*HAO*/**GDR**/**GAR**/**GAR**/*HOO*
contradiction	co-n-tra-dic-tion	*HAO*/**GDR**/**GAR**/**GAR**/*HOO*
contrary	con-tra-ry	*HAO*/*HDO*/**GDR**
contrast	con-tra-st	*HAO*/**GAR**/*HOO*
contribute	con-tri-bu-te	*HAO*/**GAR**/*HOO*/*HDO*
contribution	con-tri-bu-tion	*HAO*/**GAR**/*HOO*/*HOO*

Word	Mouthables	Mouth Movements Notations
contrivance	co-n-tri-van-ce	*HAO*/**GDR/GRR/GAR/GRR**
contrive	co-n-tri-ve	*HAO*/**GDR/GRR/GDR**
control	con-tro-l	*HAO/HOO/HDO*
controversy	co-n-tro-ver-sy	*HAO*/**GDR**/*HAO/HAO*/**GAR**
contusion	co-n-tu-sion	*HAO*/**GDR**/*HOO/HOO*
convalescent	co-n-va-les-ce-nt	*HAO*/**GDR/GAR/GAR/GAR/GDR**
convenience	co-n-ve-ni-e-nce	*HAO*/**GDR/GRR/GAR/GDR**
convenient	con-ve-ni-e-nt	*HAO*/**GDR/GRR/GAR/GAR/GDR**
convent	co-n-ven-t	*HAO*/**GDR/GAR**/*HDO*
convention	co-n-ven-tion	*HAO*/**GDR/GAR**/*HOO*
conventional	co-n-ven-tion-al	*HAO*/**GDR/GAR**/*HOO/HDO*
converge	co-n-ver-ge	*HAO*/**GDR**/*HAO/HDO*
conversational	co-n-ver-sa-tion-al	*HAO*/**GDR**/*HAO*/**GAR**/*HOO/HDO*
convert	co-n-ver-t	*HAO*/**GDR**/*HAO/HOO*
convey	co-n-vey	*HAO*/**GDR**/*HAO*
conveyance	co-n-vey-a-nce	*HAO*/**GDR**/*HAO*/**GAR/GDR**
convict	co-n-vi-ct	*HAO*/**GDR/GAR/GDR**
conviction	co-n-vi-c-tion	*HAO*/**GDR/GAR/GDR**/*HOO*
convince	co-n-vi-nce	*HAO*/**GDR/GAR/GDR**
convocation	con-vo-ca-tion	*HAO/HOO/HAO/HOO*
convulsive	con-vu-l-si-ve	*HAO*/**GDR/GAR/GDR/GAR**/*HDO*
cook	coo-k	*HOO/HDO*
cooker	coo-ker	*HOO/HDO*
cookie	coo-kie	*HOO*/**GAR**
cool	coo-l	*HOO*/**GDR**
coop	co-o-p	*HOO/HAO/HDO*
cooperate	co-o-per-a-te	*HOO/HAO/HDO/HAO/HDO*
coordinate	co-or-di-na-te	*HOO/HOO*/**GAR**/*HAO/HDO*
cop	co-p	*HAO/HDO*
cope	co-pe	*HOO/HDO*
copier	co-pi-er	*HAO*/**GAR**/*HAO*

Word	Mouthables	Mouth Movements Notations
copper	cop-per	*HAO/HDO*
copy	co-py	*HAO/***GAR**
coral	co-ral	*HAO/HDO*
cord	cor-d	*HOO/HDO*
corduroy	cor-du-roy	*HOO/HOO/HAO*
core	co-re	*HOO/HDO*
cork	cor-k	*HOO/HDO*
corn	cor-n	*HOO/***GDR**
corner	cor-ner	*HOO/HDO*
cornet	cor-ne-t	*HAO/***GAR***/HDO*
corporal	cor-po-ral	*HOO/***GAR***/***GDR**
corporate	cor-po-ra-te	*HOO/***GAR***/HAO/HDO*
corporation	cor-po-ra-tion	*HOO/***GAR***/HAO/HOO*
corps	corps	*HOO*
corpse	cor-pse	*HOO/HDO*
correct	cor-rec-t	*HAO/***GAR***/HOO*
correlate	cor-re-la-te	*HOO/***GAR***/HAO/HDO*
correlation	cor-re-la-tion	*HOO/***GAR***/HAO/HOO*
correspondence	cor-re-spon-de-nce	*HAO/***GAR***/HAO/***GAR***/***GDR**
corridor	cor-ri-dor	*HAO/***GAR***/HOO*
corroborative	cor-ro-bo-ra-ti-ve	*HOO/HAO/***GAR/GAR/GAR/GDR**
corrode	cor-ro-de	*HOO/HOO/HDO*
corrupt	cor-ru-pt	**GAR/GAR***/HDO*
cosmetic	co-s-me-ti-c	*HAO/***GDR/GAR/GAR/GDR**
cosmetician	co-s-me-ti-ci-an	*HAO/***GDR/GAR/GAR/GDR/GDR**
cost	co-st	*HAO/HOO*
costly	co-st-ly	*HAO/HOO/***GDR**
costume	cos-tu-me	*HAO/HOO/HDO*
cosy	co-sy	*HOO/***GAR**
cot	co-t	*HAO/HDO*
cottage	co-tta-ge	*HAO/HAO/HDO*

Word	Mouthables	Mouth Movements Notations
cotton	co-tto-n	*HAO/HAO/HDO*
couch	cou-ch	**GAR**/*HDO*
cough	cou-gh	*HAO/HDO*
could	coul-d	*HOO/HOO*
council	cou-n-ci-l	*HAO*/**GDR/GAR**/*GDR*
counsel	coun-sel	*HAO/HDO*
counsellor	coun-se-lor	*HAO/HDO/HOO*
count	coun-t	*HAO/HOO*
countenance	cou-n-te-na-nce	*HAO*/**GDR/GAR/GAR**/*GDR*
counter	coun-ter	*HAO/HOO*
countered	coun-tere-d	*HAO/HOO/HOO*
counter	coun-ter	*HAO/HDO*
counteract	coun-ter-a-ct	*HAO/HAO*/**GAR**/*HOO*
counterfeit	coun-ter-fei-t	*HAO/HAO*/**GRR/GRR**
counterfoil	coun-ter-foi-l	*HAO/HAO*/**GAR**/*GDR*
counterpart	coun-ter-par-t	*HAO/HAO/HAO/HOO*
countless	coun-t-le-ss	*HAO/HOO*/**GAR**/*GDR*
country	coun-t-ry	*HAO/HOO*/**GDR**
countryside	coun-t-ry-si-de	*HAO/HOO*/**GDR/GRR**/*HDO*
county	cou-n-ty	**GAR/GDR/GAR**
coupon	cou-po-n	*HOO/HAO/HDO*
courage	cou-ra-ge	**GAR**/*HAO/HDO*
course	cour-se	*HOO/HDO*
court	cour-t	*HOO/HDO*
courtesy	cour-te-sy	**GAR/GAR/GAR**
cousin	cou-si-n	**GAR/GAR/GDR**
convene	con-ve-ne	*HAO*/**GRR/GDR**
cover	co-ver	**GAR**/*HDO*
coverage	co-ve-rage	**GAR**/*HAO/HDO*
cow	cow	*HAO*
coward	co-war-d	**GAR**/*HAO/HDO*

Word	Mouthables	Mouth Movements Notations
cower	co-wer	GAR/*HDO*
cowered	co-were-d	GAR/*HDO*/*HOO*
cox	co-x	*HAO*/*HDO*
coy	coy	GAR
cozy	co-zy	*HOO*/GAR
crab	cra-b	GAR/*HDO*
crack	cra-ck	GAR/GDR
cracked	cra-cke-d	GAR/GDR/*HOO*
crack	cra-ck	GAR/*HDO*
cracker	crac-ker	GAR/*HDO*
crackers	crac-ker-s	GAR/*HDO*/*HDO*
cradle	cra-dle	*HAO*/*HOO*
craft	craf-t	*HAO*/*HOO*
craftsman	craf-ts-ma-n	GAR/*HOO*/GAR/GDR
crafty	craf-ty	GAR/GAR
cram	cra-m	GAR/*HDO*
cramp	cra-mp	GAR/*HDO*
cramped	cra-mpe-d	GAR/GDR/*HOO*
crane	cra-ne	*HAO*/GDR
crank	cran-k	GAR/*HOO*
cranky	cran-ky	GAR/GAR
crash	cra-sh	GAR/*HDO*
crate	cra-te	*HAO*/*HDO*
crave	cra-ve	*HAO*/GDR
crawl	craw-l	*HOO*/*HDO*
craze	cra-ze	*HAO*/GDR
crazy	cra-zy	*HAO*/GAR
creak	crea-k	GRR/*HDO*
cream	crea-m	GRR/*HDO*
crease	crea-se	GRR/*HDO*
create	cre-a-te	GRR/*HAO*/*HDO*

Word	Mouthables	Mouth Movements Notations
creature	crea-tu-re	**GRR**/*HOO*/*HDO*
crèche	crè-che	**GAR**/*HDO*
credible	cre-di-ble	**GAR/GAR**/*HOO*
credit	cre-di-t	**GAR/GAR**/*HOO*
creditable	cre-di-ta-ble	**GAR/GAR/GAR**/*HOO*
creditor	cre-di-tor	**GAR/GAR**/*HOO*
credulous	cre-du-lous	**GAR**/*HOO*/**GAR**
creed	cree-d	**GRR**/*HOO*
creep	cree-p	**GRR/GDR**
creeper	cree-per	**GRR**/*HDO*
creepy	cree-py	**GRR/GAR**
cremation	cre-ma-tion	**GAR**/*HAO*/*HOO*
crept	cre-p-t	**GAR/GDR/GRR**
crescent	cres-ce-nt	**GAR/GAR/GDR**
cress	cre-ss	**GAR**/*HDO*
crest	cres-t	**GAR**/*HOO*
crevasse	cre-va-sse	**GAR/GAR**/*HDO*
crevice	cre-vi-ce	**GAR/GAR/GDR**
crew	cre-w	*HOO*/*HDO*
crib	cri-b	**GAR**/*HDO*
cricket	cri-cke-t	**GAR/GAR/GDR**
criminal	cri-mi-nal	**GAR/GAR**/*HDO*
cripple	cri-p-ple	**GAR**/*HDO*/*HOO*
crisis	cri-si-s	**GRR/GAR/GDR**
crisp	cri-sp	**GAR**/*HDO*
criteria	cri-te-ri-a	**GRR/GRR/GAR/GAR**
criterion	cri-te-ri-on	**GRR/GRR/GAR/GDR**
critic	cri-ti-c	**GAR/GAR/GDR**
critical	cri-ti-cal	**GAR/GAR**/*HDO*
criticize	cri-ti-ci-ze	**GAR/GAR/GRR**/*HDO*
croak	croa-k	*HOO*/*HDO*

Word	Mouthables	Mouth Movements Notations
crocodile	cro-co-di-le	*HAO/HOO/***GRR/GDR**
crook	croo-k	*HOO/HDO*
crop	cro-p	*HAO/HDO*
croquet	cro-quet	*HOO/HAO*
cross	cro-ss	*HAO/HDO*
crouch	crou-ch	**GAR**/*HDO*
crow	cro-w	*HOO/HOO*
crowed	cro-we-d	*HOO/HOO/HOO*
crow	cro-w	*HOO/HDO*
crowd	crow-d	**GAR**/*HOO*
crown	crow-n	*HAO/***GDR**
crucial	cru-cial	*HOO/HDO*
crucifix	cru-ci-fi-x	*HOO/***GAR/GAR/GDR**
crude	cru-de	*HOO/HDO*
cruel	cru-el	*HOO/***GDR**
cruise	crui-se	*HOO/HDO*
cruiser	crui-ser	*HOO/HDO*
crumb	cru-mb	**GAR**/*HDO*
crumble	cru-m-ble	**GAR**/*HDO/HOO*
crummy	cru-mmy	**GAR/GAR**
crunch	cru-n-ch	**GAR/GDR**/*HDO*
crunchy	cru-n-chy	**GAR/GDR/GAR**
crush	cru-sh	**GAR**/*HDO*
crust	cru-st	**GAR**/*HDO*
crutch	cru-tch	**GAR**/*HDO*
crux	cru-x	**GAR/GDR**
cry	cry	**GRR**
crystal	cry-stal	**GAR/GDR**
cub	cu-b	**GAR**/*HDO*
cube	cu-be	*HOO/HDO*
cuckoo	cuc-koo	*HOO/HOO*

Word	Mouthables	Mouth Movements Notations
cucumber	cu-cu-m-ber	*HOO*/**GAR**/*HDO*/*HDO*
cuddle	cu-ddle	**GAR**/*HDO*
cudgel	cud-gel	**GAR**/*HOO*
cue	cue	*HOO*
cuff	cu-ff	**GAR**/*HDO*
cullender	cul-len-der	**GAR/GAR**/*HDO*
culminate	cu-l-mi-na-te	**GAR/GDR/GAR**/*HAO*/*HDO*
culottes	cu-lot-tes	*HOO*/*HAO*/*HDO*
culprit	cul-pri-t	**GAR/GAR**/*HOO*
cult	cu-lt	**GAR**/*HDO*
cultivate	cu-l-ti-va-te	**GAR/GDR/GAR**/*HAO*/*HDO*
cultivated	cu-l-ti-va-ted	**GAR/GDR/GAR**/*HAO*/**GRR**
culture	cu-l-tu-re	**GAR/GDR**/*HOO*/*HDO*
cultured	cu-l-ture-d	**GAR/GDR**/*HOO*/*HOO*
cumbersome	cum-ber-so-me	**GAR**/*HDO*/*HAO*/*HDO*
cunning	cu-nni-ng	**GAR/GAR/GDR**
cup	cu-p	**GAR**/*HDO*
curb	cur-b	*HAO*/*HDO*
curdle	cur-dle	**GAR**/*HOO*
cure	cu-re	*HOO*/*HDO*
curfew	cur-few	**GAR**/*HOO*
curious	cu-ri-ous	*HOO*/**GAR**/*HAO*
curl	cur-l	**GAR/GDR**
curler	cur-ler	*HAO*/*HDO*
curly	cur-ly	**GAR/GAR**
currant	cu-rra-nt	**GAR/GAR/GDR**
currency	cur-re-ncy	**GAR/GAR/GDR**
current	cur-ren-t	**GAR/GAR**/*HOO*
curriculum	cur-ri-cu-lu-m	**GAR/GAR**/*HOO*/**GAR**/*HDO*
curse	cur-se	**GAR**/*HDO*
cursory	cur-so-ry	**GAR**/*HAO*/*HDO*

Word	Mouthables	Mouth Movements Notations
curt	cur-t	GAR/*HOO*
curtail	cur-tai-l	GAR/*HAO*/GDR
curtain	cur-tain	GAR/*HDO*
curve	cur-ve	GAR/*HDO*
cushion	cu-shio-n	*HOO*/*HAO*/*HDO*
cushy	cu-shy	*HOO*/GAR
custard	cu-star-d	GAR/*HAO*/*HDO*
custodian	cu-sto-di-an	GAR/*HOO*/GAR/GDR
custody	cu-sto-dy	GAR/*HOO*/GAR
custom	cu-sto-m	GAR/*HAO*/*HDO*
customary	cu-sto-ma-ry	GAR/*HAO*/GAR/*HDO*
customer	cu-sto-mer	GAR/GAR/*HDO*
cut	cu-t	GAR/*HOO*
cute	cu-te	*HOO*/*HDO*
cutlery	cu-t-le-ry	GAR/*HOO*/GAR/GDR
cutlet	cu-t-le-t	GAR/GDR/GAR/*HDO*
cutting	cu-tting	GAR/GDR
cyclamen	cy-c-la-me-n	GAR/GDR/GAR/GAR/GDR
cycle	cy-cle	GRR/*HOO*
cyclist	cy-cli-st	GRR/GAR/GDR
cyclone	cy-clo-ne	GRR/*HOO*/GDR
cylinder	cy-li-n-der	GAR/GAR/GDR/*HDO*
cynic	cy-ni-c	GAR/GAR/GDR
cynical	cy-ni-cal	GAR/GAR/*HDO*
cypress	cy-pre-ss	GRR/GAR/*HDO*
Czech	Cze-ch	GAR/*HDO*

Word	Mouthables	Mouth Movements Notations
D		
D	D	**GRR**
dab	da-b	**GAR**/*HDO*
dabble	da-bble	**GAR**/*HOO*
dachshund	da-ch-shun-d	**GAR/GDR**/*HAO*/*HOO*
dad	da-d	**GAR**/*HDO*
daddy	dad-dy	**GAR/GAR**
daffodil	da-ffo-di-l	**GAR**/*HOO*/**GAR/GDR**
dagger	da-gger	**GAR**/*HDO*
daily	dai-ly	*HAO*/**GDR**
dainty	dai-n-ty	*HAO*/**GDR/GAR**
dairy	dair-y	*HAO*/**GDR**
dais	da-i-s	*HAO*/**GAR/GDR**
daisy	dai-sy	*HAO*/**GAR**
dam	da-m	**GAR**/*HDO*
damage	da-ma-ge	**GAR**/*HAO*/*HDO*
Damascus	Da-mas-cu-s	**GAR**/*HAO*/**GAR**/*HDO*
damask	da-ma-sk	*HAO*/**GAR**/*HDO*
damn	da-mn	**GAR**/*HDO*
damnation	da-m-na-tion	**GAR**/*HDO*/*HAO*/*HOO*
damned	da-m-ne-d	**GAR**/*HDO*/**GRR/GRR**
damp	dam-p	**GAR**/*HDO*
dampness	dam-p-ne-ss	**GAR**/*HDO*/**GAR**/*HDO*
dance	dan-ce	*HAO*/*HDO*
dandelion	da-n-de-li-on	**GAR/GDR/GAR/GRR/GDR**
dandruff	da-n-dru-ff	**GAR/GDR/GAR**/*HDO*
dandy	da-n-dy	**GAR/GDR/GAR**
danger	da-n-ger	*HAO*/**GDR/GAR**
dangerous	dan-ger-ous	*HAO*/**GAR/GAR**
dangle	dan-gle	**GAR**/*HOO*
Danish	Da-ni-sh	*HAO*/**GAR**/*HDO*

Word	Mouthables	Mouth Movements Notations
dank	dan-k	**GAR**/*HDO*
dare	dare	*HAO*
dark	dar-k	**GAR**/*HDO*
darken	dar-ke-n	**GAR/GAR/GDR**
darkness	dar-k-ne-ss	**GAR**/*HDO*/**GAR/GDR**
darling	dar-ling	*HAO*/**GDR**
darn	dar-n	*HAO*/**GRR**
darned	dar-ne-d	*HAO*/**GRR**/*HOO*
darn	dar-n	**GAR/GDR**
dart	dar-t	*HAO*/*HOO*
dash	da-sh	**GAR**/*HDO*
dashing	da-shing	**GAR/GDR**
data	da-ta	*HAO*/**GAR**
date	da-te	*HAO*/*HDO*
dated	da-ted	*HAO*/**GRR**
daub	dau-b	*HOO*/*HDO*
daughter	daugh-ter	*HOO*/*HDO*
daunt	dau-nt	*HOO*/**GDR**
dauntless	dau-nt-le-ss	*HAO*/**GDR/GAR/GDR**
dawdler	daw-d-ler	*HOO*/*HOO*/*HDO*
dawn	daw-n	*HOO*/**GDR**
day	day	*HAO*
dazzle	daz-zle	**GAR**/*HOO*
deacon	dea-co-n	**GRR**/*HAO*/*HDO*
deaconess	dea-co-ne-ss	**GRR**/*HAO*/**GAR/GDR**
dead	dea-d	**GAR**/*HOO*
deaf	dea-f	**GAR**/*HDO*
deafen	dea-fen	**GAR/GDR**
deal	dea-l	**GRR/GDR**
dealer	dea-ler	**GRR**/*HDO*
dear	de-ar	**GRR**/*HAO*

Word	Mouthables	Mouth Movements Notations
dearth	dear-th	*HOO*/*HTO*
death	dea-th	**GAR/GTR**
debar	de-bar	**GRR**/*HAO*
debase	de-ba-se	**GRR**/*HAO*/*HDO*
debate	de-ba-te	**GRR**/*HAO*/*HDO*
debauched	de-bau-che	**GRR**/*HOO*/*HDO*
debauchery	de-bau-che-ry	**GRR**/*HOO*/**GAR/GDR**
debenture	de-be-n-tu-re	**GRR/GAR/GDR**/*HOO*/*HDO*
debit	de-bi-t	**GAR/GAR**/*HDO*
debonair	de-bo-n-air	**GAR**/*HAO*/*HDO*/*HAO*
debris	de-bris	**GAR/GAR**
debtor	deb-tor	**GAR**/*HOO*
decade	de-ca-de	**GAR**/*HAO*/*HDO*
decant	de-can-t	**GRR/GAR**/*HDO*
decanter	de-ca-n-ter	**GRR/GAR/GDR**/*HDO*
decay	de-cay	**GRR**/*HAO*
deceased	de-cea-sed	**GRR/GRR**/*HOO*
deceit	de-cei-t	**GRR/GRR**/*HOO*
deceitful	de-cei-t-ful	**GRR/GRR**/*HOO*/*HDO*
deceive	de-cei-ve	**GRR/GRR**/*HDO*
deceive	de-cei-ves	**GRR/GRR**/*HDO*
December	De-cem-ber	**GAR/GAR**/*HDO*
decency	de-ce-n-cy	**GRR/GAR/GDR/GAR**
decent	de-cen-t	**GRR/GAR**/*HOO*
decentralization	de-ce-n-tra-li-za-tion	**GRR/GAR/GDR/GAR/GRR/** *HAOHOO*
deception	de-ce-p-tion	**GAR/GAR/GDR**/*HOO*
deceptive	de-ce-p-ti-ve	**GRR/GAR/GDR/GAR/GDR**
decide	de-ci-de	**GRR/GRR**/*HDO*
decided	de-ci-ded	**GRR/GRR/GRR**
decimal	de-ci-mal	**GAR/GAR**/*HDO*

Word	Mouthables	Mouth Movements Notations
decimation	de-ci-ma-tion	**GAR/GAR/**_HAO_/_HOO_
decision	de-ci-sion	**GRR/GAR/**_HOO_
deck	dec-k	**GAR/**_HDO_
declaim	de-clai-m	**GRR/**_HAO_/_HDO_
declamatory	de-cla-ma-tory	**GRR/GAR/GAR/**_HDO_
declaration	de-clar-a-tion	**GAR/**_HAO_/_HAO_/_HOO_
declare	de-cla-re	**GRR/**_HAO_/_HDO_
decline	de-cli-ne	**GRR/GRR/GDR**
delinquent	de-li-n-que-nt	**GRR/GAR/GDR/GAR/GDR**
decompose	de-co-m-po-se	**GRR/**_HAO_/_HDO_/_HOO_/_HDO_
decomposition	de-co-m-po-si-tion	**GRR/**_HAO_/_HDO_/_HOO_/**GAR/**_HOO_
décor	de-cor	_HAO_/_HOO_
decorate	de-cor-a-te	**GAR/**_HOO_/_HAO_/_HDO_
decoration	de-co-ra-tion	**GAR/**_HAO_/_HAO_/_HOO_
decorator	de-co-ra-tor	**GAR/**_HAO_/_HAO_/_HOO_
decorum	de-co-ru-m	**GAR/**_HOO_/**GAR/**_HDO_
decoy	de-coy	**GRR/GAR**
decrease	de-crea-se	**GRR/GRR/**_HDO_
decree	de-cree	**GRR/GRR**
dedicated	de-di-ca-ted	**GAR/GAR/**_HAO_/**GRR**
dedication	de-di-ca-tion	**GAR/GAR/**_HAO_/_HOO_
deduct	de-du-c-t	**GRR/GAR/GDR/**_HOO_
deduction	de-du-c-tion	**GRR/GAR/GDR/**_HOO_
deed	dee-d	**GRR/**_HDO_
deep	dee-p	**GRR/GDR**
deepen	dee-pe-n	**GRR/GAR/GDR**
deer	de-er	**GAR/**_HDO_
deface	de-fa-ce	**GRR/**_HAO_/**GDR**
default	de-faul-t	**GRR/**_HOO_/_HDO_
defeat	de-fea-t	**GRR/GRR/**_HOO_
defect	de-fe-c-t	**GRR/GAR/GDR/**_HOO_

Word	Mouthables	Mouth Movements Notations
defection	de-fe-c-tion	**GRR/GAR/GDR**/*HOO*
defection	de-fec-ti-ve	**GRR/GAR/GDR/GAR**/*HDO*
defence	de-fe-nce	**GRR/GAR/GDR**
defendant	de-fe-n-da-nt	**GAR/GAR/GDR/GAR/GDR**
defer	de-fer	**GRR**/*HDO*
deference	de-fer-e-nce	**GAR**/*HAO*/**GAR/GDR**
defiance	de-fi-a-nce	**GRR/GRR/GAR/GDR**
defiant	de-fi-a-nt	**GRR/GRR/GAR/GRR**
deficiency	de-fi-ci-e-ncy	**GAR/GAR/GAR/GAR/GDR**
deficit	de-fi-ci-t	**GAR/GAR/GAR**/*HDO*
definite	de-fi-ni-te	**GAR/GAR/GRR**/*HDO*
definitely	de-fi-ni-te-ly	**GAR/GAR/GRR**/*HDO*/**GDR**
definition	de-fi-ni-tion	**GAR/GAR/GAR**/*HOO*
deflate	de-fla-te	**GRR**/*HAO*/*HDO*
deflation	de-fla-tion	**GRR**/*HAO*/*HOO*
deflection	de-fle-c-tion	**GRR/GAR/GDR**/*HOO*
deforest	de- fo-re-st	**GRR**/*HAO*/**GAR**/*HOO*
deformation	de-for-ma-tion	**GAR/GAR**/*HAO*/*HOO*
deformity	de-for-mi-ty	**GRR**/*HAO*/**GAR/GAR**
defrost	de-fro-st	**GRR**/*HAO*/*HDO*
deft	de-ft	**GAR**/*HDO*
defuse	de-fu-se	**GRR**/*HOO*/*HOO*
defused	de-fu-se-d	**GAR**/*HOO*/*HOO*/*HOO*
defy	de-fy	**GRR/GRR**
degenerate	de-ge-ne-ra-te	**GRR/GAR/GAR**/*HAO*/*HDO*
degrade	de-gra-de	**GRR**/*HAO*/*HDO*
degree	de-gree	**GRR/GRR**
dehydration	de-hy-dra-tion	**GRR/GRR**/*HAO*/*HOO*
deify	de-i-fy	**GRR/GAR/GRR**
deity	de-i-ty	**GRR/GAR/GAR**
dejection	de-jec-tion	**GRR/GAR**/*HOO*

Word	Mouthables	Mouth Movements Notations
delay	de-lay	**GRR**/*HAO*
delegation	de-le-ga-tion	**GAR/GAR**/*HAO*/*HOO*
delete	de-le-te	**GRR/GRR**/*HOO*
deliberate	de-li-be-ra-te	**GRR/GAR/GAR**/*HAO*/*HDO*
deliberation	de-li-be-ra-tion	**GRR/GAR/GAR***HAO*/*HOO*
delicacy	de-li-ca-cy	**GAR/GAR/GAR/GAR**
delicatessen	de-li-ca-te-ssen	**GAR/GAR/GAR**/*HDO*
delicious	de-li-ci-ous	**GRR/GAR/GDR**/*HAO*
delight	de-ligh-t	**GRR/GRR**/*HDO*
delighted	de-ligh-ted	**GRR/GRR/GRR**
delirious	de-li-ri-ous	**GRR/GAR/GAR**/*HAO*
delirium	de-li-ri-u-m	**GRR/GAR/GAR**/*HDO*
deliver	de-li-ver	**GRR/GAR**/*HDO*
delivery	de-li-ver-y	**GRR/GAR**/*HAO*/**GAR**
delude	de-lu-de	**GRR**/*HOO*/*HDO*
deluge	de-lu-ge	**GAR**/*HOO*/*HDO*
delusion	de-lu-sion	**GRR**/*HOO*/*HOO*
delve	de-l-ve	**GAR/GDR**/*HDO*
demagogue	de-ma-go-gue	**GAR/GAR**/*HAO*/*HDO*
demagogy	de-ma-go-gy	**GAR/GAR**/*HAO*/**GAR**
demand	de-ma-n-d	**GRR/GAR/GDR**/*HOO*
demanding	de-ma-n-ding	**GRR/GAR/GDR/GDR**
demean	de-mea-n	**GRR/GRR/GDR**
dementia	de-me-n-ti-a	**GAR/GAR/GDR**/*HDO*/**GAR**
demobilization	de-mo-bi-li-za-tion	**GRR**/*HOO*/**GAR/GRR**/*HAO*/*HOO*
demobilize	de-mo-bi-li-ze	**GRR**/*HOO*/**GAR/GRR/GDR**
democracy	de-mo-cra-cy	**GAR**/*HAO*/**GAR/GAR**
democrat	de-mo-cra-t	**GAR**/*HOO*/**GAR**/*HOO*
democratic	de-mo-cra-ti-c	**GAR**/*HOO*/**GAR/GAR/GDR**
demography	de-mo-gra-phy	**GAR**/*HOO*/**GAR/GAR**
demolish	de-mo-li-sh	**GRR**/*HAO*/**GAR**/*HDO*

Word	Mouthables	Mouth Movements Notations
demolition	de-mo-li-tion	**GAR**/*HOO*/**GAR**/*HOO*
demon	de-mo-n	**GRR**/*HAO*/**GDR**
demonstrate	de-mo-n-stra-te	**GAR**/*HAO*/**GDR**/*HAO*/*HDO*
demonstration	de-mo-n-stra-tion	**GAR**/*HAO*/**GDR**/*HAO*/*HOO*
demoralization	de-mor-a-li-za-tion	**GRR**/*HOO*/**GAR**/**GRR**/*HAO*/*HOO*
demoralize	de-mor-a-li-ze	**GRR**/*HOO*/**GAR**/**GRR**/**GDR**
demote	de-mo-te	**GRR**/*HOO*/*HDO*
den	de-n	**GAR**/**GDR**
denationalize	de-na-tion-a-li-ze	**GRR**/**GAR**/*HOO*/**GAR**/**GRR**/**GDR**
denial	de-ni-a-l	**GRR**/**GRR**/**GAR**/**GDR**
Denmark	Den-mar-k	**GAR**/*HAO*/*HDO*
denominate	de-no-mi-na-te	**GRR**/*HAO*/**GAR**/*HAO*/*HDO*
denomination	de-no-mi-na-tion	**GRR**/*HAO*/**GAR**/*HAO*/*HOO*
denote	de-no-te	**GRR**/*HOO*/*HDO*
denounce	de-nou-nce	**GRR**/**GAR**/**GDR**
dense	de-nse	**GAR**/**GDR**
density	de-n-si-ty	**GAR**/**GDR**/**GAR**/**GAR**
dent	de-nt	**GAR**/**GDR**
dental	de-n-tal	**GAR**/**GDR**/*HDO*
detention	de-te-n-tion	**GRR**/**GAR**/**GDR**/*HOO*
dentist	de-n-ti-st	**GAR**/**GDR**/**GAR**/*HOO*
dentistry	de-n-ti-stry	**GAR**/**GDR**/**GAR**/*HDO*
dentures	de-n-tu-res	**GAR**/**GDR**/*HOO*/*HDO*
denunciation	de-nu-n-ci-a-tion	**GRR**/**GAR**/**GDR**/**GAR**/*HAO*/*HOO*
deny	de-ny	**GRR**/**GRR**
deodorant	de-o-dor-a-nt	**GRR**/*HOO*/*HOO*/**GAR**/**GDR**
depraved	de-pra-ve-d	**GRR**/*HAO*/*HDO*/*HOO*
depravity	de-pra-vi-ty	**GRR**/**GAR**/**GAR**/**GAR**
depreciation	de-pre-ci-a-tion	**GRR**/**GRR**/**GDR**/*HAO*/*HOO*
depress	de-pre-ss	**GRR**/**GAR**/*HDO*
deprive	de-pri-ve	**GRR**/**GRR**/*HDO*

Word	Mouthables	Mouth Movements Notations
deprived	de-pri-ve-d	**GRR/GRR/***HDO***/***HOO*
depth	de-pth	**GAR/GTR**
deputy	de-pu-ty	**GAR/***HOO***/GAR**
derail	de-rai-l	**GRR/***HAO***/GDR**
deranged	de-ra-n-ge-d	**GRR/***HAO***/GDR/***HOO***/***HOO*
deregulation	de-re-gu-la-tion	**GRR/GAR/***HOO***/***HAO***/***HOO*
derision	de-ri-sion	**GRR/GAR/***HOO*
derisory	de-ri-so-ry	**GRR/GRR/***HOO***/***HDO*
derivation	de-ri-va-tion	**GAR/GAR/***HAO***/***HOO*
derive	de-ri-ve	**GRR/GRR/***HDO*
dermatologist	der-ma-to-lo-gi-st	*HAO***/GAR/***HAO***/***HOO***/GAR/GDR**
derogatory	de-ro-ga-tor-y	**GRR/***HAO***/GAR/***HOO***/GAR**
desalinate	de-sa-li-na-te	**GRR/GAR/GAR/***HAO***/***HDO*
descend	de-sce-nd	**GRR/GAR/GDR**
descendant	de-sce-n-da-nt	**GRR/GAR/GDR/GAR/GDR**
descent	de-sce-nt	**GRR/GAR/GDR**
describe	de-scri-be	**GRR/GRR/***HDO*
description	de-scri-p-tion	**GRR/GAR/***HDO***/***HOO*
desert	de-ser-t	**GAR/***HOO***/***HOO*
deserter	de-ser-ter	**GRR/***HOO***/***HDO*
deserts	de-ser-ts	**GRR/GAR/***HDO*
deserve	de-ser-ve	**GRR/***HAO***/***HDO*
desiccate	de-si-cca-te	**GAR/GAR/***HAO***/***HOO*
desiccated	de-si-cca-ted	**GAR/GAR/***HAO***/GRR**
design	de-si-gn	**GRR/GRR/GDR**
designer	de-si-gn-er	**GRR/GRR/GDR/***HDO*
desire	de-si-re	**GRR/GRR/***HDO*
desk	de-sk	**GAR/***HDO*
desolate	de-so-la-te	**GAR/***HOO***/***HAO***/***HDO*
despair	de-spair	**GRR/GAR**
desperate	de-spe-ra-te	**GAR/GDR/***HAO***/***HDO*

Word	Mouthables	Mouth Movements Notations
desperation	de-spe-ra-tion	**GAR/GDR**/*HAO*/*HOO*
despise	de-spi-se	**GRR/GRR**/*HDO*
despite	de-spi-te	**GRR/GRR**/*HDO*
despondent	de-spo-n-de-nt	**GRR**/*HAO*/**GDR/GAR/GDR**
despot	de-spo-t	**GAR**/*HAO*/*HOO*
despotism	de-spo-ti-sm	**GAR**/*HAO*/**GAR/GDR**
destabilize	de-sta-bi-li-ze	**GRR**/*HAO*/**GAR/GRR/GDR**
destination	de-sti-na-tion	**GAR/GAR**/*HAO*/*HOO*
destined	de-sti-ne-d	**GAR/GAR/GRR**/*HOO*
destiny	de-sti-ny	**GAR/GAR/GAR**
destroy	de-stroy	**GRR**/*HAO*
destroyer	de-stroy-er	**GRR**/*HAO*/*HDO*
destruction	de-struc-tion	**GRR/GAR**/*HOO*
desultory	de-su-l-tor-y	**GAR/GAR/GDR**/*HOO*/**GAR**
detached	de-ta-che-d	**GRR/GAR**/*HOO*/*HOO*
detachment	de-ta-ch-me-nt	**GRR/GAR**/*HDO*/**GAR/GDR**
detail	de-tai-l	**GRR**/*HAO*/**GDR**
detain	de-tai-n	**GRR**/*HAO*/**GDR**
detainee	de-tai-nee	**GRR**/*HAO*/**GRR**
detect	de-tec-t	**GRR/GAR**/*HOO*
detection	de-tec-tion	**GRR/GAR**/*HOO*
detector	de-tec-tor	**GRR/GAR**/*HDO*
detergent	de-ter-ge-nt	**GRR**/*HAO*/**GAR/GDR**
deteriorate	de-te-ri-o-ra-te	**GRR/GRR/GAR**/*HOO*/*HAO*/*HDO*
determine	de-ter-mi-ne	**GRR**/*HAO*/**GAR/GDR**
determined	de-ter-mi-ne-d	**GRR**/*HAO*/**GAR/GRR**/*HOO*
deterrent	de-te-rre-nt	**GRR/GAR/GAR/GDR**
detest	de-te-st	**GRR/GAR**/*HOO*
detonate	de-to-na-te	**GAR**/*HOO*/*HAO*/*HDO*
detonator	de-to-na-tor	**GAR**/*HOO*/*HAO*/*HOO*
detour	de-tour	**GRR**/*HOO*

Word	Mouthables	Mouth Movements Notations
devaluation	de-va-lu-a-tion	**GRR/GAR**/*HOO/HAO/HOO*
devalue	de-va-lue	**GRR/GAR**/*HOO*
devastate	de-va-sta-te	**GAR/GAR**/*HAO/HDO*
develop	de-ve-lo-p	**GRR/GAR**/*HAO/HDO*
developer	de-ve-lo-per	**GRR/GAR**/*HAO/HDO*
development	de-ve-lo-p-me-nt	**GRR/GAR**/*HAO/HDO*/**GAR/GDR**
deviate	de-vi-a-te	**GRR/GAR**/*HAO/HOO*
deviation	de-vi-a-tion	**GRR/GAR**/*HAO/HOO*
device	de-vi-ce	**GRR/GRR/GDR**
devil	de-vi-l	**GAR/GAR/GDR**
devilish	de-vi-li-sh	**GAR/GAR/GAR**/*HDO*
devious	de-vi-ous	**GRR/GAR/GAR**
devoid	de-voi-d	**GRR/GAR**/*HOO*
devolution	de-vo-lu-tion	**GRR**/*HOO/HOO/HOO*
devote	de-vo-te	**GRR**/*HOO/HDO*
devoted	de-vo-ted	**GRR**/*HOO*/**GRR**
devotee	de-vo-tee	**GRR**/*HOO*/**GRR**
devour	de-vo-ur	**GRR/GAR**/*HAO*
devout	de-vou-t	**GRR/GAR**/*HOO*
dew	dew	*HDO*
dexterity	de-x-te-ri-ty	**GAR/GDR/GAR/GAR/GAR**
diabetes	di-a-be-te-s	**GRR/GAR/GRR/GRR/GDR**
diagnose	di-a-g-no-se	**GRR/GAR/GDR**/*HOO/HDO*
diagnosis	di-a-g-no-si-s	**GRR/GAR/GDR**/*HOO*/**GAR/GDR**
diagonal	di-a-go-nal	**GRR/GAR/GAR**/*HDO*
dial	di-a-l	**GRR/GAR/GDR**
dialect	di-a-le-c-t	**GRR/GAR/GAR/GDR**/*HOO*
dialogue	di-a-lo-gue	**GRR/GAR**/*HAO/HDO*
dialysis	di-a-ly-si-s	**GRR/GAR/GAR/GAR/GDR**
diameter	di-a-me-ter	**GRR/GAR/GAR**/*HDO*
diamond	di-a-mo-nd	**GRR/GAR**/*HAO*/**GDR**

Word	Mouthables	Mouth Movements Notations
diaper	dia-per	**GRR**/*HDO*
diaphragm	di-a-phrag-m	**GRR/GAR/GAR**/*HDO*
diarrhea	di-a-rrhe-a	**GRR/GAR/GRR/GAR**
diary	di-a-ry	**GRR/GAR**/*HDO*
dice	di-ce	**GRR/GDR**
dicey	di-cey	**GRR/GAR**
dick	di-ck	**GAR**/*HDO*
dicky	di-cky	**GAR/GAR**
dictate	di-c-ta-te	**GAR/GDR**/*HAO*/*HOO*
dictation	di-c-ta-tion	**GAR/GDR**/*HAO*/*HOO*
dictator	di-c-ta-tor	**GAR/GDR**/*HAO*/*HOO*
dictatorship	di-c-ta-tor-shi-p	**GAR/GDR**/*HAO*/*HOO***/GAR/GDR**
diction	di-c-tion	**GAR/GDR**/*HOO*
dictionary	di-c-tion-ary	**GAR/GDR**/*HOO*/*HDO*
did	di-d	**GAR/GRR**
didactic	di-da-c-ti-c	**GRR/GAR/GDR/GAR/GDR**
diddle	di-ddle	**GAR**/*HOO*
die	die	**GRR**
diesel	die-sel	**GAR**/*HDO*
diet	di-e-t	**GRR/GAR/GDR**
dietetics	di-e-te-ti-cs	**GRR/GAR**/*HDO***/GAR/GDR**
dietician	di-e-ti-ci-a-n	**GRR/GAR/GAR/GDR/GAR/GDR**
differ	di-ffer	**GAR**/*HDO*
difference	di-ffer-e-nce	**GAR**/*HAO***/GAR/GDR**
different	di-ffer-e-nt	**GAR/GAR/GAR/GDR**
differential	di-ffe-ren-tial	**GAR/GAR/GAR**/*HDO*
differentiate	di-ffe-ren-ti-a-te	**GAR/GAR/GAR**/*HDO*/*HAO*/*HDO*
difficulty	di-ffi-cu-l-ty	**GAR/GAR**/*HOO***/GDR/GAR**
diffident	di-ffi-de-nt	**GAR/GAR/GAR/GDR**
diffusion	di-ffu-sion	**GAR**/*HOO*/*HOO*
difficult	di-ffi-cu-lt	**GAR/GAR/GAR**/*HDO*

Word	Mouthables	Mouth Movements Notations
diffuse	di-ffu-se	GAR/*HOO*/*HDO*
dig	di-g	GAR/GDR
digest	di-ge-st	GRR/GAR/*HOO*
digestion	di-ge-stion	GRR/GAR/*HOO*
digestive	di-ge-sti-ve	GRR/GAR/GAR/*HDO*
digger	di-gger	GAR/*HDO*
digit	di-gi-t	GAR/GAR/*HOO*
digital	di-gi-tal	GAR/GAR/*HDO*
dignified	di-g-ni-fie-d	GAR/GDR/GAR/GRR/*HOO*
dignity	di-g-ni-ty	GAR/GDR/GAR/GAR
digression	di-gres-sion	GRR/GAR/*HOO*
dike	di-ke	GRR/*HDO*
dilate	di-la-te	GRR/*HAO*/*HDO*
dilemma	di-le-mma	GRR/GAR/GAR
diligence	di-li-ge-nce	GAR/GAR/GAR/GDR
diligent	di-li-ge-nt	GAR/GAR/GAR/GDR
dilute	di-lu-te	GRR/*HOO*/*HDO*
dim	di-m	GAR/*HDO*
dimension	di-men-sion	GRR/GAR/*HOO*
diminish	di-mi-ni-sh	GAR/GAR/GAR/*HDO*
dimple	di-m-ple	GAR/*HDO*/*HOO*
dine	di-ne	GRR/GDR
diner	di-ner	GRR/*HDO*
dinghy	di-n-ghy	GAR/GDR/GAR
dingy	di-n-gy	GAR/GDR/*HDO*
dinner	di-nner	GAR/*HDO*
dinosaur	di-no-saur	GRR/GAR/*HOO*
dint	di-nt	GAR/GDR
diocese	di-o-ce-se	GRR/*HOO*/GRR/GDR
dip	di-p	GAR/*HDO*
diphtheria	di-ph-the-ri-a	GAR/GDR/GTR/GAR/GAR

Word	Mouthables	Mouth Movements Notations
diploma	di-plo-ma	GAR/*HOO*/GAR
diplomacy	di-plo-ma-cy	GAR/*HOO*/GAR/GAR
diplomat	di-plo-ma-t	GAR/*HOO*/GAR/*HDO*
diplomatic	di-plo-ma-ti-c	GAR/*HOO*/GAR/GAR/GDR
dire	di-re	GRR/*HDO*
direct	di-re-c-t	GRR/GAR/GDR/*HOO*
direction	di-re-c-tion	GRR/GAR/GDR/*HOO*
directness	di-rec-t-ne-ss	GRR/GAR/*HDO*/GAR/GDR
director	di-re-c-tor	GRR/GAR/GDR/*HDO*
directory	di-rec-to-ry	GRR/GAR/*HOO*/*HDO*
dirge	dir-ge	*HAO*/*HDO*
dirt	dir-t	*HOO*/*HDO*
dirty	dir-ty	*HOO*/GAR
disability	di-sa-bi-li-ty	GAR/GAR/GAR/GAR/GAR
disabled	di-sa-ble-d	GRR/*HAO*/*HOO*/*HOO*
disadvantage	di-sa-d-van-ta-ge	GAR/GAR/GDR/GAR/*HAO*/*HDO*
disaffected	di-sa-ffe-c-ted	GAR/GAR/GAR/GDR/GRR
disagree	di-sa-gree	GAR/GAR/GRR
disagreeable	di-sa-gree-a-ble	GAR/GAR/GRR/GAR/*HDO*
disagreement	di-sa-gree-me-nt	GAR/GAR/GRR/GAR/GDR
disappointed	di-sa-ppoi-n-ted	GAR/GAR/GAR/GDR/GRR
disappointment	di-sa-poi-nt-me-nt	GAR/GAR/GAR/GDR/GAR/GDR
disarmament	di-sar-ma-men-t	GAR/*HAO*/GAR/GAR/*HOO*
disarming	di-sar-ming	*HAO*/*HAO*/GDR
disarray	di-sa-rray	GAR/GAR/*HAO*
disaster	di-sas-ter	GAR/*HAO*/*HDO*
disband	dis-ba-nd	GAR/GAR/GDR
disc	di-sc	GAR/*HDO*
discard	di-scar-d	GAR/*HAO*/*HOO*
discern	dis-cer-n	GAR/*HAO*/GDR
discernment	dis-cer-n-me-nt	GAR/*HAO*/GDR/GAR/GDR

Word	Mouthables	Mouth Movements Notations
discharge	dis-char-ge	**GAR**/*HAO*/*HDO*
disciple	dis-ci-ple	**GAR/GRR**/*HOO*
discipline	dis-ci-pli-ne	**GAR/GAR/GAR/GDR**
disclaim	dis-clai-m	**GAR**/*HAO*/*HDO*
disclose	dis-clo-se	**GAR**/*HOO*/*HDO*
disco	dis-co	**GAR**/*HOO*
discolour	dis-co-lour	**GAR**/*HAO*/*HAO*
discomfort	dis-co-m-for-t	**GAR**/*HAO*/*HDO*/*HOO*/*HOO*
disconcert	dis-co-n-cer-t	**GAR**/*HAO*/**GDR**/*HAO*/*HOO*
disconnect	dis-co-n-ne-c-t	**GAR**/*HAO*/**GDR/GAR/GDR**/*HOO*
disconnected	dis-co-n-ne-c-ted	**GAR**/*HAO*/**GDR/GAR/GDR/GRR**
discontent	dis-co-n-ten-t	**GAR**/*HAO*/**GDR/GAR**/*HOO*
discontinue	dis-co-n-ti-n-ue	**GAR**/*HAO*/**GDR/GAR/GDR**/*HOO*
discord	dis-cor-d	**GAR**/*HOO*/*HOO*
discordant	dis-cor-da-nt	**GAR**/*HOO*/**GAR/GDR**
discotheque	di-sco-the-que	**GAR**/*HOO*/**GAR/GDR**
discount	dis-cou-nt	**GAR/GAR/GDR**
discourage	dis-cou-ra-ge	**GAR/GAR**/*HAO*/*HDO*
discourtesy	dis-cour-te-sy	**GAR/GAR/GAR/GAR**
discover	dis-co-ver	**GAR**/*HAO*/*HDO*
discoverer	dis-co-ve-rer	**GAR**/*HAO*/*HDO*/*HDO*
discovery	dis-co-ve-ry	**GAR**/*HAO*/*HDO*/**GDR**
discredit	dis-cre-di-t	**GAR/GAR/GAR/GDR**
discreet	dis-cree-t	**GAR/GRR**/*HDO*
discretion	dis-cre-tion	**GAR/GAR**/*HOO*
discriminate	dis-cri-mi-na-te	**GAR/GAR/GAR**/*HAO*/*HDO*
discrimination	dis-cri-mi-na-tion	**GAR/GAR/GAR**/*HAO*/*HOO*
discus	dis-cu-s	**GAR/GAR/GDR**
discuss	dis-cu-ss	**GAR/GAR**/*HDO*
discussion	dis-cus-sion	**GAR/GAR**/*HOO*
disdain	dis-dai-n	**GAR**/*HAO*/**GDR**

Word	Mouthables	Mouth Movements Notations
disease	di-sea-se	**GAR/GRR/GDR**
disembark	dis-e-m-bar-k	**GAR/GAR/GDR**/*HAO*/*HDO*
disenchanted	dis-e-n-chan-ted	**GAR/GAR/GDR**/*HAO*/**GRR**
disengage	dis-e-n-ga-ge	**GAR/GAR/GDR**/*HAO*/*HDO*
disfigure	dis-fi-gu-re	**GAR/GAR**/*HOO*/*HDO*
disgorge	dis-gor-ge	**GAR**/*HOO*/*HDO*
disgrace	dis-gra-ce	**GAR**/*HAO*/**GDR**
disguise	dis-gui-se	**GAR/GRR**/*HDO*
disgust	dis-gu-st	**GAR/GAR**/*HOO*
dish	di-sh	**GAR**/*HDO*
dishearten	dis-hear-t-e-n	**GAR/GAR/GDR/GAR/GDR**
disheveled	di-she-vele-d	**GAR/GAR**/*HDO*/*HOO*
dishonest	dis-ho-ne-st	**GAR**/*HAO*/**GAR**/*HOO*
dishonour	dis-ho-no-ur	**GAR**/*HAO*/*HOO*/*HDO*
dishwater	di-sh-wa-sher	**GAR**/*HDO*/*HAO*/*HDO*
disillusion	di-si-llu-sion	**GAR/GAR**/*HOO*/*HOO*
disinfect	di-si-n-fe-c-t	**GAR/GAR/GDR/GAR/GDR**/*HOO*
disinfectant	di-si-n-fe-c-ta-nt	**GAR/GAR/GDR/GAR/GDR/GAR/ GDR**
disinherit	di-si-n-he-ri-t	**GAR/GAR/GDR/GAR/GAR/GDR**
disintegrate	di-si-n-te-gra-te	**GAR/GAR/GDR/GAR**/*HAO*/*HDO*
disinterestedness	di-si-n-te-re-sted-ness	**GAR/GAR/GDR/GAR/GAR/GRR/ GDR**
disk	di-sk	**GAR**/*HDO*
diskette	di-ske-tte	**GAR/GAR**/*HDO*
dislike	dis-li-ke	**GAR/GRR**/*HDO*
dislocation	dis-lo-ca-tion	**GAR**/*HOO*/*HAO*/*HOO*
disloyal	dis-loy-al	**GAR/GAR/GDR**
dismal	di-s-mal	**GAR/GDR**/*HOO*
dismantle	dis-ma-n-tle	**GAR/GAR/GDR**/*HOO*
dismay	di-s-may	**GAR/GDR**/*HAO*
dismiss	di-s-mi-ss	**GAR/GDR/GAR**/*HDO*

Word	Mouthables	Mouth Movements Notations
dismissal	di-s-mi-ssal	**GAR/GDR/GAR/**_HDO_
dismount	di-s-mou-nt	**GAR/GDR/GAR/GDR**
disobedience	di-so-be-di-e-nce	**GAR/**_HOO_**/GRR/GAR/GAR/GDR**
disobey	di-so-bey	**GAR/**_HOO_**/**_HAO_
disorder	di-sor-der	**GAR/**_HOO_**/**_HDO_
disorganized	di-sor-ga-ni-ze-d	**GAR/**_HOO_**/GAR/GRR/GDR/**_HOO_
disorient	di-sor-i-e-nt	**GAR/**_HOO_**/GAR/GAR/GDR**
disorientate	di-sor-i-e-n-ta-te	**GAR/**_HOO_**/GAR/GAR/GDR/**_HAO_**/** _HDO_
disown	di-sow-n	**GAR/**_HOO_**/GDR**
disparity	dis-pa-ri-ty	**GAR/GAR/GAR/GAR**
dispassionate	dis-pas-sion-a-te	**GAR/GAR/**_HOO_**/**_HAO_**/**_HDO_
dispatch	dis-pa-tch	**GAR/GAR/**_HDO_
dispense	dis-pe-nse	**GAR/GAR/GDR**
disperse	dis-per-se	**GAR/**_HAO_**/**_HDO_
dispersion	dis-per-sion	**GAR/**_HAO_**/**_HOO_
displace	dis-pla-ce	**GAR/**_HAO_**/GDR**
displacement	dis-pla-ce-me-nt	**GAR/**_HAO_**/GDR/GAR/GDR**
display	dis-play	**GAR/**_HAO_
disposable	dis-po-sa-ble	**GAR/**_HOO_**/GAR/**_HDO_
dispose	dis-po-se	**GAR/**_HOO_**/**_HDO_
disposess	dis-po-sse-ss	**GAR/**_HOO_**/GAR/**_HDO_
disposition	dis-po-si-tion	**GAR/**_HAO_**/GAR/**_HOO_
dispossesion	dis-po-sse-ssion	**GAR/**_HOO_**/GAR/**_HOO_
disproportion	dis-pro-por-tion	**GAR/**_HOO_**/**_HOO_**/**_HOO_
disqualify	dis-qua-li-fy	**GAR/GAR/GAR/GRR**
disregard	dis-re-gar-d	**GAR/GAR/**_HAO_**/**_HOO_
dissatisfied	dis-sa-ti-s-fie-d	**GAR/GAR/GAR/GDR/GRR/**_HOO_
dissect	dis-sec-t	**GAR/GAR/**_HOO_
disseminate	dis-se-mi-na-te	**GAR/GAR/GAR/**_HAO_**/**_HOO_
dissent	dis-se-nt	**GAR/GAR/GDR**

Word	Mouthables	Mouth Movements Notations
dissident	di-ssi-de-nt	GAR/GAR/GAR/GDR
dissimilar	di-ssi-mi-lar	GAR/GAR/GAR/*HAO*
dissimulate	di-ssi-mu-la-te	GAR/GAR/*HOO*/*HAO*/*HDO*
dissociate	di-sso-ci-a-te	GAR/*HOO*/*HDO*/*HAO*/*HDO*
dissolute	di-sso-lu-te	GAR/*HOO*/*HOO*/*HDO*
dissolve	di-sso-l-ve	GAR/*HAO*/GDR/*HDO*
dissuade	dis-sua-de	GAR/*HAO*/*HOO*
distance	dis-ta-nce	GAR/GAR/GDR
distant	dis-tan-t	GAR/GAR/*HDO*
distasteful	di-s-ta-ste-ful	GAR/GDR/*HAO*/*HOO*/*HDO*
distil	di-sti-l	GAR/GAR/GDR
distillery	di-sti-lle-ry	GAR/GAR/GAR/*HDO*
distinct	di-sti-nct	GAR/GAR/GDR
distinction	dis-ti-nc-tion	GAR/GAR/GDR/*HOO*
distinguish	dis-ti-n-gui-sh	GAR/GAR/GDR/GAR/*HDO*
distract	dis-trac-t	GAR/GAR/*HDO*
distress	di-stre-ss	GAR/GDR/*HDO*
distressed	di-stre-sse-d	GAR/GDR/*HDO*/*HOO*
distribute	di-stri-bu-te	GAR/GAR/*HOO*/*HDO*
distribution	di-stri-bu-tion	GAR/GAR/*HOO*/*HOO*
distributor	di-stri-bu-tor	GAR/GAR/*HOO*/*HDO*
district	di-stri-ct	GAR/GAR/*HDO*
distrust	di-stru-st	GAR/GAR/*HOO*
distrustful	di-stru-st-ful	GAR/GAR/*HOO*/*HDO*
disturb	di-stur-b	GAR/GAR/*HDO*
disturbance	di-stur-ba-nce	GAR/GAR/GAR/GDR
disuse	dis-u-se	GAR/*HOO*/*HDO*
disused	dis-u-se-d	GAR/*HOO*/*HDO*/*HOO*
ditch	di-tch	GAR/*HDO*
diuretic	di-u-re-ti-c	GRR/GAR/GAR/GAR/GDR
dive	di-ve	GRR/GDR

Word	Mouthables	Mouth Movements Notations
diver	di-ver	**GRR**/*HDO*
diverge	di-ver-ge	**GRR**/*HOO*/*HDO*
diversify	di-ver-si-fy	**GRR**/*HAO*/**GAR**/**GRR**
diversion	di-ver-sion	**GRR**/*HOO*/*HOO*
divert	di-ver-t	**GRR**/*HOO*/*HDO*
divide	di-vi-de	**GAR**/**GRR**/*HDO*
dividend	di-vi-de-nd	**GAR**/**GAR**/**GAR**/**GDR**
dividers	di-vi-ders	**GAR**/**GRR**/*HDO*
divine	di-vi-ne	**GAR**/**GRR**/**GDR**
diviner	di-vi-ner	**GAR**/**GRR**/*HDO*
divinity	di-vi-ni-ty	**GAR**/**GAR**/**GAR**/**GAR**
division	di-vi-sion	**GAR**/**GAR**/*HOO*
divorce	di-vor-ce	**GAR**/*HOO*/**GDR**
dizziness	di-zzi-ne-ss	**GAR**/**GAR**/**GAR**/*HDO*
dizzy	di-zzy	**GAR**/**GAR**
do	do	*HOO*
docile	do-ci-le	*HOO*/**GRR**/**GDR**
dock	doc-k	*HAO*/*HDO*
docker	doc-ker	*HAO*/*HDO*
doctor	doc-tor	*HAO*/*HOO*
doctrine	do-c-tri-ne	*HAO*/**GDR**/**GAR**/**GDR**
document	do-c-u-men-t	*HAO*/**GDR**/*HOO*/**GAR**/*HDO*
documentary	do-c-u-men-tar-y	*HAO*/**GDR**/*HOO*/**GAR**/*HAO*/**GDR**
doddering	do-dder-ing	*HAO*/*HAO*/**GDR**
doddle	do-ddle	*HOO*/*HOO*
dodge	dod-ge	*HAO*/*HDO*
dodgems	dod-ge-ms	*HAO*/**GAR**/*HDO*
doe	doe	*HDO*
does	doe-s	**GAR**/*HDO*
dog	do-g	*HAO*/*HDO*
doggedly	do-gged-ly	*HAO*/**GRR**/**GDR**

Word	Mouthables	Mouth Movements Notations
doing	do-ing	*HOO*/**GDR**
dole	do-le	*HOO*/*HDO*
doleful	do-le-ful	*HOO*/**GDR**/*HDO*
doll	do-ll	*HAO*/*HDO*
dollar	dol-lar	*HAO*/*HDO*
dollphin	dol-phi-n	*HAO*/**GAR**/**GDR**
dome	do-me	*HOO*/*HDO*
domed	do-me-d	*HOO*/*HDO*/*HOO*
domestic	do-me-sti-c	*HAO*/**GAR**/**GAR**/**GDR**
domesticate	do-me-sti-ca-te	*HAO*/**GAR**/**GAR**/*HAO*/*HOO*
dominate	do-mi-na-te	*HAO*/**GAR**/*HAO*/*HOO*
domineering	do-mi-nee-ring	*HAO*/**GAR**/**GRR**/**GDR**
dominion	do-mi-ni-on	*HAO*/**GAR**/**GAR**/*HDO*
don	do-n	*HAO*/*HDO*
donate	do-na-te	*HOO*/*HAO*/*HOO*
done	do-ne	**GAR**/**GDR**
donkey	do-n-key	*HAO*/*HDO*/**GDR**
donor	do-nor	*HOO*/*HDO*
doodle	doo-dle	*HOO*/*HOO*
doomed	doo-me-d	*HOO*/*HDO*/*HOO*
door	do-or	*HAO*/*HDO*
dope	do-pe	*HOO*/*HDO*
dopey	do-pey	*HOO*/**GAR**
dormant	dor-ma-nt	*HOO*/**GAR**/**GDR**
dormitory	dor-mi-to-ry	*HOO*/**GAR**/*HOO*/*HDO*
dormouse	dor-mou-se	*HOO*/**GAR**/*HDO*
dorsal	dor-sal	*HOO*/*HDO*
dose	do-se	*HOO*/*HDO*
dosser	dos-ser	*HAO*/**GAR**
dot	do-t	*HAO*/*HDO*
dotage	do-tage	*HOO*/*HDO*

Word	Mouthables	Mouth Movements Notations
dotty	dot-ty	*HAO*/**GAR**
double	dou-ble	**GAR**/*HOO*
doubles	dou-ble-s	**GAR**/*HDO*/*HDO*
doubly	dou-b-ly	**GAR**/*HDO*/**GDR**
doubte	doub-t	*HAO*/*HDO*
doubtful	doub-t-ful	*HAO*/*HDO*/*HOO*
doubtless	doub-t-le-ss	*HAO*/*HDO*/**GAR**/**GDR**
dough	do-ugh	*HOO*/*HDO*
douse	dou-se	**GAR**/*HDO*
doused	dou-se-d	**GAR**/*HDO*/*HOO*
dove	do-ve	*HOO*/*HDO*
dove	do-ve	**GAR**/*HDO*
dowdy	dow-dy	**GAR**/**GAR**
downy	dow-ny	*HAO*/**GDR**
dowry	dow-ry	*HAO*/*HDO*
dowse	dow-se	*HAO*/*HDO*
dowsed	dow-se-d	**GAR**/*HDO*/*HOO*
doze	do-ze	*HOO*/**GDR**
dozen	do-ze-n	**GAR**/**GAR**/**GDR**
drab	dra-b	**GAR**/*HDO*
draft	dra-f-t	*HAO*/*HDO*/*HOO*
drafted	dra-f-ted	*HAO*/*HDO*/**GRR**
draft	draf-t	*HAO*/*HDO*
draft	draf-t	**GAR**/**GDR**
drag	dra-g	**GAR**/*HDO*
dragnet	dra-g-ne-t	**GAR**/**GDR**/**GAR**/*HDO*
dragon	dra-go-n	**GAR**/*HAO*/*HDO*
drain	drai-n	*HAO*/**GDR**
drainage	drai-nage	*HAO*/*HDO*
drake	dra-ke	*HAO*/*HDO*
dram	dra-m	**GAR**/*HDO*

Word	Mouthables	Mouth Movements Notations
drama	dram-a	*HAO*/**GAR**
dramatic	dra-ma-ti-c	**GAR/GAR/GAR/GDR**
dramatist	dra-ma-ti-st	**GAR/GAR/GAR**/*HDO*
drank	dran-k	**GAR/GRR**
drape	dra-pe	*HAO/HDO*
draper	dra-per	*HAO/HDO*
drastic	dras-ti-c	*HAO*/**GAR/GDR**
draught	drau-gh-t	**GAR**/*HDO/HDO*
draughts	drau-gh-ts	**GAR**/*HDO/HDO*
draw	draw	*HOO*
drawer	dra-wer	*HOO/HDO*
drawing	dra-wing	*HOO*/**GDR**
drawl	dra-wl	*HOO/HDO*
drawn	draw-n	*HOO*/**GDR**
dread	drea-d	**GAR/GRR**
dreadful	drea-d-ful	**GAR/GRR**/*HOO*
dream	drea-m	**GRR/GRR**
dreamer	drea-mer	**GRR**/*HDO*
dreamily	drea-mi-ly	**GRR/GAR/GDR**
dreamt	drea-mt	**GAR/GRR**
dreariness	drea-ri-ne-ss	**GRR/GAR/GAR/GDR**
dreary	drea-ry	**GRR/GDR**
dredger	dre-d-ger	**GAR**/*HDO/HDO*
dregs	dre-gs	**GAR**/*HDO*
drench	dre-nch	**GAR/GDR**
dress	dre-ss	**GAR**/*HDO*
dressing	dre-ssing	**GAR/GDR**
drew	dre-w	*HOO/HOO*
dribble	dri-bble	**GAR**/*HOO*
drift	dri-ft	**GAR**/*HOO*
drifted	dri-f-ted	**GAR**/*HDO*/**GRR**

Word	Mouthables	Mouth Movements Notations
drift	dri-ft	**GAR**/*HDO*
drifter	dri-f-ter	**GAR**/*HDO*/*HDO*
drill	dri-ll	**GAR/GRR**
drilled	dri-lle-d	**GAR/GDR**/*HOO*
drill	dri-ll	**GAR/GDR**
drink	drin-k	**GAR/GRR**
drink	drin-k	**GAR/GDR**
drinkable	drin-k-a-ble	**GAR/GDR/GAR**/*HOO*
drip	dri-p	**GAR/GRR**
dripped	dri-ppe-d	**GAR/GDR**/*HOO*
drip	dri-p	**GAR**/*HDO*
drive	dri-ve	**GRR/GRR**
drive	dri-ve	**GRR/GDR**
driven	dri-ve-n	**GAR/GAR/GDR**
driver	dri-ver	**GRR**/*HDO*
driving	dri-ving	**GRR/GDR**
drizzle	dri-zzle	**GAR**/*HOO*
drone	dro-ne	*HOO*/**GDR**
drool	droo-l	*HOO*/**GDR**
droop	droo-p	*HOO*/*HDO*
drop	dro-p	*HAO*/*HDO*
dropper	drop-per	*HAO*/*HDO*
droppings	drop-pings	*HAO*/**GDR**
drought	drou-ght	**GAR**/*HOO*
drove	dro-ve	*HOO*/*HOO*
drown	drow-n	*HAO*/*HDO*
drowse	drow-se	**GAR**/*HDO*
drudge	dru-dge	**GAR**/*HDO*
drug	dru g	**GAR**/*HDO*
druggist	dru-ggi-st	**GAR/GAR**/*HDO*
drum	dru-m	**GAR**/*HDO*

Word	Mouthables	Mouth Movements Notations
drummer	dru-mm-er	**GAR**/*HDO*/*HDO*
drunk	drun-k	**GAR**/*HDO*
drunkard	drun-kar-d	**GAR**/*HAO*/*HDO*
drunken	drun-ke-n	**GAR/GAR/GDR**
dry	dry	**GRR**
dryer	dry-er	**GRR**/*HDO*
dual	du-al	*HOO*/*HDO*
dub	du-b	**GAR**/*HDO*
dubious	du-bi-ous	*HOO*/**GAR**/*HAO*
Dublin	Du-bli-n	**GAR/GAR/GDR**
duck	du-ck	**GAR**/*HDO*
duckling	du-ck-ling	**GAR**/*HDO*/**GDR**
ductile	du-c-ti-le	**GAR/GDR/GRR/GDR**
dud	du-d	**GAR**/*HDO*
due	due	*HOO*
duel	du-e-l	*HOO*/**GAR/GDR**
dug	du-g	**GAR**/*HDO*
duke	du-ke	*HOO*/*HDO*
dull	dul-l	**GAR**/*HDO*
dumb	du-mb	**GAR**/*HDO*
dummy	du-mmy	**GAR/GAR**
dump	du-mp	**GAR**/*HDO*
dumpy	du-mpy	**GAR/GAR**
dunce	du-nce	**GAR/GDR**
dune	du-ne	*HOO*/**GDR**
dung	dun-g	**GAR**/*HDO*
dungeon	du-n-ge-on	**GAR/GAR/GDR**
dunk	du-n-k	**GAR/GDR**/*HDO*
dupe	du-pe	*HOO*/*HDO*
duplicate	du-pli-ca-te	*HOO*/**GAR**/*HAO*/*HDO*
durable	dur-a-ble	*HOO*/**GAR**/*HOO*

Word	Mouthables	Mouth Movements Notations
during	dur-ing	*HOO*/**GDR**
dusk	du-sk	**GAR**/*HDO*
dusky	du-sky	**GAR/GAR**
dust	du-st	**GAR**/*HDO*
Dutch	Du-tch	**GAR**/*HDO*
dutiful	du-ti-ful	*HOO*/**GAR**/*HOO*
duty	du-ty	*HOO*/**GAR**
dwaft	dwa-ft	*HOO*/*HDO*
dwell	dwe-ll	**GAR/GDR**
dweller	dwe-ller	**GAR**/*HDO*
dwelt	dwe-lt	**GAR/GRR**
dye	dye	**GRR**
dyer	dy-er	**GRR**/*HDO*
dynamic	dy-na-mi-c	**GRR/GAR/GAR/GDR**
dynamite	dy-na-mi-te	**GRR/GAR/GRR**/*HDO*
dynasty	dy-na-sty	**GRR/GAR/GDR**

Word	Mouthables	Mouth Movements Notations
E		
E	E	**GRR**
e	e	**GAR**
each	ea-ch	**GRR**/*HDO*
eager	ea-ger	**GRR**/*HDO*
eagle	ea-gle	**GRR**/*HOO*
ear	e-ar	**GRR/GDR**
earl	ear-l	*HOO*/*HDO*
early	ear-ly	*HOO*/**GDR**
earn	ear-n	*HOO*/**GDR**
earnest	ear-ne-st	*HOO*/**GAR**/*HDO*
earning	ear-ning	*HOO*/**GDR**
earth	ear-th	*HOO*/*HTO*
earthen	ear-the-n	*HOO*/**GTR/GDR**
earthy	ear-thy	*HOO*/**GAR**
ease	ea-se	**GRR/GDR**
eased	ea-se-d	**GRR/GRR**/*HOO*
ease	ea-se	**GRR**/*HDO*
easel	ea-sel	**GRR**/*HDO*
east	ea-st	**GRR**/*HOO*
Easter	Ea-ster	**GRR**/*HDO*
eastern	ea-ster-n	**GRR**/*HOO*/**GDR**
eastwards	ea-st-war-ds	**GRR**/*HDO*/*HAO*/*HDO*
easy	ea-sy	**GRR/GAR**
eat	ea-t	**GRR/GRR**
eatable	ea-ta-ble	**GRR/GAR**/*HOO*
eaten	ea-te-n	**GRR/GAR/GDR**
eaves	ea-ves	**GRR**/*HDO*
ebb	e-bb	**GAR**/*HDO*
ebony	e-bo-ny	**GAR**/*HOO*/**GAR**
ebullient	e-bu-lli-e-nt	**GAR**/*HOO*/**GAR/GAR/GDR**

Word	Mouthables	Mouth Movements Notations
eccentric	e-cce-n-tri-c	GAR/GAR/GDR/GAR/GDR
ecclesiastical	e-ccle-si-as-ti-cal	GAR/GRR/GAR/GAR/GAR/*HDO*
echelon	e-che-lo-n	GAR/GAR/*HAO*/*HDO*
echo	e-cho	GAR/*HOO*
eclectic	e-c-le-c-ti-c	GAR/GDR/GAR/GDR/GAR/GDR
eclipse	e-cli-pse	GAR/GAR/*HDO*
ecology	e-co-lo-gy	GRR/*HAO*/*HOO*/GDR
economic	e-co-no-mi-c	GAR/*HOO*/*HAO*/GAR/GDR
economical	e-co-no-mi-cal	GAR/*HOO*/*HAO*/GAR/*HDO*
economics	e-co-no-mi-cs	GAR/*HOO*/*HAO*/GAR/GDR
economist	e-co-no-mi-st	GAR/*HAO*/*HOO*/GAR/*HDO*
economize	e-co-no-mi-ze	GAR/*HAO*/*HOO*/GRR/GDR
economy	e-co-no-my	GAR/*HAO*/*HOO*/GAR
ecstasy	e-c-sta-sy	GAR/GDR/GAR/GAR
ecstatic	e-c-sta-ti-c	GAR/GDR/GAR/GAR/GDR
ecumenical	e-cu-me-ni-cal	GAR/*HOO*/GAR/GAR/*HDO*
eddy	e-ddy	GAR/GAR
edge	e-dge	GAR/*HDO*
edgy	e-d-gy	GAR/*HDO*/GAR
edible	e-di-ble	GAR/GAR/*HOO*
Edinburgh	E-di-n-burgh	GAR/GAR/GDR/GAR
edit	e-di-t	GAR/GAR/GDR
edition	e-di-tion	GAR/GAR/*HOO*
editor	e-di-tor	GAR/GAR/*HDO*
editorial	e-di-to-ri-al	GAR/GAR/*HOO*/GAR/GDR
educate	e-du-ca-te	GAR/*HOO*/*HAO*/*HDO*
educational	e-du-ca-tion-al	GAR/*HOO*/*HAO*/*HOO*/*HDO*
eel	ee-l	GRR/GDR
eerie	ee-rie	GRR/GDR
efface	e-ffa-ce	GAR/*HAO*/GDR
effect	e-ffe-ct	GAR/GAR/*HDO*

Word	Mouthables	Mouth Movements Notations
effective	e-ffec-ti-ve	**GAR/GAR/GAR**/*HDO*
effeminate	e-ffe-mi-na-te	**GAR/GAR/GAR/GAR**/*HDO*
effervescent	e-ffer-ve-sce-nt	**GAR**/*HDO*/**GAR/GAR/GDR**
efficient	e-ffi-ci-e-nt	**GAR/GAR/GDR/GAR/GDR**
effort	e-ffor-t	**GAR**/*HOO*/*HDO*
effortless	e-ffort-le-ss	**GAR**/*HOO*/**GAR/GDR**
effrontery	e-ffro-n-te-ry	**GAR/GAR/GDR**/*HAO*/**GDR**
effusive	e-ffu-si-ve	**GAR**/*HOO*/**GAR**/*HDO*
egg	e-gg	**GAR**/*HDO*
egocentric	e-go-ce-n-tri-c	**GRR**/*HOO*/**GAR/GDR/GAR/GDR**
egoism	e-go-i-sm	**GRR**/*HOO*/**GAR/GDR**
egoist	e-go-i-st	**GRR**/*HOO*/**GAR/GDR**
Egyptian	E-gy-pti-a-n	**GRR/GAR/GDR/GAR/GDR**
eiderdown	ei-der-dow-n	**GRR**/*HDO*/*HAO*/*HDO*
eight	eigh-t	*HAO*/*HDO*
eighteen	eigh-tee-n	*HAO*/**GRR/GDR**
eighth	eigh-th	*HAO*/**GTR**
eighty	eigh-ty	*HAO*/**GAR**
Eire	Ei-re	*HAO*/*HDO*
either	e(i)ther	**GRR**/*HTO*
either	(e)i-ther	**GRR**/*HTO*
ejaculate	e-ja-cu-la-te	**GAR/GAR**/*HOO*/*HAO*/*HDO*
eject	e-jec-t	**GAR/GAR**/*HOO*
elaborate	e-la-bo-ra-te	**GAR/GAR**/*HAO*/*HAO*/*HDO*
elapse	e-la-pse	**GAR/GAR**/*HDO*
elastic	e-la-sti-c	**GAR/GAR/GAR/GDR**
elated	e-la-ted	**GAR**/*HAO*/**GRR**
elbow	e-l-bo-w	**GAR/GDR**/*HOO*/*HDO*
elder	e-l-der	**GAR/GDR**/*HDO*
elderly	e-l-der-ly	**GAR/GDR**/*HDO*/**GDR**
eldest	e-l-de-st	**GAR/GDR/GAR**/*HDO*

Word	Mouthables	Mouth Movements Notations
elect	e-le-ct	GAR/GAR/*HDO*
election	e-le-c-tion	GAR/GAR/GDR/*HOO*
elector	e-le-c-tor	GAR/GAR/GDR/*HOO*
electoral	e-le-c-to-ral	GAR/GAR/GDR/*HOO*/GDR
electorate	e-le-c-to-ra-te	GAR/GAR/GDR/*HOO*/*HAO*/*HDO*
electric	e-le-c-tri-c	GAR/GAR/GDR/GAR/GDR
electrical	e-le-c-tri-cal	GAR/GAR/GDR/GAR/*HDO*
electrician	e-le-c-tri-ci-a-n	GAR/GAR/GDR/GAR/GDR/GAR/ GDR
electrify	e-le-c-tri-fy	GAR/GAR/GDR/GAR/GRR
electronic	e-le-c-tro-ni-c	GAR/GAR/GDR/*HAO*/GAR/GDR
electronics	e-le-c-tro-ni-cs	GAR/GAR/GDR/*HAO*/GAR/GDR
elegance	e-le-ga-nce	GAR/GAR/GAR/GDR
elegant	e-le-gan-t	GAR/GAR/GAR/*HOO*
element	e-le-me-nt	GAR/GAR/GAR/GDR
elementary	e-le-me-n-tary	GAR/GAR/GAR/GDR/*HDO*
elephant	e-le-pha-nt	GAR/GAR/GAR/GDR
elevate	e-le-va-te	GAR/GAR/*HAO*/*HDO*
elevation	e-le-va-tion	GAR/GAR/*HAO*/*HOO*
elevator	e-le-va-tor	GAR/GAR/*HAO*/*HOO*
eleven	e-le-ven	GAR/GAR/*HDO*
elicit	e-li-ci-t	GAR/GAR/GAR/GDR
eligible	e-li-gi-ble	GAR/GAR/GAR/*HOO*
eliminate	e-li-mi-na-te	GAR/GAR/GAR/*HAO*/*HDO*
elimination	e-li-mi-na-tion	GAR/GAR/GAR/*HAO*/*HOO*
elm	e-l-m	GAR/GDR/*HDO*
elocution	e-lo-cu-tion	GAR/GAR/*HOO*/*HOO*
elongate	e-lon-ga-te	GAR/*HAO*/*HAO*/*HDO*
elopement	e-lo-pe-men-t	GAR/*HOO*/*HDO*/GAR/*HOO*
eloquence	e-lo-que-nce	GAR/*HAO*/GAR/GDR
eloquent	e-lo-que-nt	GAR/*HAO*/GAR/GDR

Word	Mouthables	Mouth Movements Notations
else	e-l-se	**GAR/GDR/***HDO*
eluciated	e-lu-ci-a-ted	**GAR/***HOO***/GAR/***HAO***/GRR**
elude	e-lu-de	**GAR/***HOO***/***HDO*
emanate	e-ma-na-te	**GAR/GAR/***HAO***/***HDO*
emanciated	e-ma-ci-a-ted	**GAR/GAR/GAR/***HAO***/GRR**
emancipation	e-ma-n-ci-pa-tion	**GAR/GAR/GDR/GAR/***HAO***/***HOO*
embalm	e-m-bal-m	**GAR/GDR/***HAO***/***HDO*
embankment	e-m-ban-k-men-t	**GAR/GDR/GAR/GDR/GAR/***HOO*
embark	e-m-bar-k	**GAR/GDR/***HAO***/***HDO*
embarkation	e-m-bar-ka-tion	**GAR/GDR/***HAO***/***HAO***/***HOO*
embarrass	e-m-ba-rra-ss	**GAR/GDR/GAR/GAR/***HDO*
embarrassment	e-m-ba-rra-ss-me-nt	**GAR/GDR/GAR/GAR/GDR/GAR/ GDR**
embassy	e-m-ba-ssy	**GAR/GDR/GAR/GAR**
embed	e-m-be-d	**GAR/GDR/GAR/***HOO*
embedded	e-m-be-dded	**GAR/GDR/GAR/GRR**
embellish	e-m-be-lli-sh	**GAR/GDR/GAR/GAR/***HDO*
ember	e-m-ber	**GAR/GDR/***HDO*
embezzle	e-m-be-zzle	**GAR/GDR/GAR/***HOO*
embezzlement	e-m-be-zzle-me-nt	**GAR/GDR/GAR/***HOO***/GAR/GDR**
embitter	e-m-bi-tter	**GAR/GDR/GAR/***HDO*
emblem	e-m-ble-m	**GAR/GDR/GAR/***HDO*
embolism	e-m-bo-li-sm	**GAR/GDR/***HAO***/GAR/GDR**
emboss	e-m-bo-ss	**GAR/GDR/***HAO***/***HDO*
embrace	e-m-bra-ce	**GAR/GDR/***HAO***/GDR**
embroider	e-m-broi-der	**GAR/GDR/GAR/***HDO*
embroidery	e-m-broi-de-ry	**GAR/GDR/GAR/***HAO***/***HDO*
embroil	e-m-broi-l	**GAR/GDR/GAR/GDR**
embryo	e-m-bry-o	**GAR/GDR/GAR/***HOO*
embryonic	e-m-bry-o-ni-c	**GAR/GDR/GAR/***HAO***/GAR/GDR**
emend	e-me-nd	**GAR/GAR/GDR**

Word	Mouthables	Mouth Movements Notations
emerald	e-me-ra-ld	GAR/GAR/*HOO*/*HDO*
emerge	e-mer-ge	GAR/*HAO*/*HDO*
emergence	e-mer-ge-nce	GAR/*HAO*/GAR/GDR
emergency	e-mer-ge-ncy	GAR/*HAO*/GAR/GDR
emery	e-me-ry	GAR/GAR/*HDO*
emigrant	e-mi-gran-t	GAR/GAR/*HOO*
emigrate	e-mi-gra-te	GAR/GAR/*HAO*/*HDO*
eminent	e-mi-nen-t	GAR/GAR/GAR/*HDO*
emir	e-mi-r	GAR/GAR/*HDO*
emirate	e-mi-ra-te	GAR/GAR/*HAO*/*HDO*
emission	e-mi-ssi-on	GAR/GAR/*HDO*/*HDO*
emotion	e-mo-tion	GAR/*HOO*/*HOO*
emotional	e-mo-tion-al	GAR/*HOO*/*HOO*/*HDO*
emotive	e-mo-ti-ve	GAR/*HOO*/GAR/*HDO*
empathy	e-m-pa-th-y	GAR/GDR/GAR/GTR/GAR
emphasis	e-m-pha-si-s	GAR/GDR/GAR/GAR/GDR
emphasize	e-m-pha-si-ze	GAR/GDR/GAR/GRR/GDR
emphatic	e-m-pha-ti-c	GAR/GDR/GAR/GAR/GDR
empire	e-m-pi-re	GAR/GDR/GRR/*HDO*
employ	e-m-ploy	GAR/GDR/*HAO*
employee	e-m-ploy-ee	GAR/GDR/*HAO*/GRR
employer	e-m-ploy-er	GAR/GDR/*HAO*/*HDO*
employment	e-m-ploy-men-t	GAR/GDR/*HAO*/GAR/*HOO*
empower	e-m-po-wer	GAR/GDR/*HAO*/*HDO*
empty	e-m-p-ty	GAR/GDR/GDR/GAR
emulate	e-mu-la-te	GAR/*HOO*/*HAOHDO*
emulsion	e-mul-sion	GAR/GAR/*HOO*
enable	e-n-a-ble	GAR/GDR/*HAO*/*HOO*
enact	e-n-a-ct	GAR/GDR/GAR/*HOO*
enamal	e-na-mal	GAR/GAR/*HDO*
enamoured	e-na-moure-d	GAR/GAR/*HAO*/*HOO*

Word	Mouthables	Mouth Movements Notations
encase	e-n-ca-se	**GAR/GDR**/*HAO*/*HDO*
enchant	e-n-chan-t	**GAR/GDR**/*HAO*/*HOO*
encirle	e-n-cir-cle	**GAR/GDR**/*HAO*/*HOO*
enclose	e-n-clo-se	**GAR/GDR**/*HOO*/*HDO*
enclosure	e-n-clo-su-re	**GAR/GDR**/*HOO*/*HOO*/*HDO*
encompass	e-n-co-m-pas-s	**GAR/GDR**/*HAO*/*HDO*/*HAO*/*HDO*
encore	e-n-co-re	*HAO*/*HDO*/*HOO*/*HDO*
encounter	e-n-coun-ter	**GAR/GDR**/*HAO*/*HOO*
encourage	e-n-cou-ra-ge	**GAR/GDR/GAR**/*HAO*/*HDO*
encouragement	e-n-cou-ra-ge-me-nt	**GAR/GDR/GAR**/*HAO*/*HDO*/**GAR/ GDR**
encroach	e-n-croa-ch	**GAR/GDR**/*HOO*/*HDO*
encumber	e-n-cu-m-ber	**GAR/GDR/GAR**/*HDO*/*HDO*
encyclical	e-n-cy-c-li-cal	**GAR/GDR/GAR/GDR/GAR**/*HDO*
end	e-n-d	**GAR/GDR**/*HOO*
endanger	e-n-dan-ger	**GAR/GDR**/*HAO*/*HDO*
endearing	e-n-dea-rin-g	**GAR/GDR/GRR/GAR/GDR**
endeavour	e-n-dea-vour	**GAR/GDR/GAR**/*HAO*
ending	e-n-din-g	**GAR/GDR/GAR/GDR**
endorse	e-n-dor-se	**GAR/GDR**/*HOO*/*HDO*
endorsement	e-n-dor-se-me-nt	**GAR/GDR**/*HOO*/*HDO*/**GAR/GDR**
endurance	e-n-du-ra-nce	**GAR/GDR**/*HOO*/**GAR/GDR**
endure	e-n-du-re	**GAR/GDR**/*HOO*/*HDO*
enemy	e-ne-my	**GAR/GAR/GAR**
energetic	e-ner-ge-ti-c	**GAR**/*HOO*/**GAR/GAR/GDR**
energy	e-ner-gy	**GAR**/*HOO*/**GAR**
enervate	e-ner-va-te	**GAR**/*HOO*/*HAO*/*HDO*
enforce	e-n-for-ce	**GAR/GDR**/*HAO*/**GDR**
engage	e-n-ga-ge	**GAR/GDR**/*HAO*/*HDO*
engaged	e-n-ga-ge-d	**GAR/GDR**/*HAO*/*HOO*/*HOO*
engaging	e-n-ga-gin-g	**GAR/GDR**/*HAO*/**GAR/GDR**

Word	Mouthables	Mouth Movements Notations
engender	e-n-ge-n-der	GAR/GDR/GAR/GDR/*HDO*
engine	e-n-gi-ne	GAR/GDR/GAR/GDR
engineer	e-n-gi-nee-r	GAR/GDR/GAR/GRR/*HDO*
engineering	e-n-gi-nee-ring	GAR/GDR/GAR/GRR/GDR
England	E-ng-lan-d	GRR/GDR/GAR/*HOO*
English	E-ng-li-sh	GRR/GDR/GAR/*HDO*
Englishman	E-ng-li-sh-ma-n	GRR/GDR/GAR/*HDO*/GAR/GDR
engrave	e-n-gra-ve	GAR/GDR/*HAO*/*HDO*
engraving	e-n-gra-vin-g	GAR/GDR/*HAO*/GAR/GDR
engrossed	e-n-gro-sse-d	GAR/GDR/*HOO*/*HOO*/*HOO*
enhance	e-n-han-ce	GAR/GDR/*HAO*/*HDO*
enigma	e-ni-g-ma	GAR/GAR/GDR/GAR
enigmatic	e-ni-g-ma-ti-c	GAR/GAR/GDR/GAR/GAR/GDR
enjoy	e-n-joy	GAR/GDR/*HAO*
enjoyable	e-n-joy-a-ble	GAR/GDR/*HAO*/GAR/*HOO*
enlarge	e-n-lar-ge	GAR/GDR/*HAO*/*HDO*
enlargement	e-n-lar-ge-men-t	GAR/GDR/*HAO*/*HDO*/GAR/*HDO*
enlighten	e-n-ligh-ten	GAR/GDR/GRR/*HDO*
enlist	e-n-li-st	GAR/GDR/GAR/*HDO*
enliven	e-n-li-ven	GAR/GDR/GRR/*HDO*
enmity	e-n-mi-ty	GAR/GDR/GAR/GAR
enormous	e-nor-mou-s	GAR/*HOO*/*HAO*/*HDO*
enough	e-nou-gh	GAR/GAR/*HDO*
enquire	e-n-gui-re	GAR/GDR/GRR/*HDO*
enrage	e-n-ra-ge	GAR/GDR/*HAO*/*HDO*
enrich	e-n-ri-ch	GAR/GDR/GAR/*HDO*
enrol	e-n-ro-l	GAR/GDR/*HOO*/*HDO*
ensconce	e-n-sco-nce	GAR/GDR/*HAO*/GDR
ensemble	e-n-se-m-ble	*HAO*/*HDO*/*HAO*/*HDO*/*HOO*
ensign	e-n-si-gn	GAR/GDR/GRR/GDR
enslave	e-n-sla-ve	GAR/GDR/*HAO*/*HDO*

Word	Mouthables	Mouth Movements Notations
ensue	e-n-sue	**GAR/GDR/***HOO*
ensure	e-n-su-re	**GAR/GDR/***HOO/HDO*
entail	e-n-tai-l	**GAR/GDR/***HAO***/GDR**
entangle	e-n-tan-gle	**GAR/GDR/GAR/***HOO*
enter	e-n-ter	**GAR/GDR/***HDO*
enterprise	e-n-ter-pri-se	**GAR/GDR/***HAO***/GRR/***HDO*
enterprising	e-n-ter-pri-sing	**GAR/GDR/***HAO***/GRR/GDR**
entertain	e-n-ter-tai-n	**GAR/GDR/***HAO/HAO***/GDR**
enthral	e-n-thra-l	**GAR/GDR/***HTO***/GDR**
enthralls	e-n-thra-lls	**GAR/GDR/***HTO/HDO*
enthuse	e-n-th-u-se	**GAR/GDR/***HTO/HOO/HDO*
enthusiasm	e-n-th-u-si-a-sm	**GAR/GDR/***HTO/HOO***/GAR/GAR/** *HDO*
entice	e-n-ti-ce	**GAR/GDR/GRR/GDR**
entire	e-n-ti-re	**GAR/GDR/GRR/***HDO*
entitle	e-n-ti-tle	**GAR/GDR/GRR/***HOO*
entity	e-n-ti-ty	**GAR/GDR/GAR/GAR**
entrance	e-n-tran-ce	**GAR/GDR/***HAO/HDO*
entrench	e-n-tre-n-ch	**GAR/GDR/GAR/GDR/***HDO*
entrepreneur	e-n-tre-pre-neur	*HAO/HDO***/GAR/GAR/***HOO*
entrust	e-n-tru-st	**GAR/GDR/GAR/***HOO*
entry	e-n-try	**GAR/GDR/***HDO*
entwine	e-n-twi-ne	**GAR/GDR/GRR/GDR**
enumerate	e-nu-me-ra-te	**GAR/***HOO***/GAR/***HAO/HDO*
enunciate	e-nun-ci-a-te	**GAR/GAR/GAR/***HAO/HDO*
envelop	e-n-ve-lo-p	**GAR/GDR/GAR/GAR/***HDO*
envelope	e-n-ve-lo-pe	**GAR/GDR/GAR/***HOO/HDO*
enveloped	e-n-ve-lo-pe-d	**GAR/GDR/GAR/GAR/***HDO/HOO*
envious	e-n-vi-ous	**GAR/GDR/GAR/***HAO*
environment	e-n-vi-ron-men-t	**GAR/GDR/GRR/***HAO***/GAR/***HOO*
environmental	e-n-vi-ron-men-tal	**GAR/GDR/GRR/***HAO***/GAR/***HDO*

Word	Mouthables	Mouth Movements Notations
environmentalist	e-n-vi-ron-men-ta-li-st	GAR/GDR/GRR/*HAO*/GAR/GAR/ GAR/GDR
envisage	e-n-vi-sa-ge	GAR/GDR/GAR/*HAOHDO*
envy	e-n-vy	GAR/GDR/GAR
epaulet	e-pau-le-t	GAR/GAR/GAR/GDR
epic	e-pi-c	GAR/GAR/GDR
epidemic	e-pi-de-mi-c	GAR/GAR/GAR/GAR/GDR
epilogue	e-pi-lo-gue	GAR/GAR/*HAO*/*HDO*
episode	e-pi-so-de	GAR/GAR/*HOO*/*HDO*
epoch	e-po-ch	GAR/*HAO*/*HDO*
equal	e-qua-l	GRR/GAR/*HDO*
equality	e-qua-li-ty	GRR/GAR/GAR/GAR
equalize	e-qua-li-ze	GRR/GAR/GAR/GDR
equation	e-qua-tion	GAR/*HAO*/*HOO*
equator	e-qua-tor	GAR/*HAO*/*HOO*
equatorial	e-qua-to-ri-a-l	GAR/GAR/*HOO*/GAR/GAR/GDR
equilibrium	e-qui-li-bri-u-m	GRR/GAR/GAR/GAR/GAR/*HDO*
equip	e-qui-p	GAR/GAR/*HDO*
equipment	e-qui-p-men-t	GAR/GAR/*HDO*/GAR/*HDO*
equity	e-qui-ty	GAR/GAR/GAR
equivalent	e-qui-va-le-nt	GAR/GAR/GAR/GAR/GDR
equivocal	e-qui-vo-cal	GAR/GAR/GAR/*HDO*
era	e-ra	GRR/GAR
erand	e-ra-nd	GAR/GAR/GDR
erase	e-ra-se	GAR/*HAO*/*HDO*
eraser	e-ra-ser	GAR/*HAO*/*HDO*
erect	e-re-c-t	GAR/GAR/GDR/*HOO*
ermine	er-mi-ne	*HAO*/GAR/GDR
erosion	e-ro-sion	GAR/*HOO*/*HOO*
erotic	e-ro-ti-c	GAR/*HAO*/GAR/GDR
err	er-r	*HAO*/*HDO*

Word	Mouthables	Mouth Movements Notations
erudition	e-ru-di-tion	GAR/GAR/GAR/*HOO*
erupt	e-ru-pt	GAR/GAR/*HDO*
escalate	e-sca-la-te	GAR/GAR/*HAO*/*HDO*
escalation	e-sca-la-tion	GAR/GAR/*HAO*/*HOO*
escalator	e-sca-la-tor	GAR/GAR/*HAO*/*HDO*
escapade	e-sca-pa-des	GAR/GAR/*HAO*/GDR
escape	e-sca-pe	GAR/*HAO*/GDR
escort	e-scor-t	GAR/*HOO*/*HOO*
escorted	e-scor-ted	GAR/*HOO*/GRR
escort	e-scor-t	GAR/*HOO*/*HDO*
Eskimo	E-ski-mo	GAR/GAR/*HOO*
especially	e-spe-ci-a-lly	GAR/GAR/GAR/GAR/GDR
espionage	e-spio-nage	GAR/GAR/*HDO*
essay	e-ssay	GAR/*HAO*
essayist	e-ssay-i-st	GAR/*HAO*/GAR/GDR
essence	e-sse-nce	GAR/GAR/GDR
essential	e-sse-n-tial	GAR/GAR/GDR/*HDO*
establish	e-sta-bli-sh	GAR/GAR/GAR/*HDO*
establishment	e-sta-bli-sh-me-nt	GRR/GAR/GAR/*HDO*/GAR/GDR
estate	e-sta-te	GAR/*HAO*/*HDO*
esteem	e-stee-m	GAR/GRR/*HDO*
estimate	e-sti-ma-te	GAR/GAR/*HAO*/*HDO*
estimation	e-sti-ma-tion	GAR/GAR/*HAO*/*HOO*
estranged	e-stra-n-ge-d	GAR/*HAO*/GDR/*HOO*/*HOO*
estuary	e-stu-ary	GAR/*HOO*/*HDO*
etching	e-t-chi-ng	GAR/GDR/GAR/GDR
eternal	e-ter-nal	GAR/*HAO*/*HDO*
eternity	e-ter-ni-ty	GAR/*HAO*/GAR/GAR
ethic	e-th-i-c	GAR/GTR/GAR/GDR
ethical	e-th-i-cal	GAR/GTR/GAR/*HDO*
ethics	e-th-i-cs	GAR/GTR/GAR/GDR

Word	Mouthables	Mouth Movements Notations
ethnic	e-th-ni-c	**GAR/GTR/GAR/GDR**
Eucharist	Eu-cha-ri-st	*HOO*/**GAR/GAR**/*HDO*
euphemism	eu-phe-mi-sm	*HOO*/**GAR/GAR**/*HDO*
euphoria	eu-phor-i-a	*HOO/HOO*/**GAR/GAR**
Eurasian	Eu-ra-si-an	*HOO/HAO*/**GAR/GDR**
Europe	Eu-ro-pe	*HOO/HOO/HDO*
European	Eu-ro-pe-an	*HOO/HOO*/**GRR/GDR**
euthanasia	eu-th-a-na-si-a	*HOO*/**GTR/GAR**/*HAO*/**GAR/GAR**
evacuate	e-va-cu-a-te	**GRR/GAR**/*HOO/HAO/HOO*
evade	e-va-de	**GRR**/*HAO/HOO*
evaluate	e-va-lu-a-te	**GRR/GAR**/*HOO/HAO/HDO*
evangelical	e-va-n-ge-li-cal	**GAR/GAR/GDR/GAR/GAR**/*HDO*
evaporate	e-va-por-a-te	**GRR/GAR**/*HOO/HAO/HDO*
evasion	e-va-sion	**GRR**/*HAO/HOO*
evasive	e-va-si-ve	**GRR**/*HAO*/**GAR/GDR**
eve	e-ve	**GRR**/*HDO*
even	e-ven	**GRR/GDR**
evening	e-ve-ning	**GRR**/*HDO*/**GDR**
event	e-ve-nt	**GRR/GAR/GDR**
eventful	e-ve-nt-ful	**GRR/GAR/GDR**/*HOO*
eventual	e-ven-tu-al	**GRR/GAR**/*HOO/HDO*
eventually	e-ven-tu-a-lly	**GRR/GAR**/*HOO*/**GAR/GDR**
ever	e-ver	**GAR**/*HAO*
every	e-ve-ry	**GAR**/*HAO/HDO*
evict	e-vi-ct	**GRR/GAR**/*HOO*
eviction	e-vi-c-tion	**GRR/GAR/GDR**/*HOO*
evidence	e-vi-de-nce	**GAR/GAR/GAR/GDR**
evident	e-vi-de-nt	**GAR/GAR/GAR/GDR**
evil	e-vil	**GRR**/*HDO*
evolution	e-vo-lu-tion	**GRR**/*HOO/HOO/HOO*
evolutionary	e-vo-lu-tion-ary	**GRR**/*HOO/HOO/HOO/HDO*

Word	Mouthables	Mouth Movements Notations
evolve	e-vo-lve	**GRR**/*HAO*/*HDO*
ewe	ewe	*HDO*
exacerbate	e-xa-cer-ba-te	**GAR/GAR**/*HOO*/*HAO*/*HDO*
exact	e-xa-ct	**GRR/GAR**/*HOO*
exacting	e-xa-cting	**GRR/GAR/GDR**
exaggerate	e-xa-gger-a-te	**GAR/GAR**/*HAO*/*HAO*/*HDO*
exalt	e-xal-t	**GAR**/*HOO*/*HDO*
exam	e-xa-m	**GAR/GAR**/*HDO*
examination	e-xa-mi-na-tion	**GAR/GAR/GAR**/*HAO*/*HOO*
examine	e-xa-mi-ne	**GAR/GAR/GAR/GDR**
example	e-xa m-ple	**GAR**/*HAO*/*HDO*/*HOO*
exasperate	e-xa-spe-ra-te	**GAR/GAR**/*HDO*/*HAO*/*HDO*
excavate	e-x-ca-va-te	**GAR/GDR/GAR**/*HAO*/*HDO*
excavation	e-x-ca-va-tion	**GAR/GDR/GAR**/*HAO*/*HOO*
excavator	e-x-ca-va-tor	**GAR/GDR/GAR**/*HAO*/*HOO*
exceed	e-x-cee-d	**GAR/GRR/GRR**/*HOO*
excel	e-x-ce-l	**GAR/GRR/GAR/GDR**
excellent	e-x-ce-lle-nt	**GAR/GRR/GAR/GAR/GDR**
except	e-x-ce-pt	**GAR/GRR/GAR**/*HDO*
exception	e-x-ce-p-tion	**GAR/GRR/GAR**/*HDO*/*HOO*
exceptional	e-x-ce-p-tion-al	**GAR/GRR/GAR**/*HDO*/*HOO*/*HDO*
excercise	e-x-cer-ci-se	**GAR/GRR**/*HAO*/**GRR**/*HDO*
excerpt	ex-cer-pt	**GAR**/*HAO*/*HDO*
excess	e-x-ce-ss	**GAR/GRR/GAR/GDR**
excessive	e-x-ce-ssi-ve	**GAR/GRR/GAR/GAR/GDR**
exchange	ex-chan-ge	**GAR**/*HAO*/*HDO*
exchequer	ex-che-quer	**GAR/GAR**/*HDO*
excise	ex-ci-se	**GAR/GRR**/*HDO*
excite	ex-ci-te	**GAR/GRR**/*HOO*
excitement	ex-ci-te-me-nt	**GAR/GRR**/*HDO*/**GAR/GDR**
exclamation	e-x-cla-ma-tion	**GAR/GRR/GAR**/*HAO*/*HOO*

Word	Mouthables	Mouth Movements Notations
exclude	ex-clu-de	GAR/*HOO*/*HOO*
exclusion	ex-clu-sion	GAR/*HAO*/*HOO*
exclusive	ex-clu-si-ve	GAR/*HOO*/GAR/*HDO*
excruciating	e-x-cru-ci-a-ting	GAR/GRR/*HOO*/GDR/*HAO*/GDR
excursion	ex-cur-sion	GAR/GAR//*HOO*
excuse	ex-cu-se	GAR/*HOO*/*HDO*
execute	e-xe-cu-te	GAR/GRR/*HOO*/*HDO*
execution	e-xe-cu-tion	GAR/GRR/*HOO*/*HOO*
executioner	e-xe-cu-tion-er	GAR/GRR/*HOO*/*HOO*/*HDO*
executive	e-xe-cu-ti-ve	GAR/GAR/*HOO*/GAR/*HDO*
exemplary	e-xe-m-plar-y	GAR/GAR/GDR/*HAO*/GAR
exemplify	e-xe-m-pli-fy	GAR/GDR/GAR/GDR
exempt	e-xem-pt	GAR/GAR/*HDO*
exemption	e-xem-p-tion	GAR/GAR/*HDO*/*HOO*
exert	e-xer-t	GAR/*HOO*/*HOO*
exertion	e-xer-tion	GAR/*HOO*/*HOO*
exhale	e-x-ha-le	GAR/GDR/*HAO*/*HDO*
exhaust	e-x-hau-st	GAR/GDR/*HOO*/*HDO*
exhaustion	e-x-haus-tion	GAR/GDR/*HOO*/*HOO*
exhaustive	e-x-haus-ti-ve	GAR/GDR/*HOO*/GAR/GDR
exhibit	e-x-hi-bi-t	GAR/GDR/GAR/GAR/*HOO*
exhibited	e-x-hi-bi-ted	GAR/GDR/GAR/GAR/GRR
exhibition	e-x-hi-bi-tion	GAR/GDR/GAR/GAR/*HOO*
exhibitor	e-x-hi-bi-tor	GAR/GDR/GAR/GAR/*HDO*
exhort	e-x-hor-t	GAR/GDR/*HOO*/*HOO*
exhume	e-x-hu-me	GAR/GDR/*HOO*/*HDO*
exile	e-x-i-le	GAR/GDR/GRR/GDR
exiles	e-x-i-les	GAR/GDR/GRR/GDR
exist	e-x-i-st	GAR/GDR/GAR/*HOO*
existence	e-x-i-ste-nce	GAR/GDR/GAR/GAR/GDR
exit	e-x-i-t	GAR/GDR/GAR/GDR

Word	Mouthables	Mouth Movements Notations
exodus	e-x-o-du-s	**GAR/GDR/**_HOO_**/GAR/**_HDO_
exotic	e-x-o-ti-c	**GAR/GDR/**_HAO_**/GAR/GDR**
expand	e-x-pa-nd	**GAR/GDR/GAR/GDR**
expanse	e-x-pa-nse	**GAR/GDR/GAR/GDR**
expansion	e-x-pa-n-sion	**GAR/GDR/GAR/GDR/**_HOO_
expansive	e-x-pa-n-si-ve	**GAR/GDR/GAR/GDR/GAR/**_HDO_
expatriate	e-x-pa-tri-a-te	**GAR/GDR/GAR/GAR/**_HAO_**/**_HDO_
expect	e-x-pec-t	**GAR/GDR/GAR/**_HOO_
expectancy	e-x-pec-ta-ncy	**GAR/GDR/GAR/GAR/GDR**
expectant	e-x-pe-c-ta-nt	**GAR/GDR/GAR/GDR/GAR/GDR**
expectation	e-x-pe-c-ta-tion	**GAR/GDR/GAR/**_HAO_**/**_HOO_
expedient	e-x-pe-di-e-nt	**GAR/GDR/GRR/GAR/GAR/GDR**
expedition	e-x-pe-di-tion	**GAR/GDR/GAR/GAR/**_HOO_
expel	e-x-pe-l	**GAR/GDR/GAR/GDR**
expenditure	e-x-pen-di-tu-re	**GAR/GDR/GAR/GAR/**_HOO_**/**_HDO_
expense	e-x-pen-se	**GAR/GDR/GAR/**_HDO_
expensive	ex-pen-si-ve	**GAR/GDR/GAR/GAR/GDR**
experience	e-x-per-i-e-nce	**GAR/GDR/**_HAO_**/GAR/GAR/GDR**
experienced	e-x-per-i-e-nce-d	**GAR/GDR/**_HAO_**/GAR/GDR/**_HOO_
experiment	e-x-pe-ri-me-nt	**GAR/GDR/GAR/GAR/GAR/GDR**
experimental	e-x-pe-ri-me-n-tal	**GAR/GDR/GAR/GAR/GAR/GDR/** _HDO_
expert	e-x-per-t	**GAR/GDR/**_HOO_**/**_HDO_
expiate	e-x-pi-a-te	**GAR/GDR/GAR/**_HAO_**/**_HDO_
expire	e-x-pi-re	**GAR/GDR/GRR/**_HDO_
expiry	e-x-pi-ry	**GAR/GDR/GRR/GDR**
explain	e-x-plai-n	**GAR/GDR/**_HAO_**/GDR**
explanation	e-x-pla-na-tion	**GAR/GDR/GAR/**_HAO_**/**_HOO_
explanatory	e-x-pla-na-tory	**GAR/GDR/GAR/**_HAO_**/**_HDO_
explicit	e-x-pli-ci-t	**GAR/GDR/GDR/GAR/GDR**
explode	e-x-plo-de	**GAR/GRR/**_HOO_**/**_HDO_

Word	Mouthables	Mouth Movements Notations
exploit	e-x-ploi-t	**GAR/GRR/GAR**/*HDO*
exploitation	e-x-ploi-ta-tion	**GAR/GRR/GAR**/*HAO/HOO*
explore	e-x-plo-re	**GAR/GRR**/*HOO/HDO*
explorer	e-x-plor-er	**GAR/GRR**/*HOO/HDO*
explosion	e-x-plo-sion	**GAR/GRR**/*HOO/HOO*
explosive	e-x-plo-si-ve	**GAR/GRR**/*HOO*/**GAR/GDR**
exponent	e-x-po-ne-nt	**GAR/GRR**/*HOO*/**GAR/GDR**
export	e-x-por-t	**GAR/GRR**/*HOO/HDO*
exporter	e-x-por-ter	**GAR/GRR**/*HOO/HDO*
expose	e-x-po-se	**GAR/GRR**/*HOO/HDO*
exposition	e-x-po-si-tion	**GAR/GRR**/*HOO*/**GAR**/*HOO*
exposure	e-x-po-su-re	**GAR/GRR**/*HOO/HOO/HDO*
express	e-x-pre-ss	**GAR/GRR/GAR**/*HDO*
expression	e-x-pre-ssion	**GAR/GRR/GAR**/*HDO*
expressive	e-x-pre-ssi-ve	**GAR/GRR/GAR/GAR**/*HDO*
expropriate	e-x-pro-pri-a-te	**GAR/GRR**/*HOO*/**GAR**/*HAO/HDO*
expulsion	e-x-pu-l-sion	**GAR/GRR/GAR/GDR**/*HOO*
exquiste	e-x-qui-si-te	**GAR/GRR/GAR/GAR**/*HDO*
extend	e-x-te-nd	**GAR/GRR/GAR/GDR**
extendable	e-x-te-n-da-ble	**GAR/GRR/GAR/GDR/GAR**/*HOO*
extension	e-x-te-n-sion	**GAR/GRR/GAR/GDR**/*HOO*
extensive	e-x-te-n-si-ve	**GAR/GRR/GAR/GDR/GAR**/*HDO*
extent	e-x-te-nt	**GAR/GRR/GAR/GDR**
extenuate	e-x-te-nu-a-te	**GAR/GRR/GAR**/*HOO/HAO/HDO*
exterior	e-x-te-ri-or	**GAR/GRR/GRR/GAR**/*HDO*
extermination	e-x-ter-mi-na-tion	**GAR/GRR**/*HAO*/**GAR**/*HAO/HOO*
external	e-x-ter-nal	**GAR/GRR**/*HAO/HDO*
extinct	e-x-ti-nct	**GAR/GRR/GAR/GDR**
extinguisher	e-x-ti-n-gui-sher	**GAR/GRR/GAR/GDR/GAR**/*HOO*
extort	e-x-tor-t	**GAR/GRR**/*HOO/HOO*
extortion	e-x-tor-tion	**GAR/GRR**/*HOO/HOO*

Word	Mouthables	Mouth Movements Notations
extra	e-x-tra	**GAR/GRR/GAR**
extract	e-x-tra-ct	**GAR/GRR/GAR/**_HDO_
extradite	e-x-tra-di-te	**GAR/GRR/GAR/GRR/**_HDO_
extradition	e-x-tra-di-tion	**GAR/GRR/GAR/GAR/**_HOO_
extramarital	e-x-tra-ma-ri-tal	**GAR/GRR/GAR/GAR/GAR/**_HDO_
extraordinary	e-x-tra-or-di-na-ry	**GAR/GRR/GAR/**_HOO_**/GAR/GAR/ GDR**
extravagant	e-x-tra-va-ga-nt	**GAR/GRR/GAR/GAR/GAR/GDR**
extreme	e-x-tre-me	**GAR/GRR/GRR/GDR**
extremity	e-x-tre-mi-ty	**GAR/GRR/GAR/GAR/GAR**
extrovert	e-x-tro-ver-t	**GAR/GRR/**_HOO_**/**_HAO_**/**_HOO_
exuberance	e-xu-ber-a-nce	**GAR/**_HOO_**/**_HAO_**/GAR/GDR**
exuberant	e-xu-ber-a-nt	**GAR/**_HOO_**/**_HAO_**/GAR/GDR**
exude	e-xu-de	**GAR/**_HOO_**/**_HDO_
exult	e-xu-lt	**GAR/GAR/GDR**
eye	eye	**GDR**

Word	Mouthables	Mouth Movements Notations
F		
F	F	**GAR**/*HDO*
fable	fa-ble	*HAO*/*HDO*
fabric	fa-bri-c	**GAR/GAR/GDR**
fabricate	fa-bri-ca-te	**GAR/GAR**/*HAO*/*HDO*
fabulous	fa-bu-lou-s	*HAO*/*HOO*/**GAR**/*HDO*
facade	fa-cade	**GAR**/*HDO*
face	fa-ce	*HAO*/**GDR**
facile	fa-ci-le	**GAR/GRR/GDR**
facility	fa-ci-li-ty	**GAR/GAR/GAR/GAR**
facing	fa-cing	*HAO*/**GDR**
fact	fa-ct	**GAR**/*HDO*
faction	fa-c-tion	**GAR/GDR**/*HOO*
factional	fa-c-tion-al	**GAR/GDR**/*HOO*/**GDR**
factor	fa-c-tor	**GAR/GDR**/*HDO*
factory	fac-tory	**GAR**/*HDO*
factual	fac-tu-al	**GAR**/*HOO*/**GDR**
faculty	fa-cu-l-ty	**GAR**/*HOO*/**GDR/GAR**
fad	fa-d	**GAR**/*HOO*
fade	fa-de	*HAO*/*HDO*
faded	fa-ded	*HAO*/**GRR**
fag	fa-g	**GAR**/*HDO*
fail	fai-l	*HAO*/**GDR**
failing	fai-ling	*HAO*/**GDR**
failure	fai-lu-re	*HAO*/*HOO*/*HDO*
faint	fai-nt	*HAO*/**GDR**
fainted	fai-n-ted	*HAO*/**GDR/GRR**
fair	fair	*HAO*
faired	faire-d	*HAO*/*HOO*
fairer	fair-er	*HAO*/*HDO*
fairest	fair-e-st	**GAR/GAR**/*HOO*

Word	Mouthables	Mouth Movements Notations
fairly	fair-ly	*HAO*/**GDR**
fairs	fair-s	*HAO*/**GDR**
fairy	fairy	*HDO*
faith	fai-th	*HAO*/**GTR**
faithful	fai-th-ful	*HAO*/**GTR**/*HOO*
faithless	fai-th-le-ss	*HAO*/**GTR**/**GAR**/**GDR**
fake	fa-ke	*HAO*/*HDO*
falcon	fal-co-n	*HOO*/*HAO*/**GDR**
fall	fall	*HOO*
fallen	fal-le-n	*HOO*/**GAR**/**GDR**
false	fa-l-se	*HAO*/**GDR**/*HDO*
falsify	fa-l-si-fy	*HAO*/**GDR**/**GAR**/**GRR**
falsity	fa-l-si-ty	*HAO*/**GDR**/**GAR**/**GAR**
falter	fal-ter	*HOO*/*HDO*
fame	fa-me	*HAO*/*HDO*
famed	fa-me-d	*HAO*/*HDO*/*HOO*
familar	fa-mi-lar	**GAR**/**GAR**/**GDR**
familiarize	fa-mi-li-ar-i-ze	**GAR**/**GAR**/*HAO*/**GRR**/**GDR**
family	fa-mi-ly	**GAR**/**GAR**/**GDR**
famished	fa-mi-she-d	**GAR**/**GAR**/*HOO*/*HOO*
famous	fa-mou-s	*HAO*/*HAO*/*HDO*
fan	fa-n	**GAR**/**GRR**
fanned	fa-nne-d	**GAR**/**GDR**/*HOO*
fan	fa-n	**GAR**/**GDR**
fanatic	fa-na-ti-c	**GAR**/**GAR**/**GAR**/**GDR**
fanatical	fa-na-ti-cal	**GAR**/**GAR**/**GAR**/*HDO*
fanciful	fan-ci-ful	**GAR**/**GAR**/*HOO*
fancy	fan-cy	**GAR**/**GAR**
fantastic	fa-n-ta-sti-c	**GAR**/**GDR**/**GAR**/**GAR**/**GDR**
fantasy	fan-ta-sy	**GAR**/**GAR**/**GAR**
far	far	*HAO*

Word	Mouthables	Mouth Movements Notations
fare	fare	*HDO*
farm	far-m	*HAO/HDO*
farmer	far-mer	*HAO/HDO*
farming	far-ming	**HAO/GDR**
farther	far-ther	*HAO/HTO*
farthest	far-th-e-st	*HAO*/**GTR/GAR**/*HDO*
fascinate	fas-ci-na-te	**GAR/GAR**/*HAO/HOO*
fascination	fas-ci-na-tion	**GAR/GAR**/*HAO/HOO*
Fascism	Fa-sc-i-sm	**GAR**/*HOO*/**GAR/GDR**
Fascist	Fa-sc-i-st	**GAR**/*HOO*/**GAR/GRR**
fashion	fa-shi-o-n	**GAR**/*HOO/HAO*/**GDR**
fashionable	fa-shi-o-na-ble	**GAR**/*HOO/HAO*/**GAR**/*HOO*
fast	fas-t	*HAO/HDO*
fasten	fas-te-n	*HAO*/**GAR/GDR**
fastener	fas-te-ner	*HAO*/**GAR**/*HDO*
fastening	fa-ste-ning	*HAO*/**GAR/GDR**
fat	fa-t	**GAR**/*HDO*
fatal	fa-tal	*HAO/HDO*
fatality	fa-ta-li-ty	*HAO*/**GAR/GAR/GAR**
fate	fa-te	*HAO/HDO*
fated	fa-ted	*HAO*/**GRR**
fateful	fa-te-ful	*HAO/HDO/HOO*
father	fa-ther	**GAR/GTR**
fatherly	fa-ther-ly	**GAR/GTR/GDR**
fathom	fath-o-m	**GTR**/*HAO/HDO*
fatigue	fa-ti-gue	**GAR/GAR**/*HDO*
fatten	fa-tten	**GAR**/*HDO*
fatty	fa-tty	**GAR/GAR**
faucet	fau-ce-t	*HOO*/**GAR**/*HDO*
fault	fau-lt	*HOO/HDO*
faulty	fau-l-ty	*HOO*/**GDR/GAR**

Word	Mouthables	Mouth Movements Notations
fauna	fau-na	*HOO*/**GAR**
favour	fa-vour	*HAO*/*HAO*
favourable	fa-vou-ra-ble	*HAO*/*HAO*/**GAR**/*HOO*
fawn	faw-n	*HOO*/**GRR**
fawned	faw-ne-d	*HAO*/**GDR**/*HOO*
fawn	faw-n	*HAO*/*HDO*
faze	fa-ze	*HAO*/**GRR**
fazed	fa-ze-d	*HAO*/**GDR**/*HOO*
fear	fe-ar	**GRR/GAR**
fearful	fe-ar-ful	**GRR/GAR**/*HOO*
feasible	fea-si-ble	**GRR/GAR**/*HOO*
feast	fea-st	**GRR**/*HOO*
feat	fea-t	**GRR/GDR**
feather	fea-ther	**GAR**/*HTO*
feature	fea-tu-re	**GRR**/*HOO*/*HDO*
February	Fe-bru-ar-y	**GAR**/*HDO*/*HAO*/**GAR**
fed	fe-d	**GAR/GRR**
federal	fe-de-ral	**GAR**/*HAO*/*HDO*
federation	fe-de-ra-tion	**GAR**/*HDO*/*HAO*/*HOO*
fee	fee	**GRR**
feeble	fee-ble	**GRR**/*HOO*
feed	fee-d	**GRR/GRR**
feeder	fee-der	**GRR**/*HDO*
feel	fee-l	**GRR/GRR**
feeling	fee-ling	**GRR/GDR**
feet	fee-t	**GRR**/*HDO*
feign	feig-n	*HAO*/**GDR**
feint	fei-nt	*HAO*/*HDO*
fell	fe-ll	**GAR/GRR**
fellow	fe-llo-w	**GAR**/*HOO*/*HDO*
felony	fe-lo-ny	**GAR/GAR/GAR**

Word	Mouthables	Mouth Movements Notations
felt	fe-lt	**GAR/GRR**
female	fe-ma-le	**GRR/**_HAO/HDO_
feminine	fe-mi-ni-ne	**GAR/GAR/GAR/GDR**
femur	fe-mur	**GAR/**_HAO_
fence	fe-n-ce	**GAR/GDR/**_HDO_
fencing	fe-n-cing	**GAR/GDR/GDR**
fend	fe-nd	**GAR/GRR**
fender	fe-n-der	**GAR/GDR/**_HDO_
fennel	fe-nnel	**GAR/**_HDO_
ferment	fer-me-nt	_HAO/_**GAR/GRR**
fern	fer-n	_HAO/HDO_
ferocious	fer-o-ci-ous	_HAO/HOO/_**GAR/**_HAO_
ferry	fe-rry	**GAR/**_HDO_
fertile	fer-ti-le	**GAR/GRR/GDR**
fertilizer	fer-ti-li-zer	**GAR/GAR/GRR/GDR**
fervent	fer-ve-nt	_HAO/_**GAR/GDR**
fervour	fer-vour	**GAR/**_HAO_
festivity	fe-sti-vi-ty	**GAR/GAR/GAR/GAR**
fete	fe-te	**GAR/GDR**
fetch	fet-ch	**GAR/**_HDO_
fetching	fet-ching	**GAR/GDR**
fetters	fet-ters	**GAR/**_HDO_
fever	fe-ver	**GRR/**_HDO_
feverish	fe-ver-i-sh	**GRR/**_HAO/_**GAR/GDR**
few	few	_HOO_
fey	fey	_HAO_
fiancée	fi-an-cée	**GAR/**_HDO/HAO_
fiasco	fi-a-sco	**GAR/GAR/**_HOO_
fib	fi-b	**GAR/**_HDO_
fiber	fi-ber	**GAR/**_HDO_
fibre	fi-bre	**GRR/**_HDO_

Word	Mouthables	Mouth Movements Notations
fickle	fi-ckle	**GAR**/*HOO*
fiction	fi-c-tion	**GAR/GDR**/*HOO*
fictional	fi-c-tion-al	**GAR/GDR**/*HOO*/**GDR**
fiddle	fi-ddle	**GAR**/*HOO*
fiddling	fi-dd-ling	**GAR**/*HDO*/**GDR**
fiddly	fi-dd-ly	**GAR**/*HDO*/**GDR**
fidelity	fi-de-li-ty	**GAR/GAR/GAR/GAR**
fidget	fi-d-ge-t	**GAR**/*HOO*/**GAR/GDR**
fidgety	fi-d-ge-ty	**GAR**/*HOO*/**GAR/GAR**
field	fie-ld	**GAR**/*HDO*
fiend	fie-nd	**GAR/GDR**
fierce	fi-er-ce	**GAR**/*HAO*/**GDR**
fiery	fie-ry	**GRR/GDR**
fifteen	fi-f-tee-n	**GAR**/*HDO*/**GRR/GDR**
fifth	fif-th	**GAR**/*HTO*
fig	fi-g	**GAR**/*HDO*
fight	figh-t	**GRR/GRR**
figure	fi-gu-re	**GAR**/*HOO*/*HDO*
filch	fi-lch	**GAR/GDR**
file	fi-le	**GRR/GRR**
filed	fi-le-d	**GRR/GDR**/*HOO*
file	fi-le	**GRR/GDR**
filet	fil-le-t	**GAR/GAR**/*HDO*
Filipino	Fi-li-pi-no	**GAR/GAR/GAR**/*HOO*
fill	fi-ll	**GAR/GRR**
filling	fil-ling	**GAR/GDR**
film	fi-l-m	**GAR/GDR**/*HDO*
filter	fil-ter	**GAR**/*HOO*
filter	fi-l-ter	**GAR/GDR**/*HDO*
filth	fi-l-th	**GAR/GDR/GTR**
filthy	fi-l-th-y	**GAR/GDR/GTR/GAR**

Word	Mouthables	Mouth Movements Notations
filtrate	fi-l-tra-te	**GAR/GDR/***HAO/HOO*
final	fi-nal	**GRR/***HDO*
finalist	fi-na-li-st	**GRR/GAR/GAR/GDR**
finalize	fi-na-li-ze	**GRR/GAR/GRR/GDR**
finally	fi-na-lly	**GRR/GAR/GDR**
finance	fi-na-nce	**GRR/GAR/GDR**
find	fi-nd	**GRR/GRR**
finding	fi-n-ding	**GRR/GDR/GDR**
fine	fi-ne	**GRR/GRR**
fined	fi-ne-d	**GRR/GDR/***HOO*
finger	fin-ger	**GAR/***HDO*
finicky	fi-ni-cky	**GAR/GAR/GAR**
finish	fi-ni-sh	**GAR/GAR/***HDO*
finite	fi-ni-te	**GRR/GRR/***HDO*
Finland	Fi-n-lan-d	**GAR/GDR/GAR/***HOO*
Finn	Fi-nn	**GAR/GDR**
fiord	fi-or-d	**GAR/***HOO/HDO*
fir	fir	*HAO*
fire	fi-re	**GRR/GDR**
firm	fir-m	*HAO/HDO*
first	fir-st	*HAO/HDO*
firth	fir-th	*HAO/HTO*
fiscal	fi-scal	**GAR/GDR**
fish	fi-sh	**GAR/***HDO*
fisherman	fi-sher-ma-n	**GAR/***HDO***/GAR/GDR**
fishing	fi-shing	**GAR/GDR**
fishy	fi-shy	**GAR/GAR**
fissure	fi-ssu-re	**GAR/***HOO/HDO*
fist	fi-st	**GAR/***HOO*
fit	fi-t	**GAR/***HOO*
fitful	fi-t-ful	**GAR/***HOO/HDO*

Word	Mouthables	Mouth Movements Notations
fitness	fi-t-ne-ss	GAR/*HOO*/GAR/GDR
fitted	fi-tted	GAR/GRR
fitting	fi-tting	GAR/GDR
five	fi-ve	GRR/*HDO*
fiver	fi-ver	GRR/*HDO*
fix	fi-x	GAR/GDR
fixation	fi-x-a-tion	GAR/GDR/*HAO*/*HOO*
fixed	fi-xe-d	GAR/GDR/*HOO*
fixings	fi-xing-s	GAR/GDR/GDR
fixture	fi-x-tu-re	GAR/GDR/*HOO*/*HDO*
fizz	fi-zz	GAR/GDR
fizzy	fi-zzy	GAR/GAR
flabbergast	flab-ber-gas-t	GAR/*HAO*/*HAO*/*HOO*
flabbergasted	flab-ber-gas-ted	GAR/*HDO*/*HAO*/GRR
flabby	fla-bby	GAR/GAR
flag	fla-g	GAR/*HDO*
flagged	fla-gge-d	GAR/*HOO*/*HOO*
flair	flair	*HAO*
flake	fla-ke	*HAO*/*HDO*
flamboyant	fla-m-boy-a-nt	GAR/GDR/*HAO*/GAR/GDR
flame	fla-me	*HAO*/*HDO*
flamingo	fla-min-go	GAR/GAR/*HOO*
flank	flan-k	GAR/*HDO*
flannel	flan-nel	GAR/*HDO*
flap	fla-p	GAR/*HDO*
flare	flare	*HDO*
flash	fla-sh	GAR/*HDO*
flashy	fla-shy	GAR/GAR
flask	flas-k	*HAO*/*HDO*
flat	fla-t	GAR/*HOO*
flatly	fla-t-ly	GAR/*HOO*/*HDO*

Word	Mouthables	Mouth Movements Notations
flatten	flat-ten	**GAR**/*HDO*
flatter	fla-tter	**GAR**/*HDO*
flattery	fla-tte-ry	**GAR**/*HAO*/**GDR**
flaunt	flau-nt	*HOO*/**GDR**
flavour	fla-vour	*HAO*/*HAO*
flaw	flaw	*HOO*
flax	fla-x	**GAR**/*HDO*
flea	f-lea	**GRR/GDR**
fleck	fle-ck	**GAR**/*HDO*
fled	fle-d	**GAR/GRR**
flee	flee	**GRR**
fleece	flee-ce	**GRR/GRR**
fleece	flee-ce	**GAR**/*HDO*
fleet	flee-t	**GRR**/*HOO*
fleeting	flee-ting	**GRR/GDR**
Flemish	Fle-mi-sh	**GAR/GAR**/*HDO*
flesh	fle-sh	**GAR**/*HDO*
fleshy	fle-shy	**GAR/GAR**
flew	flew	*HOO*
flex	fle-x	**GAR/GRR**
flexed	fle-xe-d	**GAR/GDR**/*HOO*
flexible	fle-xi-ble	**GAR/GAR**/*HOO*
flick	fli-ck	**GAR**/*HDO*
flicker	fli-cker	**GAR**/*HDO*
flight	fli-ght	**GRR**/*HOO*
flimsy	fli-m-sy	**GAR/GDR/GAR**
flinch	fli-n-ch	**GAR/GDR**/*HDO*
fling	flin-g	**GAR/GRR**
flint	fli-nt	**GAR/GDR**
flippant	fli-pp-a-nt	**GAR**/*HDO*/**GAR/GDR**
flipper	fli-p-per	**GAR**/*HDO*/*HDO*

Word	Mouthables	Mouth Movements Notations
flirtation	flir-ta-tion	*HAO/HAO/HOO*
flit	fli-t	**GAR**/*HOO*
float	floa-t	*HOO/HOO*
flock	floc-k	*HAO/HDO*
flog	flo-g	*HAO/HDO*
flood	floo-d	**GAR**/*HOO*
flooded	floo-ded	**GAR/GRR**
floor	floo-r	*HOO/HDO*
flooring	floor-i-ng	*HOO*/**GAR/GDR**
flop	flo-p	*HAO/HDO*
floppy	flo-ppy	*HAO*/**GAR**
Florence	Flo-ren-ce	*HAO*/**GAR**/*HDO*
florist	flo-ri-st	*HAO*/**GAR**/*HDO*
floss	flo-ss	*HAO/HDO*
flounder	flou-n-der	**GAR/GDR**/*HDO*
flour	flo-ur	*HAO/HDO*
flourish	flou-ri-sh	**GAR/GAR**/*HDO*
flout	flou-t	**GAR**/*HOO*
flow	flo-w	*HOO/HOO*
flowed	flo-we-d	*HOO/HOO/HOO*
flow	flo-w	*HOO/HDO*
flower	flow-er	**GAR**/*HDO*
flowery	flow-ery	**GAR/GDR**
flown	flow-n	*HOO*/**GDR**
flu	flu	*HDO*
fluctuate	fluc-tu-a-te	**GAR**/*HOO/HAO/HDO*
fluent	flu-e-nt	*HOO*/**GAR/GDR**
fluff	flu-ff	**GAR**/*HDO*
fluffy	flu-ffy	**GAR/GAR**
fluid	flu-i-d	*HOO*/**GAR/GDR**
fluke	flu-ke	*HOO/HDO*

Word	Mouthables	Mouth Movements Notations
flung	flun-g	**GAR**/*HDO*
flunk	flun-k	**GAR**/*HDO*
fluorescent	fluor-es-ce-nt	*HOO*/**GAR/GAR/GDR**
flush	flu-sh	**GAR**/*HOO*
flushed	flu-she-d	**GAR**/*HOO/HOO*
fluster	flu-ster	**GAR**/*HDO*
flute	flu-te	*HOO/HDO*
flutter	flu-tter	**GAR**/*HDO*
flux	flu-x	**GAR/GDR**
fly	fly	**GRR**
fly	fly	**GDR**
foal	foal	*HOO*
foaled	foale-d	*HOO/HOO*
foal	foa-l	*HOO/HDO*
foam	foa-m	*HOO/HDO*
foamy	foa-my	*HOO/***GAR**
focus	fo-cu-s	*HAO/***GAR**/*HDO*
fodder	fod-der	*HAO/HDO*
fog	fo-g	*HAO/HDO*
foggy	fo-ggy	*HAO/***GAR**
foil	foi-l	**GAR/GRR**
foiled	foi-le-d	**GAR/GDR**/*HOO*
foil	foi-l	**GAR**/*HDO*
fold	fo-ld	*HOO/HOO*
folded	fo-l-ded	*HOO/HDO/***GRR**
fold	fo-ld	*HOO/HDO*
folder	fo-l-der	*HAO/HDO/HDO*
foliage	fo-li-a-ge	*HAO/***GAR**/*HAO/HDO*
folk	fo-lk	*HOO/HDO*
folksy	fol-ksy	*HOO/***GAR**
follow	fo-llo-w	*HAO/HOO/HDO*

Word	Mouthables	Mouth Movements Notations
follow	fo-llo-wer	*HAO*/*HOO*/*HDO*
following	fo-llo-wing	*HAO*/*HOO*/**GDR**
folly	fo-lly	*HAO*/**GDR**
foment	fo-me-nt	*HAO*/**GAR**/**GRR**
fond	fo-nd	*HAO*/**GDR**
fondle	fo-n-dle	*HAO*/**GDR**/*HOO*
fondness	fo-nd-ne-ss	*HAO*/**GDR**/**GAR**/**GDR**
food	foo-d	*HOO*/*HOO*
fool	foo-l	*HOO*/*HDO*
foolish	foo-li-sh	*HOO*/**GAR**/*HDO*
foot	foo-t	*HOO*/*HOO*
foot	foo-t	*HOO*/*HDO*
for	for	*HOO*
forage	fo-ra-ge	*HAO*/*HAO*/**GDR**
foray	for-ay	*HOO*/*HAO*
forbade	for-ba-de	*HOO*/*HAO*/*HDO*
forbearing	for-bea-ring	*HOO*/*HAO*/**GDR**
forbid	for-bi-d	*HOO*/**GAR**/**GRR**
forbidden	for-bi-dde-n	*HOO*/**GAR**/**GAR**/**GDR**
forbidding	for-bi-dding	*HOO*/**GAR**/**GDR**
force	for-ce	*HOO*/**GRR**
force	for-ce	*HOO*/*HDO*
forced	for-ce-d	*HAO*/**GDR**/*HOO*
ford	for-d	*HOO*/*HDO*
fore	fo-re	*HAO*/*HDO*
foreign	fo-reig-n	*HAO*/*HAO*/**GDR**
foreigner	fo-reig-ner	*HAO*/*HAO*/**GDR**
forest	fo-re-st	*HAO*/**GAR**/*HDO*
forever	for-e-ver	*HAO*/**GAR**/*HDO*
forgave	for-ga-ve	*HOO*/*HAO*/**GDR**
forge	for-ge	*HOO*/*HOO*

Word	Mouthables	Mouth Movements Notations
forge	for-ge	*HOO*/*HDO*
forgery	for-ge-ry	*HOO*/**GAR**/**GDR**
forget	for-get	*HOO*/**GRR**
forgetful	for-ge-t-ful	*HOO*/**GAR**/**GRR**/*HOO*
forgivable	for-gi-va-ble	*HOO*/**GAR**/**GAR**/*HOO*
forgive	for-gi-ve	*HOO*/**GAR**/**GRR**
forgiven	for-gi-ve-n	*HAO*/**GAR**/**GAR**/**GDR**
forgiveness	for-gi-ve-ne-ss	*HOO*/**GAR**/**GAR**/**GAR**/**GDR**
forgo	for-go	*HOO*/*HOO*
forgot	for-go-t	*HOO*/*HAO*/*HOO*
forgotten	for-go-tte-n	*HOO*/*HAO*/**GAR**/**GDR**
fork	for-k	*HOO*/*HDO*
form	for-m	*HOO*/*HDO*
formal	for-ma-l	*HOO*/**GAR**/**GDR**
formality	for-ma-li-ty	*HOO*/**GAR**/**GAR**/**GAR**
format	for-ma-t	*HOO*/**GAR**/*HOO*
formation	for-ma-tion	*HOO*/*HAO*/*HOO*
former	for-mer	*HOO*/*HDO*
formidable	for-mi-da-ble	*HOO*/**GAR**/**GAR**/*HOO*
formula	for-mu-la	*HOO*/*HOO*/**GAR**
formulate	for-mu-la-te	*HOO*/*HOO*/*HAO*/*HDO*
fort	for-t	*HOO*/*HDO*
forth	for-th	*HOO*/*HTO*
fortification	for-ti-fi-ca-tion	*HOO*/**GAR**/**GAR**/*HAO*/*HOO*
fortify	for-ti-fy	*HOO*/**GAR**/**GRR**
fortitude	for-ti-tu-de	*HOO*/**GAR**/*HOO*/*HDO*
fortnight	for-t-nigh-t	*HOO*/*HOO*/**GRR**/*HDO*
fortress	for-tre-ss	*HOO*/**GAR**/*HDO*
fortuitous	for-tu-i-tous	*HOO*/*HOO*/**GAR**/*HAO*
fortunate	for-tu-na-te	*HOO*/*HOO*/*HAO*/*HDO*
fortune	for-tu-ne	*HOO*/*HOO*/**GDR**

Word	Mouthables	Mouth Movements Notations
forty	for-ty	*HOO*/**GAR**
forward	for-war-d	*HAO*/**GAR**/*HDO*
forward	for-war-d	*HOO/HAO/HOO*
forwards	for-war-ds	*HOO/HAO/HDO*
fossil	fo-ssi-l	*HAO*/**GAR/GDR**
fossilize	fo-ssi-li-ze	*HAO*/**GAR/GRR**/*HDO*
foster	fo-ster	*HAO/HDO*
fought	fough-t	*HOO/HOO*
foul	fou-l	**GAR/GDR**
found	foun-d	*HAO/HOO*
foundation	fou-n-da-tion	*HAO*/**GDR**/*HAO/HOO*
foundry	foun-dry	*HAO/HDO*
fountain	fou-n-tai-n	*HAO*/**GDR**/*HAO*/**GDR**
four	fo-ur	*HOO/HDO*
fourteen	four-tee-n	*HOO*/**GRR/GDR**
fourth	four-th	*HDO/HTO*
fowl	fow-l	*HAO/HDO*
fox	fo-x	*HAO*/**GDR**
foyer	foy-er	*HAO/HAO*
fraction	fra-c-tion	**GAR/GDR**/*HOO*
fractious	fra-c-ti-ous	**GAR/GDR/GDR/GAR**
fracture	fra-c-tu-re	**GAR/GDR**/*HOO/HDO*
fragile	fra-gi-le	**GAR/GRR/GDR**
fragment	fra-g-me-nt	**GAR/GDR/GAR/GDR**
fragmentary	fra-g-me-n-tar-y	**GAR/GDR/GAR/GDR**/*HAOHDO*
fragrancy	fra-gra-n-cy	*HAO*/**GAR/GDR/GAR**
fragrant	fra-gra-nt	*HAO*/**GAR/GDR**
frail	frai-l	*HAO*/**GDR**
frame	fra-me	*HAO/HDO*
franc	fra-n-c	**GAR/GDR/GDR**
France	Fran-ce	*HAO*/**GDR**

Word	Mouthables	Mouth Movements Notations
Francis	Fran-ci-s	*HAO*/**GAR**/*HDO*
frank	fran-k	**GAR/GDR**
frankly	fran-k-ly	**GAR/GDR/GAR**
frantic	fra-n-ti-c	**GAR/GDR/GAR/GDR**
fraternize	fra-ter-ni-ze	**GAR**/*HAO*/**GRR/GDR**
fraud	frau-d	*HOO*/*HOO*
fraudulent	frau-du-le-nt	*HOO*/*HOO*/**GAR/GDR**
fraught	frau-ght	*HOO*/*HOO*
fray	fray	*HAO*
freak	frea-k	**GRR/GDR**
free	free	**GRR**
freedom	free-do-m	**GRR**/*HAO*/*HDO*
freeze	free-ze	**GRR/GRR**
freight	freigh-t	*HAO*/*HDO*
freighter	freigh-ter	*HAO*/*HDO*
French	Fre-n-ch	**GAR/GDR**/*HDO*
frequency	fre-que-ncy	**GRR/GAR/GDR**
frequent	fre-quen-t	**GRR/GRR**/*HDO*
fresh	fre-sh	**GAR**/*HDO*
freshen	fre-shen	**GAR**/*HDO*
fresher	fre-sher	**GAR**/*HDO*
fret	fre-t	**GAR**/*HOO*
friar	fri-ar	**GRR**/*HAO*
friction	fri-c-tion	**GAR/GDR**/*HOO*
Friday	Fri-day	**GRR**/*HAO*
fridge	frid-ge	**GAR**/*HDO*
friend	fr(i)e n-d	**GAR/GDR**/*HOO*
friendly	fr(i)e-n-dly	**GAR/GDR/GDR**
friendship	fr(i)e-n-d-shi-p	**GAR/GDR**/*HDO*/**GAR**/*HDO*
frieze	fr(i)e-ze	**GRR/GDR**
fright	frigh-t	**GRR**/*HOO*

Word	Mouthables	Mouth Movements Notations
frightful	frigh-t-ful	**GRR**/*HOO*/*HDO*
frigid	fri-gi-d	**GAR/GAR**/*HDO*
fringe	fri-nge	**GAR/GDR**
frisk	fri-sk	**GAR/GDR**
frisky	fri-sky	**GAR/GAR**
fritter	fri-tter	**GAR**/*HDO*
frivolous	fri-vo-lou-s	**GAR**/*HOO*/**GAR**/*HDO*
frizzy	fri-zzy	**GAR/GAR**
frog	fro-g	*HAO*/*HDO*
frolic	fro-li-c	*HAO*/**GAR/GDR**
from	fro-m	*HAO*/*HDO*
front	fro-nt	**GAR/GDR**
frontal	fro-n-tal	**GAR/GDR**/*HDO*
frontier	fro-n-ti-er	**GAR/GDR/GAR**/*HDO*
frost	fro-st	*HAO*/*HDO*
frosted	fro-sted	*HAO*/**GRR**
froth	fr-o-th	*HAO*/*HTO*
frown	frow-n	**GAR/GDR**
froze	fro-ze	*HOO*/*HDO*
frozen	fro-ze-n	*HOO*/**GAR/GDR**
frugal	fru-gal	*HOO*/*HDO*
fruit	frui-t	*HOO*/*HOO*
frustrate	fru-stra-te	**GAR**/*HAO*/*HDO*
frustration	fru-stra-tion	**GAR**/*HAO*/*HOO*
fry	fry	**GRR**
fuck	fuc-k	**GAR**/*HDO*
fuddle	fu-ddle	**GAR**/*HOO*
fuel	fu-el	*HOO*/*HDO*
fugitive	fu-gi-ti-ve	*HOO*/**GAR/GAR/GDR**
full	ful-l	*HOO*/*HDO*
fumble	fu-m-ble	**GAR/GAR**/*HOO*

Word	Mouthables	Mouth Movements Notations
fume	fu-me	*HOO*/*HDO*
fumes	fu-me-s	*HOO*/*HDO*/**GDR**
fun	fu-n	**GAR/GDR**
function	fun-c-tion	**GAR/GDR**/*HOO*
funny	fun-ny	**GAR/GAR**
fur	fur	**GAR**
furious	fu-ri-ous	*HOO*/**GAR/GAR**
fury	fu-ry	*HOO*/**GDR**
fuse	fu-se	*HOO*/*HDO*
fuselage	fu-se-la-ge	*HOO*/**GAR/GAR**/*HDO*
fusion	fu-sion	*HOO*/*HOO*
fuss	fu-ss	**GAR/GDR**
fussy	fu-ssy	**GAR/GAR**
fustian	fu-sti-a-n	**GAR**/*HDO*/**GAR/GDR**
futile	fu-ti-le	*HOO*/**GRR/GDR**
future	fu-tu-re	*HOO*/*HOO*/*HDO*
fuzzy	fu-zzy	**GAR/GAR**

Word	Mouthables	Mouth Movements Notations
G		
G	G	*HOO*
G	**G**	**GRR**
gabble	ga-bble	**GAR**/*HOO*
gadget	gad-ge-t	**GAR**/**GAR**/*HOO*
gaffer	ga-ffer	**GAR**/*HDO*
gag	ga-g	**GAR**/*HDO*
gaga	ga-ga	*HDO*/*HDO*
gain	gai-n	*HAO*/**GDR**
gait	gai-t	*HAO*/*HOO*
gaity	ga-i-ty	*HAO*/**GAR**/**GDR**
gale	ga-le	*HAO*/*HDO*
gallery	ga-lle-ry	**GAR**/**GAR**/**GDR**
gallon	ga-llo-n	**GAR**/*HAO*/*HDO*
gallop	ga-llo-p	**GAR**/*HAO*/*HDO*
gallows	ga-llo-ws	**GAR**/*HOO*/*HDO*
galore	ga-lo-re	**GAR**/*HOO*/*HDO*
gamble	ga-m-ble	**GAR**/*HDO*/*HOO*
gambling	ga-m-bling	**GAR**/*HDO*/**GDR**
game	ga-me	*HAO*/*HDO*
gammon	ga-mmo-n	**GAR**/*HAO*/*HDO*
gang	gan-g	**GAR**/**GDR**
gangling	gan-g-ling	**GAR**/*HDO*/**GDR**
gap	ga-p	**GAR**/*HDO*
gape	ga-pe	*HAO*/*HDO*
gaping	ga-ping	*HAO*/**GDR**
Gar	Gar	**GAR**
garage	ga-ra-ge	**GAR**/*HAO*/*HDO*
garbage	gar-bage	**GAR**/*HDO*
garbled	gar-ble-d	**GAR**/*HOO*/*HOO*
garden	gar-den	**GAR**/*HDO*

Word	Mouthables	Mouth Movements Notations
gardening	gar-de-ning	GAR/GAR/GDR
gargle	gar-gle	*HAO/HOO*
garish	gar-i-sh	GAR/GAR/GDR
garland	gar-la-nd	*HAO*/GAR/GDR
garlic	gar-li-c	GAR/GAR/GDR
garment	gar-me-nt	GAR/GAR/GDR
garnish	gar-ni-sh	GAR/GAR/GDR
garett	ga-rre-t	GAR/GAR/*HOO*
garrulous	ga-rru-lous	GAR/*HOO*/GAR
garter	gar-ter	GAR/*HDO*
gas	ga-s	GAR/GDR
gash	ga-sh	GAR/*HDO*
gasoline	ga-so-li-ne	GAR/*HOO*/GAR/GDR
gassy	ga-ssy	GAR/GAR
gastronomy	ga-stro-no-my	GAR/*HOO/HAO*/GAR
gate	ga-te	*HAO/HDO*
gather	ga-ther	GAR/*HTO*
gathering	ga-the-ring	GAR/*HTO*/GDR
gaudy	gau-dy	*HOO*/GAR
gauge	gau-ge	*HAO/HDO*
gauze	gau-ze	*HOO*/GDR
gave	ga-ve	*HAO*/GRR
gay	gay	*HAO*
gaze	ga-ze	*HAO*/GRR
gazelle	ga-ze-lle	GAR/GAR/GDR
gazette	ga-ze-tte	GAR/GAR/*HDO*
gear	ge-a-r	GRR/*HAO/HDO*
geese	gee-se	GRR/*HDO*
gel	ge-l	GAR/GDR
gelatine	ge-la-ti-ne	GAR/GAR/GAR/GDR
gem	ge-m	GAR/GDR

Word	Mouthables	Mouth Movements Notations
gender	ge-n-der	**GAR/GDR**/*HDO*
genealogical	ge-ne-a-lo-gi-cal	**GRR/GRR/GAR**/*HAO*/**GAR**/*HDO*
general	ge-n-eral	**GAR/GDR**/*HDO*
generalize	ge-ne-ra-li-ze	**GAR/GAR/GAR/GRR/GDR**
generate	ge-ne-ra-te	**GAR/GAR**/*HAO*/*HDO*
generation	ge-ne-ra-tion	**GAR/GAR**/*HAO*/*HOO*
generic	ge-ne-ri-c	**GAR/GAR/GAR/GDR**
generosity	ge-ne-ro-si-ty	**GAR/GAR**/*HAO*/**GAR/GAR**
generous	ge-ne-rous	**GAR/GAR**/*HAO*
genetics	ge-ne-ti-cs	**GAR/GAR/GAR/GDR**
Geneva	Ge-ne-va	**GRR/GRR/GAR**
genial	ge-ni-a-l	**GRR/GAR/GAR/GDR**
genius	ge-ni-u-s	**GRR/GAR/GAR/GDR**
gent	ge-nt	**GAR/GDR**
gentle	gen-tle	**GAR**/*HOO*
gentleman	gen-tle-ma-n	**GAR**/*HOO*/**GAR/GDR**
genuine	gen-u-i-ne	**GAR**/*HOO*/**GAR/GDR**
geography	ge-o-gra-phy	**GRR**/*HAO*/**GAR**/*HDO*
geology	ge-o-lo-gy	**GRR**/*HAO*/*HOO*/*HDO*
geometry	ge-o-me-try	**GRR**/*HAO*/**GAR**/*HDO*
geranium	ge-ra-ni-um	**GAR**/*HAO*/**GAR**/*HDO*
geriatrician	ge-ri-a-tri-cian	**GAR/GAR/GAR/GAR**/*HDO*
geriatrics	ge-ri-a-tri-cs	**GAR/GAR/GAR/GAR/GDR**
germ	ger-m	*HOO*/*HDO*
German	Ger-ma-n	*HOO*/**GAR/GDR**
Germany	Ger-ma-ny	*HOO*/**GAR/GAR**
germicidal	ger-mi-ci-dal	*HOO*/**GAR/GRR**/*HDO*
germinal	ger-mi-nal	*HOO*/**GAR**/*HDO*
germinate	ger-mi-na-te	*HOO*/**GAR**/*HAO*/*HDO*
gesticulate	ge-sti-cu-la-te	**GAR/GAR**/*HOO*/*HAO*/*HDO*
gesture	ge-stu-re	**GAR**/*HOO*/*HDO*

Word	Mouthables	Mouth Movements Notations
get	ge-t	GAR/GRR
geyser	gey-ser	*HAO/HDO*
ghastly	ghas-t-ly	*HAO/HDO*/GDR
gherkin	gher-ki-n	*HOO*/GAR/GDR
ghetto	ghe-tto	GAR/*HOO*
ghost	gho-st	*HOO/HOO*
ghosts	gho-sts	*HOO/HDO*
giant	gi-a-nt	GRR/GAR/GDR
gibberish	gi-bber-i-sh	GAR/*HDO*/GAR/*HDO*
gibe	gi-be	GRR/*HDO*
giblets	gi-b-le-ts	GAR/*HDO*/GAR/GDR
giddy	gi-ddy	GAR/GAR
gift	gi-ft	GAR/*HDO*
gifted	gi-fted	GAR/GRR
giggle	gi-ggle	GAR/*HOO*
gild	gi-ld	GAR/*HDO*
gilt	gi-l-t	GAR/GDR/*HDO*
gimmick	gi-mmi-ck	GAR/GAR/*HDO*
gin	gi-n	GAR/GDR
ginger	gi-n-ger	GAR/GDR/*HDO*
gingerly	gi-n-ger-ly	GAR/GDR/*HOO*/GDR
gipsy	gi-p-sy	GAR/*HDO*/GAR
giraffe	gi-raf-fe	GAR/*HAO/HDO*
girder	gir-der	*HOO/HDO*
girdle	gir-dle	*HOO/HOO*
girl	gir-l	*HOO/HDO*
girlish	gir-li-sh	*HAO*/GAR/*HDO*
giro	gi-ro	GRR/*HOO*
gist	gi-st	GAR/*HDO*
give	gi-ve	GAR/GRR
given	gi-ven	GAR/*HDO*

Word	Mouthables	Mouth Movements Notations
glacier	gla-ci-er	*HAO*/**GDR**/*HDO*
glad	gla-d	**GAR**/*HDO*
gladden	gla-dden	**GAR**/*HDO*
gladly	gla-d-ly	**GAR**/*HDO*/**GDR**
glamorous	gla-mo-rous	**GAR/GAR/GAR**
glamour	gla-mour	**GAR/GAR**
glance	glan-ce	*HAO*/**GDR**
glancing	glan-cing	*HAO*/**GDR**
glare	glare	**GAR**
glass	glas-s	*HAO*/*HDO*
glassy	glas-sy	*HAO*/**GAR**
glaze	gla-ze	*HAO*/**GDR**
glazier	gla-zi-er	*HAO*/**GAR**/*HDO*
gleam	glea-m	**GRR**/*HDO*
glean	glea-n	**GRR/GDR**
glib	gli-b	**GAR**/*HDO*
glide	gli-de	**GRR**/*HDO*
glider	gli-der	**GRR**/*HDO*
glimmer	gli-mmer	**GAR**/*HDO*
glimpse	glim-pse	**GAR/GDR**
glisten	gli-sten	**GAR**/*HDO*
glitter	gli-tter	**GAR**/*HDO*
gloat	gloa-t	*HOO*/*HOO*
global	glo-bal	*HOO*/*HDO*
globe	glo-be	*HOO*/*HDO*
gloominess	gloo-mi-ne-ss	*HOO*/**GAR/GAR/GDR**
gloomy	gloo-my	*HOO*/**GAR**
glorify	glor-i-fy	*HOO*/**GAR**/*HDO*
glorious	glor-i-ous	*HOO*/**GAR**/*HAO*
glory	glor-y	*HOO*/**GAR**
gloss	glo-ss	*HAO*/*HDO*

Word	Mouthables	Mouth Movements Notations
glossary	glo-ssa-ry	*HAO*/**GAR**/**GDR**
glossy	glo-ssy	*HAO*/**GAR**
glove	glo-ve	**GAR**/*HDO*
gloved	glo-ve-d	**GAR**/*HOO*/*HOO*
glow	glo-w	*HOO*/*HDO*
glue	glue	*HOO*
glum	glu-m	**GAR**/*HDO*
glut	glu-t	**GAR**/*HOO*
glutton	glu-tto-n	**GAR**/*HAO*/*HDO*
gnat	gna-t	**GAR**/*HDO*
gnaw	gnaw	*HOO*
gnome	gno-me	*HOO*/*HDO*
go	go	*HOO*
goal	goa-l	*HOO*/*HDO*
goat	goa-t	*HOO*/*HDO*
gobble	go-bble	*HAO*/*HOO*
god	go-d	*HAO*/*HDO*
godly	go-d-ly	*HAO*/*HDO*/**GDR**
goes	go-es	*HOO*/*HDO*
going	go-ing	*HOO*/**GDR**
gold	go-ld	*HOO*/*HDO*
golden	go-lden	*HOO*/**GDR**
goldfish	go-ld-fi-sh	*HOO*/*HDO*/**GAR**/*HDO*
golf	go-lf	*HAO*/*HDO*
gone	go-ne	*HAO*/*HDO*
good	goo-d	*HOO*/*HDO*
goodbye	goo-d-bye	*HOO*/*HDO*/**GRR**
goody	goo-dy	*HOO*/**GAR**
google	goo-gle	*HAO*/*HOO*
googles	goo-gles	*HAO*/*HDO*
Google	Goo-gle	*HOO*/*HOO*

Word	Mouthables	Mouth Movements Notations
goose	goo-se	*HOO/HDO*
gorge	gor-ge	*HOO/HDO*
gorgeous	gor-ge-ous	*HOO*/**GAR/GAR**
gorilla	go-ri-lla	*HAO*/**GAR/GAR**
gormless	gor-m-le-ss	*HOO/HDO*/**GAR/GDR**
gory	go-ry	*HAO*/**GAR**
gosh	go-sh	*HAO/HDO*
gospel	go-spel	*HAO/HDO*
gossip	go-ssi-p	*HAO*/**GAR/GDR**
got	go-t	*HAO/HOO*
Gothic	Go-th-i-c	*HAO*/**GTR/GAR/GDR**
gotten	go-tte-n	*HAO*/**GAR/GDR**
gourd	gour-d	*HOO/HDO*
govern	go-ver-n	**GAR**/*HOO*/**GDR**
governess	go-ver-ne-ss	**GAR**/*HOO*/**GAR/GDR**
gradation	gra-da-tion	**GAR**/*HAO/HOO*
grade	gra-de	*HAO/HDO*
gradient	gra-di-e-nt	*HAO*/**GAR/GAR/GDR**
graduate	gra-du-a-te	**GAR**/*HOO/HAO*/**GDR**
grain	grai-n	*HAO*/**GDR**
gram	gra-m	**GAR**/*HDO*
grammar	gra-mmar	**GAR/GDR**
grammatical	gra-mma-ti-cal	**GAR/GAR/GAR**/*HDO*
gramme	gra-mme	**GAR**/*HDO*
granary	gra-nar-y	**GAR**/*HAO*/**GAR**
grand	gran-d	**GAR**/*HOO*
granite	gra-ni-te	**GAR/GAR**/*HDO*
grant	gran-t	*HAO/HOO*
grape	gra-pe	*HAO/HDO*
graph	gra-ph	*HAO/HDO*
graphic	gra-ph-i-cs	**GAR**/*HDO*/**GAR/GDR**

Word	Mouthables	Mouth Movements Notations
grapple	gra-pple	**GAR**/*HOO*
grasp	gras-p	*HAO*/*HDO*
grasping	gra-sp-ing	*HAO*/*HDO*/**GDR**
grass	gras-s	*HAO*/*HDO*
grate	gra-te	*HAO*/*HOO*
grateful	gra-te-ful	*HAO*/*HOO*/*HOO*
gratiful	gra-ti-fy	**GAR/GAR/GRR**
gratitude	gra-ti-tu-de	**GAR/GAR**/*HOO*/*HDO*
gratuitous	gra-tu-i-tous	**GAR**/*HOO*/**GAR/GAR**
gratuity	gra-tu-i-ty	**GAR**/*HOO*/**GAR/GAR**
grave	gra-ve	*HAO*/*HDO*
gravel	gra-vel	**GAR**/*HDO*
gravitate	gra-vi-ta-te	**GAR/GAR**/*HAO*/*HDO*
gravy	gra-vy	*HAO*/*HDO*
gray	gray	*HAO*
graze	gra-ze	*HAO*/*HOO*
graze	gra-ze	*HAO*/**GRR**
grease	grea-se	**GRR/GDR**
greasy	grea-sy	**GRR/GAR**
great	grea-t	*HAO*/*HOO*
greatly	grea-t-ly	*HAO*/*HOO*/**GDR**
Grecian	Gre-cian	**GRR**/*HDO*
Greece	Gree-ce	**GRR/GDR**
greed	gree-d	**GRR**/*HOO*
greedy	gree-dy	**GRR/GAR**
Greek	Gree-k	**GRR**/*HDO*
green	gree-n	**GRR/GDR**
greet	gree-t	**GRR**/*HOO*
greeting	gree-ting	**GRR/GDR**
grew	grew	*HOO*
grey	grey	*HAO*

Word	Mouthables	Mouth Movements Notations
grid	gri-d	**GAR**/*HDO*
grief	grie-f	**GAR**/*HDO*
grievance	grie-va-nce	**GAR/GAR/GDR**
grieve	grie-ve	**GAR**/*HDO*
grievous	grie-vou-s	**GAR/GAR**/*HDO*
grill	gri-ll	**GAR/GRR**
grille	gril-le	**GAR/GDR**
grim	gri-m	**GAR/GDR**
grimance	gri-ma-nce	**GAR/GAR/GDR**
grin	gri-n	**GAR/GRR**
grin	gri-n	**GAR/GDR**
grind	gri-nd	**GRR/GRR**
grinder	gri-n-der	**GRR/GDR**/*HDO*
grip	gri-p	**GAR/GRR**
grip	gri-p	**GAR/GDR**
grist	gri-st	**GAR/GDR**
grit	gri-t	**GAR**/*HOO*
grit	gri-ts	**GAR**/*HDO*
gritty	gri-tty	**GAR/GAR**
groan	groa-n	*HOO/HDO*
groat	groa-t	*HOO/HOO*
grocer	gro-cer	*HOO/HDO*
groggy	grog-gy	*HAO*/**GAR**
groin	groi-n	**GAR/GDR**
groom	groo-m	*HOO/HDO*
groove	groo-ve	*HOO/HDO*
grope	gro-pe	*HOO/HDO*
gross	gro-ss	*HOO/HDO*
grotesque	gro-te-sque	*HOO*/**GAR**/*HDO*
grouchy	grou-chy	**GAR/GAR**
ground	groun-d	*HAO/HOO*

Word	Mouthables	Mouth Movements Notations
ground	grou-n-d	*HAO/HDO/HOO*
grounding	grou-n-ding	*HAO/HDO*/**GDR**
group	grou-p	*HOO/HDO*
grove	gro-ve	*HOO/HDO*
grow	gro-w	*HOO/HOO*
growl	grow-l	**GAR/GDR**
grown	grow-n	*HOO*/**GDR**
growth	grow-th	*HOO/HTO*
grub	gru-b	**GAR**/*HDO*
grubby	gru-bby	**GAR/GAR**
grudge	gru-dge	**GAR**/*HDO*
gruelling	grue-lling	*HOO*/**GDR**
gruesome	grue-so-me	*HOO/HAO/HDO*
gruff	gru-ff	**GAR**/*HDO*
grumble	gru-m-ble	**GAR**/*HDO/HOO*
grumpy	gru-m-py	**GAR**/*HDO*/**GAR**
grunt	gru-nt	**GAR/GDR**
guage	gau-ge	*HAO/HDO*
guarantee	gua-ra-n-tee	**GAR/GAR/GDR/GRR**
guarantor	gua-ra-n-tor	**GAR/GAR/GDR**/*HOO*
guard	guar-d	**GAR**/*HOO*
guarded	guar-ded	**GAR/GRR**
guardian	guar-di-a-n	**GAR/GAR/GAR/GDR**
guardianship	guar-di-a-n-shi-p	**GAR/GAR/GAR/GDR/GDR**/*HDO*
guerrilla	guer-ri-lla	**GAR/GAR/GAR**
guess	gue-ss	**GAR**/*HDO*
guest	gue-st	**GAR**/*HOO*
guidance	gui-da-nce	**GRR/GAR/GDR**
guide	gui-de	**GRR**/*HDO*
guild	gui-ld	**GAR**/*HDO*
guile	gui-le	**GRR/GDR**

Word	Mouthables	Mouth Movements Notations
guilt	gui-l-t	**GAR/GDR**/*HDO*
guilty	gui-l-ty	**GAR/GDR/GAR**
guise	gui-se	**GRR/GDR**
guitar	gui-tar	**GAR**/*HAO*
gulf	gu-l-f	**GAR/GDR**/*HDO*
gull	gul-l	**GAR/GDR**
gullible	gul-li-ble	**GAR/GAR**/*HOO*
gulp	gu-lp	**GAR**/*HDO*
gum	gu-m	**GAR**/*HDO*
gumption	gu-mp-tion	**GAR**/*HDO*/*HOO*
gun	gu-n	**GAR/GDR**
gunwale	gu-n(wa)le	**GAR**/*HDO*/*HDO*
gurgle	gur-gle	*HOO*/*HOO*
gush	gu-sh	**GAR**/*HDO*
gushing	gu-shing	**GAR/GDR**
gust	gu-st	**GAR**/*HDO*
guts	gu-ts	**GAR**/*HDO*
gutter	gu-tter	**GAR**/*HDO*
guy	guy	**GRR**
gym	gy-m	**GAR/GDR**
gymnasium	gy-m-na-si-um	**GAR/GDR**/*HAO*/**GAR**/*HDO*
gymnastics	gy-m-na-sti-cs	**GAR/GDR/GAR/GAR/GDR**
gynaecologist	gy-nae-co-lo-gi-st	**GRR/GAR**/*HAO*/*HOO*/**GAR/GDR**
gypsy	gy-p-sy	**GAR/GDR/GAR**

Word	Mouthables	Mouth Movements Notations
H		
H	H	*HAO/HDO*
haberdashery	ha-ber-da-she-ry	**GAR**/*HDO*/**GAR**/*HOO*/*HDO*
habit	ha-bi-t	**GAR/GAR/GDR**
habitable	ha-bi-ta-ble	**GAR/GAR/GAR**/*HOO*
hack	ha-ck	**GAR**/*HDO*
hacker	ha-cker	**GAR**/*HDO*
hackney	ha-ck-ney	**GAR**/*HDO*/*HAO*
hackneyed	ha-ck-neye-d	**GAR**/*HDO*/*HAO*/*HOO*
had	ha-d	**GAR/GRR**
haggard	ha-ggar-d	**GAR/GAR**/*HDO*
hail	hai-l	*HAO/HDO*
hair	hair	*HAO*
hairy	hai-ry	*HAO*/**GDR**
hale	ha-le	*HAO/HDO*
half	hal-f	*HAO/HDO*
hall	hall	*HOO*
hallow	ha-llo-w	**GAR**/*HOO*/*HDO*
hallowed	ha-llo-we-d	**GAR**/*HOO*/*HOO*/*HOO*
halloween	ha-llo-wee-n	**GAR**/*HOO*/**GRR/GDR**
halo	ha-lo	*HAO/HOO*
halt	hal-t	*HOO/HOO*
halting	hal-ting	*HOO*/**GDR**
halucination	ha-llu-ci-na-tion	**GAR**/*HOO*/**GAR**/*HAO/HOO*
halve	hal-ve	*HAO/HDO*
ham	ha-m	**GAR**/*HDO*
hamlet	ha-m-le-t	**GAR**/*HDO*/**GAR/GDR**
hammer	ha-mmer	**GAR**/*HDO*
hammock	ha-mm-o-ck	**GAR**/*HDO*/*HAO*/*HDO*
hamper	ham-per	**GAR**/*HDO*
hamper	ha-m-per	**GAR/GDR**/*HDO*

Word	Mouthables	Mouth Movements Notations
hamster	ha-m-ster	GAR/GDR/*HDO*
hand	ha-nd	GAR/GDR
handle	han-dle	GAR/HOO
handy	han-dy	GAR/GAR
hang	ha-ng	GAR/GRR
hangar	han-gar	GAR/*HAO*
hank	ha-nk	GAR/GDR
hanky	han-ky	GAR/GAR
haphazard	ha-p-ha-zar-d	GAR/GDR/GAR/GAR/*HOO*
happen	ha-ppe-n	GAR/GAR/*HDO*
happening	ha-ppe-n-ing	GAR/GDR/GDR
happy	ha-ppy	GAR/GAR
harangue	ha-ran-gue	GAR/GAR/*HDO*
harass	ha-ra-ss	GAR/GAR/*HDO*
harassment	ha-ra-ss-me-nt	GAR/GAR/*HDO*/GAR/GDR
harbour	har-bour	*HAO/HAO*
hard	har-d	GAR/*HOO*
harden	har-den	GAR/*HDO*
hardly	har-d-ly	GAR/*HDO*/GDR
hardy	har-dy	GAR/*HDO*
haricot	ha-ri-cot	GAR/GAR/*HOO*
hark	har-k	*HAO/HDO*
harm	har-m	GAR/*HDO*
harmful	har-m-ful	GAR/*HDO/HOO*
harmless	har-m-le-ss	GAR/*HDO*/GAR/GDR
harmonious	har-mo-ni-ou-s	*HAO/HOO*/GAR/GAR/*HDO*
harmony	har-mo-ny	*HAO/HAO*/GAR
harness	har-ne-ss	*HAO*/GAR/*HDO*
harp	har-p	*HAO/HDO*
harpoon	har-poo-n	*HAO/HOO*/GDR
harrowing	har-ro-wi-ng	GAR/*HOO*/GAR/GDR

Word	Mouthables	Mouth Movements Notations
harsh	har-sh	**GAR**/*HDO*
harvest	har-ve-st	*HAO*/**GAR**/*HOO*
hash	ha-sh	**GAR**/*HDO*
hassle	ha-ss-le	**GAR**/*HOO*/*HDO*
haste	ha-ste	*HAO*/*HOO*
hasten	ha-sten	*HAO*/*HDO*
hat	ha-t	**GAR**/*HOO*
hatch	ha-tch	**GAR**/*HDO*
hatchet	ha-tch-e-t	**GAR/GDR/GAR/GDR**
hate	ha-te	*HAO*/**GRR**
hateful	ha-te-ful	*HAO*/**GDR**/*HOO*
hatred	ha-tre-d	*HAO*/**GDR**/*HOO*
haughty	haugh-ty	*HOO*/**GAR**
haul	hau-l	*HOO*/*HDO*
haulage	hau-lage	*HOO*/*HDO*
haulier	hau-li-er	*HOO*/**GAR**/*HDO*
haunch	hau-nch	*HOO*/**GDR**
haunt	hau-nt	*HOO*/**GDR**
have	ha-ve	**GAR/GRR**
haven	ha-ven	*HAO*/*HDO*
havoc	ha-vo-c	**GAR**/*HOO*/**GDR**
hawk	haw-k	*HOO*/*HDO*
hawker	haw-ker	*HOO*/*HDO*
hawthorn	haw-thor-n	*HOO*/*HTO*/**GDR**
hay	hay	*HAO*
haystack	hay-sta-ck	*HAO*/**GAR**/*HDO*
haywire	hay-wi-re	*HAO*/**GRR/GDR**
hazard	ha-zar-d	**GAR/GAR**/*HOO*
hazardous	ha-zar-dou-s	**GAR/GAR/GAR**/*HDO*
haze	ha-ze	*HAO*/**GDR**
hazel	ha-zel	*HAO*/*HDO*

Word	Mouthables	Mouth Movements Notations
head	hea-d	**GAR**/*HOO*
header	hea-der	**GAR**/*HDO*
heading	hea-ding	**GAR/GDR**
heady	hea-dy	**GAR/GAR**
heal	hea-l	**GRR/GRR**
heal	hea-l	**GRR**/*HDO*
health	hea-l-th	**GAR/GDR/GTR**
healthy	hea-l-th-y	**GAR/GDR/GTR/GAR**
heap	hea-p	**GRR**/*HDO*
hear	he-ar	**GRR**/*HAO*
heard	hear-d	*HAO/HOO*
hearer	hea-rer	**GRR**/*HDO*
hearing	hea-ring	**GRR/GDR**
hearse	hear-se	*HOO/HDO*
heart	hear-t	**GAR/GDR**
hearten	hear-ten	**GAR**/*HDO*
hearth	hear-th	**GAR/GTR**
heartless	hear-t-le-ss	**GAR/GDR/GAR**/*HDO*
hearty	hear-ty	**GAR/GAR**
heat	hea-t	**GRR**/*HDO*
heated	hea-ted	**GRR/GRR**
heath	hea-th	**GRR/GTR**
heathen	hea-th-e-n	**GRR/GTR/GAR/GDR**
heather	hea-th-er	**GAR**/*HTO/HDO*
heating	hea-ting	**GRR/GDR**
heave	hea-ve	**GRR/GDR**
heaven	hea-ven	**GAR**/*HDO*
heavenly	hea-ven-ly	**GAR**/*HDO*/**GDR**
heavy	hea-vy	**GAR/GAR**
Hebrew	He-brew	**GRR**/*HOO*
heckle	hec-kle	**GAR**/*HOO*

Word	Mouthables	Mouth Movements Notations
hectare	he-c-tare	GAR/GDR/*HAO*
hectic	hec-ti-c	GAR/GAR/GDR
hector	hec-tor	GAR/*HOO*
hedge	hed-ge	GAR/*HDO*
heed	hee-d	GRR/*HOO*
heel	hee-l	GRR/*HDO*
hefty	he-f-ty	GAR/*HDO*/GAR
heifer	hei-fer	GAR/*HDO*
height	h(e)igh-t	GRR/*HOO*
heighten	h(e)igh-ten	GRR/*HDO*
heir	hei-r	GAR/*HDO*
heiress	hei-r-e-ss	GAR/*HDO*/GAR/GDR
held	he-ld	GAR/GRR
helicopter	he-li-co-p-ter	GAR/GAR/*HAO*/*HDO*/*HDO*
hell	he-ll	GAR/GDR
hellish	he-lli-sh	GAR/GAR/GDR
hello	he-llo	GAR/*HOO*
helm	he-l-m	GAR/GDR/*HDO*
helmet	he-l-me-t	GAR/GDR/GAR/*HDO*
help	he-l-p	GAR/GDR/*HDO*
helper	he-l-per	GAR/GDR/*HDO*
helpful	he-l-p-ful	GAR/GDR/*HDO*/*HDO*
helping	he-l-ping	GAR/GDR/GDR
helpless	he-l-p-le-ss	GAR/GDR/GAR/GDR
hem	he-m	GAR/*HDO*
hemisphere	he-mi-sphe-re	GAR/GAR/GRR/*HDO*
hemorrhage	he-mor-rha-ge	GAR/*HOO*/*HAO*/*HDO*
hemorrhoids	he-mor-rhoi-ds	GAR/*HOO*/GAR/*HDO*
hemp	he-mp	GAR/*HDO*
hen	he-n	GAR/GDR
her	her	*HAO*

Word	Mouthables	Mouth Movements Notations
herald	he-ra-l-d	**GAR/GAR/GDR**/*HOO*
herb	her-b	*HAO/HDO*
herbalist	her-ba-li-st	*HAO*/**GAR/GAR/GDR**
herbicide	her-bi-ci-de	*HAO*/**GAR/GRR**/*HDO*
herd	her-d	*HAO/HDO*
here	he-re	**GRR/GDR**
hereby	he-re-by	**GRR/GDR/GRR**
hereditary	he-re-di-ta-ry	**GAR/GAR/GAR**/*HAO/HDO*
heredity	he-re-di-ty	**GAR/GAR/GAR/GAR**
heresy	he-re-sy	**GAR/GAR/GAR**
heritage	he-ri-tage	**GAR/GAR**/*HDO*
hermitage	her-mi-ta-ge	*HAO*/**GAR**/*HAO/HDO*
hernia	her-ni-a	*HOO*/**GAR/GAR**
hero	he-ro	**GRR**/*HOO*
heroic	he-ro-i-c	**GRR**/*HOO*/**GAR/GDR**
heroin	he-ro-i-n	**GAR**/*HOO*/**GAR/GDR**
heroine	he-ro-i-ne	**GAR**/*HOO*/**GAR/GDR**
heroism	he-ro-i-sm	**GAR**/*HOO*/**GAR**/*HDO*
heron	her-o-n	*HAO/HAO/HDO*
herring	he-rring	**GAR/GDR**
hers	her-s	*HAO/HDO*
herself	her-se-l-f	*HAO*/**GAR/GDR**/*HDO*
hesitancy	he-si-ta-ncy	**GAR/GAR/GAR/GDR**
hesitant	he-si-ta-nt	**GAR/GAR/GAR/GDR**
hesitate	he-si-ta-te	**GAR/GAR**/*HAO/HDO*
hessian	he-ssi-a-n	**GAR/GAR/GAR/GDR**
heterogeneous	he-te-ro-ge-ne-ous	**GAR**/*HAO/HOO*/**GRR/GRR/GAR**
heterosexual	he-te-ro-se-xu-al	**GAR**/*HAO/HOO*/**GAR**/*HOO/HDO*
hew	hew	*HOO*
hey	hey	*HAO*
hi	hi	**GRR**

Word	Mouthables	Mouth Movements Notations
hibernate	hi-ber-na-te	**GRR**/*HAO*/*HAOHDO*
hibernation	hi-ber-na-tion	**GRR**/*HAO*/*HAO*/*HOO*
hiccough	hi-ccou-gh	**GAR/GAR**/*HDO*
hiccup	hi-ccu-p	**GAR/GAR**/*HDO*
hick	hi-ck	**GAR**/*HDO*
hid	hi-d	**GRR/GRR**
hidden	hi-dden	**GAR**/*HDO*
hide	hi-de	**GRR/GDR**
hideous	hi-de-ous	**GAR/GRR/GAR**
hierarchy	hie-rar-chy	**GRR**/*HAO*/**GAR**
hifi	hi-fi	**GRR/GRR**
high	hi-gh	**GRR**/*HDO*
hijack	hi-jac-k	**GRR/GAR**/*HDO*
hike	hi-ke	**GRR**/*HDO*
hilarious	hi-lar-i-ous	**GAR**/*HAO*/**GAR**/*HAO*
hill	hi-ll	**GAR**/*HDO*
hillock	hi-llo-ck	**GAR**/*HAO*/*HDO*
hilly	hi-lly	**GAR/GDR**
hilt	hi-l-t	**GAR/GDR**/*HDO*
him	hi-m	**GAR**/*HDO*
hind	hi-nd	**GRR/GDR**
hinder	hi-n-der	**GAR/GDR**/*HDO*
hindrance	hi-n-dra-nce	**GAR/GDR/GAR/GDR**
hinge	hi-n-ge	**GAR/GDR**/*HDO*
hint	hi-nt	**GAR/GDR**
hinterland	hin-ter-lan-d	**GAR**/*HDO*/**GAR**/*HOO*
hip	hi-p	**GAR**/*HDO*
hippo	hi-pp-o	**GAR**/*HDO*/*HOO*
hire	hi-re	**GRR**/*HDO*
hireing	hi-reing	**GRR**/*HDO*
his	hi-s	**GAR/GDR**

Word	Mouthables	Mouth Movements Notations
hiss	hi-ss	**GAR**/*HDO*
historian	hi-stor-i-an	**GAR**/*HOO*/**GAR/GDR**
historic	hi-sto-ri-c	**GAR**/*HAO*/**GAR/GDR**
historical	hi-sto-ri-cal	**GAR**/*HAO*/**GAR**/*HDO*
history	hi-sto-ry	**GAR**/*HOO*/**GDR**
hit	hi-t	**GAR**/*HOO*
hit	hi-t	**GAR**/*HDO*
hitch	hi-tch	**GAR**/*HDO*
hitech	hi-te-ch	**GRR/GAR**/*HDO*
hives	hi-ves	**GRR**/*HDO*
hoard	hoar-d	*HOO*/*HOO*
hoarder	hoar-der	*HOO*/*HDO*
hoarding	hoar-ding	*HOO*/**GDR**
hoarse	hoar-se	*HOO*/*HDO*
hoax	hoa-x	*HOO*/**GDR**
hob	ho-b	*HAO*/*HDO*
hobble	ho-bble	*HAO*/*HOO*
hobby	ho-bby	*HAO*/**GAR**
hoe	hoe	*HOO*
hog	ho-g	*HAO*/*HDO*
hoist	hoi-st	**GAR**/*HDO*
hold	ho-ld	*HOO*/*HOO*
hold	ho-ld	*HOO*/*HDO*
holder	ho-lder	*HOO*/*HDO*
holding	ho-lding	*HOO*/**GDR**
hole	ho-le	*HOO*/**GDR**
holiday	ho-li-day	*HAO*/**GAR**/*HAO*
Holland	Hol-lan-d	*HAO*/**GAR**/*HOO*
hollow	hol-lo-w	*HAO*/*HOO*/*HDO*
holly	hol-ly	*HAO*/**GDR**
holocaust	ho-lo-ca-st	*HAO*/*HOO*/**GAR**/*HOO*

Word	Mouthables	Mouth Movements Notations
holy	ho-ly	*HOO*/**GDR**
homage	ho-ma-ge	*HAO*/*HAO*/*HDO*
home	ho-me	*HOO*/*HDO*
homeless	ho-me-le-ss	*HOO*/*HDO*/**GAR**/**GDR**
homely	ho-me-ly	*HOO*/*HDO*/**GDR**
homeopathic	ho-me-o-pa-th-i-c	*HOO*/**GAR**/*HOO*/**GAR**/**GTR**/**GAR**/**GDR**
homosexual	ho-mo-se-xu-al	*HOO*/*HOO*/**GAR**/*HOO*/*HDO*
hone	ho-ne	*HOO*/**GDR**
honest	ho-ne-st	*HAO*/**GAR**/*HOO*
honesty	ho-ne-sty	*HAO*/**GAR**/**GDR**
honey	ho-ney	**GAR**/**GRR**
honour	ho-nour	*HAO*/*HAO*
honourable	ho-nour-a-ble	*HAO*/*HAO*/**GAR**/*HOO*
hoo	hoo	*HOO*
hood	hoo-d	*HOO*/*HOO*
hoof	hoo-f	*HOO*/*HDO*
hook	hoo-k	*HOO*/*HDO*
hooked	hoo-ke-d	*HOO*/**GDR**/*HOO*
hooli-gan	hoo-li-ga-n	*HOO*/**GAR**/**GAR**/**GDR**
hoop	hoo-p	*HOO*/*HDO*
hoot	hoo-t	*HOO*/*HOO*
hooter	hoo-ter	*HOO*/*HDO*
hooves	hoo-ves	*HOO*/*HDO*
hop	ho-p	*HAO*/*HDO*
hope	ho-pe	*HOO*/*HDO*
hopeful	ho-pe-ful	*HOO*/*HDO*/*HDO*
hopeless	ho-pe-le-ss	*HOO*/*HDO*/**GAR**/**GDR**
horde	hor-de	*HOO*/*HDO*
horizon	ho-ri-zon	*HAO*/**GAR**/*HDO*
horizontal	ho-ri-zon-tal	*HAO*/**GAR**/*HAO*/*HDO*

Word	Mouthables	Mouth Movements Notations
hormone	hor-mo-ne	*HOO*/*HOO*/*HDO*
horn	hor-n	*HOO*/**GDR**
hornet	hor-ne-t	*HOO*/**GAR**/**GRR**
horoscope	ho-ro-sco-pe	*HAO*/*HOO*/*HOO*/*HDO*
horrible	hor-ri-ble	*HAO*/**GAR**/*HOO*
horrific	hor-ri-fi-c	*HAO*/**GAR**/**GAR**/**GDR**
horror	hor-ror	*HAO*/*HOO*
horse	hor-se	*HOO*/*HDO*
hose	ho-se	*HOO*/*HDO*
hosiery	ho-sie-ry	*HOO*/**GAR**/*HDO*
hospice	ho-spi-ce	*HAO*/**GAR**/**GDR**
hospitable	ho-spi-ta-ble	*HAO*/**GAR**/**GAR**/*HOO*
hospital	ho-spi-tal	*HAO*/**GAR**/*HDO*
hospitality	ho-spi-ta-li-ty	*HAO*/**GAR**/**GAR**/**GAR**/**GAR**
host	ho-st	*HOO*/*HOO*
host	ho-st	*HOO*/*HDO*
hostage	ho-st-a-ge	*HAO*/*HDO*/*HAO*/*HDO*
hostel	ho-stel	*HAO*/*HDO*
hostess	ho-ste-ss	*HOO*/**GAR**/**GDR**
hostile	ho-sti-le	*HAO*/**GRR**/*HDO*
hot	ho-t	*HAO*/*HDO*
hotel	ho-tel	*HOO*/**GDR**
hotelier	ho-te-li-er	*HOO*/**GAR**/**GAR**/*HDO*
hour	ho-ur	*HAO*/*HDO*
hourly	ho-ur-ly	*HAO*/*HDO*/**GDR**
house	hou-se	*HAO*/*HDO*
housewife	hou-se-wi-fe	*HAO*/*HDO*/**GRR**/*HDO*
housing	hou-sing	*HAO*/**GDR**
hovel	ho-vel	*HAO*/*HDO*
hover	ho-ver	*HAO*/*HDO*
hovercraft	ho-ver-cra-ft	*HAO*/*HDO*/**GAR**/*HDO*

Word	Mouthables	Mouth Movements Notations
how	how	*HAO*
however	how-e-ver	*HAO*/**GAR**/*HDO*
howl	ho-wl	*HAO*/*HDO*
howler	ho-w-ler	*HAO*/*HDO*/*HDO*
huddle	hu-ddle	**GAR**/*HOO*
hue	hue	*HOO*
huff	hu-ff	**GAR**/*HDO*
hug	hu-g	**GAR**/*HDO*
huge	hu-ge	*HOO*/*HDO*
hulk	hu-lk	**GAR**/*HDO*
hull	hu-ll	**GAR/GDR**
hum	hu-m	**GAR**/*HDO*
human	hu-ma-n	*HOO*/**GAR/GDR**
humane	hu-ma-ne	*HOO*/*HAO*/**GDR**
humanitarian	hu-ma-ni-tar-i-an	*HOO*/**GAR/GAR**/*HAO*/**GAR/GDR**
humble	hu-m-ble	**GAR**/*HDO*/*HOO*
humbug	hu-m-bu-g	**GAR**/*HDO*/**GAR**/*HDO*
humdrum	hu-m-dr-u-m	**GAR**/*HDO*/*HOO*/**GAR**/*HDO*
humid	hu-mi-d	*HOO*/**GAR**/*HOO*
humiliate	hu-mi-li-a-te	*HOO*/**GAR/GAR**/*HAO*/*HDO*
humility	hu-mi-li-ty	*HOO*/**GAR/GAR/GAR**
humming	hu-mm-ing	**GAR**/*HDO*/**GDR**
humour	hu-mour	*HOO*/*HAO*
hump	hu-mp	**GAR**/*HDO*
hunch	hu-nch	**GAR/GDR**
hundred	hu-n-dre-d	**GAR/GDR/GAR**/*HOO*
hung	hun-g	**GAR**/*HDO*
Hungarian	Hu-gar-i-an	**GAR**/*HAO*/**GAR/GDR**
Hungary	Hun-ga-ry	**GAR/GAR**/*HDO*
hunger	hun-ger	**GAR**/*HDO*
hungry	hun-g-ry	**GAR**/*HDO*/*HDO*

Word	Mouthables	Mouth Movements Notations
hunk	hun-k	**GAR**/*HDO*
hunt	hu-nt	**GAR/GRR**
hunt	hun-t	**GAR**/*HDO*
hunting	hun-ting	**GAR/GDR**
hurdle	hur-dle	*HAO/HOO*
huricane	hu-rri-ca-ne	**GAR/GAR**/*HAO*/**GDR**
hurl	hur-l	*HOO/HOO*
hurry	hur-ry	**GAR/GDR**
hurt	hur-t	**GAR**/*HOO*
hurt	hur-t	*HAO/HDO*
hurtful	hur-t-ful	*HAO/HOO/HDO*
hurtle	hur-tle	*HOO/HOO*
husband	hu-s-ban-d	**GAR/GDR/GAR**/*HOO*
hush	hu-sh	**GAR**/*HDO*
husk	hu-sk	**GAR**/*HDO*
husky	hu-sky	**GAR/GAR**
hustle	hu-stle	**GAR**/*HOO*
hut	hu-t	**GAR**/*HOO*
hutch	hu-tch	**GAR**/*HDO*
hyacinth	hy-a-ci-nth	**GRR/GAR/GAR/GTR**
hyaenas	hy-(a)e-na-s	**GRR/GRR/GAR/GDR**
hybrid	hy-bri-d	**GRR/GAR**/*HOO*
hydrangea	hy-dra-n-gea	**GRR**/*HAO*/**GDR/GDR**
hydraulic	hy-drau-li-c	**GRR**/*HOO*/**GAR/GDR**
hydro	hy-dro	**GRR**/*HOO*
hydrocarbon	hy-dro-car-bon	**GRR**/*HOO*/**GAR**/*HDO*
hydrofoil	hy-dro-foi-l	**GRR**/*HOO*/**GAR/GDR**
hydrogen	hy-dro-ge-n	**GRR**/*HOO*/**GAR/GDR**
hydroplane	hy-dro-pla-ne	**GRR**/*HOO/HAO*/**GDR**
hyena	hy-e-na	**GRR/GRR/GAR**
hygiene	hy-gie-ne	**GRR/GAR/GDR**

Word	Mouthables	Mouth Movements Notations
hygienic	hy-gie-ni-c	**GRR/GAR/GAR/GDR**
hymn	hy-mn	**GAR**/*HDO*
hype	hy-pe	**GRR**/*HDO*
hyper	hy-per	**GRR**/*HDO*
hypermarket	hy-per-mar-ke-t	**GRR**/*HAO*/*HAO*/**GAR/GDR**
hyphen	hy-ph-en	**GRR**/*HOO*/*HDO*
hyphenate	hy-ph-e-na-te	**GRR**/*HOO*/**GAR**/*HAO*/*HDO*
hypnosis	hy-p-no-si-s	**GAR**/*HDO*/*HOO*/**GAR/GDR**
hypocrisy	hy-po-cri-sy	**GAR**/*HAO*/**GAR/GAR**
hypocrite	hy-po-cri-te	**GAR**/*HOO*/**GAR**/*HDO*
hypocritical	hy-po-cri-ti-cal	**GAR**/*HOO*/**GAR/GAR**/*HDO*
hypothesis	hy-po-th-e-si-s	**GRR**/*HAO*/**GTR/GAR/GAR/GDR**
hypothetical	hy-po-th-e-ti-cal	**GRR/GAR/GTR/GAR/GAR**/*HDO*
hysteria	hy-ste-ri-a	**GAR/GRR/GAR/GAR**
hysterical	hy-ste-ri-cal	**GAR/GAR/GAR**/*HDO*
hysterics	hy-ste-ri-cs	**GAR/GAR/GAR/GDR**

Word	Mouthables	Mouth Movements Notations
I		
I	I	**GRR**
i	i	**GAR**
ice	i-ce	**GRR/GDR**
icon	i-co-n	**GRR/*HAO*/*HDO***
idea	i-de-a	**GRR/GRR/GAR**
ideal	i-de-al	**GRR/GRR/*HDO***
idealize	i-de-a-li-ze	**GRR/GRR/GAR/GRR/GDR**
identical	i-de-n-ti-cal	**GRR/GAR/GDR/GAR/*HDO***
identify	i-de-n-ti-fy	**GRR/GAR/GDR/GAR/GRR**
ideological	i-de-o-lo-gi-cal	**GRR/GRR/GAR/*HAO*/*HDO*/*HDO***
ideologist	i-de-o-lo-gi-st	**GRR/GRR/GAR/*HAO*/*HDO*/*HOO***
idiocy	i-di-o-cy	**GAR/GAR/*HAO*/GAR**
idiom	i-di-o-m	**GAR/GAR/*HAO*/*HDO***
idiomatic	i-di-o-ma-ti-c	**GAR/GAR/*HOO*/GAR/GAR/GDR**
idiot	i-di-o-t	**GAR/GAR/*HAO*/*HOO***
idle	i-dle	**GRR/*HOO***
idyll	i-dy-ll	**GRR/GAR/*HDO***
idyllic	i-dy-lli-c	**GRR/GAR/GAR/GDR**
if	i-f	**GAR/*HDO***
ignominious	i-g-no-mi-ni-ous	**GAR/*HDO*/GAR/GAR/GAR/GAR**
ignorant	i-g-no-ra-nt	**GAR/*HDO*/GAR/GAR/GDR**
ignore	i-g-no-re	**GAR/*HDO*/*HOO*/*HDO***
ilk	i-l-k	**GAR/GDR/*HDO***
ill	i-ll	**GAR/GDR**
illegal	i-lle-gal	**GAR/GRR/*HDO***
illegible	i-lle-gi-ble	**GAR/GAR/GAR/*HOO***
illegitimate	i-lle-gi-ti-ma-te	**GAR/GAR/GAR/GAR/*HAO*/*HDO***
illicit	i-lli-ci-t	**GAR/GAR/GAR/GRR**
illiterate	i-lli-te-ra-te	**GAR/GAR/*HAO*/*HAO*/*HDO***
illness	i-ll-ne-ss	**GAR/GDR/GAR/GDR**

Word	Mouthables	Mouth Movements Notations
illogical	i-llo-gi-cal	GAR/*HAO*/GAR/*HDO*
illuminate	i-llu-mi-na-te	GAR/*HOO*/GAR/*HAO*/*HDO*
illusion	i-llu-sion	GAR/*HOO*/*HOO*
illusory	i-llu-so-ry	GAR/*HOO*/GAR/*HDO*
illustrate	i-llu-stra-te	GAR/GAR/*HAO*/*HDO*
illustration	i-llu-stra-tion	GAR/GAR/*HAO*/*HOO*
illustrative	i-llu-stra-ti-ve	GAR/GAR/*HAO*/GAR/GDR
illustrious	i-llus-tri-ous	GAR/GAR/*HDO*/*HAO*
image	i-ma-ge	GAR/*HAO*/*HDO*
imagination	i-ma-gi-na-tion	GAR/GAR/GAR/*HAO*/*HOO*
imagine	i-ma-gi-ne	GAR/GAR/GAR/GDR
imbecile	i-m-be-ci-le	GAR/GDR/GAR/GAR/GDR
imbibe	i-m-bi-be	GAR/GDR/GRR/*HDO*
imitate	i-mi-ta-te	GAR/GAR/*HAO*/*HDO*
imitation	i-mi-ta-tion	GAR/GAR/*HAO*/*HOO*
immaculate	i-mma-cu-la-te	GAR/GAR/*HOO*/*HAO*/*HDO*
immature	i-mma-tu-re	GAR/GAR/*HOO*/*HDO*
immeasurable	i-mmea-su-ra-ble	GAR/GAR/*HOO*/GAR/*HOO*
immediacy	i-mme-di-a-cy	GAR/GRR/GAR/GAR/GDR
immediate	i-mme-di-a-te	GAR/GRR/GAR/*HAO*/*HOO*
immediately	i-mme-di-a-te-ly	GAR/GRR/GAR/*HAO*/*HDO*/GDR
immense	i-m-me-n-se	GAR/GDR/GAR/GDR/*HDO*
immerse	i-m-mer-se	GAR/GDR/*HAO*/*HDO*
immersion	i-m-mer-sion	GAR/GDR/*HAO*/*HOO*
immigrant	i-mmi-gra-nt	GAR/GAR/GAR/GDR
imminent	i-mmi-ne-nt	GAR/GAR/GAR/GDR
immobilize	i-mmo-bi-li-ze	GAR/*HOO*/GAR/GRR/GDR
immolate	i-mmo-la-te	GAR/*HOO*/*HAO*/GRR
immoral	i-mmo-ral	GAR/*HAO*/*HDO*
immemorial	i-mme-mor-i-al	GAR/GAR/*HOO*/GAR/*HDO*
immortal	i-mmor-tal	GAR/*HOO*/*HDO*

Word	Mouthables	Mouth Movements Notations
immortalize	i-mmor-ta-li-ze	**GAR**/*HOO*/**GAR**/**GRR**/**GDR**
immovable	i-mmo-va-ble	**GAR**/*HOO*/**GAR**/*HOO*
immune	i-mmu-ne	**GAR**/*HOO*/**GDR**
immunize	i-mmu-ni-ze	**GAR**/*HOO*/**GRR**/**GDR**
immutable	i-mmu-ta-ble	**GDR**/*HOO*/**GAR**/*HOO*
imp	i-mp	**GAR**/*HDO*
impact	i-m-pa-ct	**GAR**/**GDR**/**GAR**/*HOO*
impair	i-m-pair	**GAR**/**GDR**/*HAO*
impalpable	i-m-pa-l-pa-ble	**GAR**/**GDR**/**GAR**/**GDR**/**GAR**/*HOO*
impartial	i-m-par-tial	**GAR**/**GDR**/*HAO*/*HDO*
impassable	i-m-pas-sa-ble	**GAR**/**GDR**/*HAO*/**GAR**/*HOO*
impasse	i-m-pas-se	**GAR**/**GDR**/*HAO*/*HDO*
impassive	i-m-pas-si-ve	**GAR**/**GDR**/**GAR**/**GAR**/**GDR**
impatience	i-m-pa-ti-e-nce	**GAR**/**GDR**/*HAO*/*HDO*/**GAR**/**GDR**
impatient	i-m-pa-ti-e-nt	**GAR**/**GDR**/*HAO*/*HDO*/**GAR**/**GDR**
impeach	i-m-pea-ch	**GAR**/**GDR**/**GRR**/*HDO*
impeachment	i-m-pea-ch-me-nt	**GAR**/**GDR**/**GRR**/*HDO*/**GAR**/**GDR**
impeccable	i-m-pec-ca-ble	**GAR**/**GDR**/**GAR**/**GAR**/*HOO*
impede	i-m-pe-de	**GAR**/**GDR**/**GRR**/*HOO*
impel	i-m-pe-l	**GAR**/**GDR**/**GAR**/**GDR**
impenetrable	i-m-pe-ne-tra-ble	**GAR**/**GDR**/**GAR**/**GAR**/*HAO*/*HOO*
imperative	i-m-pe-ra-ti-ve	**GAR**/**GDR**/**GAR**/**GAR**/**GAR**/**GDR**
imperceptible	i-m-per-ce-p-ti-ble	**GAR**/**GDR**/*HAO*/**GAR**/**GDR**/**GAR**/*HOO*
imperfect	i-m-per-fec-t	**GAR**/**GDR**/*HAO*/**GAR**/*HOO*
imperfection	i-m-per-fec-tion	**GAR**/**GDR**/*HAO*/**GAR**/*HOO*
implicit	i-m-pli-ci-t	**GAR**/**GDR**/**GAR**/**GAR**/**GDR**
implore	i-m-plo-re	**GAR**/**GDR**/*HAO*/*HDO*
imply	i-m-ply	**GAR**/**GDR**/**GRR**
impolite	i-m-po-li-te	**GAR**/**GDR**/*HOO*/**GRR**/*HDO*
import	i-m-por-t	**GAR**/**GDR**/*HOO*/*HDO*

Word	Mouthables	Mouth Movements Notations
import	i-m-por-t-s	**GAR/GDR**/*HOO*/*HDO*/*HDO*
importance	i-m-por-ta-nce	**GAR/GDR**/*HOO*/**GAR/GDR**
important	i-m-por-ta-nt	**GAR/GDR**/*HOO*/**GAR/GDR**
importation	i-m-por-ta-tion	**GAR/GDR**/*HOO*/*HAO*/*HOO*
importer	i-m-por-ter	**GAR/GDR**/*HOO*/*HDO*
impose	i-m-po-se	**GAR/GDR**/*HOO*/*HDO*
imposing	i-m-po-sing	**GDR**/*HOO*/**GDR**
imposition	i-m-po-si-tion	**GAR/GDR**/*HOO*/**GAR**/*HOO*
impossible	i-m-pos-si-ble	**GAR/GDR**/*HAO*/**GAR**/*HOO*
impotent	i-m-po-te-nt	**GAR/GDR**/*HOO*/**GAR/GDR**
impracticable	i-m-prac-ti-ca-ble	**GAR/GDR/GAR/GAR/GAR**/*HOO*
imprecise	i-m-pre-ci-se	**GAR/GDR/GAR/GRR**/*HDO*
impregnate	i-m-pre-g-na-te	**GAR/GDR/GAR/GDR**/*HAO*/*HDO*
impress	i-m-pres-s	**GAR/GDR/GAR**/*HDO*
impression	i-m-pres-sion	**GAR/GDR/GAR**/*HOO*
impressive	i-m-pres-si-ve	**GAR/GDR/GAR/GAR/GDR**
imprint	i-m-prin-t	**GAR/GDR/GAR**/*HOO*
imprison	i-m-pri-so-n	**GAR/GDR/GAR**/*HAO*/*HDO*
improbable	i-m-pro-ba-ble	**GAR/GDR**/*HAO*/**GAR**/*HOO*
impromptu	i-m-pro-mp-tu	**GAR/GDR**/*HAO*/*HDO*/*HOO*
improper	i-m-pro-per	**GAR/GDR**/*HAO*/*HDO*
improve	i-m-pro-ve	**GAR/GDR**/*HOO*/*HDO*
improvisation	i-m-pro-vi-sa-tion	**GAR/GDR**/*HOO*/**GRR**/*HAO*/*HOO*
improvise	i-m-pro-vi-se	**GAR/GDR**/*HOO*/**GRR**/*HDO*
imprudent	i-m-pru-den-t	**GAR/GDR**/*HOO*/**GAR**/*HOO*
impulse	i-m-pu-l-se	**GAR/GDR/GAR/GDR**/*HDO*
impulsive	i-m-pu-l-si-ve	**GAR/GDR/GAR/GDR/GAR/GDR**
impure	i-m-pu-re	**GAR/GDR**/*HOO*/*HDO*
imputation	i-m-pu-ta-tion	**GAR/GDR**/*HOO*/*HAO*/*HOO*
in	i-n	**GAR/GDR**
inaccessible	i-n-a-cce-ssi-ble	**GAR/GDR/GAR/GAR/GAR**/*HOO*

Word	Mouthables	Mouth Movements Notations
inaccurate	i-n-a-ccu-ra-te	**GAR/GDR/GAR/***HOO/HAO/HDO*
inactive	i-n-ac-ti-ve	**GAR/GDR/GAR/GAR/***HDO*
inadequate	i-n-a-de-qua-te	**GAR/GDR/GAR/GAR/***HAO/HDO*
inadvisable	i-n-ad-vi-sa-ble	**GAR/GDR/GAR/GRR/GAR/***HOO*
inanimate	i-na-ni-ma-te	**GAR/GAR/GAR/***HAO/HDO*
inapplicable	i-na-ppli-ca-ble	**GAR/GAR/GAR/GAR/***HOO*
inaudible	i-n-au-di-ble	**GAR/GDR/***HOO/**GAR/***HOO*
inaugurate	i-n-au-gu-ra-te	**GAR/GDR/***HOO/HOO/HAO/HDO*
inauguration	i-n-au-gu-ra-tion	**GAR/GDR/***HOO/HOO/HAO/HOO*
inauspicious	i-n-au-spi-ci-ous	**GAR/GDR/***HOO/**GAR/***HDO/HAO*
inborn	i-n-bor-n	**GAR/GDR/***HOO/HDO*
inbred	i-n-bre-d	**GAR/GDR/GAR/***HOO*
incalculable	i-n-ca-l-cu-la-ble	**GAR/GDR/GAR/GDR/***HOO/**GAR/***HOO*
incandescent	i-n-ca-n-de-sce-nt	**GAR/GDR/GAR/GDR/GAR/GAR/GDR**
incapable	i-n-ca-pa-ble	**GAR/GDR/***HAO/**GAR/***HOO*
incarnation	i-n-car-na-tion	**GAR/GDR/GAR/***HAO/HOO*
incautious	i-n-cau-ti-ous	**GAR/GDR/***HOO/HDO/HAO*
incense	i-n-ce-nse	**GAR/GDR/GAR/GDR**
incentive	i-n-cen-ti-ve	**GAR/GDR/GAR/GAR/GDR**
incessant	i-n-ce-ssa-nt	**GAR/GDR/GAR/GAR/GDR**
inch	i-n-ch	**GAR/GDR/***HDO*
incident	i-n-ci-de-nt	**GAR/GDR/GAR/GAR/GDR**
incinerator	i-n-ci-ne-ra-tor	**GAR/GDR/GAR/GAR/***HAO/HOO*
incision	i-n-ci-sion	**GAR/GDR/GAR/***HOO*
incisive	i-n-ci-si-ve	**GAR/GDR/GRR/GAR/GDR**
incisor	i-n-ci-sor	**GAR/GDR/GRR/***HOO*
incite	i-n-ci-te	**GAR/GDR/GRR/***HDO*
incitement	i-n-ci-te-me-nt	**GAR/GDR/GRR/***HDO/**GAR/GDR**
inclement	i-n-cle-me-nt	**GAR/GDR/GAR/GAR/GDR**
incline	i-n-cli-ne	**GAR/GDR/GRR/GDR**

Word	Mouthables	Mouth Movements Notations
inclined	i-n-cli-ne-d	GAR/GDR/GRR/GDR/*HOO*
include	i-n-clu-de	GAR/GDR/*HOO*/*HOO*
inclusive	i-n-clu-si-ve	GAR/GDR/*HOO*/GAR/GDR
income	i-n-co-me	GAR/GDR/*HAO*/*HDO*
incoming	i-n-co-mi-ng	GAR/GDR/*HAO*/GAR/GDR
incomparable	i-n-co-m-pa-ra-ble	GAR/GDR/*HAO*/*HDO*/GAR/GAR/*HOO*
incompatible	i-n-co-m-pa-ti-ble	GAR/GDR/*HAO*/*HDO*/GAR/GAR/*HOO*
incompetent	i-n-co-m-pe-te-nt	GAR/GDR/*HAO*/*HDO*/GAR/GAR/GDR
incomplete	i-n-co-m-ple-te	GAR/GDR/*HAO*/*HDO*/GRR/*HDO*
incomprehensible	i-n-com-pre-he-n-si-ble	GAR/GDR/*HAO*/GRR/GAR/GDR/GAR/*HOO*
inconceivable	i-n-co-n-cei-va-ble	GAR/GDR/*HAO*/GDR/GRR/GAR/*HOO*
inconclusive	i-n-co-n-clu-si-ve	GAR/GDR/*HAO*/GDR/*HOO*/GAR/GDR
incongruous	i-n-con-gru-ous	GAR/GDR/*HAO*/*HOO*/*HAO*
inconsiderate	i-n-co-n-si-der-a-te	GAR/GDR/*HAO*/GDR/GAR/*HAO*/*HAO*/*HDO*
inconsistent	i-n-co-n-si-ste-nt	GAR/GDR/*HAO*/GDR/GAR/GAR/GDR
inconstant	i-n-co-n-sta-nt	GAR/GDR/*HAO*/GDR/GAR/GDR
inconvenience	i-n-co-n-ve-ni-e-nce	GAR/GDR/*HAO*/GDR/GRR/GAR/GAR/GDR
inconvenient	i-n-co-n-ve-ni-e-nt	GAR/GDR/*HAO*/GDR/GAR/GAR/GAR/GDR
incorporate	i-n-cor-po-ra-te	GAR/GDR/*HOO*/*HOO*/*HAO*/*HDO*
incorrect	i-n-cor-rec-t	GAR/GDR/*HOO*/GAR/*HOO*
incorrigible	i-n-cor-ri-gi-ble	GAR/GDR/*HOO*/GAR/GDR/*HOO*
incorrupt	i-n-cor-ru-pt	GAR/GDR/*HOO*/GAR/*HDO*
increase	i-n-crea-se	GAR/GDR/GRR/*HDO*

Word	Mouthables	Mouth Movements Notations
increased	i-n-crea-se-d	GAR/GDR/GRR/*HDO*/*HOO*
incredible	i-n-cre-di-ble	GAR/GDR/GAR/GAR/*HOO*
incredulous	i-n-cre-du-lous	GAR/GDR/GAR/*HOO*/GAR
increment	i-n-cre-me-nt	GAR/GDR/GRR/GAR/GDR
incriminate	i-n-cri-mi-na-te	GAR/GDR/GAR/GAR/*HAO*/GDR
incubate	i-n-cu-ba-te	GAR/GDR/*HOO*/*HAO*/*HOO*
incubator	i-n-cu-ba-tor	GAR/GDR/*HOO*/*HAO*/*HDO*
incumbent	i-n-cu-m-be-nt	GAR/GDR/GAR/*HDO*/GAR/GDR
incur	i-n-cur	GAR/GDR/*HAO*
incurable	i-n-cu-ra-ble	GAR/GDR/*HOO*/GAR/*HOO*
incursion	i-n-cur-sion	GAR/GDR/GAR/*HOO*
indebted	i-n-deb-ted	GAR/GDR/GAR/GRR
indecency	i-n-de-ce-ncy	GAR/GDR/GRR/GAR/GDR
indecent	i-n-de-ce-nt	GAR/GDR/GRR/GAR/GDR
indecision	i-n-de-ci-sion	GAR/GDR/GRR/GAR/*HOO*
indeed	i-n-dee-d	GAR/GDR/GRR/*HOO*
indefinable	i-n-de-fi-na-ble	GAR/GDR/GAR/GRR/GAR/*HOO*
indefinite	i-n-de-fi-ni-te	GAR/GDR/GAR/GAR/GAR/*HOO*
indelible	i-n-de-li-ble	GAR/GDR/*HAO*/GAR/*HOO*
indelicate	i-n-de-li-ca-te	GAR/GDR/GAR/GAR/*HAO*/*HDO*
indemnity	i-n-de-m-ni-ty	GAR/GDR/GAR/GDR/GAR/GAR
indent	i-n-den-t	GAR/GDR/GAR/*HOO*
independent	i-n-de-pen-de-nt	GAR/GDR/GAR/GAR/GDR
indepth	i-n-de-pth	GAR/GDR/GAR/*HTO*
indescribable	i-n-de-scri-ba-ble	GAR/GDR/GAR/GRR/GAR/*HOO*
indestructible	i-n-de-struc-ti-ble	GAR/GDR/GAR/GAR/GAR*HOO*
indeterminate	i-n-de-ter-mi-na-te	GAR/GDR/GAR/*HAO*/GAR/*HAO*/ *HDO*
index	i-n-de-x	GAR/GDR/GAR/GDR
India	I-n-di-a	GAR/GDR/GAR/GAR
Indian	I-n-di-a-n	GAR/GDR/GAR/GAR/GDR

Word	Mouthables	Mouth Movements Notations
indicate	i-n-di-ca-te	**GAR/GDR/GAR/**_HAO_/_HOO_
indicative	i-n-di-ca-ti-ve	**GAR/GDR/GAR/GAR/GAR/GDR**
indict	i-n-dic-t	**GAR/GDR/GRR/**_HOO_
indicted	i-n-dic-ted	**GAR/GDR/GRR/GRR**
indictment	i-n-dic-t-men-t	**GAR/GDR/GRR/**_HOO_/**GAR/**_HOO_
indifferent	i-n-di-ffe-re-nt	**GAR/GDR/GAR/**_HDO_/**GAR/GDR**
indigenous	i-n-di-ge-nous	**GAR/GDR/GAR/GAR/**_HAO_
indigestible	i-n-di-ge-sti-ble	**GAR/GDR/GAR/GAR/GAR/**_HOO_
indignant	i-n-di-g-na-nt	**GAR/GDR/GAR/GDR/GAR/GDR**
indignity	i-n-di-g-ni-ty	**GAR/GDR/GAR/GDR/GAR/GAR**
indirect	i-n-di-rec-t	**GAR/GDR/GAR/GAR/**_HOO_
indiscreet	i-n-di-scree-t	**GAR/GDR/GAR/GRR/**_HOO_
indispensable	i-n-di-spe-n-sa-ble	**GAR/GDR/GAR/GAR/GDR/GAR/**_HOO_
indisposed	i-n-di-spo-se-d	**GAR/GDR/GAR/**_HOO_/**GDR/**_HOO_
indistinct	i-n-di-sti-nct	**GAR/GDR/GAR/GAR/GDR**
individual	i-n-di-vi-du-al	**GAR/GDR/GAR/GAR/**_HOO_/_HDO_
indivisible	i-n-di-vi-si-ble	**GAR/GDR/GAR/GAR/GAR/**_HOO_
indolent	i-n-do-le-nt	**GAR/GDR/**_HOO_/**GAR/GDR**
Indonesian	In-do-ne-si-an	**GAR/GDR/**_HOO_/**GRR/GAR/GDR**
indoor	i-n-door	**GAR/GDR/**_HOO_
indoors	i-n-door-s	**GAR/GDR/**_HOO_/_HDO_
induce	i-n-du-ce	**GAR/GDR/**_HOO_/**GDR**
inducement	i-n-du-ce-me-nt	**GAR/GDR/**_HOO_/**GDR/GAR/GDR**
induction	i-n-duc-tion	**GAR/GDR/GAR/**_HOO_
inductive	i-n-duc-ti-ve	**GAR/GDR/GAR/GAR/GDR**
indulge	i-n-du-l-ge	**GAR/GDR/GAR/GDR/**_HDO_
indulgent	i-n-du-l-ge-nt	**GAR/GDR/GAR/GDR/GAR/GDR**
industrial	i-n-du-stri-al	**GAR/GDR/GAR/GDR/**_HDO_
industrialist	i-n-du-stri-a-li-st	**GAR/GDR/GAR/GDR/GAR/GAR/**_HDO_
industrious	i-n-du-stri-ous	**GAR/GDR/GAR/GDR/**_HAO_

Word	Mouthables	Mouth Movements Notations
industry	i-n-du-stry	**GAR/GDR/GAR/***HDO*
inedible	i-n-e-di-ble	**GAR/GDR/GAR/GAR/***HOO*
ineffable	i-n-e-ffa-ble	**GAR/GDR/GAR/GAR/***HOO*
inefficient	i-n-e-ffi-ci-e-nt	**GAR/GDR/GAR/GAR/GAR/GDR**
ineptitude	i-n-e-pti-tu-de	**GAR/GDR/GAR/GAR/***HOO/HDO*
inert	i-ner-t	**GAR/***HAO/HOO*
inestimable	i-n-e-sti-ma-ble	**GAR/GDR/GAR/GAR/GAR/***HOO*
inevitable	i-n-e-vi-ta-ble	**GAR/GDR/GAR/GAR/GAR/***HOO*
inexhaustible	i-n-ex-hau-sti-ble	**GAR/GDR/GDR/***HOO/***GAR/***HOO*
inexpensive	i-n-ex-pe-n-si-ve	**GAR/GDR/GDR/GAR/GDR/GAR/ GDR**
inexperience	i-n-ex-per-i-e-nce	**GAR/GDR/GDR/***HAO/***GAR/GAR/ GDR**
infallible	i-n-fa-lli-ble	**GAR/GDR/GAR/GAR/***HOO*
infamous	i-n-fa-mous	**GAR/GDR/GAR/GAR**
infancy	i-n-fa-n-cy	**GAR/GDR/GAR/GDR/GAR**
infant	i-n-fan-t	**GAR/GDR/GAR/***HOO*
infantry	i-n-fa-n-try	**GAR/GDR/GAR/GDR/***HDO*
infect	i-n-fec-t	**GAR/GDR/GAR/***HOO*
infectious	i-n-fec-ti-ous	**GAR/GDR/GAR/***HDO/HAO*
infer	i-n-fer	**GAR/GDR/***HDO*
inferior	i-n-fe-ri-or	**GAR/GDR/GRR/GAR/***HDO*
infernal	i-n-fer-nal	**GAR/GDR/***HAO/HDO*
infertility	i-n-fer-ti-li-ty	**GAR/GDR/***HAO/***GAR/GAR/GAR**
infest	i-n-fe-st	**GAR/GDR/GAR/GDR**
infiltrate	i-n-fi-l-tra-te	**GAR/GDR/GAR/GDR/***HAO/HDO*
infinite	i-n-fi-ni-te	**GAR/GDR/GAR/GRR/***HDO*
infirm	i-n-fir-m	**GAR/GDR/***HOO/HDO*
infirmary	i-n-fir-ma-ry	**GAR/GDR/***HOO/***GAR/***HDO*
inflame	i-n-fla-me	**GAR/GDR/***HAO/HDO*
inflate	i-n-fla-te	**GAR/GDR/***HAO/HDO*
inflation	i-n-fla-tion	**GAR/GDR/***HAO/HOO*

Word	Mouthables	Mouth Movements Notations
inflexible	i-n-fle-xi-ble	GAR/GDR/GAR/GAR/*HOO*
inflict	i-n-flic-t	GAR/GDR/GAR/*HOO*
influence	i-n-flu-e-nce	GAR/GDR/*HOO*/GAR/GDR
influenza	i-n-flu-e-n-za	GAR/GDR/*HOO*/GAR/GDR/GAR
info	i-n-fo	GAR/GDR/*HOO*
inform	i-n-for-m	GAR/GDR/*HOO*/*HDO*
informal	i-n-for-mal	GAR/GDR/*HOO*/*HDO*
informant	i-n-for-ma-nt	GAR/GDR/*HOO*/GAR/GDR
information	i-n-for-ma-tion	GAR/GDR/*HOO*/*HAO*/*HOO*
infrared	i-n-fra-re-d	GAR/GDR/GAR/GAR/*HOO*
infrastructure	i-n-fra-stru-c-tu-re	GAR/GDR/GAR/GAR/GDR/*HOO*/*HDO*
infringe	i-n-fri-n-ge	GAR/GDR/GAR/GDR/*HDO*
infuse	i-n-fu-se	GAR/GDR/*HOO*/*HDO*
infusion	i-n-fu-sion	GAR/GDR/*HOO*/*HOO*
ingenious	i-n-ge-ni-ous	GAR/GDR/GRR/GAR/*HAO*
ingenuous	i-n-ge-nu-ous	GAR/GDR/GAR/*HOO*/GAR
ingoing	i-n-go-ing	GAR/GDR/*HOO*/GDR
ingot	i-n-go-t	GAR/GDR/*HAO*/*HDO*
ingratiate	i-n-gra-ti-a-te	GAR/GDR/*HAO*/*HDO*/*HAO*/*HDO*
ingredient	i-n-gre-di-e-nt	GAR/GDR/GRR/GAR/GAR/GDR
inhabitant	i-n-ha-bi-ta-nt	GAR/GDR/GAR/GAR/GDR
inhale	i-n-ha-le	GAR/GDR/*HAO*/GDR
inherent	i-n-he-re-nt	GAR/GDR/GAR/GAR/GDR
inherit	i-n-he-ri-t	GAR/GDR/GAR/GAR/*HDO*
inhibited	i-n-hi-bi-ted	GAR/GDR/GAR/GAR/GRR
inhospitable	i-n-hos-pi-ta-ble	GAR/GDR/*HAO*/GAR/GAR/*HOO*
inhuman	i-n-hu-ma-n	GAR/GDR/*HOO*/GAR/GDR
inhumane	i-n-hu-ma-ne	GAR/GDR/*HOO*/*HAO*/*HDO*
inimitable	i-ni-mi-ta-ble	GAR/GAR/GAR/GAR/*HOO*
iniquitous	i-n-i-qui-tous	GAR/GAR/GAR/GAR

Word	Mouthables	Mouth Movements Notations
initial	i-ni-tial	**GAR/GAR/***HDO*
initiate	i-ni-ti-a-te	**GAR/GAR/GDR/***HAO/HDO*
initiative	i-ni-tia-ti-ve	**GAR/GAR/GDR/GAR/***HDO*
inject	i-n-jec-t	**GAR/GDR/GAR/***HOO*
injunction	i-n-jun-c-tion	**GAR/GDR/GAR/GDR/***HOO*
injure	i-n-ju-re	**GAR/GDR/***HOO/HDO*
injured	i-n-ju-re-d	**GAR/GDR/***HOO/HDO/HOO*
injurious	i-n-ju-ri-ous	**GAR/GDR/***HOO/***GAR/GAR**
injury	i-n-ju-ry	**GAR/GDR/***HOO/***GDR**
injustice	i-n-ju-sti-ce	**GAR/GDR/GAR/GAR/GDR**
ink	i-n-k	**GAR/GDR/***HDO*
inkling	i-nk-li-ng	**GAR/GDR/GAR/GDR**
inlaid	i-n-lai-d	**GAR/GDR/***HAO/HOO*
inland	i-n-lan-d	**GAR/GDR/GAR/***HOO*
inlay	i-n-lay	**GAR/GDR/***HAO*
inlet	i-n-le-t	**GAR/GDR/GAR/***HDO*
inmate	i-n-ma-te	**GAR/GDR/***HAO/HDO*
inmost	i-n-mo-st	**GAR/GDR/***HOO/HOO*
inn	i-nn	**GAR/GDR**
innards	i-n-nar-ds	**GAR/GDR/GAR/***HDO*
innate	i-n-na-te	**GAR/GDR/***HAO/HDO*
inner	i-n-ner	**GAR/GDR/***HDO*
innocent	i-n-no-cen-t	**GAR/GDR/***HOO/***GAR/***HOO*
innocuous	i-n-no-cu-ous	**GAR/GDR/***HAO/HOO/***GAR**
innovation	i-n-no-va-tion	**GAR/GDR/***HOO/HAO/HOO*
inoculation	i-no-cu-la-tion	**GAR/***HAO/HOO/HAO/HOO*
input	i-n-put	**GAR/GDR/***HOO*
inquire	i-n-qui-re	**GAR/GDR/GRR/***HDO*
inquirer	i-n-qui-rer	**GAR/GDR/GRR/***HDO*
inquiring	i-n-qui-ring	**GAR/GDR/GRR/GDR**
inquiry	i-n-qui-ry	**GAR/GDR/GRR/GDR**

Word	Mouthables	Mouth Movements Notations
inquisitive	i-n-qui-si-ti-ve	GAR/GDR/GAR/GAR/GAR/GDR
inroad	i-n-roa-d	GAR/GDR/*HOO*/*HOO*
insane	i-n-sa-ne	GAR/GDR/*HAO*/GDR
insanitary	i-n-sa-ni-tary	GAR/GDR/GAR/GAR/*HDO*
insatiable	i-n-sa-ti-a-ble	GAR/GDR/*HAO*/*HDO*/GAR/*HOO*
inscription	i-n-scri-p-tion	GAR/GDR/GAR/*HDO*/*HOO*
insect	i-n-sec-t	GAR/GDR/GAR/*HOO*
insecticide	i-n-se-c-ti-ci-de	GAR/GDR/GAR/GDR/GAR/GRR/*HDO*
insecure	i-n-se-cu-re	GAR/GDR/GAR/*HOO*/*HDO*
inseminate	i-n-se-mi-na-te	GAR/GDR/GAR/GAR/*HAO*/*HDO*
insensible	i-n-sen-si-ble	GAR/GDR/GAR/GAR/*HOO*
insensitive	i-n-sen-si-ti-ve	GAR/GDR/GAR/GAR/GAR/*HDO*
insert	i-n-ser-t	GAR/GDR/*HOO*/*HOO*
inshore	i-n-sho-re	GAR/GDR/*HOO*/*HDO*
inside	i-n-si-de	GAR/GDR/GRR/*HDO*
insidious	i-n-si-di-ous	GAR/GDR/GAR/GAR/GAR
insight	i-n-sigh-t	GAR/GDR/GRR/*HOO*
insignificant	i-n-si-g-ni-fi-ca-nt	GAR/GDR/GAR/GDR/GAR/GAR/GAR/GDR
insincere	i-n-si-n-ce-re	GAR/GDR/GAR/GDR/GRR/*HDO*
insinuate	i-n-si-nu-a-te	GAR/GDR/GAR/*HOO*/*HAO*/*HDO*
insipid	i-n-si-pi-d	GAR/GDR/GAR/GAR/GDR
insist	i-n-si-st	GAR/GDR/GAR/*HDO*
insistent	i-n-si-ste-nt	GAR/GDR/GAR/GAR/GDR
insole	i-n-so-le	GAR/GDR/*HOO*/GDR
insolent	i-n-so-le-nt	GAR/GDR/*HOO*/GAR/GDR
insolubility	i-n-so-lu-bi-li-ty	GAR/GDR/*HAO*/*HOO*/GAR/GAR/GAR
insoluble	i-n-so-lu-ble	GAR/GDR/*HAO*/*HOO*/*HOO*
insolvent	i-n-so-l-ve-nt	GAR/GDR/*HAO*/GDR/GAR/GDR
insomnia	i-n-so-m-ni-a	GAR/GDR/*HAO*/*HDO*/GAR/GAR

Word	Mouthables	Mouth Movements Notations
inspection	i-n-spe-c-tion	**GAR/GDR/GAR/GDR**/*HOO*
inspector	i-n-spe-c-tor	**GAR/GDR/GAR/GDR**/*HOO*
inspiration	i-n-spi-ra-tion	**GAR/GDR/GAR**/*HAO*/*HOO*
inspire	i-n-spi-re	**GAR/GDR/GRR**/*HDO*
install	i-n-stal-l	**GAR/GDR**/*HOO*/*HDO*
installation	i-n-stal-la-tion	**GAR/GDR**/*HOO*/*HAO*/*HOO*
installment	i-n-stal-l-me-nt	**GAR/GDR**/*HOO*/*HDO*/**GAR/GDR**
instance	i-n-sta-nce	**GAR/GDR/GAR/GDR**
instant	i-n-sta-nt	**GAR/GDR/GAR/GDR**
instantaneous	i-n-sta-n-ta-ne-ous	**GAR/GDR/GAR/GDR**/*HAO*/**GRR**/*HAO*
instead	i-n-stea-d	**GAR/GDR/GAR**/*HOO*
instep	i-n-ste-p	**GAR/GDR/GAR**/*HDO*
instigate	i-n-sti-ga-te	**GAR/GDR/GAR**/*HAO*/*HDO*
instill	i-n-sti-ll	**GAR/GDR/GAR/GDR**
instinct	i-n-stin-ct	**GAR/GDR/GAR**/*HOO*
institute	i-n-sti-tu-te	**GAR/GDR/GAR**/*HOO*/*HDO*
institution	i-n-sti-tu-tion	**GAR/GDR/GAR**/*HOO*/*HOO*
instruct	i-n-stru-ct	**GAR/GDR/GAR**/*HOO*
instruction	i-n-struc-tion	**GAR/GDR/GAR**/*HOO*
instrument	i-n-stru-me-nt	**GAR/GDR/GAR/GAR/GDR**
instrumentalist	i-n-stru-men-ta-li-st	**GAR/GDR**/*HOO*/**GAR/GAR/GAR**/*HDO*
insubstantial	i-n-sub-sta-n-tial	**GAR/GDR/GAR/GAR/GDR**/*HDO*
insufficient	i-n-su-ffi-ci-e-nt	**GAR/GDR/GAR**/*HDO*/**GAR/GDR**
insulate	i-n-su-la-te	**GAR/GDR/GAR**/*HAO*/*HDO*
insulating	i-n-su-la-ting	**GAR/GDR/GAR**/*HAO*/**GDR**
insulation	i-n-su-la-tion	**GAR/GDR/GAR**/*HAO*/*HOO*
insult	i-n-su-l-t	**GAR/GDR/GAR**/*GRR*
insult	i-n-sul-t	**GAR/GDR/GAR**/*HDO*
insurance	i-n-su-ra-nce	**GAR/GDR**/*HOO*/**GAR/GDR**
insure	i-n-su-re	**GAR/GDR**/*HOO*/*HDO*

Word	Mouthables	Mouth Movements Notations
insurer	i-n-su-rer	**GAR/GDR**/*HOO*/*HDO*
insurrection	i-n-su-rrec-tion	**GAR/GDR/GAR/GAR**/*HOO*
intact	i-n-tac-t	**GAR/GDR/GAR**/*HOO*
intake	i-n-ta-ke	**GAR/GDR**/*HAO*/*HDO*
integral	i-n-te-gral	**GAR/GDR/GAR**/*HDO*
integrate	i-n-te-gra-te	**GAR/GDR**/*HAO*/*HAO*/*HDO*
intellectual	i-n-te-llec-tu-al	**GAR/GDR/GAR/GAR**/*HOO*/*HDO*
intelligence	i-n-te-lli-ge-nce	**GAR/GDR/GAR/GAR/GAR/GDR**
intend	i-n-ten-d	**GAR/GDR/GAR**/*HOO*
intense	i-n-te-nse	**GAR/GDR/GAR/GDR**
intensify	i-n-te-n-si-fy	**GAR/GDR/GAR/GDR/GAR/GRR**
intention	i-n-te-n-tion	**GAR/GDR/GAR/GDR**/*HOO*
intentional	i-n-te-n-tion-al	**GAR/GDR/GAR/GDR**/*HOO*/*HDO*
interact	i-n-ter-a-ct	**GAR/GDR**/*HAO*/**GAR/GDR**
intercept	i-n-ter-ce-pt	**GAR/GDR**/*HAO*/**GAR**/*HDO*
intercession	i-n-ter-ces-sion	**GAR/GDR**/*HAO*/**GAR**/*HOO*
interchange	i-n-ter-cha-n-ge	**GAR/GDR**/*HAO*/*HAO*/**GDR**/*HDO*
intercourse	i-n-ter-cour-se	**GAR/GDR**/*HAO*/*HOO*/*HDO*
interest	i-n-te-re-st	**GAR/GDR/GAR/GAR**/*HDO*
interestingly	i-n-te-re-sti-ng-ly	**GAR/GDR/GAR/GAR/GAR/GDR/ GDR**
interfere	i-n-ter-fe-re	**GAR/GDR**/*HAO*/**GRR**/*HDO*
interior	i-n-te-ri-or	**GAR/GDR/GAR/GAR**/*HOO*
interlace	i-n-ter-la-ce	**GAR/GDR**/*HAO*/*HAO*/**GDR**
intermediary	i-n-ter-me-di-ar-y	**GAR/GDR**/*HAO*/**GRR/GAR**/*HAO*/ **GDR**
intermediate	i-n-ter-me-di-a-te	**GAR/GDR**/*HAO*/**GRR/GAR**/*HAO*/ *HOO*
international	i-n-ter-na-tion-al	**GAR/GDR**/*HAO*/**GAR**/*HOO*/*HDO*
internment	i-n-ter-n-me-nt	**GAR/GDR**/*HAO*/**GDR/GAR/GRR**
interpret	i-n-ter-pre-t	**GAR/GDR**/*HAO*/**GAR**/*HOO*
interpreter	i-n-ter-pre-ter	**GAR/GDR**/*HAO*/**GAR**/*HDO*

Word	Mouthables	Mouth Movements Notations
interrogate	i-n-te-rro-ga-te	**GAR/GDR/GAR**/*HOO*/*HAO*/*HDO*
interrupt	i-n-ter-ru-pt	**GAR/GDR**/*HAO*/**GAR**/*HDO*
interval	i-n-ter-val	**GAR/GDR**/*HAO*/*HDO*
intervene	i-n-ter-ve-ne	**GAR/GDR**/*HAO*/**GRR/GDR**
intervention	i-n-ter-ve-n-tion	**GAR/GDR**/*HAO*/**GAR/GDR**/*HOO*
interview	i-n-ter-view	**GAR/GDR**/*HAO*/*HOO*
intestine	i-n-te-sti-ne	**GAR/GDR/GAR/GRR/GDR**
intimate	i-n-ti-ma-te	**GAR/GDR/GAR**/*HAO*/*HDO*
intimidate	i-n-ti-mi-da-te	**GAR/GDR/GAR/GAR**/*HAO*/*HDO*
into	i-n-to	**GAR/GDR**/*HOO*
intolerant	i-n-to-le-ra-nt	**GAR/GDR**/*HAO*/**GAR/GAR/GDR**
intoxicating	i-n-to-xi-ca-ting	**GAR/GDR**/*HAO*/**GAR**/*HAO*/**GDR**
intoxication	i-n-to-xi-ca-tion	**GAR/GDR**/*HAO*/**GAR**/*HAO*/*HOO*
intransigent	i-n-tra-n-si-ge-nt	**GAR/GDR/GAR/GDR/GAR/GAR/ GDR**
intravenous	i-n-tra-ve-n-ous	**GAR/GDR/GAR/GRR/GDR/GAR**
intrepid	i-n-tre-pi-d	**GAR/GDR/GAR/GAR**/*HOO*
intricacy	i-n-tri-ca-cy	**GAR/GDR/GAR/GAR/GAR**
intricate	i-n-tri-ca-te	**GAR/GDR/GAR**/*HAO*/*HDO*
intrigue	i-n-tri-gue	**GAR/GDR/GAR**/*HDO*
introduce	i-n-tro-du-ce	**GAR/GDR**/*HOO*/*HOO*/*HDO*
introvert	i-n-tro-ver-t	**GAR/GDR**/*HOO*/*HAO*/*HOO*
intruder	i-n-tru-der	**GAR/GDR**/*HOO*/*HDO*
intrusive	i-n-tru-si-ve	**GAR/GDR**/*HOO*/**GAR**/*HDO*
intuition	i-n-tu-i-tion	**GAR/GDR**/*HOO*/**GAR**/*HOO*
invade	i-n-va-de	**GAR/GDR**/*HAO*/*HOO*
invader	i-n-va-der	**GAR/GDR**/*HAO*/*HDO*
invalid	i-n-va-li-d	**GAR/GDR/GAR/GAR**/*HDO*
invaluable	i-n-va-lu-a-ble	**GAR/GDR/GAR**/*HOO*/**GAR**/*HOO*
invariable	i-n-var-i-a-ble	**GAR/GDR**/*HAO*/**GAR/GAR**/*HOO*
invasion	i-n-va-sion	**GAR/GDR**/*HAO*/*HOO*

Word	Mouthables	Mouth Movements Notations
invent	i-n-ve-nt	GAR/GDR/GAR/GDR
invention	i-n-ven-tion	GAR/GDR/GAR/*HOO*
inventor	i-n-ven-tor	GAR/GDR/GAR/*HOO*
inventory	i-n-ve-n-to-ry	GAR/GDR/GAR/GDR/*HOO*/*HDO*
inverse	i-n-ver-se	GAR/GDR/*HAO*/*HDO*
inversion	i-n-ver-sion	GAR/GDR/*HAO*/*HOO*
invert	i-n-ver-t	GAR/GDR/*HAO*/*HOO*
invest	i-n-ve-st	GAR/GDR/GAR/*HOO*
investigate	i-n-ve-sti-ga-te	GAR/GDR/GAR/GAR/*HAO*/*HDO*
investment	i-n-ve-st-me-nt	GAR/GDR/GAR/*HOO*/GAR/GDR
investor	i-n-ve-stor	GAR/GDR/GAR/*HOO*
invidious	i-n-vi-di-ous	GAR/GDR/GAR/GAR/GAR
invisible	i-n-vi-si-ble	GAR/GDR/GAR/GAR/*HOO*
invitation	i-n-vi-ta-tion	GAR/GDR/GAR/*HAO*/*HOO*
invite	i-n-vi-te	GAR/GDR/GRR/*HOO*
invoice	i-n-voi-ce	GAR/GDR/GAR/GDR
invoke	i-n-vo-ke	GAR/GDR/*HOO*/*HDO*
involuntary	i-n-vo-lu-n-ta-ry	GAR/GDR/*HAO*/GAR/GDR/GAR/*HDO*
involve	i-n-vol-ve	GAR/GDR/*HAO*/*HDO*
involvement	i-n-vol-ve-me-nt	GAR/GDR/*HAO*/*HDO*/GAR/GDR
inward	i-n-war-d	GAR/GDR/*HAO*/*HOO*
inwards	i-n-war-d-s	GAR/GDR/*HAO*/*HOO*/*HDO*
iodine	i-o-di-ne	GRR/*HOO*/GAR/GDR
Iranian	I-ra-ni-a-n	GAR/*HAO*/GAR/GAR/GDR
Iraqi	I-raq-i	GAR/*HAO*/GAR
irascible	i-ra-sci-ble	GAR/GAR/GAR/*HOO*
Ireland	I-re-lan-d	GRR/*HDO*/GAR/*HOO*
iridescent	i-ri-de-sce-nt	GAR/GAR/GAR/GAR/GDR
iris	i-ri-s	GRR/GAR/GDR
Irish	I-ri-sh	GRR/GAR/*HDO*

Word	Mouthables	Mouth Movements Notations
iron	i-ro-n	**GRR**/*HAO*/*HDO*
ironical	i-ro-ni-cal	**GRR**/*HAO*/**GAR**/*HDO*
ironmonger	i-ro-n-mon-ger	**GRR**/*HAO*/*HDO*/**GAR**/*HDO*
irony	i-ro-ny	**GRR**/*HAO*/**GAR**
irrational	i-rra-tion-al	**GAR**/**GAR**/*HOO*/*HDO*
irregular	i-rre-gu-lar	**GAR**/**GAR**/*HOO*/*HDO*
irreplaceable	i-rre-pla-ce-a-ble	**GAR**/**GRR**/*HAO*/**GRR**/**GAR**/*HOO*
irrepressible	i-rre-pre-ssi-ble	**GAR**/**GRR**/**GAR**/**GAR**/*HOO*
irresistible	i-rre-si-sti-ble	**GAR**/**GRR**/**GAR**/**GAR**/*HOO*
irresponsible	i-rre-spo-n-si-ble	**GAR**/**GRR**/*HAO*/**GDR**/**GAR**/*HOO*
irrigate	i-rri-ga-te	**GAR**/**GAR**/*HAO*/*HDO*
irritate	i-rri-ta-te	**GAR**/**GAR**/*HAOHDO*
is	i-s	**GAR**/**GDR**
Islam	I-s-lam	**GAR**/**GDR**/*HAO*
Islamic	I-sla-mi-c	**GAR**/**GAR**/**GAR**/**GDR**
island	i-(s)lan-d	**GRR**/**GAR**/*HDO*
isolate	i-so-la-te	**GRR**/*HOO*/*HAO*/*HDO*
isolation	i-so-la-tion	**GRR**/*HOO*/*HAO*/*HOO*
Israe	I-s-ra-el	**GAR**/**GDR**/*HAO*/**GDR**
Issue	i-ss-ue	**GAR**/*HDO*/*HOO*
it	i-t	**GAR**/**GDR**
Italian	I-ta-li-a-n	**GAR**/**GAR**/**GAR**/**GAR**/**GDR**
italics	i-ta-li-cs	**GRR**/**GAR**/**GAR**/**GDR**
Italy	I-ta-ly	**GAR**/**GAR**/**GDR**
itch	i-tch	**GAR**/*HDO*
item	i-te-m	**GRR**/**GAR**/*HDO*
itinerant	i-ti-ne-ra-nt	**GRR**/**GAR**/**GAR**/**GAR**/**GDR**
itinerary	i-ti-ner-a-ry	**GRR**/**GAR**/*HAO*/**GAR**/*HDO*
its	i-ts	**GAR**/**GDR**
itself	i-t-se-l-f	**GAR**/**GDR**/**GAR**/**GDR**/*HDO*
ivory	i-vo-ry	**GRR**/*HOO*/*HDO*
ivy	i-vy	**GRR**/**GDR**

Word	Mouthables	Mouth Movements Notations
J		
J	J	*HAO*
jack	ja-ck	**GAR/GDR**
Jack	Jac-k	**GAR**/*HDO*
jackal	jac-kal	**GAR**/*HDO*
jacket	jac-ke-t	**GAR/GAR**/*HDO*
jackpot	jac-k-po-t	**GAR**/*HDO/HAO/HOO*
jade	ja-de	*HAO/HDO*
jaded	ja-ded	*HAO*/**GRR**
jagged	jag-ged	**GAR/GRR**
jaguar	ja-gu-ar	**GAR**/*HOO/HAO*
jail	jai-l	*HAO/HDO*
jalopy	ja-lo-py	**GAR**/*HAO*/**GAR**
jam	ja-m	**GAR/GRR**
jam	ja-m	**GAR**/*HDO*
jammed	ja-mme-d	**GAR/GDR**/*HOO*
jammy	ja-mmy	**GAR/GAR**
janitor	jan-i-tor	**GAR/GAR**/*HOO*
January	Ja-n-u-ar-y	**GAR/GDR**/*HOO/HAO*/**GAR**
Japan	Ja-pa-n	**GAR/GAR/GDR**
Japanese	Ja-pa-ne-se	**GAR/GAR/GRR**/*HDO*
jar	jar	*HAO*
jargon	jar-go-n	*HAO/HAO/HDO*
jasmine	ja-s-mi-ne	**GAR/GDR/GAR**/*HDO*
jaunt	jau-nt	*HOO/HDO*
jaw	jaw	*HOO*
jazz	ja-zz	**GAR/GDR**
jazzy	ja-zzy	**GAR/GAR**
jealous	jca-lou-s	**GAR/GAR**/*HDO*
jeer	je-er	**GRR/GDR**
jelly	je-lly	**GAR/GAR**

Word	Mouthables	Mouth Movements Notations
jeopardise	jeo-par-di-se	**GAR**/*HAO*/**GRR/GDR**
jerk	jer-k	*HOO/HOO*
jerk	jer-k	*HOO/HDO*
jerkin	jer-ki-n	*HOO*/**GAR/GDR**
jerky	jer-ky	*HOO*/**GAR**
jersey	jer-sey	**GAR/GDR**
Jersey	Jer-sey	*HAO/HDO*
jest	je-st	**GAR**/*HDO*
Jesus	Je-su-s	**GRR/GAR**/*HDO*
jet	je-t	**GAR**/*HOO*
jettison	je-tti-so-n	**GAR/GAR**/*HAO/HDO*
jetty	je-tty	**GAR/GDR**
jew	jew	*HOO*
jewel	jew-e-l	*HOO*/**GAR/GDR**
jeweller	jew-e-ller	*HOO*/**GAR**/*HDO*
Jewish	Jew-i-sh	*HOO*/**GAR**/*HDO*
jibe	ji-be	**GRR**/*HDO*
jiffy	ji-ffy	**GAR**/*HDO*
jigsaw	ji-g-saw	**GAR/GDR**/*HOO*
jimmy	ji-mmy	**GAR/GAR**
jimmy	ji-m-my	**GAR**/*HDO*/**GDR**
jingle	ji-n-gle	**GAR/GDR**/*HOO*
jink	ji-nx	**GAR/GDR**
jitters	ji-tter-s	**GAR**/*HAO/HDO*
jittery	ji-tte-ry	**GAR/GAR**/*HDO*
job	jo-b	*HAO/HDO*
jobbing	jo-bbing	*HAO*/**GDR**
jockey	joc-key	*HAO*/**GRR**
jog	jo-g	*HAO/HDO*
John	Joh-n	*HAO/HDO*
join	joi-n	**GAR/GRR**

Word	Mouthables	Mouth Movements Notations
joined	joi-ne-d	GAR/GDR/*HOO*
joiner	joi-ner	GAR/*HDO*
joint	joi-nt	*HAO*/GDR
joke	jo-ke	*HOO*/*HDO*
jokey	jo-key	*HOO*/GRR
jolly	jo-lly	*HAO*/GDR
jolt	jo-lt	*HOO*/*HOO*
Jordan	Jor-da-n	*HOO*/GAR/GDR
Jordanian	Jor-da-ni-a-n	*HOO*/*HAO*/GAR/GAR/GDR
jostle	jo-stle	*HAO*/*HOO*
jot	jo-t	*HAO*/*HOO*
jotter	jo-tter	*HAO*/*HDO*
journal	jour-nal	GAR/*HDO*
journalism	jour-na-li-sm	GAR/GAR/GAR/*HDO*
journey	jour-ney	*HOO*/GRR
jowl	jow-l	*HAO*/*HDO*
joy	joy	*HAO*
jubilee	ju-bi-lee	*HOO*/GAR/GRR
judge	ju-d-ge	GAR/*HDO*/*HDO*
judgement	ju-d-ge-me-nt	GAR/*HDO*/*HDO*/GAR/GDR
judicial	ju-di-cial	*HOO*/GAR/*HDO*
jug	ju-g	GAR/*HDO*
juggernaut	ju-gger-nau-t	GAR/*HDO*/*HOO*/*HOO*
juggle	ju-ggle	GAR/*HOO*
juice	jui-ce	*HOO*/GDR
juicy	jui-cy	*HOO*/GAR
July	Ju-ly	*HOO*/GDR
jumble	ju-m-ble	GAR/*HDO*/*HOO*
jumbo	ju-m-bo	GAR/*HDO*/*HOO*
jump	ju-mp	GAR/*HDO*
jumped	ju-mpe-d	GAR/*HOO*/*HOO*

Word	Mouthables	Mouth Movements Notations
jumper	ju-m-per	**GAR**/*HDO*/*HDO*
jumpy	jum-py	**GAR/GAR**
junction	jun-c-tion	**GAR/GDR**/*HOO*
juncture	jun-c-tu-re	**GAR/GDR**/*HOO*/*HDO*
June	Ju-ne	*HOO*/*HDO*
jungle	jun-gle	**GAR**/*HOO*
junior	ju-ni-or	*HOO*/**GAR**/*HDO*
juniper	ju-ni-per	*HOO*/**GAR**/*HDO*
junk	jun-k	**GAR**/*HDO*
junkie	jun-kie	**GAR/GAR**
juridical	ju-ri-di-cal	*HOO*/**GAR/GAR**/*HDO*
jurisdiction	ju-ri-s-di-c-tion	*HOO*/**GAR/GDR/GAR/GDR**/*HOO*
jurisprudence	ju-ri-s-pru-de-nce	*HOO*/**GAR/GDR**/*HOO*/**GAR/GDR**
jurist	ju-ri-st	*HOO*/**GAR**/*HOO*
juror	ju-ror	*HOO*/*HDO*
jury	ju-ry	*HOO*/**GDR**
just	ju-st	**GAR**/*HOO*
justice	ju-sti-ce	**GAR/GAR/GDR**
justifiable	ju-sti-fi-a-ble	**GAR/GAR/GRR/GAR**/*HOO*
justification	ju-sti-fi-ca-tion	**GAR/GAR/GAR**/*HAO*/*HOO*
justify	ju-sti-fy	**GAR/GAR/GRR**
jut	ju-t	**GAR**/*HDO*
juvenile	ju-ve-ni-le	*HOO*/**GAR/GRR/GDR**
juxtapose	ju-xta-po-se	**GAR/GAR**/*HOO*/**GDR**

Word	Mouthables	Mouth Movements Notations
K		
K	K	*HAO*
kangaroo	kan-ga-roo	**GAR/GAR/***HOO*
keel	kee-l	**GRR/GDR**
keen	kee-n	**GRR/GDR**
keep	kee-p	**GRR/GDR**
keeper	kee-per	**GRR/***HDO*
kennel	ke-nnel	**GAR/***HDO*
kept	ke-pt	**GAR/GRR**
kerb	ker-b	*HOO/HDO*
kernel	ker-nel	*HOO/HDO*
kettle	ket-tle	**GAR/***HOO*
key	key	**GRR**
kick	ki-ck	**GAR/***HDO*
kid	ki-d	**GAR/***HOO*
kidnap	ki-d-na-p	**GAR/***HDO***/GAR/***HDO*
kidnapping	ki-d-na-pi-ng	**GAR/***HDO***/GAR/GAR/GDR**
kidney	ki-d-ney	**GAR/***HOO***/GRR**
kill	ki-ll	**GAR/GRR**
killing	ki-lling	**GAR/GDR**
kiln	ki-l-n	**GAR/GDR/GDR**
kilogram	ki-lo-gra-m	**GAR/***HOO***/GAR/***HDO*
kilometre	ki-lo-me-tre	**GAR/***HOO***/GAR/***HDO*
kind	ki-nd	**GRR/GDR**
kindegarten	ki-n-de-gar-ten	**GAR/GDR/GAR/GAR/***HDO*
kindle	ki-n-dle	**GAR/GDR/***HOO*
kindly	ki-n-dly	**GRR/GDR/***HDO*
kindness	kin-d-ne-ss	**GRR/***HDO***/GAR/GDR**
king	kin-g	**GAR/***HDO*
kingdom	kin-g-do-m	**GAR/***HDO***/***HAO***/***HDO*
kingsize	kin-g-si-ze	**GAR/***HDO***/GRR/GDR**

Word	Mouthables	Mouth Movements Notations
kinship	ki-n-ship	**GAR/GDR**/*HDO*
kiosk	ki-o-sk	**GAR**/*HAO*/*HDO*
kip	ki-p	**GAR**/*HDO*
kiss	ki-ss	**GAR**/*HDO*
kit	ki-t	**GAR**/*HDO*
kitchen	kit-che-n	**GAR/GAR/GDR**
kitchenette	kit-che-ne-tte	**GAR/GAR/GAR**/*HDO*
kite	ki-te	**GRR**/*HDO*
kitten	kit-ten	**GAR**/*HDO*
kitty	kit-ty	**GAR/GAR**
klaxon	kla-xo-n	**GAR**/*HAO*/*HDO*
knack	kna-ck	**GAR**/*HDO*
knead	knea-d	**GRR**/*HOO*
knee	knee	**GRR**
kneel	knee-l	**GRR/GDR**
knell	kne-ll	**GAR/GDR**
knelt	kne-lt	**GAR/GRR**
knew	knew	*HOO*
knickerbockers	kni-cker-boc-kers	**GAR**/*HDO*/*HAO*/*HDO*
knickers	kni-cker-s	**GAR**/*HDO*/*HDO*
knife	kni-fe	**GRR**/*HDO*
knight	knigh-t	**GRR**/*HOO*
knit	kni-t	**GAR**/*HOO*
knitwear	kni-t-wear	**GAR**/*HOO*/*HAO*
knives	kni-ve-s	**GRR**/*HDO*/*HDO*
knob	kno-b	*HAO*/*HDO*
knock	kno-ck	*HAO*/*HDO*
knocker	kno-cker	*HAO*/*HDO*
knot	kno-t	*HAO*/*HDO*
knotty	kno-tty	*HAO*/**GAR**
know	know	*HOO*

Word	Mouthables	Mouth Movements Notations
knowing	kno-wing	*HOO*/**GDR**
knowledge	know-led-ge	*HAO*/**GAR**/*HDO*
knowledgeable	know-led-gea-ble	*HAO*/**GAR**/**GDR**/*HOO*
knuckle	kn-u-ckle	**GDR**/**GAR**/*HOO*
Koran	Ko-ra-n	*HOO*/**GAR**/**GDR**
Korea	Ko-re-a	*HAO*/**GRR**/**GAR**

Word	Mouthables	Mouth Movements Notations
L		
L	L	**GAR/GDR**
lab	la-b	**GAR/**_HDO_
label	la-bel	_HAO/HDO_
laboratory	la-bo-ra-to-ry	**GAR/**_HAO/_**GAR/**_HOO/HDO_
labour	la-bour	_HAO/HAO_
labyrinth	la-by-ri-nth	**GAR/GAR/GAR/GTR**
lace	la-ce	_HAO/_**GDR**
lacerate	la-ce-ra-te	**GAR/GAR/**_HAO/HDO_
lack	lac-k	**GAR/**_HDO_
lackadaisical	lac-ka-dai-si-cal	**GAR/GAR/**_HAO/_**GAR/**_HDO_
lackey	lac-key	**GAR/GRR**
lacquer	lac-quer	**GAR/**_HDO_
lad	la-d	**GAR/**_HOO_
ladder	la-d-der	**GAR/**_HOO/HDO_
laden	la-den	_HAO/HDO_
ladle	la-dle	_HAO/HOO_
lady	la-dy	_HAO/HDO_
lag	la-g	**GAR/**_HDO_
lager	lag-er	_HAO/HDO_
lagging	la-gging	**GAR/GDR**
lagoon	la-goo-n	**GAR/**_HOO/HDO_
laid	lai-d	_HAO/_**GRR**
lain	lai-n	_HAO/_**GRR**
lair	lair	_HAO_
lake	la-ke	_HAO/HDO_
lamb	la-mb	**GAR/**_HDO_
lame	la-me	_HAO/HDO_
lament	la-me-nt	**GAR/GAR/GDR**
lamp	la-mp	**GAR/GDR**
lance	lan-ce	_HAO/_**GDR**

Word	Mouthables	Mouth Movements Notations
lancet	lan-ce-t	*HAO*/**GAR**/*HOO*
land	la-nd	**GAR/GRR**
land	lan-d	**GAR**/*HDO*
landed	la-n-ded	**GAR/GDR/GRR**
landing	la-n-ding	**GAR/GDR/GDR**
lane	la-ne	*HAO*/**GDR**
language	lan-guage	**GAR**/*HDO*
languish	lan-gui-sh	**GAR/GAR**/*HDO*
lank	lan-k	**GAR**/*HDO*
lanky	lan-ky	**GAR/GAR**
lantern	la-n-ter-n	**GAR/GDR**/*HOO*/*HDO*
lap	la-p	**GAR**/*HDO*
lapse	la-pse	**GAR**/*HDO*
larceny	lar-ce-ny	**GAR/GAR/GDR**
larch	lar-ch	*HAO*/*HDO*
large	lar-ge	**GAR**/*HDO*
larger	lar-ger	**GAR**/*HDO*
lash	la-sh	**GAR/GDR**
lashings	la-sh-ings	**GAR/GDR/GDR**
lassie	la-ssie	**GAR/GAR**
last	las-t	*HAO*/*HOO*
lastly	las-t-ly	*HAO*/*HDO*/**GDR**
latch	lat-ch	**GAR**/*HDO*
late	la-te	*HAO*/*HOO*
lately	la-te-ly	*HAO*/*HDO*/**GDR**
later	la-ter	*HAO*/*HOO*
lateral	la-te-ral	**GAR**/*HAO*/*HDO*
latest	la-te-st	*HAO*/**GAR**/*HDO*
lathe	la-the	*HAO*/**GTR**
lather	la-ther	**GAR**/*HTO*
latice	lat-ti-ce	**GAR/GAR/GDR**

Word	Mouthables	Mouth Movements Notations
Latin	La-ti-n	**GAR/GAR/GDR**
latter	lat-ter	*HAO/HDO*
laugh	lau-gh	*HAOHDO*
laughter	lau-gh-ter	*HAO/HDO/HDO*
launch	lau-nch	*HOO/***GRR**
launch	laun-ch	*HOO/HDO*
launching	lau-n-ching	*HOO/***GDR/GDR**
launder	lau-n-der	*HOO/***GDR/***HDO*
launderette	lau-n-der-e-tte	*HOO/***GDR/***HDO/***GAR/***HDO*
laundromat	lau-n-dro-ma-t	*HOO/***GDR/***HOO/***GAR/***HDO*
laundry	lau-n-dry	*HOO/***GDR/GDR**
laurel	lau-rel	*HAO/HDO*
lavatory	la-va-to-ry	**GAR/GAR/***HOO/HDO*
lavender	la-ve-n-der	**GAR/GAR/GDR/***HDO*
lavish	la-vi-sh	**GAR/GAR/***HDO*
law	law	*HOO*
lawful	law-ful	*HOO/HDO*
lawn	law-n	*HOO/***GDR**
lawyer	law-yer	*HOO/***GAR**
laxative	la-xa-ti-ve	**GAR/GAR/GAR/***HDO*
lay	lay	*HAO*
layer	lay-er	*HAO/***GDR**
laze	la-ze	*HAO/***GRR**
lazy	la-zy	*HAO/***GAR**
leached	lea-che-d	**GRR/***HDO/HOO*
lead	lea-d	**GRR/GRR**
leaden	lea-den	**GAR/***HDO*
leader	lea-der	**GRR/***HDO*
leading	lea-ding	**GRR/GDR**
leaf	lea-f	**GRR/***HDO*
leaflet	lea-f-le-t	**GRR/***HDO/***GAR/***HDO*

Word	Mouthables	Mouth Movements Notations
league	lea-gue	**GRR**/*HDO*
leak	lea-k	**GRR/GDR**
leakage	lea-kage	**GRR**/*HDO*
lean	lea-n	**GRR/GRR**
leaning	lea-ning	**GRR/GDR**
leap	lea-p	**GRR/GDR**
learn	lear-n	**GAR/GRR**
learning	lear-ning	**GAR/GDR**
learnt	learn-t	*HOO/HOO*
lease	lea-se	**GRR/GDR**
leash	lea-sh	**GRR**/*HDO*
least	lea-st	**GRR/GRR**
leather	lea-th-er	**GAR/GTR**/*HDO*
leave	lea-ve	**GRR/GDR**
leaves	lea-ve-s	**GRR**/*HDO/HDO*
Lebanese	Le-ba-ne-se	**GAR/GAR/GRR/GDR**
Lebanon	Le-ba-no-n	**GAR/GAR**/*HAO/HDO*
lecture	lec-tu-re	**GAR**/*HOO/HDO*
led	le-d	**GAR/GRR**
ledge	led-ge	**GAR**/*HDO*
ledger	led-ger	**GAR**/*HDO*
leech	lee-ch	**GRR/GRR**
leeched	lee-che-d	**GRR/GRR**/*HOO*
leek	lee-k	**GRR**/*HDO*
leer	le-er	**GRR/GDR**
leery	lee-ry	**GRR/GDR**
lees	lee-s	**GRR/GDR**
left	le-ft	**GAR/GR**R
left	le-ft	**GAR**/*HDO*
leg	le-g	**GAR**/*HDO*
legacy	le-ga-cy	**GAR/GAR/GDR**

Word	Mouthables	Mouth Movements Notations
legal	le-gal	**GRR**/*HDO*
legend	le-g-e-nd	**GAR**/*HDO*/**GAR/GDR**
legible	le-gi-ble	**GAR/GAR**/*HOO*
legislative	le-gi-sla-ti-ve	**GAR/GAR**/*HAO*/**GAR**/*HDO*
legitimate	le-gi-ti-ma-te	**GAR/GAR/GAR**/*HAO*/*HDO*
leisure	lei-su-re	**GAR**/*HOO*/*HDO*
leisurely	lei-su-re-ly	**GAR**/*HOO*/*HDO*/**GDR**
lemon	le-mo-n	**GAR**/*HAO*/*HDO*
lemonade	le-mo-na-de	**GAR**/*HAO*/*HAO*/*HDO*
lend	le-nd	**GAR/GRR**
length	len-gth	**GAR**/*HTO*
lengthen	len-gth-en	**GAR**/*HTO*/*HDO*
lengthy	len-gth-y	**GAR**/*HTO*/**GAR**
lenient	le-ni-e-nt	**GRR/GAR/GAR/GDR**
lens	le-n-s	**GAR/GDR**/*HDO*
lent	le-nt	**GAR/GRR**
Lent	Len-t	*HAO*/*HOO*
lentil	len-til	*HAO*/*HDO*
leopard	leo-par-d	**GAR**/*HAO*/*HOO*
leopardess	leo-par-de-ss	**GAR**/*HAO*/**GAR/GDR**
leotard	le-o-tar-d	**GRR**/*HOO*/*HAO*/*HOO*
lesion	le-sion	**GRR**/*HOO*
less	les-s	**GAR/GDR**
lessen	les-sen	**GAR**/*HDO*
lesser	les-ser	**GAR**/*HDO*
lesson	les-so-n	**GAR**/*HAO*/*HDO*
let	le-t	**GAR**/*HOO*
lethargy	le-th-ar-gy	**GAR**/*HTO*/*HAO*/**GDR**
letter	let-ter	**GAR**/*HDO*
lettering	let-te-ring	**GAR/GAR/GDR**
lettuce	let-tu-ce	**GAR/GAR**/*HDO*

Word	Mouthables	Mouth Movements Notations
leukaemia	leu-k(a)e-mi-a	*HOO*/**GRR/GAR/GAR**
levee	le-vee	**GAR**/*HAO*
level	le-vel	**GAR**/*HDO*
levy	le-vy	**GAR/GAR**
lewd	lew-d	*HOO/HOO*
liability	li-a-bi-li-ty	**GRR/GAR/GAR/GAR/GAR**
liable	li-a-ble	**GRR/GAR**/*HOO*
liar	li-ar	**GRR/GAR**
lib	li-b	**GAR**/*HOO*
libel	li-bel	**GRR**/*HOO*
libelious	li-bel-i-ous	**GRR**/*HOO*/**GAR**/*HDO*
liberal	li-be-ral	**GAR**/*HAO/HDO*
liberalize	li-be-ra-li-ze	**GAR**/*HAO*/**GAR/GAR/GDR**
liberation	li-be-ra-tion	**GAR**/*HAO/HAO/HOO*
liberty	li-ber-ty	**GAR**/*HAO*/**GAR**
librarian	li-b-rar-i-a-n	**GRR**/*HDO*/**GAR/GAR/GDR**
library	li-b-rar-y	**GRR**/*HDO*/**GAR**/*HDO*
Libya	Li-by-a	**GAR/GAR/GAR**
Libyan	Li-by-a-n	**GAR/GAR/GAR/GDR**
lice	li-ce	**GRR/GDR**
licence	li-ce-nce	**GRR/GAR/GDR**
license	li-cen-se	**GRR/GAR**/*HDO*
lichen	li-ch-e-n	**GAR/GDR/GAR/GDR**
lick	li-ck	**GAR**/*HDO*
licker	li-cker	**GAR**/*HDO*
licorice	li-co-ri-ce	**GAR/GAR/GAR/GDR**
lid	li-d	**GAR**/*HDO*
lie	lie	**GRR**
licd	lie d	**GRR**/*HOO*
lien	li-e-n	**GAR/GAR/GDR**
lieutenant	lieu-te-na-nt	*HOO*/**GAR/GAR/GDR**

Word	Mouthables	Mouth Movements Notations
lieu	lieu	*HDO*
life	li-fe	**GRR**/*HDO*
lift	li-ft	**GAR**/*HDO*
light	ligh-t	**GRR**/*HDO*
lighten	ligh-ten	**GRR**/*HDO*
lighter	ligh-ter	**GRR**/*HDO*
lighting	light-ing	**GRR/GDR**
likable	li-ka-ble	**GRR/GAR**/*HOO*
like	li-ke	**GRR**/*HDO*
likely	li-ke-ly	**GRR**/*HDO*/**GDR**
liken	li-ken	**GRR**/*HDO*
likeness	li-ke-ne-ss	**GRR**/*HDO*/**GAR/GDR**
liking	li-king	**GRR/GDR**
lilt	li-lt	**GAR/GDR**
lily	li-ly	**GAR/GDR**
limb	li-mb	**GAR**/*HDO*
lime	li-me	**GRR/GDR**
line	li-ne	**GRR/GDR**
lineage	li-nea-ge	**GAR**/*HAO*/*HDO*
linen	li-ne-n	**GAR/GAR/GDR**
liner	li-ner	**GRR**/*HDO*
linger	lin-ger	**GAR**/*HDO*
lingo	lin-go	**GAR**/*HOO*
lining	li-ni-ng	**GRR/GAR/GDR**
link	lin-k	**GAR**/*HDO*
linkage	lin-kage	**GAR**/*HDO*
links	lin-ks	**GAR**/*HDO*
lino	li-no	**GAR**/*HOO*
lint	li-nt	**GAR/GDR**
lintel	li-n-tel	**GAR/GDR**/*HDO*
lion	li-o-n	**GRR**/*HAO*/*HDO*

Word	Mouthables	Mouth Movements Notations
lioness	li-o-ne-ss	**GRR**/*HAO*/**GAR/GDR**
lip	li-p	**GAR**/*HDO*
liqueur	li-que-ur	**GAR**/*HOO*/*HDO*
liquid	li-qui-d	**GAR/GAR**/*HOO*
liquidate	li-qui-da-te	**GAR/GAR**/*HAO*/*HDO*
liquidizer	li-qui-di-zer	**GAR/GAR/GRR**/*HDO*
liquor	li-quor	**GAR/GAR**
liquorice	li-quo-rice	**GAR**/*HOO*/*HDO*
Lisbon	Li-s-bo-n	**GAR/GDR**/*HAO*/*HDO*
lisp	li-s-p	**GAR/GDR**/*HDO*
list	li-st	**GAR/GDR**
listen	li-sten	**GAR**/*HDO*
listener	li-sten-er	**GAR**/*HDO*/*HDO*
listless	li-st-le-ss	**GAR**/*HDO*/**GAR/GDR**
liter	li-ter	**GAR**/*HDO*
literal	li-ter-al	**GAR**/*HDO*/*HDO*
literary	li-ter-ary	**GAR**/*HAO*/*HDO*
literate	li-ter-a-te	**GAR**/*HAO*/*HAO*/*HDO*
literature	li-ter-a-tu-re	**GAR**/*HAO*/*HAO*/*HOO*/*HDO*
litigation	li-ti-ga-tion	**GAR/GAR**/*HAO*/*HOO*
lithe	li-the	**GRR/GTR**
lithograph	li-th-o-gra-ph	**GAR/GTR**/*HOO*/*HAO*/*HDO*
litre	li-tre	**GAR**/*HDO*
litter	lit-ter	**GAR**/*HDO*
littered	lit-tere-d	**GAR**/*HOO*/*HOO*
little	lit-tle	**GAR**/*HOO*
liturgical	li-tur-gi-cal	**GAR**/*HOO*/**GAR**/*HDO*
live	li-ve	**GAR**/*HDO*
lively	li-ve-ly	**GRR**/*HDO*/**GDR**
liven	li-v-en	**GRR**/*HDO*/*HDO*
liver	li-ver	**GAR**/*HDO*

Word	Mouthables	Mouth Movements Notations
lives	li-ves	**GRR**/*HDO*
livid	li-vi-d	**GAR/GAR/GDR**
living	li-ving	**GAR/GDR**
lizard	li-zar-d	**GAR**/*HAO/HOO*
load	loa-d	*HOO/HOO*
loaded	loa-ded	*HOO/***GRR**
loaf	loa-f	*HOO/HDO*
loan	lo(a)-n	*HOO/***GRR**
loaned	lo(a)-ne-d	*HOO/***GDR**/*HOO*
lone	lo-ne	*HOO/***GDR**
loathe	loa-the	*HOO/***GTR**
loath	loa-th	*HOO/HDO*
loathing	loa-th-i-ng	*HOO/***GTR/GAR/GDR**
loathsome	loa-th-so-me	*HOO/***GTR**/*HAO/HDO*
loaves	loa-ves	*HOO/HDO*
lobby	lob-by	*HAO/***GAR**
lobbied	lob-bie-d	*HAO/***GAR**/*HOO*
lobby	lo-bby	*HAO/HDO*
lobe	lo-be	*HOO/HDO*
local	lo-cal	*HOO/HDO*
localize	lo-ca-li-ze	*HOO/***GAR/GRR/GDR**
locate	lo-ca-te	*HOO/***HAO/GDR**
location	lo-ca-tion	*HOO/HAO/HOO*
loch	lo-ch	*HAO/HDO*
lock	lo-ck	*HAO/***GDR**
locked	lo-cke-d	*HAO/***GDR**/*HOO*
locker	lo-cker	*HAO/HDO*
locomotive	lo-co-mo-ti-ve	*HOO/HOO/HOO/***GAR/GDR**
locum	lo-cu-m	*HOO/***GAR**/*HDO*
locks	lo-cks	*HAO/***GDR**
locks	lo-ck-s	*HOO/HDO/***GDR**

Word	Mouthables	Mouth Movements Notations
lodge	lo-d-ge	*HAO/HDO/HDO*
lodgings	lo-d-gi-ngs	*HAO/HDO/***GAR/GDR**
loft	lo-ft	*HAO/HDO*
lofty	lo-f-ty	*HAO/HDO/***GAR**
logic	lo-gi-c	*HAO/***GAR/GDR**
logical	lo-gi-cal	*HAO/***GAR***/HDO*
logistic	lo-gi-sti-c	*HAO/***GAR/GAR/GDR**
logo	lo-go	*HOO/HOO*
loiter	loi-ter	**GAR***/HDO*
lollipop	lo-lli-po-p	*HAO/***GAR***/HAO/HDO*
lolly	lo-lly	*HAO/***GAR**
London	Lon-do-n	**GAR***/HAO/HDO*
Londoner	Lon-do-ner	**GAR***/HAO/HDO*
lonely	lo-ne-ly	*HOO/HDO/***GDR**
loner	lo-ner	*HOO/HDO*
long	lon-g	*HAO/HDO*
loo	loo	*HOO*
look	loo-k	*HOO/HDO*
loom	loo-m	*HOO/HDO*
loony	loo-ney	*HOO/***GAR**
loop	loo-p	*HOO/HDO*
loops	loo-ps	*HOO/HDO*
loose	loo-se	*HOO/HDO*
loosen	loo-sen	*HOO/HDO*
loot	loo-t	*HOO/HOO*
looted	loo-ted	*HOO/***GRR**
loot	loo-t	*HOO/HDO*
loquacious	lo-qua-ci-ous	*HOO/HAO/HDO/HAO*
lord	lor-d	*HOO/HOO*
lore	lo-re	*HOO/HDO*
lorry	lor-ry	*HAO/***GDR**

Word	Mouthables	Mouth Movements Notations
lose	lo-se	*HOO*/**GDR**
loser	lo-ser	*HOO*/*HDO*
loss	lo-ss	*HAO*/*HDO*
lost	lo-st	*HAO*/*HOO*
lot	lo-t	*HAO*/*HOO*
lotion	lo-tion	*HOO*/*HOO*
lottery	lo-tte-ry	*HAO*/*HAO*/**GDR**
lotto	lo-tto	*HAO*/*HOO*
loud	lou-d	**GAR**/*HOO*
loudly	lou-d-ly	**GAR**/*HOO*/**GDR**
lounge	loun-ge	*HAO*/*HDO*
loup	lo(u)p	*HOO*/*HDO*
louped	lo(u)pe-d	*HOO*/*HDO*/*HOO*
louse	lou-se	**GAR**/*HDO*
lousy	lou-sy	**GAR/GAR**
lout	lou-t	**GAR**/*HOO*
love	lo-ve	**GAR**/*HOO*
loved	lo-ve-d	**GAR**/*HOO*/*HOO*
lovely	lo-ve-ly	**GAR**/*HDO*/**GDR**
lover	lo-ver	**GAR**/*HDO*
loving	lo-ving	**GAR/GDR**
low	lo-w	*HOO*/*HDO*
lower	lo-wer	*HOO*/*HDO*
lowly	low-ly	*HOO*/**GDR**
loyal	loy-a-l	**GAR/GAR/GDR**
lozenge	lo-ze-nge	*HAO*/**GAR/GDR**
lubricant	lu-bri-ca-nt	*HOO*/**GAR/GAR**/GDR
lubricate	lu-bri-ca-te	*HOO*/**GAR**/ *HAO*/*HDO*
lucid	lu-ci-d	*HOO*/**GAR/GDR**
luck	lu-ck	**GAR**/*HDO*
lucky	lu-cky	**GAR/GAR**
ludicrous	lu-di-cro-us	*HOO*/**GAR/GAR/GDR**

Word	Mouthables	Mouth Movements Notations
lug	lu-g	**GAR**/*HDO*
luggage	lu-g-gage	**GAR**/*HDO*/*HDO*
lullaby	lu-lla-by	**GAR/GAR/GRR**
lull	lul-l	**GAR**/*HDO*
lumbago	lu-m-ba-go	**GAR**/*HDO*/*HAO*/*HOO*
lumber	lu-m-ber	**GAR**/*HDO*/*HDO*
lump	lu-mp	**GAR**/*HDO*
lunatic	lu-na-ti-c	*HOO*/**GAR/GAR/GDR**
lunch	lu-n-ch	**GAR/GDR**/*HDO*
luncheon	lu-n-che-o-n	**GAR/GDR**/*HDO*/*HAO*/*HDO*
luncheonette	lu-n-che-o-n-e-tte	**GAR/GDR**/*HDO*/*HAO*/*HDO*/**GAR/ GDR**
lung	lun-g	**GAR**/*HDO*
lurch	lur-ch	**GAR**/*HDO*
lure	lu-re	*HOO*/*HDO*
lurk	lur-k	**GAR**/*HDO*
luscious	lu-sci-ous	**GAR/GDR/GAR**
lush	lu-sh	**GAR**/*HDO*
lustily	lu-sti-ly	**GAR/GAR/GDR**
lute	lu-te	*HOO*/**GDR**
Luxemburg	Lu-xe-m-bur-g	**GAR/GAR/GDR**/*HAO*/*HDO*
luxuriant	lu-xu-ri-a-nt	**GAR**/*HOO*/**GAR/GAR/GDR**
luxurious	lu-xu-ri-ous	**GAR**/*HOO*/**GAR**/*HAO*
luxury	lu-xu-ry	**GAR**/*HOO*/*HDO*
lymph	ly-m-ph	**GAR/GDR**/*HDO*
lynch	ly-n-ch	**GAR/GDR**/*HDO*
lynx	ly-nx	**GAR/GDR**
lyre	ly-re	**GAR**/*HDO*
lyrical	ly-ri-cal	**GAR/GAR**/*HOO*
lyricist	ly-ri-ci-st	**GAR/GAR/GAR**/*HDO*
lyrics	ly-ri-cs	**GAR/GAR/GDR**

Word	Mouthables	Mouth Movements Notations
M		
M	M	**GAR**/*HDO*
mac	ma-c	**GAR**/*HDO*
macaroni	ma-ca-ro-ni	**GAR/GAR**/*HOO*/**GAR**
macaroon	ma-ca-roo-n	**GAR/GAR**/*HOO*/*HDO*
machine	ma-chi-ne	**GAR/GAR/GDR**
machinery	ma-chi-ne-ry	**GAR/GDR/GAR**/*HDO*
machinist	ma-chi-ni-st	**GAR/GAR/GAR**/*HDO*
mackerel	ma-cke-rel	**GAR/GAR**/*HDO*
mackintosh	ma-cki-n-to-sh	**GAR/GAR/GDR**/*HAO*/*HDO*
macrobiotics	ma-cro-bi-o-ti-cs	**GAR**/*HOO*/**GRR**/*HAO*/**GAR/GDR**
Macugnaga	Ma-cu-gna-ga	**GAR**/*HOO*/**GDR/GAR**
mad	ma-d	**GAR/GRR**
madam	ma-da-m	**GAR/GAR**/*HDO*
madden	ma-d-den	**GAR/GDR**/*HDO*
made	ma-de	*HAO*/**GRR**
madness	ma-d-ne-ss	**GAR/GDR/GAR**/*HDO*
magazine	ma-ga-zi-ne	**GAR/GAR/GAR/GDR**
maggot	ma-ggo-t	**GAR**/*HAO*/*HOO*
magic	ma-gi-c	**GAR/GAR/GDR**
magical	ma-gi-cal	**GAR/GAR**/*HDO*
magician	ma-gi-ci-a-n	**GAR/GAR/GDR/GAR/GDR**
magistrate	ma-gi-stra-te	**GAR/GAR**/*HAO*/*HDO*
magnanimous	ma-g-na-ni-mou-s	**GAR**/*HDO*/**GAR/GAR**/*HAO*/*HDO*
magnate	ma-g-na-te	**GAR**/*HDO*/*HAO*/*HDO*
magnesium	ma-g-ne-si-u-m	**GAR/GDR/GRR/GAR/GAR**/*HDO*
magnet	ma-g-ne-t	**GAR**/*HDO*/**GAR/GDR**
magnetic	ma-g-ne-ti-c	**GAR**/*HDO*/**GAR/GAR/GDR**
magneto	ma-g-ne-to	**GAR**/*HDO*/**GRR**/*HOO*
magnificent	ma-g-ni-fi-ce-nt	**GAR**/*HDO*/**GAR/GAR/GAR/GDR**
magnify	ma-g-ni-fy	**GAR**/*HDO*/**GAR/GRR**
magpie	ma-g-pie	**GAR**/*HDO*/**GRR**

Word	Mouthables	Mouth Movements Notations
mahogany	ma-ho-ga-ny	GAR/*HAO*/GAR/GDR
maid	mai-d	*HAO/HOO*
maiden	mai-den	*HAO/HDO*
mail	mai-l	*HAO*/GDR
maim	mai-m	*HAO/HDO*
main	mai-n	*HAO*/GDR
maintain	mai-n-tai-n	*HAO*/GDR/*HAO*/GDR
maintenance	mai-n-te-na-nce	*HAO*/GDR/GAR/GAR/GDR
maize	mai-ze	*HAO/HDO*
majestic	ma-je-sti-c	GAR/GAR/GAR/GDR
majesty	ma-je-sty	GAR/GAR/*HDO*
major	ma-jor	*HAO*/GDR
majority	ma-jo-ri-ty	GAR/*HAO*/GAR/GAR
make	ma-ke	*HAO*/GRR
maker	ma-ker	*HAO/HDO*
making	ma-king	*HAO*/GDR
maladjusted	ma-lad-ju-sted	GAR/GAR/GAR/GRR
malaria	ma-lar-i-a	GAR/*HAO*/GAR/GAR
male	ma-le	*HAO/HDO*
malfunction	ma-l-fun-c-tion	GAR/GDR/GAR/GDR/*HOO*
malice	ma-li-ce	GAR/GAR/GDR
malicious	ma-li-ci-ou-s	GAR/GAR/*HDO/HAO/HDO*
malignant	ma-li-g-na-nt	GAR/GAR/GDR/GAR/GDR
malinger	ma-lin-ger	GAR/GAR/*HDO*
mall	mal-l	*HOO/HDO*
malleable	ma-lle-a-ble	GAR/GAR/GAR/*HOO*
mallet	ma-le-tt	GAR/GAR/*HDO*
malpractice	ma-l-prac-ti-ce	GAR/GDR/GAR/GAR/GDR
malt	mal-t	*HOO/HOO*
Maltese	Mal-te-se	*HOO*/GRR/*HDO*
maltreat	ma-l-trea-t	GAR/GDR/GRR/*HOO*

Word	Mouthables	Mouth Movements Notations
mamma	ma-mma	**GAR/GAR**
man	ma-n	**GAR/GDR**
mane	ma-ne	*HAO/HDO*
manage	ma-na-ge	**GAR**/*HAO/HDO*
manageable	ma-na-ge-a-ble	**GAR**/*HAO/HDO*/**GAR**/*HOO*
management	ma-na-ge-me-nt	**GAR**/*HAO/HDO*/**GAR/GDR**
manager	ma-na-ger	**GAR**/*HAO/HDO*
managerial	ma-na-ger-i-al	**GAR**/*HAO/HOO*/**GAR/GDR**
mandarin	ma-n-da-ri-n	**GAR/GDR/GAR/GAR/GDR**
mandate	ma-n-da-te	**GAR/GDR**/*HAO/HDO*
mandatory	ma-n-da-to-ry	**GAR/GDR**/*HAO/HOO*/**GDR**
mandolin	ma-n-do-li-n	**GAR/GDR**/*HOO*/**GAR/GDR**
mane	ma-ne	*HAO*/**GDR**
manerism	ma-nner-i-sm	**GAR**/*HDO*/**GAR/GDR**
maneuver	ma-neu-ver	**GAR**/*HOO/HDO*
manful	ma-n-ful	**GAR/GDR**/*HOO*
manhole	ma-n-ho-le	**GAR/GDR**/*HOO/HDO*
mania	ma-ni-a	*HAO*/**GAR/GAR**
maniac	ma-ni-a-c	*HAO*/**GAR/GAR/GDR**
maniacal	ma-ni-a-cal	*HAO*/**GAR/GAR**/*HDO*
manicure	ma-ni-cu-re	**GAR/GAR**/*HOO/HDO*
manicurist	ma-ni-cu-rist	**GAR/GAR**/*HOO/HDO*
manifest	ma-ni-fe-st	**GAR/GAR/GAR**/*HOO*
manifestation	ma-ni-fe-sta-tion	**GAR/GAR/GAR**/*HAO/HOO*
manipulate	ma-ni-p-u-la-te	**GAR/GAR**/*HDO/HOO/HAO/HDO*
mankind	ma-n-ki-nd	**GAR/GDR/GRR/GDR**
manly	ma-n-ly	**GAR/GDR/GDR**
manna	ma-nna	**GAR/GAR**
manned	ma-nne-d	**GAR/GDR**/*HOO*
manner	ma-nner	**GAR**/*HDO*
mannish	ma-nni-sh	**GAR/GAR**/*HDO*
manoeuvre	ma-n-oeu-vre	**GAR/GDR**/*HOO/HDO*

Word	Mouthables	Mouth Movements Notations
manoeuvring	ma-n-oeu-vring	GAR/GDR/*HOO*/GDR
manor	ma-nor	GAR/*HOO*
manpower	ma-n-pow-er	GAR/GDR/GAR/*HDO*
mansion	ma-n-sion	GAR/GDR/*HOO*
manslaughter	ma-n-slaugh-ter	GAR/GDR/*HOO*/*HDO*
mantel	man-te-l	GAR/GAR/*HDO*
mantle	ma-n-tle	GAR/GDR/*HOO*
manual	ma-n-u-al	GAR/GDR/*HOO*/GDR
manufacture	ma-n-u-fac-tu-re	GAR/GDR/*HOO*/GAR/*HOO*/*HDO*
manufacturer	ma-n-u-fac-tu-rer	GAR/GDR/*HOO*/GAR/*HOO*/*HDO*
manure	ma-nu-re	GAR/*HOO*/*HDO*
manuscript	ma-nu-scri-pt	GAR/*HOO*/GAR/*HDO*
many	ma-ny	*HAO*/GAR
map	ma-p	GAR/*HDO*
maple	ma-ple	*HAO*/*HOO*
maul	mau-l	*HOO*/GRR
mauled	mau-le-d	*HOO*/GDR /*HOO*
mar	mar	GAR
marathon	ma-ra-th-o-n	GAR/GAR/*HTO*/*HAO*/*HDO*
marble	mar-ble	*HAO*/*HOO*
march	mar-ch	GAR/*HDO*
March	Mar-ch	*HAO*/*HOO*
marched	mar-che-d	GAR/*HDO*/*HOO*
marcher	mar-cher	GAR/*HDO*
mare	mare	*HAO*
margarine	mar-ga-ri-ne	*HAO*/GAR/GAR/GDR
margin	mar-gi-n	*HAO*/GAR/GDR
marginal	mar-gi-nal	*HAO*/GAR/*HDO*
marginalize	mar-gi-na-li-ze	*HAO*/GAR/GAR/GRR/GDR
marginally	mar-gi-na-lly	*HAO*/GAR/GAR/GDR
Maria	Ma-ri-a	GAR/GAR/GAR
marina	ma-ri-na	GAR/GAR/GDR

Word	Mouthables	Mouth Movements Notations
marinade	ma-ri-na-de	**GAR**/**GAR**/*HAO*/*HDO*
marine	ma-ri-ne	**GAR**/**GAR**/**GDR**
marital	ma-ri-tal	**GAR**/**GAR**/*HDO*
maritime	ma-ri-ti-me	**GAR**/**GAR**/**GRR**/*HDO*
mark	mar-k	*HAO*/**GRR**
marked	mar-ke-d	*HAO*/**GDR**/*HOO*
mark	mar-k	*HAO*/**GDR**
marker	mar-ker	*HAO*/*HDO*
market	mar-ke-t	*HAO*/**GAR**/**GDR**
marmot	mar-mo-t	*HAO*/*HAO*/*HDO*
marque	mar-que	*HAO*/*HDO*
marquee	mar-quee	*HAO*/**GRR**
marquis	mar-qui-s	*HAO*/**GAR**/*HDO*
marriage	ma-rria-ge	**GAR**/**GAR**/*HDO*
marrow	ma-rro-w	**GAR**/*HOO*/*HDO*
marry	ma-rry	**GAR**/**GDR**
marsh	mar-sh	*HAO*/*HDO*
marshal	mar-shal	*HAO*/*HDO*
mart	mar-t	*HAO*/*HOO*
martial	mar-tia-l	*HAO*/*HDO*/**GDR**
marten	mar-ten	*HAO*/*HDO*
Martin	Mar-ti-n	*HAO*/**GAR**/**GDR**
martyr	mar-tyr	*HAO*/*HDO*
marvel	mar-vel	*HAO*/*HOO*
marvellous	mar-ve-llou-s	*HAO*/**GAR**/*HAO*/*HDO*
Marxist	Mar-xi-st	**GAR**/**GAR**/**GRR**
mascot	ma-sco-t	**GAR**/*HAO*/*HOO*
masculine	ma-scu-li-ne	**GAR**/*HOO*/**GAR**/**GDR**
mash	ma-sh	**GAR**/*HDO*
masher	ma-sher	**GAR**/*HDO*
mask	mas-k	*HAO*/**GRR**

Word	Mouthables	Mouth Movements Notations
masked	mas-ke-d	*HAO*/**GDR**/*HOO*
mask	mas-k	*HAO*/**GDR**
mason	ma-so-n	*HAO*/*HAO*/*HDO*
masonry	ma-so-n-ry	*HAO*/*HAO*/*HDO*/**GDR**
masque	mas-que	*HAO*/*HDO*
masquerade	mas-que-ra-de	*HAO*/**GAR**/*HAO*/*HDO*
mass	ma-ss	**GAR**/*HDO*
massacre	ma-ssa-cre	**GAR**/**GAR**/*HDO*
massage	ma-ssage	**GAR**/*HDO*
masseur	ma-sseur	**GAR**/*HOO*
masseuse	ma-sseu-se	**GAR**/*HOO*/*HDO*
massif	ma-ssi-f	**GAR**/**GAR**/**GDR**
massive	mas-si-ve	**GAR**/**GAR**/*HDO*
mast	mas-t	*HAO*/*HOO*
master	mas-ter	*HAO*/*HDO*
masterly	mas-ter-ly	*HAO*/*HOO*/**GDR**
mastery	mas-te-ry	*HAO*/*HOO*/*HDO*
mastiff	ma-sti-ff	**GAR**/**GAR**/*HDO*
mat	ma-t	**GAR**/*HDO*
match	mat-ch	**GAR**/*HOO*
match	ma-tch	**GAR**/*HDO*
matchless	ma-tch-le-ss	**GAR**/*HDO*/**GAR**/**GDR**
mate	ma-te	*HAO*/*HOO*
mate	ma-te	*HAO*/*HDO*
material	ma-te-ri al	**GAR**/**GAR**/**GAR**/*HDO*
maternal	ma-ter-nal	**GAR**/*HOO*/*HDO*
maternity	ma-ter-ni-ty	**GAR**/*HOO*/**GAR**/**GAR**
matey	ma-tey	*HAO*/**GAR**
math	ma-th	**GAR**/**GTR**
mathematical	ma-the-ma-ti-cal	**GAR**/**GTR**/**GAR**/**GAR**/*HDO*
mathematician	ma-the-ma-ti-cian	**GAR**/**GTR**/**GAR**/**GAR**/*HDO*

Word	Mouthables	Mouth Movements Notations
mathematics	ma-the-ma-ti-cs	GAR/GTR/GAR/GAR/GDR
maths	ma-th-s	GAR/GTR/GDR
matriculate	ma-tri-cu-la-te	GAR/GAR/*HOO*/*HAO*/*HDO*
matrix	ma-tri-x	*HAO*/GAR/GDR
matt	ma-tt	GAR/*HDO*
matter	mat-ter	GAR/*HDO*
mattress	ma-ttre-ss	GAR/GAR/*HDO*
mature	ma-tu-re	GAR/*HOO*/*HDO*
mauve	mau-ve	*HOO*/*HDO*
maverick	ma-ver-i-ck	GAR/*HDO*/GAR/*HDO*
maw	maw	*HOO*
mawkish	maw-ki-sh	*HOO*/GAR/*HDO*
maxim	ma-xi-m	GAR/GAR/GDR
maximum	ma-xi-mu-m	GAR/GAR/GAR/*HDO*
May	May	*HAO*
maybe	may-be	*HAO*/GRR
mayhem	may-he-m	*HAO*/GAR/*HDO*
mayonnaise	may-o-nnai-se	*HAO*/*HAO*/*HAO*/*HDO*
mayor	may-or	*HAO*/*HDO*
maze	ma-ze	*HAO*/GDR
me	me	GRR
meadow	mea-do-w	GAR/*HOO*/*HDO*
meagre	mea-gre	GRR/*HDO*
meal	mea-l	GRR/GDR
mean	mea-n	GRR/GRR
meaning	mea-ni-ng	GRR/GAR/GDR
meant	mea-nt	GAR/GRR
meaner	mea-ner	GRR/*HDO*
measles	mea-sles	GRR/*HOO*
measly	mea-sly	GRR/GAR
measurably	mea-su-ra-bly	GAR/*HOO*/GAR/*HDO*

Word	Mouthables	Mouth Movements Notations
measure	mea-su-re	GAR/*HOO*/*HDO*
meat	mea-t	GRR/*HDO*
meaty	mea-ty	GRR/GAR
mechanic	me-cha-ni-c	GAR/GAR/GAR/GDR
mechanical	me-cha-ni-cal	GAR/GAR/GAR/*HDO*
mechanics	me-cha-ni-cs	GAR/GAR/GAR/GDR
mechanize	me-cha-ni-ze	GAR/GAR/GRR/GDR
medal	me-da-l	GAR/GAR/*HDO*
meddle	me-ddle	GAR/*HOO*
media	me-di-a	GAR/GAR/GAR
medic	me-di-c	GAR/GAR/GDR
medical	me-di-cal	GAR/GAR/*HDO*
medication	me-di-ca-tion	GAR/GAR/*HAO*/*HOO*
medicine	me-di-ci-ne	GAR/GAR/GAR/GDR
mediocre	me-di-o-cre	GRR/GAR/*HOO*/*HDO*
meditate	me-di-ta-te	GAR/GAR/*HAO*/*HDO*
meditation	me-di-ta-tion	GAR/GAR/*HAO*/*HOO*
Mediterranean	Me-di-ter-ra-ne-an	GAR/GAR/*HOO*/*HAO*/GRR/GDR
medium	me-di-um	GAR/GAR/*HDO*
medley	me-d-ley	GAR/GDR/GDR
meek	mee-k	GRR/GDR
meet	mee-t	GRR/GRR
meeting	mee-ti-ng	GRR/GAR/GDR
melancholic	me-la-n-cho-li-c	GAR/GAR/GDR/*HAO*/GAR/GDR
melancholy	me-la-n-cho-ly	GAR/GAR/GDR/*HAO*/GDR
mellow	me-llo-w	GAR/*HOO*/*HDO*
melodious	me-lo-di-ous	GAR/*HOO*/GAR/GAR
melodramatic	me-lo-dra-ma-ti-c	GAR/*HOO*/GAR/GAR/GAR/GDR
melody	me-lo-dy	GAR/*HOO*/GAR
melon	me-lo-n	GAR/*HAO*/*HDO*
melt	me-lt	GAR/GRR

Word	Mouthables	Mouth Movements Notations
member	me-m-ber	GAR/*HDO*/*HDO*
membership	me-m-ber-shi-p	GAR/*HDO*/*HAO*/*HDO*/GDR
memento	me-me-n-to	GAR/GAR/GDR/*HOO*
memo	me-mo	GAR/*HOO*
memorable	me-mo-ra-ble	GAR/GAR/GAR/*HOO*
memorial	me-mor-i-al	GAR/*HOO*/GAR/GDR
memorize	me-mo-ri-ze	GAR/GAR/GRR/GDR
memory	me-mo-ry	GAR/GAR/GDR
men	me-n	GAR/GDR
menace	me-na-ce	GAR/GAR/GDR
mend	me-nd	GAR/GRR
menstruation	me-n-stru-a-tion	GAR/GDR/*HOO*/*HAO*/*HOO*
menswear	me-ns-wear	GAR/GDR/*HAO*
mental	me-n-tal	GAR/GDR/*HDO*
mentality	me-n-ta-li-ty	GAR/GDR/GAR/GAR/GAR
mention	me-n-tion	GAR/GDR/*HOO*
menu	me-nu	GAR/*HOO*
mercantile	mer-ca-n-ti-le	*HAO*/GAR/GDR/GRR/GDR
merchant	mer-cha-nt	*HAO*/GAR/GDR
merciful	mer-ci-ful	GAR/GAR/*HOO*
merciless	mer-ci-le-ss	GAR/GAR/GAR/GDR
mercurial	mer-cu-rial	*HAO*/*HOO*/*HDO*
mercury	mer-cu-ry	*HAO*/*HOO*/GDR
mercy	mer-cy	GAR/GAR
merge	mer-ge	*HOO*/*HDO*
merger	mer-ger	*HOO*/*HDO*
meridian	me-ri-di-a-n	GAR/GAR/GAR/GAR/GDR
meringue	me-rin-gue	GAR/*HAO*/*HDO*
merit	me-ri-t	GAR/GAR/GRR
merry	mer-ry	GAR/GDR
mesh	me-sh	GAR/*HDO*

Word	Mouthables	Mouth Movements Notations
mesmerize	me-s-mer-i-ze	GAR/GDR/*HAO*/GRR/GDR
mess	me-ss	GAR/*HDO*
message	mes-sage	GAR/*HDO*
messenger	mes-se-n-ger	GAR/GAR/GDR/*HDO*
messy	mes-sy	GAR/GAR
met	me-t	GAR/GRR
metal	me-ta-l	GAR/GAR/*HDO*
metallic	me-ta-lli-c	GAR/GAR/GAR/GDR
meteor	me-te-or	GRR/GRR/*HOO*
meteorology	me-te-oro-lo-gy	GAR/GRR/*HDO*/GAR/GDR
meter	me-ter	GRR/*HDO*
methane	me-th-a-ne	GRR/GTR/*HAO*/GDR
method	me-th-o-d	GAR/*HTO*/*HAO*/*HDO*
methodical	me-th-o-di-cal	GAR/*HTO*/*HAO*/GAR/*HDO*
meticulous	me-ti-cu-lou-s	GAR/GAR/*HOO*/GAR/GDR
metre	me-tre	GRR/*HDO*
metropolitan	me-tro-po-li-ta-n	GAR/*HOO*/*HAO*/GAR/GAR/GDR
mettle	me-ttle	GAR/*HOO*
mew	mew	*HOO*
mews	mew-s	*HOO*/*HDO*
Mexico	Me-xi-co	GAR/GAR/*HOO*
mezzanine	me-zza-ni-ne	GAR/GAR/GAR/GDR
mi	mi	GAR
mice	mi-ce	GRR/GDR
micky	mi-cky	GAR/GAR
micro	mi-cro	GRR/*HOO*
microbe	mi-cro-be	GRR/*HOO*/*HDO*
microphone	mi-cro-pho-ne	GRR/*HOO*/*HOO*/GDR
microscope	mi-cro-sco-pe	GRR/*HOO*/*HOO*/*HDO*
middle	mi-ddle	GAR/*HOO*
middling	mi-dd-ling	GAR/*HDO*/GDR

Word	Mouthables	Mouth Movements Notations
midge	mid-ge	**GAR**/*HDO*
midget	mi-d-ge-t	**GAR/GDR/GAR/GDR**
midnight	mi-d-nigh-t	**GAR/GDR/GRR**/*HOO*
mien	m(i)e-n	**GRR**/*HDO*
might	migh-t	**GRR/GRR**
mighty	migh-ty	**GRR/GAR**
migraine	mi-grai-ne	**GAR**/*HAO*/**GDR**
migrant	mi-gra-nt	**GRR/GAR**/*HOO*
mike	mi-ke	**GRR**/*HDO*
mild	mi-ld	**GRR/GDR**
mildew	mi-l-dew	**GAR/GDR**/*HOO*
mile	mi-le	**GRR**/*HDO*
military	mi-li-tar-y	**GAR/GAR/GAR/GAR**
militate	mi-li-ta-te	**GAR/GAR**/*HAO*/*HDO*
milk	mi-lk	**GAR**/*HDO*
milky	mi-l-ky	**GAR/GDR/GAR**
mill	mi-ll	**GAR/GDR**
miller	mi-ller	**GAR**/*HDO*
millet	mi-lle-t	**GAR/GAR**/*HDO*
millimetre	mi-lli-me-tre	**GAR/GAR/GRR**/*HDO*
million	mi-lli-o-n	**GAR/GAR**/*HAO*/*HDO*
millionaire	mi-lli-o-n-aire	**GAR/GAR**/*HAO*/*HDO*/*HAO*
mime	mi-me	**GRR**/*HDO*
mimic	mi-mi-c	**GAR/GAR/GDR**
mince	mi-n-ce	**GAR/GDR/GDR**
mincer	mi-n-cer	**GAR/GDR**/*HDO*
mincing	mi-n-ci-ng	**GAR/GDR/GAR/GDR**
mind	min-d	**GRR**/*HOO*
minder	mi-n-der	**GAR/GDR**/*HDO*
mindful	min-d-ful	**GRR**/*HOO*/*HOO*
mindless	min-d-le-ss	**GRR**/*HOO*/**GAR**/*HDO*

Word	Mouthables	Mouth Movements Notations
mine	mi-ne	**GRR/GRR**
mined	mi-ne-d	**GRR/GDR**/*HOO*
mine	mi-ne	**GRR**/*HDO*
mine	mi-ne	**GRR/GDR**
miner	mi-ner	**GRR**/*HDO*
mineral	mi-ner-al	**GAR**/*HDO*/*HDO*
mingle	min-gle	**GAR**/*HOO*
mingy	mi-n-gy	**GAR/GDR**/*HDO*
miniature	mi-ni-a-tu-re	**GAR/GAR/GAR**/*HOO*/*HDO*
miniaturize	mi-ni-a-tur-i-ze	**GAR/GAR/GAR**/*HOO*/**GRR/GDR**
minimal	mi-ni-mal	**GAR/GAR**/*HDO*
minimize	mi-ni-mi-ze	**GAR/GAR/GRR/GDR**
minimum	mi-ni-mu-m	**GAR/GAR/GAR**/*HDO*
mining	mi-ning	**GRR/GDR**
miniskirt	mi-ni-skir-t	**GAR/GAR**/*HOO*/*HDO*
minister	mi-ni-ster	**GAR/GAR**/*HDO*
ministerial	mi-ni-ste-rial	**GAR/GAR/GRR**/*HDO*
ministry	mi-ni-stry	**GAR/GAR**/*HDO*
mink	min-k	**GAR**/*HDO*
minor	mi-nor	**GRR**/*HOO*
minority	mi-no-ri-ty	**GRR**/*HAO*/**GAR/GAR**
mint	mi-n-t	**GAR/GDR**/*HOO*
minus	mi-nu-s	**GRR/GAR**/*HDO*
minute	mi-nu-te	**GRR**/*HOO*/*HDO*
miow	mi-ow	**GAR**/*HAO*
miracle	mi-ra-cle	**GAR/GAR**/*HOO*
miraculous	mi-ra-cu-lou-s	**GAR/GAR**/*HOO*/*HAO*/*HDO*
mirage	mi-ra-ge	**GAR/GAR**/*HDO*
mire	mi-re	**GRR**/*IIDO*
mirror	mi-rror	**GAR**/*HDO*
mirth	mir-th	**GAR/GTR**

Word	Mouthables	Mouth Movements Notations
misappropriation	mi-sa-ppro-pri-a-tion	GAR/GAR/*HOO*/GAR/*HAO*/*HOO*
misbehave	mi-s-be-ha-ve	GAR/GDR/GRR/*HAO*/*HDO*
miscalculate	mi-s-cal-cu-la-te	GAR/GDR/GAR/*HOO*/*HAO*/*HDO*
miscarriage	mi-s-car-ria-ge	GAR/GDR/GAR/*HAO*/*HDO*
mischance	mi-s-chan-ce	GAR/GDR/*HAO*/GDR
mischief	mi-s-chie-f	GAR/GDR/GAR/*HDO*
mischievous	mi-s-chie-v-ou-s	GAR/GDR/GAR/GDR/GAR/GDR
misconduct	mi-sco-n-duc-t	GAR/*HAO*/GDR/GAR/*HOO*
misdemeanor	mi-s-de-mea-nor	GAR/GDR/GRR/GRR/GAR
miser	mi-ser	GRR/*HDO*
miserable	mi-se-ra-ble	GAR/GAR/GAR/*HOO*
misery	mi-se-ry	GAR/GAR/GDR
misfire	mi-s-fi-re	GAR/GDR/GRR/*HDO*
misfit	mi-s-fi-t	GAR/GDR/GAR/*HOO*
misfortune	mi-s-for-tu-ne	GAR/GDR/*HOO*/*HOO*/*HDO*
misguided	mi-s-gui-ded	GAR/GDR/GRR/GRR
mishap	mi-s-ha-p	GAR/GDR/GAR/*HDO*
misinformation	mi-si-n-for-ma-tion	GAR/GAR/GDR/*HOO*/*HAO*/*HOO*
misinterpret	mi-si-n-ter-pre-t	GAR/GAR/GDR/*HOO*/GAR/*HOO*
misjudgement	mi-s-jud-ge-me-nt	GAR/GDR/GAR/*HDO*/GAR/GDR
mislaid	mi-s-lai-d	GAR/GDR/*HAO*/GRR
mislay	mi-s-lay	GAR/GDR/*HAO*
mislead	mi-s-lea-d	GAR/GDR/GRR/GRR
misrepresent	mi-s-re-pre-se-nt	GAR/GDR/GAR/GRR/GAR/GDR
misrule	mi-s-ru-le	GAR/GDR/*HOO*/*HDO*
miss	mi-ss	GAR/GRR
missed	mi-sse-d	GAR/GDR/*HOO*
missile	mi-ssi-le	GAR/GRR/GDR
missing	mi-ssi-ng	GAR/GAR/GDR
mission	mi-ssi-on	GAR/*HOO*/*HDO*
missionary	mi-ssion-ar-y	GAR/*HOO*/*HAO*/*HDO*

Word	Mouthables	Mouth Movements Notations
misspell	mi-s-spe-ll	GAR/GDR/GAR/GDR
mist	mi-st	GAR/*HOO*
mistake	mi-sta-ke	GRR/*HAO/HDO*
mister	mi-ster	GAR/*HDO*
mistletoe	mi-stle-toe	GAR/*HOO/HOO*
mistook	mi-stoo-k	GAR/*HOO/HDO*
mistreat	mi-strea-t	GAR/GRR/*HOO*
mistress	mi-stre-ss	GAR/GAR/*HDO*
mistrust	mi-stru-st	GAR/GAR/*HOO*
misty	mi-sty	GAR/*HDO*
misunderstand	mi-sun-der-sta-nd	GAR/GAR/*HAO*/GAR/GDR
misunderstanding	mi-sun-der-sta-nding	GAR/GAR/*HAO*/GAR/GDR
misunderstood	mi-sun-der-stoo-d	GAR/GAR/*HAO/HOO/HOO*
misuse	mi-s-u-se	GAR/GDR/*HOO/HOO*
mite	mi-te	GRR/*HDO*
mitigate	mi-ti-ga-te	GAR/GAR/*HAO/HDO*
mitt	mi-tt	GAR/*HDO*
mix	mi-x	GAR/GRR
mixed	mi-xe-d	GAR/GDR/*HOO*
mixer	mi-xer	GAR/*HDO*
mixture	mi-x-tu-re	GAR/GDR/*HOO/HDO*
moan	moa-n	*HOO*/GDR
moat	moa-t	*HOO/HOO*
mob	mo-b	*HAO/HDO*
mobile	mo-bi-le	*HOO*/GRR/GDR
mobilize	mo-bi-li-ze	*HOO*/GAR/GRR/GDR
moccasin	mo-cca-si-n	*HAO*/GAR/GAR/GDR
mock	moc-k	*HAO/HDO*
mocker	moc-ker	*HAO/HDO*
mockery	moc-ke-ry	*HAO*/GAR/GDR
modal	mo-dal	*HOOHDO*

Word	Mouthables	Mouth Movements Notations
mode	mo-de	*HOO*/*HDO*
model	mo-del	*HAO*/*HDO*
moderate	mo-de-ra-te	*HAO*/*HAO*/*HAO*/*HDO*
moderation	mo-de-ra-tion	*HAO*/*HAO*/*HAO*/*HOO*
modern	mo-der-n	*HAO*/*HAO*/*HDO*
modernize	mo-der-ni-ze	*HAO*/*HOO*/**GRR**/**GDR**
molar	mo-lar	*HOO*/*HAO*
mold	mo-ld	*HOO*/*HDO*
mole	mo-le	*HOO*/*HDO*
molest	mo-le-st	*HOO*/**GAR**/*HOO*
molestation	mo-le-sta-tion	*HOO*/**GAR**/*HAO*/*HOO*
mollify	mo-lli-fy	*HAO*/**GAR**/**GRR**
mollusc	mo-llu-sc	*HOO*/**GAR**/*HDO*
molten	mo-l-ten	*HOO*/**GDR**/*HDO*
mom	mo-m	**GAR**/*HDO*
moment	mo-me-nt	*HOO*/**GAR**/**GDR**
momentous	mo-men-tous	*HOO*/**GAR**/**GAR**
momma	mo-mma	**GAR**/**GAR**
monarchy	mo-nar-chy	*HAO*/**GAR**/**GAR**
monastic	mo-na-sti-c	*HAO*/**GAR**/**GAR**/**GDR**
Monday	Mo-n-day	**GAR**/**GDR**/*HAO*
monetary	mo-ne-tary	*HAO*/**GAR**/*HDO*
money	mo-ney	*HAO*/**GRR**
mongrel	mon-grel	**GAR**/*HDO*
monied	mo-nie-d	**GAR**/**GAR**/*HDO*
monitor	mo-ni-tor	*HAO*/**GAR**/*HOO*
monk	mon-k	*HAO*/*HDO*
monkey	mon-key	**GAR**/**GRR**
monogram	mo-no-gra-m	*HAO*/*HOO*/**GAR**/**GDR**
monograph	mo-no-graph	*HAO*/*HOO*/*HDO*
monolingual	mo-no-lin-gual	*HAO*/*HOO*/**GAR**/*HDO*

Word	Mouthables	Mouth Movements Notations
monologue	mo-no-lo-gue	*HAO/HOO/HAO/HDO*
monopolize	mo-no-po-li-ze	*HAO/HAO/HOO/***GRR/GDR**
monopoly	mo-no-po-ly	*HAO/HAO/HOO/HDO*
monotonous	mo-no-to-nou-s	*HAO/HAO/HOO/***GAR/GDR**
monster	mo-n-ster	*HAO/HDO/HDO*
monstrous	mo-n-strou-s	*HAO/HDO/***GAR***/HDO*
montage	mo-n-ta-ge	*HAO/HDO/HAO/HDO*
month	mon-th	**GAR/GTR**
monthly	mon-th-ly	**GAR/GTR/GAR**
monument	mo-nu-me-nt	*HAO/HOO/***GAR/GDR**
moo	moo	*HOO*
mood	moo-d	*HOO/HDO*
moody	moo-dy	*HOO/***GAR**
moon	moo-n	*HOO/HDO*
moony	moo-ny	*HOO/***GAR**
moor	moor	*HOO*
moored	moore-d	*HOO/HOO*
mooring	moor-ing	*HOO/***GDR**
moor	mo-or	*HAO/HDO*
Moor	Moor	*HAO*
mop	mo-p	*HAO/HDO*
mope	mo-pe	*HOO/HDO*
moped	mo-pe-d	*HAO/HOO/HOO*
moped	mo-pe-d	*HOO/***GAR***/HOO*
moral	mo-ral	*HAO/HDO*
morale	mo-ra-le	*HAO/***GAR/GDR**
moralist	mo-ra-li-st	*HAO/HDO/***GAR/GDR**
morality	mo-ra-li-ty	*HAO/***GAR/GAR/GAR**
morass	mo-ra-ss	**GAR/GAR***/HDO*
morbid	mor-bi-d	*HOO/***GAR/GDR**
more	mo-re	*HOO/HDO*

Word	Mouthables	Mouth Movements Notations
morgue	mor-gue	*HOO/HDO*
morning	mor-ning	*HOO*/**GDR**
Moroccan	Mo-roc-ca-n	*HAO/HAO*/**GAR/GDR**
Morocco	Mo-roc-co	*HAO/HAO/HOO*
Moron	mo-ro-n	*HOO/HAO/HDO*
morose	mo-ro-se	*HOO/HOO/HDO*
morphine	mor-phi-ne	*HOO*/**GAR/GDR**
morsel	mor-sel	*HOO/HDO*
mortal	mor-tal	*HOO/HDO*
mortar	mor-tar	*HAO/HAO*
mortgage	mort-ga-ge	*HAO/HAO/HDO*
mortician	mor-ti-ci-a-n	*HOO*/**GAR/GDR/GAR/GDR**
mortify	mor-ti-fy	*HOO*/**GAR/GRR**
mortuary	mor-tu-a-ry	*HOO/HOO*/**GAR**/*HDO*
mosaic	mo-sa-i-c	*HOO/HAO*/**GAR/GDR**
Moscow	Mo-sco-w	*HAO/HOO/HDO*
Moslem	Mo-s-le-m	*HAO*/**GDR/GAR/GDR**
mosque	mo-sque	*HAO/HDO*
mosquito	mo-squi-to	*HAO*/**GAR**/*HOO*
moss	mos-s	*HAO/HDO*
most	mo-st	*HOO/HOO*
mostly	mo-st-ly	*HOO/HOO*/**GDR**
moth	mo-th	*HAO/HTO*
mother	mo-ther	**GAR/GTR**
motherly	mo-ther-ly	**GAR/GTR/GDR**
mote	mo-te	*HOO*/**GDR**
motif	mo-ti-f	*HOO*/**GAR/GDR**
motion	mo-tion	*HOO/HOO*
motivate	mo-ti-va-te	*HOO*/**GAR**/*HAO/HDO*
motivation	mo-ti-va-tion	*HOO*/**GAR**/*HAO/HOO*
motive	mo-ti-ve	*HOO*/**GAR**/*HDO*

Word	Mouthables	Mouth Movements Notations
motor	mo-tor	*HOO/HDO*
motoring	mo-to-ring	*HOO/HDO/*GDR
motorist	mo-to-ri-st	*HAO/HOO/*GAR/GDR
motorway	mo-tor-way	*HAO/HOO/HAO*
mould	mou-ld	*HOO/HDO*
mount	mou-nt	GAR/GDR
mountain	mou-n-tia-n	GAR/GDR/*HAO/HDO*
mountaineer	mou-n-tia-ne-er	GAR/GDR/*HAO/*GRR/GDR
mountainous	mou-n-tai-nou-s	GAR/GDR/*HAO/HAO/HDO*
mounted	mou-nted	*HAO/*GRR
Mountie	Mou-ntie	*HAO/*GAR
mourn	mour-n	*HOO/HDO*
mourning	mour-ning	*HOO/*GDR
mouse	mou-se	*HAO/HDO*
moustache	mou-sta-che	*HOO/*GAR*/HDO*
mouth	mou-th	GAR/GTR
mouthful	mou-th-ful	GAR/GTR/*HOO*
move	mo-ve	*HOO/HDO*
moveable	mo-ve-a-ble	*HOO/HDO/*GAR*/HOO*
movement	mo-ve-me-nt	*HOO/HDO/*GAR/GDR
mover	mo-ver	*HOO/HDO*
movie	mo-vie	*HOO/*GAR
moving	mo-ving	*HOO/*GDR
mow	mo-w	*HOO/HDO*
mowed	mo-we-d	*HOO/HDO/HOO*
much	mu-ch	GAR*/HDO*
muck	muc-k	GAR*/HDO*
mud	mu-d	GAR*/HOO*
muddle	mu-ddle	GAR*/HOO*
muddy	mu-ddy	GAR*/*GAR
muffle	mu-ffle	GAR*/HOO*

Word	Mouthables	Mouth Movements Notations
muffler	mu-ff-ler	GAR/*HOO*/*HDO*
mug	mu-g	GAR/*HDO*
muggy	mu-gg-y	GAR/*HDO*/GAR
mulatto	mu-la-tto	*HOO*/GAR/*HOO*
mulberry	mu-l-ber-ry	GAR/GDR/*HAO*/GDR
mule	mu-le	*HOO*/GDR
mull	mu-ll	GAR/*HDO*
mullet	mu-lle-t	GAR/GAR/GDR
multinational	mu-l-ti-na-tion-al	GAR/GDR/GAR/GAR/*HOO*/*HDO*
multiple	mu-l-ti-ple	GAR/GDR/GAR/*HOO*
multiply	mu-l-ti-ply	GAR/GDR/GAR/GRR
multitude	mu-l-ti-tu-de	GAR/GDR/GAR/*HOO*/*HDO*
mum	mu-m	GAR/*HDO*
mumble	mu-m-ble	*HAO*/*HDO*/*HOO*
mumdane	mu-n-da-ne	GAR/GDR/*HAO*/GDR
mummy	mu-mmy	GAR/GAR
mumps	mu-mps	GAR/*HDO*
munch	mu-n-ch	GAR/GDR/*HDO*
municipal	mu-ni-ci-pal	*HOO*/GAR/GAR/*HDO*
mural	mu-ral	*HOO*/*HDO*
murder	mur-der	GAR/GAR
murderer	mur-de-rer	GAR/GAR/*HDO*
murderous	mur-de-rou-s	GAR/GAR/GAR/*HDO*
murky	mur-ky	GAR/GAR
murmur	mur-mur	*HAO*/*HAO*
muscatel	mu-sca-te-l	GAR/GAR/GAR/GDR
muscle	mu-scle	GAR/*HOO*
Muscovite	Mu-sco-vi-te	GAR/*HOO*/GRR/*HDO*
muse	mu-se	*HOO*/*HDO*
mused	mu-se-d	*HOO*/*HOO*/*HOO*
muse	mu-se	*HOO*/GDR

Word	Mouthables	Mouth Movements Notations
museum	mu-se-u-m	*HOO*/**GRR**/**GAR**/*HDO*
mushroom	mu-shroo-m	**GAR**/*HOO*/*HDO*
music	mu-si-c	*HOO*/**GAR**/**GDR**
musical	mu-si-cal	*HOO*/**GAR**/*HDO*
musician	mu-si-cian	*HOO*/**GRR**/*HDO*
Muslim	Mu-s-li-m	**GAR**/**GDR**/**GAR**/**GDR**
mussel	mus-se-l	**GAR**/**GAR**/**GDR**
must	mu-st	**GAR**/*HOO*
mustache	mu-sta-che	**GAR**/**GAR**/*HDO*
mustard	mu-star-d	**GAR**/*HAO*/*HDO*
muster	mu-ster	**GAR**/*HDO*
musty	mu-sty	**GAR**/**GAR**
mute	mu-te	*HOO*/*HDO*
mutiny	mu-ti-ny	*HOO*/**GAR**/**GAR**
mutter	mut-ter	**GAR**/*HDO*
mutton	mut-to-n	**GAR**/*HAO*/*HDO*
mutual	mu-tu-al	*HOO*/*HOO*/*HDO*
muzzle	muz-zle	**GAR**/*HOO*
my	my	**GRR**
myrtle	myr-tle	*HAO*/*HOO*
myself	my-se-lf	**GRR**/**GAR**/**GDR**
mysterious	my-ste-ri-ou-s	**GAR**/**GRR**/**GAR**/*HAO*/*HDO*
mystery	my-ste-ry	**GAR**/**GAR**/*HDO*
mystify	my-sti-fy	**GAR**/**GAR**/**GRR**
myth	my th	**GAR**/**GTR**
mythology	my-tho-lo-gy	**GAR**/*HTO*/*HOO*/**GDR**

Word	Mouthables	Mouth Movements Notations
N		
N	N	**GAR/GDR**
nag	na-g	**GAR**/*HDO*
nail	nai-l	*HAO*/**GDR**
naive	na-i-ve	**GAR/GAR**/*HDO*
naked	na-ked	*HAO*/**GRR**
name	na-me	*HAO/HDO*
nameless	na-me-le-ss	*HAO/HDO*/**GAR/GDR**
namely	na-me-ly	*HO/HDO*/**GDR**
nanny	nan-ny	**GAR/GAR**
nap	na-p	**GAR**/*HDO*
nape	na-pe	*HAO/HDO*
napkin	na-p-ki-n	**GAR**/*HDO*/**GAR/GDR**
Naples	Na-ples	*HAO/HOO*
nappy	na-ppy	**GAR**/*HDO*
narcissus	nar-cis-su-s	**GAR/GAR/GAR/GDR**
narcotic	nar-co-ti-c	**GAR**/*HAO*/**GAR/GDR**
nark	nar-k	*HAO/HDO*
narrowly	na-rro-w-ly	**GAR**/*HOO/HDO*/**GDR**
narrration	nar-ra-tion	*HAO/HAO/HOO*
narrrow	na-rro-w	**GAR**/*HOO/HDO*
nasal	na-sal	*HAO/IIDO*
nasty	nas-ty	*HAO*/**GAR**
nation	na-tion	*HAO/HOO*
national	na-tion-al	**GAR**/*HOO*/**GDR**
nationality	na-tion-a-li-ty	**GAR**/*HOO*/**GAR/GAR/GAR**
nationalize	na-tion-a-li-ze	**GAR**/*HOO*/**GAR/GRR/GDR**
native	na-ti-ve	*HAO*/**GAR**/*HDO*
natty	nat-ty	**GAR/GAR**
natural	na-tu-ral	**GAR**/*HOO*/**GDR**
naturalist	na-tu-ra-li-st	**GAR**/*HOO*/**GDR/GAR/GDR**

Word	Mouthables	Mouth Movements Notations
naturally	na-tu-ra-lly	GAR/*HOO*/GAR/GDR
nature	na-tu-re	*HAO*/*HOO*/*HDO*
naughty	naugh-ty	*HOO*/GAR
nausea	nau-se-a	*HOO*/GRR/GAR
nauseate	nau-se-a-te	*HOO*/GRR/*HAO*/*HDO*
nauseous	nau-se-ou-s	*HOO*/GRR/GAR/*HDO*
nautical	nau-ti-cal	*HOO*/GAR/*HDO*
navel	na-vel	*HAO*/*HDO*
navigate	na-vi-ga-te	GAR/GAR/*HAO*/*HDO*
navigation	na-vi-ga-tion	GAR/GAR/*HAO*/*HOO*
navy	na-vy	*HAO*/*HDO*
Nazi	Na-zi	GAR/GAR
Naziism	Na-zi-sm	GAR/GDR/*HDO*
Neapolitan	Ne-a-po-li-ta-n	GRR/GAR/*HAO*/GAR/GAR/GDR
near	ne-ar	GRR/*HAO*
nearby	ne-ar-by	GRR/*HAO*/GRR
nearly	ne-ar-ly	GRR/*HAO*/GDR
neat	nea-t	GRR/*HOO*
necessary	ne-ces-sar-y	GAR/GAR/*HAO*/GDR
necessity	ne-ce-ssi-ty	GAR/GAR/GAR/GAR
necklace	ne-ck-la-ce	GAR/*HDO*/*HAO*/GDR
nectar	ne-c-tar	GAR/GDR/*HAO*
need	nee-d	GRR/*HOO*
needle	nee-dle	GRR/*HOO*
negative	ne-ga-ti-ve	GAR/GAR/GAR/*HDO*
neglect	ne-g-le-ct	GAR/GDR/GAR/*HOO*
negligent	ne-g-li-ge-nt	GAR/GDR/GAR/GAR/GDR
negotiate	ne-go-ti-a-te	GAR/*HOO*/*HDO*/*HAO*/*HDO*
negotiation	ne-go-ti-a-tion	GAR/*HOO*/*HDO*/*HAO*/*HOO*
neighbour	neigh-bour	*HAO*/*HAO*
neighbourhood	neigh-bour-hoo-d	*HAO*/*HAO*/*HOO*/*HOO*/*HDO*

Word	Mouthables	Mouth Movements Notations
neither	nei-ther	**GRR**/*HTO*
neither	n(e)i-ther	**GDR**/*HTO*
neologism	ne-o-lo-gi-sm	**GRR**/*HOO*/*HAO*/**GAR/GDR**
Nepalese	Ne-pa-le-se	**GAR/GAR/GRR**/*HDO*
nephew	ne-phe-w	**GAR**/*HOO*/*HDO*
nerve	ner-ve	*HOO*/*HDO*
nervous	ner-vou-s	*HOO*/**GAR**/*HDO*
nest	ne-st	**GAR**/*HOO*
nestling	ne-st-li-ng	**GAR**/*HDO*/**GAR/GDR**
net	ne-t	**GAR/GRR**
net	ne-t	**GAR**/*HDO*
Netherlands	Ne-ther-lan-ds	**GAR**/*HTO*/**GAR**/*HDO*
netted	ne-t-ted	**GAR/GDR/GRR**
netting	ne-tting	**GAR/GDR**
nettle	ne-ttle	**GAR**/*HOO*
network	ne-t-wor-k	**GRR**/*HOO*/*HAO*/*HDO*
neuro	neu-ro	*HOO*/*HOO*
neurotic	neu-ro-ti-c	*HOO*/*HAO*/**GAR/GDR**
neutral	neu-tral	*HOO*/*HDO*
neutralize	neu-tra-li-ze	*HOO*/**GAR/GRR/GDR**
never	ne-ver	**GAR**/*HDO*
new	ne-w	*HOO*/*HDO*
New Zealand	New Zea-lan-d	*HOO*/**GRR/GAR**/*HOO*
New Zealander	New Zea-lan-der	*HOO*/**GRR/GAR**/*HDO*
newly	ne-w-ly	*HOO*/*HDO*/**GDR**
news	new-s	*HOO*/*HDO*
newsy	new-sy	*HOO*/**GAR**
next	ne-xt	**GAR**/*HOO*
nibble	ni-bble	**GAR**/*HOO*
nice	ni-ce	**GRR/GDR**
Nice	Ni-ce	**GAR**/*HDO*

Word	Mouthables	Mouth Movements Notations
nicely	ni-ce-ly	GRR/GDR/GAR
nicety	nic-e-ty	GRR/GAR/GAR
niche	ni-che	GAR/*HDO*
nick	ni-ck	GAR/GRR
nicked	ni-cke-d	GAR/GDR/*HOO*
Nick	Ni-ck	GAR/*HDO*
nicotine	ni-co-ti-ne	GAR/*HOO*/GAR/GDR
niece	nie-ce	GAR/*HDO*
Nigerian	Ni-ge-ri-a-n	GRR/*HDO*/GAR/GAR/GDR
niggle	ni-ggle	GAR/*HOO*
night	nigh-t	GRR/*HOO*
nightly	nigh-t-ly	GRR/*HOO*/GDR
nightmare	nigh-t-mare	GRR/*HOO*/*HAO*
nighty	nigh-ty	GRR/GAR
nil	ni-l	GAR/GDR
nimble	ni-m-ble	GAR/*HDO*/*HOO*
nine	ni-ne	GRR/GDR
nineteen	ni-ne-tee-n	GRR/GDR/GRR/GDR
ninety	ni-ne-ty	GRR/GDR/GAR
ninth	ni-n-th	GRR/GDR/GTR
nip	ni-p	GAR/*HDO*
nipper	ni-pper	GAR/*HDO*
nipple	ni-pple	GAR/*HOO*
nippy	ni-ppy	GAR/GAR
nitrogen	ni-tro-ge-n	GRR/*HOO*/GAR/GDR
nitrogenous	ni-tro-ge-n-ous	GRR/*HOO*/GAR/GDR/GAR
nitty	ni-tty	GAR/GAR
no	no	*HOO*
nobility	no-bi-li-ty	*HOO*/GAR/GAR/GAR
noble	no-ble	*HOO*/*HOO*
nobody	no-bo-dy	*HOO*/*HAO*/GAR

Word	Mouthables	Mouth Movements Notations
nocturnal	no-c-tur-nal	*HAO*/**GDR**/*HAO*/*HDO*
nod	no-d	*HAO*/*HOO*
noddle	no-ddle	*HOO*/*HDO*
node	no-de	*HOO*/*HDO*
noise	noi-se	**GAR/GDR**
noiseless	noi-se-le-ss	**GAR/GDR/GAR/GDR**
nomad	no-ma-d	*HOO*/**GAR**/*HOO*
nomadic	no-ma-di-c	*HOO*/**GAR/GAR/GDR**
nominal	no-mi-nal	*HAO*/**GAR**/*HDO*
nominate	no-mi-na-te	*HAO*/**GAR**/*HAO*/*HDO*
nominee	no-mi-nee	*HAO*/**GAR/GRR**
none	no-ne	*HAO*/*HDO*
nonentity	no-ne-n-ti-ty	*HAO*/**GAR/GDR/GAR/GAR**
nook	noo-k	*HOO*/*HDO*
noon	noo-n	*HOO*/**GDR**
nor	nor	*HOO*
Nordic	Nor-di-c	*HOO*/**GAR/GDR**
norm	nor-m	*HOO*/*HDO*
normal	nor-mal	*HOO*/*HDO*
normalize	nor-ma-li-ze	*HOO*/**GAR/GRR/GDR**
north	nor-th	*HOO*/*HTO*
northerly	nor-ther-ly	*HOO*/*HTO*/**GDR**
northern	nor-ther-n	*HAO*/*HTO*/**GDR**
Norway	Nor-way	*HOO*/*HAO*
Norwegian	Nor-we-gi-an	*HOO*/**GRR/GAR/GDR**
nose	no-se	*HOO*/*HDO*
nosey	no-s(e)y	*HAO*/**GAR**
nosh	no-sh	*HAO*/*HDO*
nostalgia	no-sta-l-gi-a	*HAO*/**GAR/GDR/GAR/GAR**
nostalgic	no-sta-l-gi-c	*HAO*/**GAR/GDR/GAR/GDR**
nostril	no-stri-l	*HAO*/**GAR/GDR**

Word	Mouthables	Mouth Movements Notations
not	no-t	*HAO*/*HOO*
notable	no-ta-ble	*HOO*/**GAR**/*HOO*
notary	no-ta-ry	*HOO*/**GAR**/*HDO*
notch	no-tch	*HAO*/*HDO*
note	no-te	*HOO*/*HDO*
nothing	no-thi-ng	**GAR/GTR/GDR**
notice	no-ti-ce	*HOO*/**GAR/GDR**
noticeable	no-ti-ce-a-ble	*HOO*/**GAR/GDR**/**GAR**/*HOO*
notify	no-ti-fy	*HOO*/**GAR/GRR**
notion	no-tion	*HOO*/*HOO*
notional	no-tion-al	*HOO*/*HOO*/*HDO*
notorious	no-tor-i-ou-s	*HOO*/*HOO*/**GAR/GAR**/*HDO*
nougat	nou-gat	*HOO*/*HAO*
nought	nough-t	*HOO*/*HOO*
noun	nou-n	*HAO*/**GDR**
nourish	nou-ri-sh	**GAR/GAR**/*HDO*
nourishing	nou-ri-shi-ng	**GAR/GAR/GAR/GDR**
nourishment	nou-ri-sh-men-t	**GAR/GAR/GDR/GAR**/*HOO*
novel	no-vel	*HAO*/*HDO*
novelist	no-ve-li-st	*HAO*/*HDO*/**GAR/GDR**
novelty	no-ve-l-ty	*HAO*/**GAR/GDR/GAR**
November	No-ve-m-ber	*HOO*/**GAR**/*HDO*/*HDO*
now	now	*HAO*
noxious	no-xi-ous	*HAO*/**GAR/GAR**
nozzle	noz-zle	*HAO*/*HOO*
nuance	nu-an-ce	*HOO*/*HAO*/**GDR**
nubile	nu-bi-le	*HOO*/**GRR/GDR**
nuclear	nu-cle-ar	*HOO*/**GRR**/*HAO*
nucleus	nu-cle-u-s	*HOO*/**GRR/GAR**/*HDO*
nudge	nu-d-ge	**GAR**/*HDO*/*HDO*
nudist	nu-di-st	*HOO*/**GAR**/*HOO*

Word	Mouthables	Mouth Movements Notations
nugget	nu-gge-t	**GAR/GAR/GDR**
nuisance	nui-sa-nce	*HOO*/**GAR/GDR**
nuke	nu-ke	*HOO/HDO*
nulify	nu-li-fy	**GAR/GAR/GRR**
null	nu-ll	**GAR/GDR**
numb	nu-mb	**GAR**/*HDO*
number	nu-m-ber	**GAR**/*HDO/HDO*
numberless	nu-m-ber-le-ss	**GAR**/*HDO/HAO*/**GAR/GDR**
numeracy	nu-me-ra-cy	*HOO/HAO*/**GAR/GDR**
numeral	nu-me-ra-l	*HOO/HAO*/**GAR/GDR**
numerical	nu-me-ri-cal	*HOO*/**GAR/GAR**/*HDO*
numerous	nu-mer-ou-s	*HOO/HAO/HAO/HDO*
nun	nu-n	**GAR/GDR**
nunnery	nu-nne-ry	**GAR/GAR/GDR**
nurse	nur-se	*HAO/HDO*
nursery	nur-se-ry	*HAO*/**GAR/GDR**
nursing	nur-sing	*HAO*/**GDR**
nut	nu-t	**GAR**/*HOO*
nutrient	nu-tri-e-nt	*HOO*/**GAR/GAR/GDR**
nutrition	nu-tri-tion	*HOO*/**GAR**/*HOO*
nutritious	nu-tri-ti-ous	*HOO*/**GAR**/*HDO*/**GAR**
nuts	nu-t-s	**GAR**/*HOO/HDO*
nutty	nu-tty	**GAR/GAR**
nuzzle	nu-zzle	**GAR**/*HOO*
nymph	ny-mph	**GAR**/*HDO*

Word	Mouthables	Mouth Movements Notations
O		
O	O	*HOO*
o	o	*HAO*
oaf	oa-f	*HOO/HDO*
oak	oa-k	*HOO/HDO*
oar	oar	*HDO*
oasis	o-a-si-s	*HOO/HAO/*GAR/GDR
oath	oa-th	*HOO/HTO*
oats	oa-ts	*HOO/HDO*
obedient	o-be-di-e-nt	*HOO/*GRR/GAR/GAR/GDR
obese	o-be-se	*HOO/*GRR/*HDO*
obey	o-bey	*HOO/HAO*
obituary	o-bi-tu-ary	*HOO/*GAR/*HOO/HDO*
object	o-b-jec-t	*HAO/HDO/*GAR/*HOO*
objected	o-b-jec-ted	*HAO/HDO/*GAR/GRR
objection	o-b-jec-tion	*HAO/HDO/*GAR/*HOO*
objectionable	o-b-jec-tion-a-ble	*HAO/HDO/*GAR/*HOO/*GAR/*HOO*
objective	o-b-jec-ti-ve	*HAO/HDO/*GAR/GAR/*HDO*
objector	o-b-jec-tor	*HAO/HDO/*GAR/*HDO*
obligate	o-bli-ga-te	*HAO/*GAR/*HAO/HDO*
obligation	o-bli-ga-tion	*HAO/*GAR/*HAO/HOO*
oblige	o-bli-ge	*HAO/*GRR/*HDO*
obliging	o-bli-ging	*HAO/*GRR/GDR
oblique	o-bli-que	*HOO/*GAR/*HDO*
obnoxious	o-b-no-xi-ous	*HAO/HDO/HAO/*GAR/GAR
obscene	o-b-sce-ne	*HAO/HDO/*GRR/GDR
obscure	o-b-scu-re	*HAO/HDO/HOO/HDO*
obscurity	o-b-scu-ri-ty	*HAO/HDO/HOO/*GAR/GAR
observant	o-b-ser-va-nt	*HAO/HDO/HOO/*GAR/GDR
observatory	o-b-ser-va-to-ry	*HAO/HDO/HOO/*GAR/*HOO/HDO*
observe	o-b-ser-ve	*HAO/HDO/*GAR/*HDO*

Word	Mouthables	Mouth Movements Notations
observed	o-b-ser-ve-d	*HAO*/*HDO*/**GAR**/*HDO*/*HOO*
obsess	o-b-se-ss	*HAO*/*HDO*/**GAR**/*HDO*
obsession	o-b-se-ssion	*HAO*/*HDO*/**GAR**/*HOO*
obsessive	o-b-se-ssi-ve	*HAO*/*HDO*/**GAR/GAR/GDR**
obsolete	o-b-so-le-te	*HAO*/*HDO*/*HOO*/**GRR**/*HDO*
obstacle	o-b-sta-cle	*HAO*/*HDO*/**GAR**/*HOO*
obstetrician	o-b-ste-tri-cian	*HAO*/*HDO*/**GAR/GAR**/*HDO*
obstinacy	o-b-sti-na-cy	*HAO*/*HDO*/**GAR/GAR/GAR**
obstinate	o-b-sti-na-te	*HAO*/*HDO*/**GAR/GAR**/*HDO*
obstruct	o-b-stru-c-t	*HAO*/*HDO*/**GAR/GDR**/*HOO*
obtain	o-b-tai-n	*HAO*/*HDO*/*HAO*/**GDR**
obtuse	o-b-tu-se	*HAO*/*HDO*/*HOO*/*HDO*
obvious	o-b-vi-ous	*HAO*/*HDO*/**GAR/GAR**
occasion	o-cca-sion	*HOO*/*HAO*/*HOO*
occasional	o-cca-sion-al	*HOO*/*HAO*/*HOO*/*HDO*
occlusion	o-cclu-sion	*HAO*/*HOO*/*HOO*
occult	o-ccu-lt	*HAO*/**GAR/GDR**
occupation	o-ccu-pa-tion	*HAO*/*HOO*/*HAO*/*HOO*
occupational	o-ccu-pa-tion-al	*HAO*/*HOO*/*HAO*/*HOO*/*HDO*
occupy	o-ccu-py	*HAO*/*HOO*/**GRR**
occur	o-ccur	*HAO*/**GAR**
ocean	o-ce-an	*HOO*/**GAR**/*HDO*
ochre	o-ch-re	*HAO*/*HDO*/*HDO*
octane	o-c-ta-ne	*HAO*/*HDO*/*HAO*/**GDR**
October	O-c-to-ber	*HAO*/*HDO*/*HOO*/*HDO*
octopus	o-c-to-pu-s	*HAO*/**GDR**/*HAO*/*HOO*/*HDO*
ocular	o-cu-lar	*HAO*/*HOO*/*HAO*
odd	o-dd	*HAO*/*HOO*
oddity	o-dd-i-ty	*HAO*/*HDO*/**GAR/GAR**
oddments	o-dd-me-nts	*HAO*/*HDO*/**GAR/GDR**
odds	o-dds	*HAO*/*HDO*

Word	Mouthables	Mouth Movements Notations
ode	o-de	*HOO/HDO*
odour	o-dour	*HOO/HAO*
odyssey	o-dy-ssey	**HAO/GAR/GRR**
of	o-f	*HAO/HDO*
off	o-f-f	*HAO/HOO/HDO*
offal	o-ffal	*HAO/HDO*
offence	o-ffe-nce	**GAR/GAR/GDR**
offend	o-ffe-nd	**GAR/GAR/GDR**
offended	o-ffe-n-ded	**GAR/GAR/GDR/GRR**
offender	o-ffe-n-der	**GAR/GAR/GDR**/*HDO*
offense	o-ffe-nse	**GAR/GAR/GDR**
offensive	o-ffe-n-si-ve	**GAR/GAR/GDR/GAR/GDR**
offer	o-ff-er	*HAO/HDO/HAO*
offering	o-ffe-ri-ng	*HAO/HAO/***GAR/GDR**
officate	o-ffi-ci-a-te	*HOO/***GAR/GDR**/*HAO/HDO*
office	o-ffi-ce	*HAO/***GAR/GDR**
officer	o-ff-i-cer	*HAO/HDO/***GAR**/*HDO*
officious	o-ffi-ci-ous	*HOO/***GAR/GDR/GAR**
offing	o-ffi-ng	*HAO/***GAR/GDR**
often	o-ften	*HAO/HDO*
ogle	o-gle	*HAO/HOO*
ogre	o-gre	*HOO/HDO*
oil	oi-l	**GAR**/*HDO*
ointment	oi-nt-me-nt	**GAR/GDR/GAR/GDR**
okay	o-kay	*HOO/HAO*
old	o-ld	*HOO/HDO*
olive	o-li-ve	*HAO/***GAR**/*HDO*
olympic	o-ly-m-pi-c	*HOO/***GAR/GDR/GAR/GDR**
omelette	o-me-le-tte	*HAO/HDO/***GAR**/*HDO*
omen	o-me-n	*HOO/***GAR/GDR**
ominous	o-mi-nou-s	*HAO/***GAR/GAR**/*HDO*

Word	Mouthables	Mouth Movements Notations
omission	o-mi-ssion	*HOO*/**GAR**/*HOO*
omit	o-mi-t	*HOO*/**GAR**/*HDO*
omnipotent	o-m-ni-po-te-nt	*HAO*/*HDO*/**GAR**/*HOO*/**GAR/GDR**
on	o-n	*HAO*/*HDO*
once	on-ce	**GAR/GDR**
one	o-ne	**GAR**/*HDO*
onion	o-nion	**GAR**/*HDO*
only	o-n-ly	*HOO*/*HDO*/**GDR**
onomatopoeia	o-no-ma-to-p(o)ei-a	*HAO*/*HOO*/**GAR**/*HAO*/**GRR/GAR**
ooze	oo-ze	*HOO*/*HDO*
opaque	o-pa-que	*HOO*/*HAO*/*HDO*
open	o-pe-n	*HOO*/**GAR/GDR**
opener	o-pe-ner	*HOO*/**GAR**/*HDO*
opera	o-pe-ra	*HAO*/*HAO*/**GAR**
operate	o-pe-ra-te	*HAO*/*HAO*/*HAO*/*HDO*
operatic	o-pe-ra-ti-c	*HAO*/*HAO*/**GAR/GAR/GDR**
operation	o-pe-ra-tion	*HAO*/*HAO*/*HAO*/*HOO*
operational	o-pe-ra-tion-al	*HAO*/*HAO*/*HAO*/*HOO*/*HDO*
operative	o-pe-ra-ti-ve	*HAO*/*HAO*/*HAO*/**GAR/GDR**
operator	o-pe-ra-tor	*HAO*/*HAO*/*HAO*/*HDO*
ophthalmologist	o-ph-tha-l-mo-lo-gi-st	*HAO*/*HDO*/**GTR/GDR**/*HOO*/**GAR/ GAR/GDR**
opinion	o-pi-ni-o-n	**GAR/GAR/GAR**/*HAO*/*HDO*
opinionated	o-pi-ni-o-na-ted	**GAR/GAR/GAR**/*HAO*/*HAO*/**GRR**
opium	o-pi-u-m	*HOO*/**GAR/GAR**/*HDO*
opponent	o-ppo-ne-nt	**GAR**/*HOO*/**GAR/GDR**
opportune	o-ppor-tu-ne	*HAO*/*HOO*/*HOO*/*HDO*
opportunist	o-ppor-tu-ni-st	*HAO*/*HOO*/*HOO*/**GAR/GDR**
opportunity	o-ppor-tu-ni-ty	*HAO*/*HOO*/*HOO*/**GAR/GAR**
oppose	o-ppo-se	**GAR**/*HOO*/*HDO*
opposite	o-ppo-si-te	*HAO*/*HOO*/**GAR**/*HDO*

Word	Mouthables	Mouth Movements Notations
opposition	o-ppo-si-tion	*HAO/HOO/*GAR*/HOO*
oppress	o-ppre-ss	GAR/GAR/GDR
oppression	o-ppre-ssion	GAR/GAR/*HOO*
opt	o-pt	*HAO/HDO*
optical	o-p-ti-cal	*HAO/*GDR/GAR*/HDO*
optician	o-p-ti-cian	*HAO/*GDR/GAR*/HDO*
optimist	o-p-ti-mi-st	*HAO/HDO/*GAR/GAR*/HDO*
optimize	o-p-ti-mi-ze	*HAO/HDO/*GAR/GRR/GDR
option	o-p-tion	*HAO/HDO/HOO*
optional	o-p-tion-al	*HAO/HDO/HOO/HDO*
or	o-r	*HOO/HDO*
oracle	o-ra-cle	*HAO/*GAR*/HOO*
oral	or-a-l	*HAO/*GAR/GDR
orally	or-a-lly	*HAO/*GAR/GDR
orange	o-ran-ge	*HAO/HAO/HDO*
orangeade	o-ran-ge-a-de	*HAO/HAO/HDO/HAO/HDO*
orator	o-ra-tor	*HAO/HAO/HOO*
orbit	or-bi-t	*HOO/*GAR/GDR
orca	or-ca	*HOO/*GAR
orchard	or-char-d	*HOO/HAO/HDO*
orchestra	or-che-st-ra	*HOO/*GAR*/HDO/*GAR
orchid	or-chi-d	*HOO/*GAR*/HDO*
ordeal	or-dea-l	*HOO/*GRR/GDR
order	or-der	*HOO/HDO*
orderly	or-der-ly	*HOO/HAO/*GDR
ordinary	or-di-nar-y	*HOO/*GAR*/HAO/HDO*
ore	o-re	*HOO/HDO*
oregano	o-re-ga-no	*HAO/*GAR/GAR*/HOO*
organ	or-ga-n	*HOO/*GAR/GDR
organic	or-ga-ni-c	*HOO/*GAR/GAR/GDR
organism	or-ga-ni-sm	*HOO/*GAR/GAR*/HDO*

Word	Mouthables	Mouth Movements Notations
organization	or-ga-ni-za-tion	*HOO*/**GAR**/**GRR**/*HAO*/*HOO*
organize	or-ga-ni-ze	*HOO*/**GAR**/**GRR**/**GDR**
orgasm	or-ga-sm	*HOO*/**GAR**/**GDR**
orgy	or-gy	*HOO*/**GAR**
oriental	o-ri-e-n-tal	*HAO*/**GAR**/**GAR**/**GDR**/*HDO*
orientate	o-ri-e-n-ta-te	*HAO*/**GAR**/**GAR**/**GDR**/*HAO*/*HDO*
orientation	o-ri-e-n-ta-tion	*HAO*/**GAR**/**GAR**/**GDR**/*HAO*/*HOO*
origin	o-ri-gi-n	*HAO*/**GAR**/**GAR**/*HDO*
original	o-ri-gi-nal	*HAO*/**GAR**/**GAR**//*HDO*
ornament	or-na-me-nt	*HOO*/**GAR**/**GAR**/**GDR**
ornate	or-na-te	*HOO*/*HAO*/*HDO*
orphan	or-pha-n	*HOO*/**GAR**/**GDR**
orphanage	or-pha-na-ge	*HOO*/**GAR**/*HAO*/*HDO*
orthodox	or-tho-do-x	*HOO*/**GTR**/*HAO*/**GDR**
orthopedic	or-tho-pe-di-c	*HOO*/**GTR**/**GRR**/**GAR**/**GDR**
ostrich	o-stri-ch	*HAO*/**GAR**/*HDO*
other	o-th-er	**GAR**/*HTO*/*HDO*
otter	o-tter	*HAO*/*HDO*
ouch	ou-ch	**GAR**/*HDO*
ought	ough-t	*HOO*/*HOO*
ounce	ou-nce	**GAR**/**GDR**
our	ou-r	**GAR**/*HDO*
ours	ou-r-s	**GAR**/*HDO*/*HDO*
oust	ou-st	**GAR**/*HOO*
out	ou-t	**GAR**/*HOO*
oval	o-val	*HOO*/*HDO*
ovation	o-va-tion	*HOO*/*HAO*/*HOO*
oven	o-ven	**GAR**/*HDO*
over	o-ver	*HOO*/*HDO*
owe	o-we	*HOO*/*HDO*
owl	ow-l	*HAO*/*HDO*

Word	Mouthables	Mouth Movements Notations
own	o-w-n	*HOO*/*HDO*/**GDR**
owner	o-w-ner	*HOO*/*HDO*/**GDR**
ox	o-x	*HAO*/*HDO*
oxide	o-xi-de	*HAO*/**GRR**/*HDO*
oxygen	o-xy-gen	*HAO*/**GAR**/**GDR**
oyster	oy-ster	**GAR**/*HDO*
ozone	o-zo-ne	*HOO*/*HOO*/**GDR**

Word	Mouthables	Mouth Movements Notations
P		
P	P	**GRR**
pace	pa-ce	*HAO*/**GDR**
Pacific	Pa-ci-fi-c	**GAR/GAR/GAR/GDR**
pacify	pa-ci-fy	*HAO*/**GAR/GRR**
pack	pa-ck	**GAR**/*HDO*
package	pa-ck-a-ge	**GAR**/*HDO/HAO/HDO*
packet	pa-cke-t	**GAR/GAR**/*HOO*
pact	pa-ct	**GAR**/*HOO*
pad	pa-d	**GAR**/*HOO*
paddle	pa-ddle	**GAR**/*HOO*
paddlock	pa-dd-loc-k	**GAR**/*HOO/HAO/HDO*
paddock	pa-ddoc-k	*HAO/HAO/HDO*
paediatrician	p(a)e-di-a-tri-cian	**GRR/GAR/GAR/GAR/GDR**
pagan	pa-ga-n	*HAO*/**GAR/GDR**
page	pa-ge	*HAO/HDO*
pageant	pa-gea-nt	**GAR/GAR/GDR**
paid	pai-d	*HAO*/**GRR**
pail	pai-l	*HAO/HDO*
pain	pai-n	*HAO*/**GDR**
painful	pai-n-ful	*HAO*/**GDR**/*HOO*
paint	pai-nt	*HAO*/**GDR**
painter	pain-ter	*HAO/HDO*
painting	pain-ti-ng	*HAO*/**GAR/GDR**
pair	pair	*HAO*
pajamas	pa-ja-ma-s	**GAR/GAR/GAR**/*HDO*
pal	pa-l	**GAR/GDR**
palace	pa-la-ce	**GAR/GAR/GDR**
palatable	pa-la-ta-ble	**GAR/GAR/GAR**/*HOO*
palate	pa-la-te	**GAR/GAR**/*HDO*
pale	pa-le	*HAO*/**GDR**

Word	Mouthables	Mouth Movements Notations
Palestine	Pa-le-sti-ne	**GAR**/*HAO*/**GRR/GDR**
Palestinian	Pa-le-sti-ni-a-n	**GAR**/*HAO*/**GAR/GAR/GAR/GDR**
palette	pa-let-te	**GAR**/*HAO/HDO*
pall	pal-l	*HOO/HDO*
palliative	pa-lli-a-ti-ve	**GAR/GAR**/*HAO*/**GAR/GDR**
palm	pal-m	*HAO/HDO*
palmist	pal-mi-st	*HAO*/**GAR/GDR**
palpitate	pa-l-pi-ta-te	**GAR/GDR/GAR**/*HAO/HDO*
paltry	pal-try	*HOO/HDO*
pamper	pam-per	**GAR**/*HDO*
pamphlet	pam-ph-le-t	**GAR/GDR/GAR/GDR**
pan	pa-n	**GAR/GDR**
panache	pa-na-che	**GAR/GAR**/*HDO*
pancake	pa-n-ca-ke	**GAR/GDR**/*HAO/HDO*
pander	pa-n-der	**GAR/GDR**/*HDO*
pane	pa-ne	*HAO/HDO*
panel	pa-nel	**GAR**/*HDO*
pang	pan-g	**GAR/GDR**
panic	pa-ni-c	**GAR/GAR/GDR**
panorama	pa-no-ra-ma	**GAR**/*HOO*/**GAR/GAR**
pansy	pa-n-sy	**GAR/GDR/GAR**
pant	pa-nt	**GAR/GDR**
panther	pa-n-th-er	**GAR/GDR/GTR/GDR**
pantry	pa-n-try	**GAR/GDR**/*HDO*
pants	pa-nt-s	**GAR/GDR/GDR**
papal	pa-pal	*HAO/HOO*
paper	pa-per	*HAO/HDO*
paprika	pa-pri-ka	**GAR/GAR/GAR**
papyrus	pa-py-ru-s	**GAR/GRR/GAR**/*IIDO*
par	par	*HAO*
parable	pa-ra-ble	**GAR/GAR**/*HOO*

Word	Mouthables	Mouth Movements Notations
parachute	pa-ra-chu-te	GAR/GAR/*HOO*/*HDO*
parachutist	pa-ra-chu-ti-st	GAR/GAR/*HOO*/GAR/GDR
parade	pa-ra-de	GAR/*HAO*/*HDO*
paradise	pa-ra-di-se	GAR/GAR/GRR/*HDO*
paradox	pa-ra-do-x	GAR/GAR/*HAO*/GDR
paradoxical	pa-ra-do-xi-cal	GAR/GAR/*HAO*/GAR/*HOO*
paraffin	pa-ra-ffi-n	GAR/GAR/GAR/GDR
paragraph	pa-ra-gra-ph	GAR/GAR/GAR/*HDO*
parallel	pa-ra-lle-l	GAR/GAR/GAR/GDR
paralyse	pa-ra-ly-se	GAR/GAR/GRR/*HDO*
paralysed	pa-ra-ly-se-d	GAR/GAR/GRR/*HOO*/*HOO*
paralysis	pa-ra-ly-si-s	GAR/GAR/GAR/GAR/GDR
paralyze	pa-ra-ly-ze	GAR/GAR/GRR/GDR
parameter	pa-ra-me-ter	GAR/GAR/GRR/*HDO*
paramount	pa-ra-mou-nt	GAR/GAR/GAR/GDR
paranormal	pa-ra-nor-mal	GAR/GAR/*HOO*/*HDO*
parapet	pa-ra-pe-t	GAR/GAR/GAR/*HOO*
paraphernalia	pa-ra-pher-na-li-a	GAR/GAR/*HOO*/*HAO*/GAR/GAR
parasite	pa-ra-si-te	GAR/GAR/GRR/*HDO*
paratrooper	pa-ra-troo-per	GAR/GAR/*HOO*/*HDO*
parcel	par-cel	*HAO*/*HDO*
parchment	par-ch-me-nt	*HAO*/*HDO*/GAR/GDR
pardon	par-do-n	*HAO*/*HAO*/*HDO*
parent	par-e-nt	GAR/GAR/GDR
parenthesis	pa-re-n-th-e-si-s	GAR/GAR/GDR/GTR/GAR/GAR/ GDR
Paris	Pa-ri-s	GAR/GAR/GDR
parish	pa-ri-sh	GAR/GAR/*HDO*
parishioner	pa-ri-shi-o-ner	GAR/GAR/*HDO*/*HAO*/*HDO*
parity	pa-ri-ty	GAR/GAR/GAR
park	par-k	*HAO*/*HDO*

Word	Mouthables	Mouth Movements Notations
parking	par-ki-ng	*HAO*/**GAR/GDR**
parliament	par-lia-me-nt	*HAO*/**GAR/GAR/GDR**
parliamentary	par-lia-me-n-tar-y	*HAO*/**GAR/GAR/GDR**/*HAO/HDO*
parlour	par-lour	*HAO/HAO*
Parmesan	Par-me-sa-n	*HAO*/**GRR/GAR/GDR**
parody	pa-ro-dy	**GAR/GAR/GAR**
parole	pa-ro-le	**GAR**/*HOO/HDO*
parricide	par-ri-ci-de	**GAR/GAR/GRR/GDR**
parrot	par-ro-t	*HAO/HAO/HOO*
parry	par-ry	**GAR/GDR**
parsley	par-s-ley	*HAO/HDO/HAO*
parson	par-so-n	*HAO/HAO/HDO*
part	par-t	*HAO/HOO*
part	par-t	*HAO/HDO*
partake	par-ta-ke	*HAO/HAO/HDO*
parted	par-ted	*HAO*/**GRR**
partial	par-tial	*HAO/HDO*
participant	par-ti-ci-pa-nt	*HAO*/**GAR/GAR/GAR/GDR**
participate	par-ti-ci-pa-te	*HAO*/**GAR/GAR**/*HAO/HDO*
participation	par-ti-ci-pa-tion	*HAO*/**GAR/GAR**/*HAO/HOO*
particle	par-ti-cle	*HAO*/**GAR**/*HOO*
particular	par-ti-cu-lar	*HAO*/**GAR**/*HOO/HDO*
partime	par-ti-me	*HAO*/**GRR**/*HDO*
partisan	par-ti-sa-n	*HAO*/**GAR/GAR/GDR**
partition	par-ti-tion	*HAO*/**GAR**/*HOO*
partly	par-t-ly	*HAO/HOO*/**GDR**
partner	par-t-ner	*HAO/HOO/HDO*
partnership	par-t-ner-shi-p	*HAO/HOO/HDO*/**GAR/GDR**
partook	par-too-k	*HAO/HOO/HDO*
partridge	par-tri-dge	*HAO*/**GAR**/*HDO*
party	par-ty	*HAO*/**GAR**

Word	Mouthables	Mouth Movements Notations
pass	pas-s	*HAO/HDO*
passable	pas-sa-ble	*HAO/***GAR***/HOO*
passage	pa-ssa-ge	**GAR**/*HAO/HDO*
passenger	pas-se-n-ger	**GAR/GAR/GDR**/*HDO*
passion	pas-sion	**GAR**/*HOO*
passionate	pas-sion-a-te	**GAR**/*HOO/HAO/HDO*
passive	pa-ssi-ve	**GAR/GAR**/*HDO*
past	pas-t	*HAO/HOO*
paste	pa-ste	*HAO/HDO*
pastel	pa-stel	**GAR**/*HOO*
pasteurize	pas-teu-ri-ze	*HAO/HOO/***GRR/GDR**
pastille	pa-sti-lle	**GAR/GAR/GDR**
pastime	pas-ti-me	*HAO/***GRR**/*HDO*
pastoral	pas-tor-al	*HAO/HOO/HDO*
pastry	pa-stry	*HAO/HDO*
pasture	pas-tu-re	*HAO/HOO/HDO*
pasty	pa-sty	**GAR/GAR**
pat	pa-t	**GAR**/*HOO*
patch	pa-tch	**GAR**/*HDO*
patchy	pa-t-chy	**GAR**/*HDO*/**GAR**
patent	pa-te-nt	*HAO/***GAR/GDR**
paternal	pa-ter-nal	**GAR**/*HOO/HDO*
paternity	pa-ter-ni-ty	**GAR**/*HOO/***GAR/GAR**
path	pa-th	*HAO/HTO*
pathetic	pa-th-e-ti-c	**GAR/GTR/GAR/GAR/GDR**
pathological	pa-tho-lo-gi-cal	**GAR**/*HTO/HAO/***GAR**/*HDO*
patience	pa-ti-e-nce	*HAO/HDO/***GAR/GDR**
patient	pa-ti-e-nt	*HAO/HDO/***GAR/GDR**
patriarch	pa-tri-ar-ch	**GAR/GAR**/*HAO/HDO*
patriot	pa-tri-o-t	*HAO/***GAR**/*HAO/HOO*
patrol	pa-tro-l	**GAR**/*HOO/HDO*

Word	Mouthables	Mouth Movements Notations
patron	pa-tro-n	*HAO*/*HAO*/**GDR**
patronage	pa-tro-na-ge	*HAO*/*HAO*/*HAO*/*HDO*
patronizing	pa-tro-ni-zi-ng	*HAO*/*HAO*/**GRR**/**GAR**/**GDR**
patter	pa-tter	**GAR**/*HDO*
pattern	pa-tter-n	**GAR**/*HOO*/**GDR**
paunch	pau-nch	*HOO*/**GDR**
pause	pau-se	*HOO*/*HDO*
pave	pa-ve	*HAO*/*HDO*
pavement	pa-ve-men-t	*HAO*/*HDO*/**GAR**/*HDO*
pavilion	pa-vi-lli-o-n	**GAR**/**GAR**/**GAR**/*HAO*/*HDO*
paw	paw	*HOO*
pawn	paw-n	*HOO*/**GDR**
pay	pay	*HAO*
payee	pay-ee	*HAO*/**GRR**
payment	pay-me-nt	*HAO*/**GAR**/**GDR**
pea	pea	**GRR**
peace	pea-ce	**GRR**/**GDR**
peaceable	pea-ce-a-ble	**GRR**/**GDR**/**GAR**/*HOO*
peaceful	pea-ce-ful	**GRR**/**GDR**/*HOO*
peach	pea-ch	**GRR**/*HDO*
peacock	pea-co-ck	**GRR**/*HAO*/*HDO*
peak	pea-k	**GRR**/*HDO*
peaky	pea-ky	**GRR**/**GAR**
peal	pea-l	**GRR**/**GDR**
peanut	pea-nu-t	**GRR**/**GAR**/*HDO*
pear	pear	*HAO*
pearl	pear-l	*HOO*/**GDR**
peasant	pea-sa-nt	**GAR**/**GAR**/**GDR**
pebble	pe-bble	**GAR**/*HOO*
peck	pe-ck	**GAR**/*HDO*
peckish	pe-ck-i-sh	**GAR**/*HDO*/**GAR**/*HDO*

Word	Mouthables	Mouth Movements Notations
peculiar	pe-cu-li-ar	**GAR**/*HOO*/**GAR**/*HAO*
pedal	pe-dal	**GAR**/*HDO*
pedant	pe-da-nt	**GAR/GAR/GDR**
pedantic	pe-da-n-ti-c	**GAR/GAR/GDR/GAR/GDR**
peddle	pe-ddle	**GAR**/*HOO*
pedestrian	pe-de-stri-an	**GAR/GAR/GAR/GDR**
pediatrician	pe-di-a-tri-ci-an	**GRR/GAR/GAR/GAR/GDR/GDR**
pedicure	pe-di-cu-re	**GAR/GAR**/*HOO*/*HDO*
pedlar	pe-d-lar	**GAR**/*HDO*/*HAO*
peek	pee-k	**GRR**/*HDO*
peel	pee-l	**GRR/GDR**
peelings	pee-ling-s	**GRR/GDR/GDR**
peep	pee-p	**GRR**/*HDO*
peer	pe-er	**GRR**/*HDO*
peevish	pee-vi-sh	**GRR/GAR**/*HDO*
peg	pe-g	**GAR/GDR**
Pekinese	Pe-ki-ne-se	**GRR/GAR/GRR/GDR**
Peking	Pe-ki-ng	**GRR/GAR**/*HDO*
pelican	pe-li-ca-n	**GAR/GAR/GAR/GDR**
pellet	pe-lle-t	**GAR/GAR/GDR**
pelt	pe-lt	**GAR/GDR**
pelt	pel-t	**GAR**/*HDO*
pelted	pe-l-ted	**GAR/GDR/GRR**
pen	pe-n	**GAR/GRR**
pen	pe-n	**GAR/GDR**
penal	pe-nal	**GRR**/*HDO*
penal	pe-na-li-ze	**GRR/GAR/GRR/GDR**
penalty	pe-na-l-ty	**GAR/GAR/GDR/GAR**
penance	pe-na-nce	**GAR/GAR/GDR**
pence	pen-ce	**GAR/GDR**
pencil	pe-n-ci-l	**GAR/GDR/GAR/GDR**

Word	Mouthables	Mouth Movements Notations
pendant	pe-n-da-nt	**GAR/GDR/GAR/GDR**
pending	pe-n-ding	**GAR/GDR/GDR**
pendulum	pen-du-lu-m	**GAR**/*HOO*/**GAR**/*HDO*
penetrate	pe-ne-tra-te	**GAR/GAR**/*HAO*/*HDO*
penetrating	pe-ne-tra-ting	**GAR/GAR**/*HAO*/**GDR**
penguin	pen-gui-n	**GAR/GAR/GDR**
peninsula	pe-ni-n-su-la	**GAR/GAR/GDR**/*HOO*/**GAR**
penitentiary	pe-ni-ten-ti-a-ry	**GAR/GAR/GAR/GDR**/*HAO*/*HDO*
penned	pe-nne-d	**GAR/GDR**/*HOO*
penny	pe-nny	**GAR/GAR**
pension	pe-n-sion	**GAR/GDR**/*HOO*
pensioner	pe-n-sion-er	**GAR/GDR**/*HOO*/*HDO*
pensive	pe-n-si-ve	**GAR/GDR/GAR**/*HDO*
penthouse	pe-nt-hou-se	**GAR/GDR**/*HAO*/*HDO*
penultimate	pe-n-u-l-ti-ma-te	**GAR/GDR/GAR/GDR/GAR**/*HAO*/*HDO*
penury	pe-nu-ry	**GAR**/*HOO*/*HDO*
people	peo-ple	**GRR**/*HOO*
pep	pe-p	**GAR**/*HDO*
pepper	pe-pper	**GAR**/*HDO*
peppermint	pe-pper-mi-nt	**GAR**/*HAO*/**GAR/GDR**
peppery	pe-ppe-ry	**GAR**/*HAO*/*HDO*
per	per	*HAO*
perceive	per-cei-ve	*HAO*/**GRR**/*HDO*
percentage	per-cen-ta-ge	*HAO*/**GAR**/*HAO*/*HDO*
perceptive	per-ce-p-ti-ve	*HAO*/**GAR/GDR/GAR**/*HDO*
perch	per-ch	*HAO*/*HOO*
perch	per-ch	*HOO*/*HDO*
perched	per-che-d	*HOO*/*HDO*/*HOO*
percolate	per-co-la-te	*HAO*/*HOO*/*HAO*/*HDO*
percolator	per-co-la-tor	*HAO*/*HAO*/*HAO*/*HDO*

Word	Mouthables	Mouth Movements Notations
percussion	per-cus-sion	**GAR/GAR/***HOO*
peremptory	pe-re-mp-to-ry	**GAR/GAR/***HDO/HAO/HDO*
perennial	pe-re-nni-al	**GAR/GAR/GAR/***HDO*
perfect	per-fec-t	*HAO/***GAR/***HOO*
perfection	per-fe-c-tion	*HAO/***GAR/GDR/***HOO*
perfidious	per-fi-di-ous	*HAO/***GAR/GAR/***HAO*
perforate	per-fo-ra-te	*HAO/HOO/HAO/HDO*
perform	per-for-m	*HAO/HOO/HDO*
performance	per-for-ma-nce	*HAO/HOO/***GAR/GDR**
performer	per-for-mer	*HAO/HOO/HDO*
perfume	per-fu-me	*HAO/HOO/HDO*
perfunctory	per-fun-c-to-ry	*HAO/***GAR/GDR/***HOO/HDO*
perhaps	per-ha-ps	*HAO/***GAR/***HDO*
peril	pe-ri-l	**GAR/GAR/GDR**
perimeter	pe-ri-me-ter	*HAO/***GAR/GAR/***HDO*
period	pe-ri-o-d	**GRR/GAR/***HAO/HOO*
periodical	pe-ri-o-di-cal	**GRR/GAR/***HAO/***GAR/***HDO*
peripheral	per-i-pher-al	*HAO/***GAR/***HDO/GDR**
perish	pe-ri-sh	**GAR/GAR/***HDO*
perishable	pe-ri-sha-ble	**GAR/GAR/GAR/***HOO*
perishing	pe-ri-shing	**GAR/GAR/GDR**
peritonitis	pe-ri-to-ni-ti-s	**GAR/GAR/***HOO/***GRR/GAR/GDR**
periwinkle	pe-ri-win-kle	**GAR/GAR/GAR/***HOO*
perjury	per-ju-ry	*HAO/***GAR/GDR**
perk	per-k	**GAR/***HDO*
perm	per-m	*HAO/HDO*
permanence	per-ma-ne-nce	*HAO/***GAR/GAR/GDR**
permanency	per-ma-ne-ncy	*HAO/***GAR/GAR/GDR**
permanent	per-ma-ne-nt	*HAO/***GAR/GAR/GDR**
permeable	per-me-a-ble	**GAR/GRR/GAR/***HOO*
permeate	per-me-a-te	**GAR/GRR/***HAO/HDO*

Word	Mouthables	Mouth Movements Notations
permission	per-mi-ssion	*HAO*/**GAR**/*HOO*
permissive	per-mi-ssi-ve	*HAO*/**GAR/GAR/GDR**
permit	per-mi-t	*HAO*/**GAR**/*HOO*
perpendicular	per-pe-n-di-cu-lar	*HAO*/**GAR/GDR/GAR**/*HOO/HAO*
perpetual	per-pe-tu-al	*HOO*/**GAR**/*HOO/HDO*
perplexed	per-ple-xe-d	*HAO*/**GAR/GDR**/*HOO*
persecute	per-se-cu-te	*HOO*/**GAR**/*HOO/HOO*
persecution	per-se-cu-tion	*HOO*/**GAR**/*HOO/HOO*
persevere	per-se-ve-re	*HOO*/**GAR/GRR**/*HDO*
Persian	Per-sian	*HAO/HDO*
persist	per-si-st	*HOO*/**GAR**/*HOO*
persistent	per-si-ste-nt	*HOO*/**GAR/GAR/GDR**
person	per-so-n	*HAO/HAO/HDO*
personal	per-so-nal	*HAO/HAO/HDO*
personality	per-so-na-li-ty	*HAO/HAO*/**GAR/GAR/GAR**
personify	per-so-ni-fy	*HAO/HAO*/**GAR/GRR**
personnel	per-so-nne-l	*HAO/HOO*/**GAR/GDR**
perspective	per-spe-c-ti-ve	*HAO*/**GAR/GDR/GAR/GAR/GDR**
perspiration	per-spi-ra-tion	*HAO*/**GAR**/*HAO/HOO*
persuade	per-su-a-de	*HOO/HOO/HAO/HOO*
persuasion	per-su-a-sion	*HOO/HOO/HAO/HOO*
pert	per-t	*HAO/HOO*
pertain	per-tai-n	*HAO/HAO*/**GDR**
pertinent	per-ti-ne-nt	*HAO*/**GAR/GAR/GDR**
peruse	pe-ru-se	*HAO/HOO/HDO*
pervade	per-va-de	*HAOHAO/HDO*
perverse	per-ver-se	*HAO*/**GAR**/*HDO*
pervert	per-ver-t	*HAO*/**GAR**/*HOO*
pessimist	pe-ssi-mi-st	**GAR/GAR/GAR/GDR**
pest	pe-st	**GAR/GRR**
pester	pe-ster	**GAR**/*HDO*

Word	Mouthables	Mouth Movements Notations
pestered	pe-stere-d	**GAR**/*HDO*/*HOO*
pesticide	pe-sti-ci-de	**GAR/GAR/GRR**/*HDO*
pet	pe-t	**GAR**/*HOO*
pet	pe-t	**GAR**/*HDO*
petal	pe-tal	**GAR**/*HDO*
Peter	Pe-ter	**GRR**/*HDO*
petition	pe-ti-tion	**GAR/GAR**/*HOO*
petrol	pe-tro-l	**GAR**/*HAO*/**GDR**
petroleum	pe-tro-le-u-m	**GAR**/*HOO*/**GAR/GAR**/*HDO*
petted	pe-t-ted	**GAR**/*HDO*/**GRR**
petticoat	pe-tti-coa-t	**GAR/GAR**/*HOO*/*HDO*
petty	pe-tty	**GAR/GAR**
petulant	pe-tu-la-nt	**GAR**/*HOO*/**GAR/GDR**
pew	pe-w	*HOO*/*HDO*
pewter	pe-w-ter	*HOO*/*HDO*/*HDO*
phantom	pha-n-to-m	**GAR/GDR**/*HAO*/*HDO*
pharmaceutical	phar-ma-ceu-ti-cal	**GAR/GAR**/*HOO*/**GAR**/*HDO*
pharmacist	phar-ma-ci-st	**GAR/GAR/GAR**/*HDO*
pharmacy	phar-ma-cy	**GAR/GAR/GAR**
phase	pha-se	*HAO*/*HDO*
phase	pha-se	*HAO*/*HDO*
pheasant	phea-sa-nt	**GAR/GAR/GDR**
phenomenon	phe-no-me-no-n	**GAR**/*HAO*/**GAR**/*HAO*/*HDO*
phial	phi-a-l	**GRR/GAR/GDR**
philately	phi-la-te-ly	**GAR/GAR**/*HAO*/**GDR**
Philippine	Phi-li-ppi-ne	**GAR/GAR/GAR/GDR**
philistine	phi-li-sti-ne	**GAR/GAR/GRR/GDR**
philosopher	phi-lo-so-pher	**GAR**/*HAO*/*HOO*/*HDO*
philosophy	phi-lo-so-phy	**GAR**/*HAO*/*HOO*/**GAR**
philtre	phi-l-tre	**GAR/GDR**/*HAO*
phlegm	phl-e(g)-m	**GDR/GAR**/*HDO*

Word	Mouthables	Mouth Movements Notations
phlegmatic	phl-e(g)-ma-ti-c	**GDR/GAR/GAR/GAR/GDR**
phone	pho-ne	*HOO/HDO*
phonetics	pho-ne-ti-cs	**GAR/GAR/GAR/GDR**
photo	pho-to	*HOO/HOO*
photocopier	pho-to-co-pi-er	*HOO/HOO/HAO/***GAR/GDR**
photocopy	pho-to-co-py	*HOO/HOO/HAO/***GAR**
photograph	pho-to-gra-ph	*HOO/HOO/***GAR**/*HDO*
photographer	pho-to-gra-pher	*HOO/HOO/***GAR**/*HDO*
photography	pho-to-gra-phy	*HOO/HAO/***GAR/GAR**
physical	phy-si-cal	**GAR/GAR**/*HDO*
physician	phy-si-ci-an	**GAR/GAR/GDR**/*HDO*
physicist	phy-si-ci-st	**GAR/GAR/GAR/GDR**
physics	phy-si-cs	**GAR/GAR/GDR**
physique	phy-si-que	**GAR/GAR**/*HDO*
pianist	pi-a-ni-st	**GAR/GAR/GAR**/*HDO*
piano	pi-a-no	**GAR/GAR**/*HOO*
pick	pi-ck	**GAR/GRR**
picked	pi-cke-d	**GAR/GDR**/*HOO*
pick	pi-ck	**GAR**/*HDO*
picket	pi-ck-e-t	**GAR/GDR/GAR/GDR**
pickle	pi-ckle	**GAR**/*HOO*
picnic	pi-c-ni-c	**GAR/GDR/GAR/GDR**
pictorial	pi-c-to-rial	**GAR/GDR**/*HOO/HDO*
picture	pi-c-tu-re	**GAR/GDR**/*HOO/HDO*
picturesque	pi-c-tur-e-sque	**GAR/GDR**/*HOO/***GAR/GDR**
piddling	pi-dd-li-ng	**GAR**/*HOO/***GAR/GDR**
pie	pie	**GRR**
piece	pie-ce	**GAR**/*HDO*
pier	pi-er	**GAR**/*HDO*
pierce	pi-er-ce	**GAR**/*HAO/***GDR**
piercing	pi-er-ci-ng	**GAR**/*HAO/***GAR/GDR**

Word	Mouthables	Mouth Movements Notations
piety	pi-e-ty	GRR/GAR/GAR
piffle	pi-ffle	GAR/*HOO*
pig	pi-g	GAR/*HDO*
pigeon	pi-ge-o-n	GAR/GAR/*HAO/HDO*
piggy	pi-ggy	GAR/GAR
pigment	pi-g-men-t	GAR/GDR/GAR/*HDO*
pigsty	pi-g-sty	GAR/GDR/GRR
pike	pi-ke	GRR/*HDO*
pilchard	pi-l-char-d	GAR/GDR/*HAO/HDO*
pile	pi-le	GRR/*HDO*
piled	pi-le-d	GRR/*HDO/HOO*
piles	pi-le-s	GRR/GDR/GDR
pilfer	pi-l-fer	GAR/GDR/*HDO*
pilgrim	pi-l-gri-m	GAR/GDR/GAR/*HDO*
pilgrimage	pi-l-gri-ma-ge	GAR/GDR/GAR/*HAO/HDO*
pill	pi-ll	GAR/GDR
pillage	pi-lla-ge	GAR/*HAO/HDO*
pillar	pi-llar	GAR/*HAO*
pillory	pi-llo-ry	GAR/*HAO*/GDR
pillow	pi-llo-w	GAR/*HOO/HDO*
pilot	pi-lo-t	GRR/*HAO/HDO*
pimp	pi-mp	GAR/GDR
pimple	pi-m-ple	GAR/GDR/*HOO*
pin	pi-n	GAR/GDR
pinacle	pi-na-cle	GAR/GAR/*HOO*
pinafore	pi-na-fo-re	GRR/GAR/*HOO/HDO*
pincers	pi-n-cer-s	GAR/GDR/GAR/*HDO*
pinch	pi-n-ch	GAR/GDR/*HDO*
pine	pi-ne	GRR/GRR
pine	pi-ne	GRR/GDR
pined	pi-ne-d	GRR/GRR/*HOO*

Word	Mouthables	Mouth Movements Notations
pinion	pi-ni-on	**GAR/GAR/***HDO*
pink	pin-k	**GAR/***HDO*
pint	pin-t	**GRR/***HOO*
pioneer	pi-o-ne-er	**GRR/***HOO***/GRR/GDR**
pious	pi-ou-s	**GRR/GAR/***HDO*
pip	pi-p	**GAR/***HDO*
pipe	pi-pe	**GRR/***HDO*
piped	pi-pe-d	**GRR/***HDO***/***HOO*
piping	pi-ping	**GRR/GDR**
piquant	pi-qua-nt	**GAR/***HOO***/GDR**
pique	pi-que	**GAR/***HDO*
pirate	pi-ra-te	**GRR/GAR/***HDO*
piss	pi-ss	**GAR/***HDO*
pistachio	pi-sta-chi-o	**GAR/GAR/***HDO***/***HOO*
pistol	pi-sto-l	**GAR/***HAO***/GDR**
piston	pi-sto-n	**GAR/***HAO***/***HDO*
pit	pi-t	**GAR/***HOO*
pitance	pi-ta-nce	**GAR/GAR/GDR**
pitch	pit-ch	**GAR/GDR**
pitched	pit-che-d	**GAR/GDR/***HOO*
pitch	pit-ch	**GAR/***HDO*
pitcher	pit-cher	**GAR/***HDO*
pithy	pi-th-y	**GAR/GTR/GAR**
pitiful	pi-ti-ful	**GAR/GAR/***HOO*
pitiless	pi-ti-le-ss	**GAR/GAR/GAR/GDR**
pitted	pi-t-ted	**GAR/***HOO***/GRR**
pity	pi-ty	**GAR/GAR**
pivot	pi-vo-t	**GAR/GAR/***HOO*
placard	pla-car-d	**GAR/GAR/***HOO*
place	pla-ce	*HAO***/GDR**
placement	pla-ce-me-nt	*HAO***/GDR/GAR/GDR**

Word	Mouthables	Mouth Movements Notations
placid	pla-ci-d	**GAR/GAR/GDR**
plagiarism	pla-gia-ri-sm	*HAO*/**GDR/GAR/GDR**
plagiarize	pla-gia-ri-se	*HAO*/**GDR/GRR**/*HDO*
plague	pla-gue	*HAO/HOO*
plaid	plai-d	**GAR**/*HOO*
plain	plai-n	*HAO*/**GDR**
plaintiff	plai-n-ti-ff	*HAO*/**GDR/GAR**/*HDO*
plait	plai-t	**GAR**/*HOO*
plan	pla-n	**GAR/GDR**
plane	pla-ne	*HAO/HDO*
planet	pla-ne-t	**GAR/GAR**/*HOO*
planetarium	pla-ne-tar-i-um	**GAR/GAR/GAR/GAR/GDR**
planetary	pla-ne-tar-y	**GAR/GRR/GAR/GAR**
plank	plan-k	**GAR**/*HDO*
planned	pla-nne-d	**GAR/GRR**/*HOO*
planning	pla-nni-ng	**GAR/GAR/GDR**
plant	plan-t	*HAO/HOO*
plantation	plan-ta-tion	*HAO/HAO/HOO*
plaque	pla-que	**GAR**/*HDO*
plaster	plas-ter	*HAO/HDO*
plastered	plas-tere-d	*HAO/HDO/HOO*
plastic	plas-ti-c	*HAO*/**GAR/GDR**
plasticine	plas-ti-ci-ne	*HAO*/**GAR/GAR/GDR**
plate	pla-te	*HAO/HDO*
platform	pla-t-for-m	**GAR**/*HOO/HOO/HDO*
platinum	pla-ti-n-u-m	**GAR/GAR/GDR/GAR**/*HDO*
platoon	pla-too-n	**GAR**/*HOO/HDO*
plausible	plau-si-ble	*HOO*/**GAR**/*HOO*
play	play	*HAO*
played	playe-d	*HAO/HOO*
player	pla-yer	*HAO/HDO*

Word	Mouthables	Mouth Movements Notations
playful	play-ful	*HAO/HOO*
plea	plea	**GRR**
plead	plea-d	**GRR/GRR**
pleasant	plea-san-t	**GAR/GAR**/*HDO*
please	plea-se	**GRR**/*HDO*
pleasure	plea-su-re	**GAR**/*HOO/HDO*
pleat	plea-t	**GRR/GRR**
pledge	pled-ge	**GAR**/*HDO*
plenary	ple-na-ry	**GAR/GAR**/*HDO*
plentiful	ple-n-ti-ful	**GAR/GDR/GAR**/*HOO*
plenty	ple-n-ty	**GAR/GDR/GAR**
pleonastic	ple-o-na-sti-c	**GRR**/*HAO*/**GAR/GAR/GDR**
pleurisy	pleu-ri-sy	*HAO*/**GAR/GAR**
pliable	pli-a-ble	**GRR/GAR**/*HOO*
pliers	pli-er-s	**GRR**/*HDO/HDO*
plight	pligh-t	**GRR**/*HOO*
plimsoll	pli-m-so-ll	**GAR/GDR**/*HOO/HDO*
plod	plo-d	*HAO/HOO*
plonk	plon-k	*HAO/HDO*
plop	plo-p	*HAO/HDO*
plot	plo-t	*HAO/HOO*
plot	plo-t	*HAO/HDO*
plotted	plo-t-ted	*HAO/HOO*/**GRR**
plough	plou-gh	*HAO/HDO*
ploy	ploy	**GAR**
pluck	pluc-k	**GAR**/*HDO*
plucky	pluc-ky	**GAR/GAR**
plug	plu-g	**GAR**/*HDO*
plum	plu-m	**GAR**/*HDO*
plumb	plu-mb	**GAR**/*HDO*
plumbed	plu-mbe-d	**GAR**/*HDO/HOO*

Word	Mouthables	Mouth Movements Notations
plumber	plu-mb-er	**GAR**/*HDO*/*HDO*
plumbing	plu-mb-ing	**GAR**/*HDO*/**GDR**
plummet	plu-m-me-t	**GAR**/*HDO*/**GAR**/**GDR**
plump	plu-m-p	**GAR**/*HDO*/*HDO*
plunder	plu-n-der	**GAR**/**GDR**/*HDO*
plunge	plu-n-ge	**GAR**/**GDR**/*HDO*
plunger	plu-n-ger	**GAR**/**GDR**/*HDO*
plunging	plu-n-ging	**GAR**/**GDR**/**GDR**
plural	plu-ra-l	*HOO*/**GAR**/**GDR**
plus	plu-s	**GAR**/*HDO*
plush	plu-sh	**GAR**/*HDO*
ply	ply	**GRR**
pneumatic	pneu-ma-ti-c	*HOO*/**GAR**/**GAR**/**GDR**
pneumonia	pneu-mo-ni-a	*HOO*/*HOO*/**GAR**/**GAR**
poach	poa-ch	*HOO*/*HDO*
poached	poa-che-d	*HOO*/*HOO*/*HOO*
poacher	poa-cher	*HOO*/*HDO*
pocket	po-cke-t	*HAO*/**GAR**/*HOO*
pod	po-d	*HAO*/*HOO*
podgy	po-d-gy	*HAO*/*HOO*/**GAR**
podium	po-di-u-m	*HOO*/**GAR**/**GAR**/*HDO*
pocm	po-e-m	*HOO*/**GAR**/*HDO*
poet	po-e-t	*HOO*/**GAR**/*HOO*
poetic	po-e-ti-c	*HOO*/**GAR**/**GAR**/**GDR**
poetical	po-e-ti-cal	*HOO*/**GAR**/**GAR**/*HDO*
poetry	po-e-try	*HOO*/**GAR**/*HDO*
poignant	poi-gna-nt	**GAR**/**GAR**/**GDR**
point	poi-nt	**GAR**/**GDR**
pointed	poi-n-ted	**GAR**/**GDR**/**GRR**
pointer	poi-n-ter	**GAR**/**GDR***HDO*
pointless	poi-nt-le-ss	**GAR**/**GDR**/**GAR**/**GAR**/**GDR**

Word	Mouthables	Mouth Movements Notations
poise	poi-se	**GAR**/*HDO*
poison	poi-so-n	**GAR/GAR/GDR**
poisonous	poi-so-nou-s	**GAR/GAR/GAR**/*HDO*
poke	po-ke	*HOO/HDO*
poker	po-ker	*HOO/HDO*
poky	po-ky	*HOO*/**GAR**
Poland	Po-lan-d	*HOO*/**GAR**/*HOO*
polar	po-lar	*HOO/HAO*
pole	po-le	*HOO/HDO*
polemic	po-le-mi-c	*HOO*/**GAR/GAR/GDR**
polemical	po-le-mi-cal	*HOO*/**GAR/GAR**/*HDO*
police	po-li-ce	*HOO*/**GAR/GDR**
policy	po-li-cy	*HAO*/**GAR/GAR**
polio	po-li-o	*HOO*/**GAR**/*HOO*
poliomyelitis	po-li-o-mye-li-ti-s	*HOO*/**GAR**/*HOO*/**GRR/GAR/GAR/GDR**
polish	po-li-sh	*HAO*/**GAR/GDR**
Polish	Po-li-sh	*HOO*/**GAR**/*HDO*
polite	po-li-te	*HAO*/**GRR**/*HDO*
political	po-li-ti-cal	*HAO*/**GAR/GAR**/*HDO*
politician	po-li-ti-cian	*HAO*/**GAR/GAR**/*HDO*
politicized	po-li-ti-ci-ze-d	*HAO*/**GAR/GAR/GRR/GDR**/*HOO*
politics	po-li-ti-cs	*HAO*/**GAR/GAR/GDR**
poll	po-ll	*HOO/HDO*
pollen	pol-le-n	*HAO*/**GAR/GDR**
polling	po-lli-ng	*HOO*/**GAR/GDR**
pollutant	po-llu-tan-t	*HOO/HOO*/**GAR**/*HDO*
pollute	po-llu-te	*HOO/HOO/HDO*
pollution	po-llu-tion	*HOO/HOO/HOO*
polo	po-lo	*HOO/HOO*
polystyrene	po-ly-sty-re-ne	*HAO*/**GAR/GRR/GRR/GDR**

Word	Mouthables	Mouth Movements Notations
polytechnic	po-ly-te-ch-ni-c	*HAO*/**GAR/GAR/GDR/GAR/GDR**
pomander	po-man-der	*HOO*/**GAR**/*HDO*
pomegranate	po-me-gra-na-te	*HOO*/**GAR/GAR/GAR**/*HDO*
pompous	po-mp-ous	*HAO/HDO/HAO*
pond	po-n-d	*HAO/HDO/HOO*
ponder	po-n-der	*HAO/HDO/HDO*
pong	pon-g	*HAO/HDO*
pontificate	po-n-ti-fi-ca-te	*HAO*/**GDR/GAR/GAR**/*HAO/HDO*
pontoon	po-n-too-n	*HAO/HDO/HOO/HDO*
pony	po-ny	*HOO*/**GAR**
poodle	poo-dle	*HOO/HOO*
pool	poo-l	*HOO*/**GDR**
pool	poo-l	*HOO/HDO*
pool	poo-le-d	*HOO*/**GDR**/*HOO*
poor	poo-r	*HOO/HDO*
poorly	poor-ly	*HOO*/**GDR**
pop	po-p	*HAO/HDO*
Pope	Po-pe	*HOO/HDO*
poplar	po-p-lar	*HAO/HDO/HAO*
poppet	po-pp-e-t	*HAO/HDO*/**GAR/GDR**
poppy	po-ppy	*HAO*/**GAR**
popular	po-pu-lar	*HAO/HOO/HDO*
populate	po-pu-la-te	*HAO/HOO/HAO/HDO*
population	po-pu-la-tion	*HAO/HOO/HAO/HOO*
porcelain	por-ce-lai-n	*HOO*/**GAR/GAR/GDR**
porch	por-ch	*HOO/HDO*
porcupine	por-cu-pi-ne	*HOO/HOO*/**GRR/GDR**
pore	po-re	*HOO/HDO*
pork	por-k	*HOO/HDO*
pornographic	por-no-gra-phi-c	*HOO/HOO*/**GAR/GAR/GDR**
porous	por-ou-s	*HOO*/**GAR**/*HDO*

Word	Mouthables	Mouth Movements Notations
porridge	por-ri-dge	*HOO*/**GAR**/*HDO*
port	por-t	*HOO*/*HOO*
portable	por-ta-ble	*HOO*/**GAR**/*HOO*
portal	por-tal	*HOO*/*HDO*
portent	por-te-nt	*HOO*/**GAR**/**GDR**
porter	por-ter	*HOO*/*HDO*
portfolio	port-fo-li-o	*HOO*/*HOO*/**GAR**/*HOO*
porthole	port-ho-le	*HOO*/*HOO*/*HDO*
portion	por-tion	*HOO*/*HOO*
portrait	por-trai-t	*HOO*/*HAO*/*HOO*
portray	por-tray	*HOO*/*HAO*
Portugal	Por-tu-ga-l	*HOO*/*HOO*/**GAR**/**GDR**
Portugese	Por-tu-gue-se	*HOO*/*HOO*/**GRR**/*HDO*
pose	po-se	*HOO*/*HDO*
posh	po-sh	*HAO*/*HDO*
position	po-si-tion	*HOO*/**GAR**/*HOO*
positive	po-si-ti-ve	*HAO*/**GAR**/**GAR**/**GDR**
possess	po-sse-ss	*HOO*/**GAR**/*HDO*
possession	po-sse-ssion	*HOO*/**GAR**/*HOO*
possessive	po-sse-ssi-ve	*HOO*/**GAR**/**GAR**/**GDR**
possessor	po-sse-ssor	*HOO*/**GAR**/*HDO*
possible	po-ssi-ble	*HAO*/**GAR**/*HOO*
possibility	po-ssi-bi-li-ty	*HAO*/**GAR**/**GAR**/**GAR**/**GAR**
possibly	po-ssi-bly	*HAO*/**GAR**/**GDR**
post	po-st	*HOO*/*HOO*
post	po-st	*HOO*/*HDO*
postage	po-stage	*HOO*/*HDO*
postal	po-stal	*HOO*/*HDO*
posted	po-sted	*HOO*/**GRR**
poster	po-ster	*HOO*/*HDO*
posterior	po-ste-ri-or	*HAO*/**GRR**/**GAR**/*HDO*

Word	Mouthables	Mouth Movements Notations
postpone	po-st-po-ne	*HOO/HOO/HOO/HDO*
posy	po-sy	*HOO*/**GAR**
pot	po-t	*HAO/HOO*
pot	po-t	*HAO/HDO*
potato	po-ta-to	*HOO/HAO/HOO*
potted	po-t-ted	*HAO/HDO*/**GRR**
potter	po-t-ter	*HAO/HDO/HDO*
pottery	pot-te-ry	*HAO*/**GAR**/*HDO*
potty	po-tty	*HAO*/**GAR**
pouch	pou-ch	**GAR**/*HDO*
poulterer	pou-l-ter-er	*HAO/HDO/HAO/HDO*
poultry	pou-l-try	*HAO/HDO/HDO*
pounce	pou-n-ce	**GAR/GDR/GDR**
pound	pou-nd	*HAO*/**GDR**
pound	pou-nd	*HAO/HDO*
pounded	pou-n-ded	*HAO*/**GDR/GRR**
pour	pou-r	*HOO/HDO*
pout	pou-t	**GAR**/*HOO*
poverty	po-ver-ty	*HAO/HAO*/**GAR**
power	pow-er	*HAO/HDO*
powered	po-were-d	*HAO/HOO/HOO*
powerful	po-wer-fu-l	*HAO/HOO/HOO/HDO*
powerless	po-wer-le-ss	*HAO/HOO*/**GAR/GDR**
practical	pra-c-ti-cal	**GAR/GDR/GAR**/*HDO*
practice	pra-c-ti-ce	**GAR/GDR/GAR/GDR**
practise	pra-c-ti-se	**GAR/GDR/GAR**/*HDO*
practitioner	pra-c-ti-tion-er	**GAR/GDR/GAR**/*HOO/HDO*
Prague	Pra-gue	*HAO/HDO*
prairie	prai-rie	*HAO*/**GAR**
praise	prai-se	*HAO/HDO*
pram	pra-m	**GAR**/*HDO*

Word	Mouthables	Mouth Movements Notations
prank	pra-nk	**GAR/GDR**
prattle	pra-ttle	**GAR**/*HOO*
prawn	praw-n	*HOO*/**GDR**
pray	pray	*HAO*
prayer	pray-er	*HAO/HDO*
preach	prea-ch	**GRR**/*HDO*
preamble	pre-a-m-ble	**GRR/GAR**/*HDO/HOO*
precarious	pre-ca-ri-ous	**GRR/GAR/GAR**/*HAO*
precaution	pre-cau-tion	**GRR**/*HOO/HOO*
precede	pre-ce-de	**GRR/GRR**/*HDO*
precedence	pre-ce-de-nce	**GAR/GAR/GAR/GDR**
precedent	pre-ce-de-nt	**GAR/GAR/GAR/GDR**
precinct	pre-ci-nct	**GRR/GAR/GDR**
precious	pre-ci-ous	**GAR/GDR/GAR**
precipice	pre-ci-pi-ce	**GAR/GAR/GAR/GDR**
precipitous	pre-ci-pi-tous	**GAR/GAR/GAR**/*HDO*
précis	pre-cis	*HAO*/**GAR**
precise	pre-ci-se	**GRR/GRR**/*HDO*
precision	pre-ci-sion	**GRR/GAR**/*HOO*
precocious	pre-co-ci-ous	**GAR**/*HOO*/**GDR**/*HAO*
predatory	pre-da-to-ry	**GAR/GAR**/*HOO*/**GDR**
predecessor	pre-de-ces-sor	**GRR/GAR/GAR**/*HOO*
predestination	pre-de-sti-na-tion	**GRR/GAR/GAR**/*HAO/HOO*
predicament	pre-di-ca-men-t	**GRR/GAR/GAR/GAR**/*HDO*
predicate	pre-di-ca-te	**GAR/GAR**/*HAO/HDO*
predict	pre-di-ct	**GRR/GAR**/*HOO*
predominance	pre-do-mi-na-nce	**GRR**/*HAO*/**GAR/GAR/GDR**
preempt	pre-e-mp-t	**GRR/GAR**/*HDO/HDO*
preface	pre-fa-ce	**GRR**/*HAO/HDO*
prefect	pre-fec-t	**GRR/GAR**/*HOO*
prefer	pre-fer	**GRR**/*HDO*

Word	Mouthables	Mouth Movements Notations
preference	pre-fer-e-nce	**GAR**/*HAO*/**GAR**/**GDR**
preferential	pre-fer-e-n-tial	**GAR**/*HAO*/**GAR**/**GDR**/*HDO*
pregnancy	pre-g-na-cy	**GAR**/**GDR**/**GAR**/**GAR**
pregnant	pre-g-na-nt	**GAR**/**GDR**/**GAR**/**GDR**
prehistory	pre-hi-sto-ry	**GRR**/**GAR**/*HOO*/**GDR**
prejudge	pre-jud-ge	**GRR**/**GAR**/*HDO*
prejudice	pre-ju-di-ce	**GAR**/*HOO*/**GAR**/**GDR**
prejudiced	pre-ju-di-ce-d	**GAR**/*HOO*/**GAR**/**GDR**/*HOO*
prelate	pre-la-te	**GRR**/*HAO*/*HDO*
preliminary	pre-li-mi-na-ry	**GRR**/**GAR**/**GAR**/**GAR**/*HDO*
prelude	pre-lu-de	**GAR**/*HOO*/*HDO*
premarital	pre-ma-ri-tal	**GRR**/**GAR**/**GAR**/*HDO*
premature	pre-ma-tu-re	**GAR**/**GAR**/*HOO*/*HDO*
premediation	pre-me-di-ta-tion	**GRR**/**GAR**/**GAR**/*HAO*/*HOO*
premeditate	pre-me-di-ta-te	**GRR**/**GAR**/**GAR**/*HAO*/*HDO*
premier	pre-mi-er	**GAR**/**GAR**/*HDO*
premiere	pre-mi-ere	**GAR**/**GAR**/*HDO*
premise	pre-mi-se	**GAR**/**GAR**/*HDO*
premiss	pre-mi-ss	**GAR**/**GAR**/*HDO*
premium	pre-mi-u-m	**GRR**/**GAR**/**GAR**/*HDO*
preoccupation	pre-o-ccu-pa-tion	**GRR**/*HAO*/*HOOHAO*/*HOO*
prep	pre-p	**GAR**/*HDO*
preparation	pre-par-a-tion	**GAR**/*HAO*/*HAO*/*HOO*
preparatory	pre-par-a-to-ry	**GAR**/*HAO*/*HAO*/*HOO*/*HDO*
prepare	pre-pare	**GRR**/*HAO*
prepossessing	pre-po-sse-ssi-ng	**GRR**/*HAO*/**GAR**/**GAR**/**GDR**
preposterous	pre-po-ster-ous	**GRR**/*HAO*/*HAO*/**GAR**
prerequisite	pre-re-qui-si-te	**GRR**/**GAR**/**GAR**/**GAR**/**GDR**
prerogative	pre-ro-ga-ti-ve	**GRR**/*HAO*/**GAR**/**GAR**/**GDR**
prescribe	pre-scr-i-be	**GRR**/**GDR**/**GRR**/*HDO*
prescription	pre-scri-p-tion	**GRR**/**GAR**/*HDO*/*HOO*

Word	Mouthables	Mouth Movements Notations
presence	pre-se-nce	GAR/GAR/GDR
present	pre-se-nt	GAR/GAR/GDR
presenter	pre-sen-ter	GAR/GAR/*HDO*
presentiment	pre-se-n-ti-me-nt	GAR/GAR/GDR/GAR/GAR/GDR
presently	pre-sen-tly	GAR/GAR/*HDO*
preserve	pre-ser-ve	GAR/*HAO*/*HDO*
preside	pre-si-de	GAR/GRR/*HDO*
presidency	pre-si-de-ncy	GAR/GAR/GAR/GDR
president	pre-si-den-t	GAR/GAR/GAR/*HOO*
press	pre-ss	GAR/*HDO*
pressing	pre-ssing	GAR/GDR
pressure	pre-ssu-re	GAR/*HOO*/*HDO*
prestige	pre-sti-ge	GAR/GAR/*HDO*
presume	pre-su-me	GRR/*HOO*/*HDO*
presumptive	pre-su-mp-ti-ve	GRR/GAR/*HDO*/GAR/*HDO*
presumptuous	pre-su-mp-tu-ous	GRR/GAR/*HDO*/*HOO*/*HAO*
presurize	pre-su-ri-ze	GAR/*HOO*/GRR/GDR
pretence	pre-te-nce	GRR/GAR/GDR
pretend	pre-ten-d	GRR/GAR/*HOO*
pretender	pre-ten-der	GRR/GAR/*HDO*
pretension	pre-ten-sion	GRR/GAR/*HOO*
pretext	pre-te-xt	GRR/GAR/GDR
pretty	pre-tty	GRR/GAR
prevail	pre-vai-l	GRR/*HAO*/GDR
prevalent	pre-va-len-t	GAR/GAR/GAR/*HDO*
prevaricate	pre-va-ri-ca-te	GRR/GAR/GAR/*HAO*/*HDO*
prevent	pre-ven-t	GRR/GAR/*HOO*
prevention	pre-ven-tion	GRR/GDR/*HOO*
preventive	pre-ve-n-ti-ve	GRR/GAR/GDR/GAR/GDR
preview	pre-view	GRR/*HOO*
previous	pre-vi-ous	GRR/GAR/*HAO*

Word	Mouthables	Mouth Movements Notations
prewar	pre-war	**GRR**/*HOO*
prey	prey	*HAO*
price	pri-ce	**GAR/GDR**
priceless	pri-ce-les-s	**GAR/GDR/GAR/GDR**
prick	pri-ck	**GAR**/*HDO*
prickle	pri-ckle	**GAR**/*HOO*
pride	pri-de	**GRR**/*HDO*
priest	prie-st	**GAR**/*HOO*
prig	pri-g	**GAR**/*HDO*
primary	pri-ma-ry	**GRR/GAR**/*HDO*
prime	pri-me	**GRR**/*HDO*
primer	pri-mer	**GRR**/*HDO*
primitive	pri-mi-ti-ve	**GAR/GAR/GAR**/*HDO*
primrose	pri-m-ro-se	**GAR/GDR**/*HOO*/*HDO*
prince	pri-n-ce	**GAR/GDR/GDR**
principal	pri-n-ci-pa-l	**GAR/GDR/GAR/GAR/GDR**
principle	pri-n-ci-ple	**GAR/GDR/GAR**/*HOO*
print	pri-n-t	**GAR/GDR**/*HOO*
printer	pri-n-ter	**GAR/GDR**/*HDO*
prior	pri-or	**GRR/GAR**
prior	pri-or	**GRR**/*HDO*
priority	pri-or-i-ty	**GRR**/*HAO*/**GAR/GAR**
prison	pri-so-n	**GAR**/*HAO*/*HDO*
prisoner	pri-so-ner	**GAR**/*HAO*/*HDO*
privacy	pri-va-cy	**GRR/GAR/GAR**
private	pri-va-te	**GRR/GAR**/*HDO*
privation	pri-va-tion	**GRR**/*HAO*/*HOO*
privatize	pri-va-ti-ze	**GRR/GAR/GRR/GDR**
privilege	pri-vi-le-ge	**GAR/GAR/GAR**/*HDO*
privileged	pri-vi-le-ge-d	**GAR/GAR/GAR**/*HOO*/*HOO*
privy	pri-vy	**GAR/GAR**

Word	Mouthables	Mouth Movements Notations
prize	pri-ze	**GRR/GDR**
pro	pro	*HOO*
probable	pro-ba-ble	*HAO/***GAR***/HOO*
probation	pro-ba-tion	*HOO/HAO/HOO*
probe	pro-be	*HOO/HDO*
problem	pro-ble-m	*HAO/***GAR/GDR**
procedure	pro-ce-du-re	*HOO/***GRR***/HOO/HDO*
proceed	pro-cee-d	*HOO/***GRR***/HOO*
proceedings	pro-cee-dings	*HOO/***GRR/GDR**
proceeds	pro-cee-ds	*HOO/***GRR***/HDO*
process	pro-ce-ss	*HDO/***GAR***/HDO*
processes	pro-ce-ss-es	*HDO/***GAR***/HDO/***GDR**
procession	pro-ces-sion	*HOO/***GAR***/HOO*
processor	pro-ces-sor	*HOO/***GAR/GAR**
proclaim	pro-clai-m	*HOO/HAO/HDO*
prod	pro-d	*HAO/HOO*
prod	pro-d	*HAO/HDO*
prodded	pro-d-ded	*HAO/HOO/***GRR**
prodigy	pro-di-gy	*HAO/***GAR/GAR**
produce	pro-du-ce	*HOO/HOO/***GDR**
producer	pro-du-cer	*HOO/HOO/HDO*
product	pro-duc-t	*HAO/***GAR***/HOO*
productive	pro-duc-ti-ve	*HAO/***GAR/GAR/GDR**
profane	pro-fa-ne	*HOO/HAO/***GDR**
profession	pro-fes-sion	*HOO/***GAR***/HOO*
professional	pro-fes-sion-al	*HOO/***GAR***/HOO/HDO*
professionalism	pro-fes-sion-al-i-sm	*HOO/***GAR***/HOO/HDO/***GAR/GDR**
professor	pro-fes-sor	*HOO/***GAR***/HOO*
proficiency	pro-fi-ci-e-ncy	*HOO/***GAR/GAR/GAR/GDR**
profile	pro-fi-le	*HOO/***GRR/GDR**
profit	pro-fi-t	*HAO/***GAR***/HOO*

Word	Mouthables	Mouth Movements Notations
profitable	pro-fi-ta-ble	*HAO*/**GAR**/**GAR**/*HOO*
profiteer	pro-fi-tee-r	*HAO*/**GAR**/**GRR**/*HDO*
progamme	pro-gra-mme	*HOO*/**GAR**/*HDO*
prognosis	pro-g-no-si-s	*HAO*/*HDO*/*HOO*/**GAR**/**GDR**
progress	pro-gre-ss	*HOO*/**GAR**/*HDO*
progressive	pro-gre-ssi-ve	*HOO*/**GAR**/**GAR**/**GDR**
prohibit	pro-hi-bi-t	*HOO*/**GAR**/**GAR**/*HOO*
prohibition	pro-hi-bi-tion	*HOO*/**GAR**/**GAR**/*HOO*
prohibitive	pro-hi-bi-ti-ve	*HOO*/**GAR**/**GAR**/**GAR**/*HDO*
project	pro-jec-t	*HOO*/**GAR**/*HOO*
projection	pro-jec-tion	*HOO*/**GAR**/*HOO*
projector	pro-jec-tor	*HOO*/**GAR**/*HOO*
proletarian	pro-le-tar-i-an	*HAO*/**GAR**/*HAO*/**GAR**/**GDR**
prolific	pro-li-fi-c	*HOO*/**GAR**/**GAR**/**GDR**
prolix	pro-li-x	*HOO*/**GAR**/**GDR**
prologue	pro-lo-gue	*HOO*/*HAO*/*HDO*
prolong	pro-lon-g	*HOO*/*HAO*/*HDO*
promenade	pro-me-nade	*HAO*/**GAR**/*HDO*
promiscuity	pro-mi-scu-i-ty	*HAO*/**GAR**/*HOO*/**GAR**/**GAR**
promiscuous	pro-mi-scu-ous	*HAO*/**GAR**/**GAR**/*HDO*
promise	pro-mi-se	*HAO*/**GAR**/*HDO*
promontory	pro-mo-n-to-ry	*HOO*/**GAR**/**GDR**/*HOO*/*HDO*
promote	pro-mo-te	*HOO*/*HOO*/*HDO*
promoter	pro-mo-ter	*HOO*/*HOO*/*HDO*
promotion	pro-mo-tion	*HOO*/*HOO*/*HOO*
promotional	pro-mo-tion-al	*HOO*/*HOO*/*HOO*/*HDO*
prompt	pro-mp-t	*HAO*/*HDO*/*HOO*
prompter	pro-mp-ter	*HAO*/*HDO*/*HDO*
prong	pron-g	*HAO*/*HDO*
pronoun	pro-nou-n	*HOO*/*HAO*/**GDR**
pronounce	pro-nou-nce	*HOO*/**GAR**/**GDR**

Word	Mouthables	Mouth Movements Notations
pronounced	pro-nou-nce-d	*HOO*/**GAR**/**GDR**/*HOO*
pronto	pro-n-to	*HAO*/**GDR**/*HOO*
pronunciation	pro-nun-ci-a-tion	*HOO*/**GAR**/**GAR**/*HAO*/*HOO*
proof	proo-f	*HOO*/*HDO*
prop	pro-p	*HAO*/*HOO*
prop	pro-p	*HAO*/*HDO*
propagate	pro-pa-ga-te	*HAO*/**GAR**/*HAO*/*HDO*
propellant	pro-pe-lla-nt	*HOO*/**GAR**/**GAR**/**GDR**
propeller	pro-pe-ller	*HOO*/**GAR**/*HDO*
proper	pro-per	*HAO*/*HDO*
property	pro-per-ty	*HAO*/*HAO*/**GAR**
prophecy	pro-phe-cy	*HAO*/**GAR**/**GAR**
prophet	pro-phe-t	*HAO*/**GAR**/*HOO*
propitious	pro-pi-ti-ous	*HOO*/**GAR**/**GDR**/**GAR**
propliferate	pro-li-fer-a-te	*HOO*/**GAR**/*HAO*/*HAO*/*HDO*
proportion	pro-por-tion	*HOO*/*HOO*/*HOO*
proportional	pro-por-tion-al	*HOO*/*HOO*/*HOO*/*HDO*
proportionate	pro-por-tion-a-te	*HOO*/*HOO*/*HOO*/*HAOHDO*
proposal	pro-po-sal	*HOO*/*HOO*/*HDO*
propose	pro-po-se	*HOO*/*HOO*/*HDO*
proposition	pro-po-si-tion	*HAO*/*HOO*/**GAR**/*HOO*
propped	pro-ppe-d	*HAO*/*HDO*/*HOO*
proprietor	pro-pri-e-tor	*HOO*/**GRR**/**GAR**/*HDO*
propriety	pro-pri-e-ty	*HOO*/**GRR**/**GAR**/**GAR**
prosaic	pro-sa-i-c	*HOO*/*HAO*/**GAR**/**GDR**
prose	pro-se	*HOO*/*HDO*
prosecute	pro-se-cu-te	*HAO*/**GAR**/*HOO*/*HDO*
prosecutor	pro-se-cu-tor	*HAO*/**GAR**/*HOO*/*HOO*
prospect	pro-spe-c-t	*HAO*/**GAR**/**GDR**/*HOO*
prospectus	pro-spe-c-tus	*HDO*/**GAR**/**GDR**/**GAR**
prostitute	pro-sti-tu-te	*HAO*/**GAR**/*HOO*/*HDO*

Word	Mouthables	Mouth Movements Notations
prostrate	pro-stra-te	*HAO/HAO/HDO*
protagonist	pro-ta-go-ni-st	*HOO/***GAR/GAR/GAR**/*HDO*
protect	pro-te-c-t	*HOO/***GAR/GDR**/*HOO*
protection	pro-te-c-tion	*HOO/***GAR/GDR**/*HOO*
protective	pro-te-c-ti-ve	*HOO/***GAR/GDR/GAR**/*HDO*
protector	pro-te-c-tor	*HOO/***GAR/GDR**/*HDO*
protein	pro-tei-n	*HOO/***GRR/GDR**
protest	pro-te-st	*HOO/***GAR**/*HOO*
Protestant	Pro-te-sta-nt	*HAO/***GAR/GAR/GDR**
protester	pro-te-ster	*HOO/***GAR**/*HDO*
protocol	pro-to-co-l	*HOO/***GAR**/*HAO/***GDR**
prototype	pro-to-ty-pe	*HOO/***GAR/GRR**/*HDO*
protrusion	pro-tru-sion	*HOO/HOO/HOO*
protuberance	pro-tu-be-ra-nce	*HOO/HOO/***GAR/GAR/GDR**
protuberant	pro-tu-be-ra-nt	*HOO/HOO/***GAR/GAR/GDR**
proud	pr-ou-d	*HDO/HAO/HOO*
prove	pro-ve	*HOO/HDO*
proven	pro-ve-n	*HOO/***GAR/GDR**
proverb	pro-ver-b	*HAO/HAO/HDO*
provide	pro-vi-de	*HOO/***GRR**/*HOO*
provided	pro-vi-ded	*HOO/***GRR/GRR**
providence	pro-vi-de-nce	*HAO/***GAR/GAR/GDR**
providing	pro-vi-ding	*HOO/***GRR/GDR**
province	pro-vi-nce	*HAO/***GAR/GDR**
provincial	pro-vi-n-cial	*HOO/***GAR/GDR**/*HDO*
provision	pro-vi-sion	*HOO/***GAR**/*HOO*
provisional	pro-vi-sion-al	*HOO/***GAR**/*HAO/HOO/HDO*
provoke	pro-vo-ke	*HOO/HOO/HDO*
prow	prow	*HAO*
proxy	pro-xy	*HAO/***GAR**
prude	pru-de	*HOO/HDO*

Word	Mouthables	Mouth Movements Notations
prudence	pru-de-nce	*HOO*/**GAR**/**GDR**
prudent	pru-de-nt	*HOO*/**GAR**/**GDR**
prudish	pru-di-sh	*HOO*/**GAR**/*HDO*
prune	pru-ne	*HOO*/**GRR**
prune	pru-ne	*HOO*/*HDO*
pruned	pru-ne-d	*HOO*/**GDR**/*HOO*
pry	pry	**GRR**
psalm	psal-m	*HAO*/**GDR**
pseudonym	pseu-do-ny-m	*HOO*/*HOO*/**GAR**/**GDR**
psyche	psy-che	**GRR/GAR**
psychedelic	psy-che-de-li-c	**GRR/GAR/GAR/GAR/GDR**
psychiatrist	psy-chi-a-tri-st	**GRR/GRR/GAR/GAR**/*HOO*
psychic	psy-chi-c	**GRR/GAR/GDR**
psychoanalysis	psy-cho-a-na-ly-si-s	**GRR**/*HOO*/**GAR/GAR/GAR/GAR/ GDR**
psychoanalyst	psy-cho-a-na-ly-st	**GRR**/*HOO*/**GAR/GAR/GAR**/*HOO*
psychologist	psy-cho-lo-gi-st	**GRR**/*HAO*/*HOO*/**GAR**/*HOO*
psychology	psy-cho-lo-gy	**GRR**/*HAO*/*HOO*/**GAR**
psychomatic	psy-cho-so-ma-ti-c	**GRR**/*HOO*/*HOO*/**GAR/GAR/GDR**
psychosis	psy-cho-si-s	**GRR**/*HOO*/**GAR/GDR**
pub	pu-b	**GAR**/*HDO*
public	pu-b-li-c	**GAR**/*HDO*/**GAR/GDR**
publican	pu-b-li-ca-n	**GAR**/*HDO*/**GAR/GAR/GDR**
publicity	pu-b-li-ci-ty	**GAR**/*HDO*/**GAR/GAR/GAR**
publish	pu-b-li-sh	**GAR**/*HDO*/**GAR**/*HDO*
published	pu-b-li-she-d	**GAR**/*HDO*/**GAR**/*HOO*/*HOO*
publisher	pu-b-li-sher	**GAR**/*HDO*/**GAR**/*HDO*
publishing	pu-b-li-shing	**GAR**/*HDO*/**GAR/GDR**
pudding	pud-ding	*HOO*/**GDR**
puddle	pu-ddle	**GAR**/*HOO*
puerile	pue-ri-le	**GAR/GRR/GDR**

Word	Mouthables	Mouth Movements Notations
puff	pu-ff	**GAR**/*HDO*
pull	pul-l	*HOO/HDO*
pulp	pu-l-p	**GAR/GDR**/*HDO*
pulpit	pul-pi-t	*HOO/***GAR/GDR**
pulsation	pu-l-sa-tion	**GAR/GDR**/*HAO/HOO*
pulse	pu-l-se	**GAR/GDR**/*HDO*
pulverize	pu-l-ve-ri-ze	**GAR/GDR/GAR/GRR/GDR**
pummel	pu-m-mel	**GAR**/*HDO/HOO*
pump	pu-mp	**GAR**/*HDO*
pumpkin	pu-mp-ki-n	**GAR**/*HDO/***GAR/GDR**
pumps	pu-mp-s	**GAR**/*HDO/HDO*
pun	pu-n	**GAR/GDR**
punch	pu-n-ch	**GAR/GDR**/*HOO*
punctual	pun-c-tu-al	**GAR/GDR**/*HOO/***GDR**
puncture	pun-c-tu-re	**GAR/GDR**/*HOO/HDO*
pungent	pu-n-ge-nt	**GAR/GDR/GAR/GDR**
punish	pu-ni-sh	**GAR/GAR**/*HDO*
punishment	pu-ni-sh-men-t	**GAR/GAR**/*HDO/***GAR**/*HOO*
punt	pun-t	**GAR**/*HOO*
punter	pun-ter	**GAR**/*HDO*
puny	pu-ny	*HOO/***GAR**
pup	pu-p	**GAR**/*HDO*
pupil	pu-pil	*HOO/HDO*
pupil	pu-pi-l	*HOO/***GAR/GDR**
puposeful	pur-po-se-ful	*HAO/HAO/HDO/HOO*
purple	pur-ple	*HAO/HOO*
purpose	pur-po-se	*HAO/HAO/HDO*
purposely	pur-po-se-ly	*HAO/HAO/HDO/***GDR**
purr	pur-r	**GAR/GDR**
purse	pur-se	**GAR**/*HDO*
pursue	pur-sue	*HAO/HOO*

Word	Mouthables	Mouth Movements Notations
pus	pu-s	GAR/GDR
push	pu-sh	*HOO/HDO*
pusher	pu-sher	*HOO/HDO*
pushy	pu-shy	*HOO*/GAR
puss	pu-ss	*HOO/HDO*
pusuit	pur-sui-t	*HAO/HOO/HOO*
put	put	*HOO*
putrid	pu-tri-d	*HOO*/GAR/GRR
putty	put-ty	GAR/GAR
puzzle	pu-zzle	GAR/*HOO*
pyjamas	py-ja-ma-s	GRR/GAR/GAR/*HDO*
pyramid	py-ra-mi-d	GAR/GAR/GAR/*HOO*
pyromaniac	py-ro-ma-ni-a-c	GRR/*HOO/HAO*/GAR/GAR/GDR
python	py-tho-n	GRR/*HTO*/GDR

Word	Mouthables	Mouth Movements Notations
Q		
Q	Q	*HOO*
quack	qua-ck	**GAR**/*HDO*
quagmire	qua-g-mi-re	**GAR**/*HDO*/**GRR**/*HDO*
quail	quai-l	*HAO*/**GDR**
quaint	quai-nt	*HAO*/**GDR**
quake	qua-ke	*HAO*/*HDO*
qualification	qua-li-fi-ca-tion	*HOO*/**GAR**/**GAR**/*HAO*/*HOO*
qualified	qua-li-fie-d	*HOO*/**GAR**/**GRR**/*HOO*
qualify	qua-li-fy	*HOO*/**GAR**/**GRR**
qualitative	qua-li-ta-ti-ve	*HOO*/**GAR**/*HAO*/**GAR**/**GDR**
qualm	qual-m	*HAO*/*HDO*
quandary	quan-dary	*HAO*/*HDO*
quantify	quan-ti-fy	*HAO*/**GAR**/**GRR**
quarrel	quar-re-l	**GAR**/**GAR**/**GDR**
quarrelsome	quar-re-l-so-me	**GAR**/**GAR**/**GDR**/*HAO*/*HDO*
quarry	quar-ry	*HAO*/*HDO*
quarried	quar-rie-d	*HAO*/*HDO*/*HOO*
quarry	quar-ry	**GAR**/**GAR**
quarter	quar-ter	*HOO*/*HDO*
quartz	quar-tz	*HOO*/**GDR**
quaterly	qua-ter-ly	*HOO*/*HDO*/**GDR**
quay	qu(a)y	**GAR**
queasy	quea-sy	**GRR**/**GAR**
queen	quee-n	**GRR**/**GDR**
queer	que-er	**GAR**/*HDO*
quench	que-n-ch	**GAR**/**GDR**/*HDO*
query	que-ry	**GRR**/**GDR**
question	que-stion	**GAR**/*HOO*
questionable	que-stion-a-ble	**GAR**/*HOO*/**GAR**/*HOO*
questionnaire	que-stion-aire	**GAR**/*HOO*/*HAO*

Word	Mouthables	Mouth Movements Notations
queue	que-ue	*HOO/HDO*
quick	qui-ck	**GAR/GDR**
quicken	qui-ck-e-n	**GAR/GDR/GAR/GDR**
quicksand	qui-ck-sa-n-d	**GAR/GDR/GAR/GDR**/*HOO*
quid	qui-d	**GAR**/*HOO*
quiet	qui-e-t	**GRR/GAR/GDR**
quilt	qui-l-t	**GAR/GDR**/*HDO*
quip	qui-p	**GAR/GDR**
quirk	quir-k	*HOO/HDO*
quit	qui-t	**GAR**/*HOO*
quite	qui-te	**GRR**/*HDO*
quits	qui-ts	**GAR/GDR**
quiver	qui-ver	**GAR**/*HDO*
quiver	qui-ver	**GAR/GDR**
quivered	qui-vere-d	**GAR**/*HDO/HOO*
quizzical	qui-zzi-cal	**GAR/GAR**/*HDO*
quota	quo-ta	*HOO*/**GAR**
quotation	quo-ta-tion	*HOO/HAO/HOO*
quote	quo-te	*HOO/HDO*
quotient	quo-ti-e-nt	*HOO/HDO*/**GAR/GDR**

Word	Mouthables	Mouth Movements Notations
R		
R	R	*HAO*
rabbi	ra-bbi	**GAR/GRR**
rabbit	ra-b-bi-t	**GAR**/*HDO*/**GAR/GDR**
rabid	ra-bi-d	**GAR/GAR/GDR**
rabies	ra-bi-es	*HAO*/**GAR/GDR**
race	ra-ce	*HAO*/**GDR**
race	ra-ce	*HAO/HDO*
raced	ra-ce-d	*HAO*/**GDR**/*HOO*
racer	ra-cer	*HAO/HDO*
Rachel	Ra-ch-e-l	*HAO/HDO*/**GAR/GDR**
racial	ra-cial	*HAO/HDO*
racialism	ra-cial-i-sm	*HAO/HDO*/**GAR**/*HDO*
racing	ra-cing	*HAO*/**GDR**
racist	ra-ci-st	*HAO*/**GAR**/*HOO*
rack	ra-ck	**GAR**/*HDO*
racket	ra-ck-e-t	**GAR**/*HDO*/**GAR/GDR**
racketeer	ra-ck-e-te-er	**GAR**/*HDO*/**GAR/GRR/GDR**
racoon	rac-coo-n	**GAR**/*HOO/HDO*
racy	ra-cy	*HAO*/**GAR**
radiant	ra-di-a-nt	*HAO*/**GAR/GAR/GDR**
radiator	ra-di-a-tor	*HAO*/**GAR**/*HAO/HDO*
radical	ra-di-cal	**GAR/GAR**/*HDO*
radio	ra-di-o	*HAO*/**GAR**/*HOO*
radish	ra-di-sh	**GAR/GAR**/*HDO*
radius	ra-di-us	*HAO*/**GAR/GAR**
raffish	ra-ffi-sh	*HAO*/**GAR**/*HDO*
raffle	ra-f-fle	**GAR**/*HDO/HOO*
raft	raf-t	*HAO/HOO*
rag	ra-g	**GAR**/*HDO*
ragamuffin	ra-ga-mu-ffi-n	**GAR/GAR/GAR/GAR/GDR**

Word	Mouthables	Mouth Movements Notations
rage	ra-ge	*HAO*/**GDR**
ragged	rag-ged	**GAR/GRR**
raid	rai-d	*HAO/HOO*
raider	rai-der	*HAO/HDO*
rail	rai-l	*HAO*/**GDR**
railing	rai-ling	*HAO*/**GDR**
rain	rai-n	*HAO*/**GRR**
rain	rai-n	*HAO*/**GDR**
rainbow	rai-n-bo-w	*HAO*/**GDR**/*HOO/HDO*
raining	rai-ni-ng	*HAO*/**GAR/GDR**
raise	rai-se	*HAO*/**GRR**
raisin	rai-si-n	*HAO*/**GAR/GDR**
rake	ra-ke	*HAO/HDO*
rally	ra-lly	**GAR/GDR**
ram	ra-m	**GAR**/*HDO*
ramble	ra-m-ble	**GAR**/*HDO/HOO*
rambling	ra-m-bli-ng	**GAR**/*HDO*/**GAR/GDR**
rampant	ra-m-pa-nt	**GAR/GDR/GAR/GDR**
rampart	ra-m-par-t	**GAR/GDR**/*HAO/HDO*
ramshackle	ra-m-sha-ckle	**GAR/GDR/GAR**/*HOO*
ran	ra-n	**GAR/GRR**
ranch	ran-ch	*HAO/HDO*
rancid	ra-n-ci-d	**GAR/GDR/GAR/GDR**
rancour	ra-n-cou-r	**GAR/GDR/GAR**/*HDO*
random	ra-n-do-m	**GAR/GDR**/*HAO/HDO*
rang	ra-ng	**GAR/GRR**
range	ra-nge	*HAO/HDO*
ranger	ra-ng-er	*HAO/HDO/HDO*
rank	ra-nk	**GAR/GRR**
ransack	ra-n-sa-ck	**GAR/GDR/GAR**/*HDO*
ransom	ra-n-so-m	**GAR/GDR**/*HAO/HDO*

Word	Mouthables	Mouth Movements Notations
rant	ra-nt	**GAR/GRR**
rap	ra-p	**GAR**/*HDO*
rapacious	ra-pa-ci-ous	**GAR**/*HAO*/**GDR/GAR**
rape	ra-pe	*HAO/HDO*
rapid	ra-pi-d	**GAR/GAR**/*HDO*
rapist	ra-pi-st	*HAO*/**GAR/GDR**
rapt	ra-pt	**GAR**/*HDO*
rapture	ra-p-tu-re	**GAR**/*HDO/HOO/HDO*
rare	rare	*HAO*
rarity	rar-i-ty	*HAO*/**GAR/GAR**
rascal	ras-cal	*HAO/HOO*
rash	ra-sh	**GAR**/*HDO*
rasher	ra-sher	**GAR**/*HDO*
rasp	ras-p	*HAO/HDO*
raspberry	ras-p-ber-ry	*HAO/HDO/HAO/HDO*
rat	ra-t	**GAR/GRR**
rate	ra-te	*HAO/HDO*
rather	rath-er	*HTO/HDO*
ratify	ra-ti-fy	**GAR/GAR/GRR**
rating	ra-ting	*HAO*/**GDR**
ratio	ra-ti-o	*HAO/HDO/HOO*
ration	ra-tion	**GAR**/*HOO*
rational	ra-tion-al	**GAR**/*HOO/HDO*
rationalize	ra-tion-a-li-ze	**GAR**/*HOO*/**GAR/GRR/GDR**
rattle	ra-ttle	**GAR**/*HOO*
ratty	rat-ty	**GAR/GAR**
ravage	ra-va-ge	**GAR**/*HAO/HDO*
rave	ra-ve	*HAO/HDO*
raven	ra-ve-n	*HAO*/**GAR/GDR**
ravenous	ra-ve-nous	**GAR/GAR/GAR**
ravine	ra-vi-ne	**GAR/GAR/GDR**

Word	Mouthables	Mouth Movements Notations
raving	ra-vi-ng	*HAO*/**GAR**/**GDR**
raw	raw	*HOO*
ray	ray	*HAO*
razor	ra-zor	*HAO*/*HDO*
reach	rea-ch	**GRR**/*HDO*
react	re-a-c-t	**GRR**/**GAR**/**GDR**/*HOO*
reactionary	re-a-c-tion-ar-y	**GRR**/**GAR**/**GDR**/*HOO*/*HAO*/**GAR**
reactor	re-ac-tor	**GRR**/**GAR**/*HDO*
read	rea-d	**GRR**/**GRR**
read	rea-d	**GAR**/**GRR**
readable	rea-da-ble	**GRR**/**GAR**/*HOO*
reading	rea-di-ng	**GRR**/**GAR**/**GDR**
ready	rea-dy	**GAR**/**GAR**
reaforestation	rea-for-e-sta-tion	**GRR**/*HOO*/**GAR**/*HAO*/*HOO*
real	re-al	**GRR**/*HDO*
realism	re-a-li-sm	**GRR**/**GAR**/**GAR**/**GDR**
realistic	re-a-li-sti-c	**GRR**/**GAR**/**GAR**/**GAR**/**GDR**
reality	re-a-li-ty	**GRR**/**GAR**/**GAR**/**GAR**
realization	re-a-li-za-tion	**GRR**/**GAR**/**GRR**/*HAO*/*HOO*
realize	re-a-li-ze	**GRR**/**GAR**/**GRR**/**GDR**
really	rea-lly	**GRR**/**GDR**
reanimate	re-a-ni-ma-te	**GRR**/**GAR**/**GAR**/*HAO*/*HDO*
reap	rea-p	**GRR**/*HDO*
rear	re-ar	**GRR**/*HAO*
rearmament	re-ar-ma-me-nt	**GRR**/*HAO*/**GAR**/**GAR**/**GDR**
reason	rea-so-n	**GRR**/*HAO*/*HDO*
reasonable	rea-so-na-ble	**GRR**/*HAO*/**GAR**/*HOO*
reasoning	rea-so-ning	**GRR**/*HAO*/**GDR**
reassessment	re-a-sse-ss-me-nt	**GRR**/**GAR**/**GAR**/**GDR**/**GAR**/*HOO*
reassuring	re-a-ssu-ring	**GRR**/**GAR**/*HOO*/**GDR**
rebel	re-be-l	**GRR**/**GAR**/**GDR**

Word	Mouthables	Mouth Movements Notations
rebel	re-bel	**GAR**/*HOO*
rebelled	re-be-lle-d	**GRR/GAR/GDR**/*HOO*
rebellion	re-be-lli-o-n	**GRR/GAR/GAR**/*HAO/HDO*
rebellious	re-be-lli-ous	**GRR/GAR/GAR**/*HAO*
rebound	re-bou-nd	**GRR**/*HAO*/**GDR**
rebuke	re-bu-ke	**GRR**/*HOO/HDO*
recall	re-cal-l	**GRR**/*HOO/HDO*
recede	re-ce-de	**GRR/GRR**/*HDO*
receipt	re-cei(p)t	**GRR/GRR/GDR**
receive	re-cei-ve	**GRR/GRR**/*HDO*
receiver	re-cei-ver	**GRR/GRR**/*HDO*
recent	re-ce-nt	**GRR/GAR/GDR**
reception	re-ce-p-tion	**GRR/GAR**/*HDO/HOO*
recess	re-ce-ss	**GRR/GAR**/*HDO*
recidivist	re-ci-di-vi-st	**GRR/GAR/GAR/GAR**/*HDO*
recipe	re-ci-pe	**GAR/GAR/GRR**
reciprocal	re-ci-pro-cal	**GRR/GAR**/*HOO/HDO*
recite	re-ci-te	**GRR/GRR**/*HOO*
reckless	re-ck-le-ss	**GAR/GDR/GAR**/*HDO*
reckon	re-cko-n	**GAR**/*HAO/HDO*
reckoning	re-cko-ning	**GAR**/*HAO*/**GDR**
reclamation	re-cla-ma-tion	**GAR/GAR**/*HAO/HOO*
recognition	re-co-g-ni-tion	**GAR**/*HAO/HDO*/**GAR**/*HOO*
recognize	re-co-g-ni-ze	**GAR**/*HAO/HDO*/**GRR/GDR**
recommend	re-co-me-nd	**GAR**/*HOO*/**GAR/GDR**
recompense	re-co-m-pe-nse	**GAR**/*HAO/HDO*/**GAR/GDR**
reconcile	re-co-n-ci-le	**GAR**/*HAO*/**GDR/GRR/GDR**
reconnaissance	re-con-nai-ssance	**GAR/GAR/GAR**/*HDO*
reconstruct	re-con-stru-ct	**GRR**/*HAO*/**GAR**/*HOO*
record	re-cor-d	**GRR**/*HOO/HDO*
recorder	re-cor-der	**GRR**/*HOO/HDO*

Word	Mouthables	Mouth Movements Notations
recourse	re-cour-se	**GRR**/*HOO*/*HDO*
recover	re-co-ver	**GRR/GAR**/*HDO*
recovery	re-co-ve-ry	**GRR/GAR**/*HDO*/*HDO*
recreation	re-cre-a-tion	**GAR/GRR**/*HAO*/*HOO*
recruit	re-crui-t	**GAR**/*HOO*/*HOO*
rectifacation	re-c-ti-fi-ca-tion	**GAR/GDR/GAR/GAR**/*HAO*/*HOO*
rectify	re-c-ti-fy	**GAR/GDR/GAR/GRR**
rectitude	re-c-ti-tu-de	**GAR/GDR/GAR**/*HOO*/*HDO*
rector	re-c-tor	**GAR/GDR**/*HDO*
recur	re-cur	**GRR/GAR**
recycle	re-cy-cle	**GRR/GRR**/*HOO*
recycling	re-cy-cli-ng	**GRR/GRR/GAR/GDR**
red	re-d	**GAR**/*HDO*
redden	re-dde-n	**GAR/GAR/GDR**
redeem	re-dee-m	**GRR/GRR**/*HDO*
redeemer	re-dee-mer	**GRR/GRR**/*HDO*
redemption	re-de-mp-tion	**GRR/GAR**/*HDO*/*HOO*
reduce	re-du-ce	**GRR**/*HOO*/**GDR**
reduction	re-duc-tion	**GRR/GAR**/*HOO*
redundant	re-du-n-da-nt	**GRR/GAR/GDR/GAR/GDR**
reed	ree-d	**GRR**/*HDO*
reef	ree-f	**GRR**/*HDO*
reek	ree-k	**GRR**/*HDO*
reel	ree-l	**GRR/GDR**
refer	re-fer	**GRR**/*HDO*
referee	re-fer-ee	**GAR**/*HAO*/**GRR**
reference	re-fer-e-nce	**GAR**/*HAO*/**GAR/GDR**
refined	re-fi-ne-d	**GRR/GRR/GDR**/*HOO*
refinement	re-fi-ne-men-t	**GRR/GRR/GDR/GAR**/*HDO*
refinery	re-fi-ne-ry	**GRR/GRR**/*HAO*/*HDO*
reflect	re-fle-ct	**GRR/GAR**/*HOO*

Word	Mouthables	Mouth Movements Notations
reflection	re-flec-tion	GRR/GAR/*HOO*
reflex	re-fle-x	GRR/GAR/GDR
reforestation	re-fo-re-sta-tion	GRR/*HAO*/*HAO*/*HOO*
reform	re-for-m	GRR/*HOO*/*HDO*
refractory	re-fra-c-to-ry	GRR/GAR/GDR/GAR/GDR
refrain	re-frai-n	GRR/*HAO*/GRR
refrain	re-frai-n	GRR/*HAO*/GDR
refrained	re-frai-ne-d	GRR/*HAO*/GRR/*HOO*
refresh	re-fre-sh	GRR/GAR/*HDO*
refreshment	re-fre-sh-men-t	GRR/GAR/*HDO*/GAR/*HOO*
refrigerate	re-fri-ge-ra-te	GRR/GAR/*HDO*/*HAO*/*HDO*
refrigerator	re-fri-ge-ra-tor	GRR/GAR/*HDO*/*HAO*/*HOO*
refuge	re-fu-ge	GAR/*HOO*/*HDO*
refund	re-fu-nd	GRR/GAR/GRR
refund	re-fu-nd	GRR/GAR/GDR
refunded	re-fu-n-ded	GRR/GAR/GDR/GRR
refusal	re-fu-sal	GRR/*HOO*/*HDO*
refuse	re-fu-se	GRR/*HOO*/*HOO*
refuse	re-fu-se	GAR/*HOO*/GDR
refused	re-fu-se-d	GRR/*HOO*/*HOO*/*HOO*
refute	re-fu-te	GRR/*HOO*/*HDO*
regal	re-gal	GRR/*HDO*
regale	re-ga-le	GRR/*HAO*/*HDO*
regard	re-gar-d	GRR/*HAO*/*HOO*
regards	re-gar-ds	GRR/*HAO*/*HDO*
regarded	re-gar-ded	GRR/*HAO*/GRR
regarding	re-gar-di-ng	GRR/*HAO*/GAR/GDR
regardless	re-gar-d-le-ss	GRR/*HAO*/*HDO*/GAR/GDR
regatta	re-ga-tta	GRR/GAR/GAR
regency	re-ge-n-cy	GRR/GAR/GDR/GAR
regent	re-ge-nt	GRR/GAR/GDR

Word	Mouthables	Mouth Movements Notations
regime	re-gi-me	GAR/GAR/GDR
regiment	re-gi-men-t	GAR/GAR/GAR/*HOO*
region	re-gi-o-n	GRR/GAR/*HAO*/GDR
regional	re-gi-o-nal	GRR/GAR/*HAO*/HDO
register	re-gi-ster	GAR/GAR/*HDO*
registration	re-gi-stra-tion	GAR/GAR/*HAO*/HOO
registry	re-gi-stry	GAR/GAR/*HDO*
regress	re-gre-ss	GRR/GAR/*HDO*
regret	re-gre-t	GRR/GAR/*HDO*
regrettable	re-gre-tta-ble	GRR/GAR/GAR/*HOO*
regular	re-gu-lar	GAR/*HOO*/HDO
regulate	re-gu-la-te	GAR/*HOO*/HAO/HDO
regulation	re-gu-la-tion	GAR/*HOO*/HAO/HOO
regurgitate	re-gur-gi-ta-te	GRR/*HOO*/GAR/*HAO*/HDO
rehabilitate	re-ha-bi-li-ta-te	GRR/GAR/GAR/GAR/*HAO*/HDO
rehearsal	re-hear-sal	GRR/*HAO*/HDO
rehearse	re-hear-se	GRR/*HAO*/HDO
reign	reig-n	*HAO*/GRR
reigning	reig-ning	*HAO*/GDR
reindeer	rei-n-de-er	*HAO*/GDR/GRR/*HDO*
reinforce	re-i-n-for-ce	GRR/GAR/GDR/*HOO*/GDR
reinforcement	re-i-n-for-ce-me-nt	GRR/GAR/GDR/*HOO*/GDR/GAR/ GDR
reinstate	re-i-n-sta-te	GRR/GAR/GDR/*HAO*/HDO
reissue	re-i-ssue	GRR/GAR/*HOO*
reject	re-je-ct	GRR/GAR/*HOO*
rejection	re-je-c-tion	GRR/GAR/GDR/*HOO*
rejoice	re-joi-ce	GRR/GAR/GDR
rejoin	re-joi-n	GRR/GAR/GDR
relapse	re-la-pse	GRR/GAR/GDR
relate	re-la-te	GRR/*HAO*/HDO

Word	Mouthables	Mouth Movements Notations
related	re-la-ted	**GRR**/*HAO*/**GRR**
relating	re-la-ti-ng	**GRR**/*HAO*/**GAR/GDR**
relation	re-la-tion	**GRR**/*HAO/HOO*
relative	re-la-ti-ve	**GAR/GAR/GAR**/*HDO*
relax	re-la-x	**GRR/GAR**/*HDO*
relaxation	re-la-x-a-tion	**GRR/GAR**/*HDO/HAO/HOO*
relay	re-lay	**GRR**/*HAO*
release	re-lea-se	**GRR/GRR**/*HDO*
relegate	re-le-ga-te	**GAR/GAR**/*HAO/HDO*
relentless	re-le-nt-le-ss	**GRR/GAR/GDR/GAR/GDR**
relevant	re-le-va-nt	**GAR/GAR/GAR/GDR**
reliable	re-li-a-ble	**GRR/GRR/GAR**/*HOO*
reliant	re-li-a-nt	**GRR/GRR/GAR/GDR**
relic	re-li-c	**GAR/GAR/GDR**
relief	re-lie-f	**GRR/GAR**/*HDO*
relieve	re-lie-ve	**GRR/GAR**/*HDO*
religion	re-li-gi-o-n	**GRR/GAR/GAR**/*HAO/HOO*
religious	re-li-gi-ous	**GRR/GAR/GAR**/*HAO*
relinquish	re-li-n-qui-sh	**GRR/GAR/GDR/GAR**/*HDO*
relish	re-li-sh	**GAR/GAR**/*HDO*
relocation	re-lo-ca-tion	**GRR**/*HOO/HAO/HOO*
reluctant	re-lu-c-ta-nt	**GRR/GAR/GDR/GAR/GDR**
reluctantly	re-lu-c-ta-nt-ly	**GRR/GAR/GDR/GAR/GDR/GDR**
rely	re-ly	**GRR/GRR**
remade	re-ma-de	**GRR**/*HAOHDO*
remain	re-mai-n	**GRR**/*HAO*/**GDR**
remainder	re-mai-n-der	**GRR**/*HAO*/**GDR**/*HDO*
remains	re-mai-ns	**GRR**/*HAO*/**GDR**
remake	re-ma-ke	**GRR**/*HAO/HDO*
remark	re-mar-k	**GRR**/*HAO/HDO*
remarkable	re-mar-ka-ble	**GRR**/*HAO*/**GAR**/*HOO*

Word	Mouthables	Mouth Movements Notations
remedy	re-me-dy	**GAR/GAR/GAR**
remembrance	re-me-m-bra-nce	**GRR/GAR/**_HDO_**/GAR/GDR**
remember	re-me-m-ber	**GRR/GAR/**_HDO/HDO_
remind	re-mi-nd	**GRR/GRR/GRR**
reminder	re-mi-n-der	**GRR/GRR/GDR/**_HDO_
reminiscence	re-mi-ni-sce-nce	**GAR/GAR/GAR/GAR/GDR**
remission	re-mi-ssion	**GRR/GAR/**_HOO_
remit	re-mi-t	**GRR/GAR/**_HOO_
remittance	re-mi-tta-nce	**GRR/GAR/GAR/GDR**
remnant	re-m-na-nt	**GAR/**_HDO_**/GAR/GDR**
remorse	re-mor-se	**GRR/**_HOO/HDO_
remorseless	re-mor-se-le-ss	**GRR/**_HOO/HDO_**/GAR/GDR**
remote	re-mo-te	**GRR/**_HOO/HDO_
removal	re-mo-val	**GRR/**_HOO/HDO_
remove	re-mo-ve	**GRR/**_HOO/HDO_
removed	re-mo-ve-d	**GRR/**_HOO/HOO/HOO_
remover	re-mo-ver	**GRR/**_HOO/HDO_
remuneration	re-mu-ne-ra-tion	**GRR/**_HOO_**/GAR/**_HAO/HOO_
renal	re-nal	**GRR/**_HDO_
rend	re-nd	**GAR/GRR**
renegade	re-ne-ga-de	**GAR/GAR/**_HAO/HDO_
renew	re-ne-w	**GRR/**_HOO/HDO_
renewable	re-new-a-ble	**GRR/**_HOO_**/GAR/**_HOO_
renewal	re-new-al	**GRR/**_HOO_**/GDR**
renounce	re-nou-nce	**GRR/GAR/GDR**
renovate	re-no-va-te	**GAR/**_HOO/HAO/HDO_
renovated	re-no-va-ted	**GAR/**_HOO/HAO_**/GRR**
renown	re-now-n	**GRR/**_HAO_**/GDR**
renowned	re-now-ne-d	**GRR/**_HAO_**/GDR/**_HOO_
rent	re-nt	**GAR/GRR**
rent	ren-t	**GAR/**_HDO_

Word	Mouthables	Mouth Movements Notations
rental	ren-tal	**GAR**/*HDO*
rented	re-n-ted	**GAR/GDR/GRR**
renunciation	re-nu-n-ci-a-tion	**GRR/GAR/GDR/GAR**/*HAO*/*HOO*
reopen	re-o-pen	**GRR**/*HOO*/*HDO*
reorganize	re-or-ga-ni-ze	**GRR**/*HOO*/**GAR/GRR/GRR**
rep	re-p	**GAR**/*HDO*
repaid	re-pai-d	**GRR**/*HAO*/*HDO*
repair	re-pair	**GRR**/*HAO*
reparation	re-pa-ra-tion	**GAR/GAR**/*HAO*/*HOO*
repartee	re-par-tee	**GAR**/*HAO*/**GRR**
repatriate	re-pa-tri-a-te	**GRR/GAR/GAR**/*HAO*/*HDO*
repatriation	re-pa-tri-a-tion	**GRR/GAR/GAR**/*HAO*/*HOO*
repay	re-pay	**GRR**/*HAO*
repayable	re-pay-a-ble	**GRR**/*HAO*/**GAR**/*HOO*
repeal	re-pea-l	**GRR/GRR/GDR**
repeat	re-pea-t	**GRR/GRR/GRR**
repel	re-pe-l	**GRR/GAR/GDR**
repellent	re-pe-ll-e-nt	**GRR/GAR/GDR/GAR/GDR**
repent	re-pe-nt	**GRR/GAR/GDR**
repentance	re-pe-n-ta-nce	**GRR/GAR/GDR/GAR/GDR**
repentant	re-pe-n-ta-nt	**GRR/GAR/GDR/GAR/GDR**
repertoire	re-per-toire	**GAR**/*HAO*/*HAO*
repertory	re-per-to-ry	**GAR**/*HAO*/*HAO*/*HDO*
repetition	re-pe-ti-tion	**GAR**/*HAO*/**GAR**/*HOO*
repetitious	re-pe-ti-ti-ous	**GAR**/*HAO*/**GAR/GDR/GAR**
replace	re-pla-ce	**GRR**/*HAO*/**GDR**
reply	re-ply	**GRR/GRR**
report	re-por-t	**GRR**/*HOO*/*HOO*
reportage	re-por-ta-ge	**GRR**/*HOO*/**GAR**/*HDO*
reportedly	re-por-ted-ly	**GRR**/*HOO*/**GRR/GDR**
reporter	re-por-ter	**GRR**/*HOO*/*HDO*

Word	Mouthables	Mouth Movements Notations
represent	re-pre-se-nt	**GAR/GRR/GAR/GRR**
representation	re-pre-se-n-ta-tion	**GAR/GRR/GAR/GDR**/*HAO*/*HOO*
representative	re-pre-sen-ta-ti-ve	**GAR/GRR/GAR/GDR/GAR/GAR**/*HDO*
repress	re-pre-ss	**GRR/GAR/GDR**
repression	re-pre-ssion	**GRR/GAR**/*HOO*
repressive	re-pre-ssi-ve	**GRR/GAR/GAR/GDR**
reprieve	re-prie-ve	**GRR/GAR**/*HDO*
reprint	re-prin-t	**GRR/GAR**/*HOO*
reprisal	re-pri-sal	**GRR/GRR**/*HOO*
reproach	re-proa-ch	**GRR**/*HOO*/*HDO*
reproachful	re-proa-ch-ful	**GRR**/*HOO*/*HDO*/*HOO*
reproduce	re-pro-du-ce	**GRR**/*HOO*/*HOO*/**GDR**
reproof	re-proo-f	**GRR**/*HOO*/*HDO*
reptile	re-p-ti-le	**GAR/GDR/GRR/GDR**
republic	re-pu-b-li-c	**GRR/GAR**/*HDO*/**GAR/GDR**
republican	re-pu-b-li-ca-n	**GRR/GAR**/*HDO*/**GAR/GAR/GDR**
repudiate	re-pu-dia-te	**GRR**/*HOO*/*HAO*/*HDO*
repugnant	re-pu-g-na-nt	**GRR/GAR**/*HDO*/**GAR/GDR**
repulsion	re-pu-l-sion	**GRR/GAR/GDR**/*HOO*
repulsive	re-pu-l-si-ve	**GRR/GAR/GDR/GAR/GDR**
reputable	re-pu-ta-ble	**GAR**/*HOO*/**GAR**/*HOO*
reputation	re-pu-ta-tion	**GAR**/*HOO*/*HAO*/*HOO*
reputed	re-pu-ted	**GRR**/*HOO*/**GRR**
request	re-que-st	**GAR/GAR**/*HOO*
require	re-qui-re	**GRR/GRR**/*HDO*
requirement	re-qui-re-me-nt	**GRR/GRR**/*HDO*/**GAR/GDR**
requisite	re-qui-si-te	**GAR/GAR/GAR**/*HDO*
requisition	re-qui-si-tion	**GAR/GAR/GAR**/*HOO*
rescue	re-scue	**GAR**/*HOO*
rescuer	re-scu-er	**GAR**/*HOO*/*HDO*

Word	Mouthables	Mouth Movements Notations
research	re-sear-ch	**GRR**/*HOO*/*HDO*
researcher	re-sear-cher	**GRR**/*HOO*/*HDO*
resemblance	re-se-m-bla-nce	**GRR/GAR**/*HDO*/**GAR/GDR**
resemble	re-se-m-ble	**GRR/GAR/GDR**/*HOO*
resent	re-se-nt	**GRR/GAR/GDR**
resentment	re-se-nt-me-nt	**GRR/GAR/GDR/GAR/GDR**
reservation	re-ser-va-tion	**GAR**/*HAO*/*HAO*/*HOO*
reserve	re-ser-ve	**GRR**/*HOO*/*HDO*
reservoir	re-ser-voir	**GAR**/*HOO*/*HAO*
reside	re-si-de	**GRR/GRR**/*HDO*
residence	re-si-de-nce	**GAR/GAR/GAR/GDR**
residue	re-si-due	**GAR/GAR**/*HOO*
resign	re-si-gn	**GRR/GRR/GRR**
resignation	re-si-g-na-tion	**GAR/GAR/GDR**/*HAO*/*HOO*
resin	re-si-n	**GAR/GAR/GDR**
resist	re-si-st	**GRR/GAR**/*HOO*
resistance	re-si-sta-nce	**GRR/GAR/GAR/GDR**
resolution	re-so-lu-tion	**GAR**/*HOO*/*HOO*/*HOO*
resolve	re-so-lve	**GRR**/*HAO*/*HDO*
resolved	re-so-lve-d	**GRR**/*HAO*/*HOO*/*HOO*
resonance	re-so-na-nce	**GAR**/*HOO*/**GAR/GDR**
resort	re-sor-t	**GRR**/*HOO*/*HOO*
resort	re-sor-t	**GRR**/*HOO*/*HDO*
resorted	re-sor-ted	**GRR**/*HOO*/**GRR**
resound	re-sou-nd	**GRR/GAR/GDR**
resounding	re-sou-n-ding	**GRR/GAR/GDR/GDR**
resource	re-sour-ce	**GRR**/*HAO*/**GDR**
respect	re-spe-c-t	**GRR/GAR/GDR**/*HOO*
respectable	re-spe-c-ta-ble	**GRR/GAR/GDR/GAR**/*HOO*
respecting	re-spe-c-ti-ng	**GRR/GAR/GAR/GAR/GDR**
respiration	re-spi-ra-tion	**GAR/GAR**/*HAO*/*HOO*

Word	Mouthables	Mouth Movements Notations
respond	re-spon-d	**GRR**/*HAO*/*HOO*
response	re-spon-se	**GRR**/*HAO*/*HDO*
responsible	re-spon-si-ble	**GRR**/*HAO*/**GAR**/*HOO*
responsive	re-spon-si-ve	**GRR**/*HAO*/**GAR**/*HDO*
rest	re-st	**GAR**/*HOO*
restaurant	re-stau-ra-nt	**GAR**/*HOO*/**GAR**/**GDR**
restaurateur	re-stau-ra-teur	**GAR**/*HOO*/**GAR**/*HOO*
restful	re-st-ful	**GAR**/*HOO*/*HOO*
restless	re-st-le-ss	**GAR**/*HOO*/**GAR**/**GDR**
restoration	re-sto-ra-tion	**GAR**/*HOO*/*HAO*/*HOO*
restorative	re-sto-ra-ti-ve	**GAR**/*HOO*/**GAR**/**GAR**/*HDO*
restore	re-sto-re	**GRR**/*HOO*/*HDO*
restorer	re-sto-rer	**GRR**/*HOO*/*HDO*
restrain	re-strai-n	**GRR**/*HAO*/**GDR**
restrained	re-strai-ne-d	**GRR**/*HAO*/**GDR**/*HOO*
restricted	re-stri-c-ted	**GRR**/**GAR**/**GDR**/**GRR**
restriction	re-stri-c-tion	**GRR**/**GAR**/**GDR**/*HOO*
restructure	re-stru-c-ture	**GRR**/**GAR**/**GDR**/*HDO*
result	re-sul-t	**GAR**/**GAR**/*HOO*
resurrect	re-sur-re-ct	**GAR**/*HOO*/**GAR**/*HOO*
resurrection	re-sur-rec-tion	**GAR**/*HOO*/**GAR**/*HOO*
resuscitate	re-sus-ci-ta-te	**GRR**/**GAR**/**GAR**/*HAO*/*HDO*
retail	re-tai-l	**GRR**/*HAO*/**GDR**
retailer	re-tai-ler	**GRR**/*HAO*/*HDO*
retain	re-tai-n	**GRR**/*HAO*/**GDR**
retaliation	re-ta-li-a-tion	**GRR**/**GAR**/**GAR**/*HAO*/*HOO*
retch	re-tch	**GAR**/*HDO*
reticent	re-ti-ce-nt	**GAR**/**GAR**/**GAR**/**GDR**
retire	re-ti-re	**GRR**/**GRR**/*HDO*
retired	re-ti-re-d	**GRR**/**GRR**/*HDO*/*HOO*
retiree	re-ti-ree	**GRR**/**GRR**/**GRR**

Word	Mouthables	Mouth Movements Notations
retiring	re-ti-ring	**GRR/GRR/GDR**
retouch	re-tou-ch	**GRR/GAR/***HDO*
retract	re-tra-ct	**GRR/GAR/***HOO*
retreat	re-trea-t	**GRR/GRR/***HOO*
retrieve	re-trie-ve	**GRR/GAR/***HDO*
retriever	re-trie-ver	**GRR/GAR/***HDO*
retro	re-tro	**GAR/***HOO*
retroactive	re-tro-a-c-ti-ve	**GAR/***HOO***/GAR/GDR/GAR/GDR**
retrograde	re-tro-gra-de	**GAR/***HOO/HAO/HDO*
retrospective	re-tro-spec-ti-ve	**GAR/***HOO***/GAR/GAR/***HDO*
return	re-tur-n	**GRR/***HAO/HDO*
returnable	re-tur-na-ble	**GRR/***HAO***/GAR/***HOO*
reunion	re-u-ni-o-n	**GRR/***HOO***/GAR/***HAO/HDO*
reunite	re-u-ni-te	**GRR/***HOO***/GRR/***HDO*
revberation	re-ver-be-ra-tion	**GRR/***HAO/HAO/HAO/HOO*
reveal	re-ve-al	**GRR/GRR/GDR**
revelry	re-ve-l-ry	**GAR/GAR/GDR/***HDO*
revenge	re-ve-n-ge	**GRR/GAR/GDR/***HDO*
revengeful	re-ve-n-ge-ful	**GRR/GAR/GDR/***HDO/HOO*
revenue	re-ve-nue	**GAR/GAR/***HOO*
reverend	re-ve-re-nd	**GAR/GAR/GAR/GDR**
reverse	re-ver-se	**GRR/***HAO/HDO*
reversible	re-ver-si-ble	**GRR/***HAO***/GAR/***HOO*
revert	re-ver-t	**GRR/***HAO/HOO*
review	re-view	**GRR/***HOO*
reviewer	re-view-er	**GRR/***HOO/HDO*
revile	re-vi-le	**GRR/GRR/GDR**
revise	re-vi-se	**GRR/GRR/***HDO*
revision	re-vi-sion	**GRR/GAR/***HOO*
revival	re-vi-val	**GRR/GRR/***HDO*
revive	re-vi-ve	**GRR/GRR/***HDO*

Word	Mouthables	Mouth Movements Notations
revoke	re-vo-ke	**GRR**/*HOO*/*HDO*
revolt	re-vol-t	**GRR**/*HOO*/**GRR**
revolting	re-vol-ting	**GRR**/*HOO*/**GDR**
revolution	re-vo-lu-tion	**GAR**/*HOO*/*HOO*/*HOO*
revolutionary	re-vo-lu-tion-ary	**GAR**/*HOO*/*HOO*/*HOO*/*HDO*
revolve	re-vo-l-ve	**GRR**/*HAO*/**GDR**/*HDO*
revolver	re-vo-l-ver	**GRR**/*HAO*/**GDR**/*HDO*
revue	re-vue	**GRR**/*HOO*
revulsion	re-vu-l-sion	**GRR**/**GAR**/**GDR**/*HOO*
reward	re-war-d	**GRR**/*HAO*/*HOO*
rewarding	re-war-ding	**GRR**/*HAO*/**GDR**
rhetorical	rhe-tor-i-cal	**GAR**/*HOO*/**GAR**/*HDO*
rheumatic	rheu-ma-ti-c	*HOO*/**GAR**/**GAR**/**GDR**
rheumatism	rheu-ma-ti-sm	*HOO*/**GAR**/**GAR**/*HDO*
rhinoceros	rhi-no-ce-ro-s	**GRR**/*HAO*/**GAR**/**GAR**/*HDO*
rhododendron	rho-do-de-n-dro-n	*HOO*/*HAO*/**GAR**/**GDR**/*HAO*/*HDO*
rhubarb	rhu-bar-b	*HOO*/*HAO*/*HDO*
rhyme	rhy-me	**GRR**/*HDO*
rhythm	rhy-th-m	**GAR**/**GTR**/**GDR**
rhythmical	rhy-th-mi-cal	**GAR**/**GTR**/**GAR**/*HDO*
rib	ri-b	**GAR**/*HDO*
ribbed	ri-bbe-d	**GAR**/*HDO*/*HOO*
ribbon	ri-bb-o-n	**GAR**/*HDO*/*HAO*/*HDO*
rice	ri-ce	**GRR**/**GDR**
rich	ri-ch	**GAR**/*IIDO*
riches	ri-ch-es	**GAR**/*HDO*/**GDR**
rickets	ri-cke-ts	**GAR**/**GAR**/*HDO*
rickety	ri-cke-ty	**GAR**/**GDR**/**GAR**
rid	ri d	**GAR**/*HOO*
ridden	ri-dden	**GAR**/*HDO*
ridding	ri-d-ding	**GRR**/**GDR**/**GDR**

Word	Mouthables	Mouth Movements Notations
riddle	rid-dle	**GAR**/*HOO*
ride	ri-de	**GRR/GRR**
rider	ri-der	**GRR**/*HDO*
ridge	ri-d-ge	**GAR**/*HDO/HDO*
ridicule	ri-di-cu-le	**GAR/GAR**/*HOO/HDO*
ridiculous	ri-di-cu-lous	**GAR/GAR**/*HOO/HAO*
rife	ri-fe	**GRR**/*HDO*
rifle	ri-fle	**GRR**/*HOO*
rift	ri-ft	**GAR**/*HDO*
rig	ri-g	**GAR/GRR**
rig	ri-g	**GAR**/*HDO*
rigged	ri-gge-d	**GAR/GDR**/*HOO*
right	ri-ght	**GRR**/*HOO*
rightful	ri-ght-ful	**GRR**/*HOO/HOO*
rigid	ri-gi-d	**GAR/GAR**/*HDO*
rigour	ri-gour	**GAR**/*HAO*
rile	ri-le	**GRR/GDR**
rim	ri-m	**GAR**/*HDO*
rind	ri-nd	**GRR/GDR**
ring	rin-g	**GAR**/*HDO*
ring	ri-ng	**GAR/GRR**
ringing	ri-ng-ing	**GAR/GDR/GDR**
ringlet	ri-ng-le-t	**GAR/GDR/GAR/GDR**
rink	rin-k	**GAR**/*HDO*
rinse	ri-n-se	**GAR/GDR**/*HDO*
riot	ri-o-t	**GRR**/*HAO/HOO*
rioter	ri-o-ter	**GAR**/*HAO/HDO*
riotous	ri-o-t-ous	**GAR**/*HAO/HDO/HAO*
rip	ri-p	**GAR**/*HDO*
ripe	ri-pe	**GRR**/*HDO*
ripen	ri-pen	**GRR/GDR**

Word	Mouthables	Mouth Movements Notations
ripple	ri-pple	GAR/*HOO*
rise	ri-se	GRR/GRR
risen	ri-sen	GAR/*HDO*
rising	ri-sing	GRR/GDR
risk	ri-sk	GAR/GRR
risk	ri-sk	GAR/*HDO*
risked	ri-ske-d	GAR/GDR/*HOO*
risky	ri-sky	GAR/GAR
risole	ri-so-le	GAR/*HOO*/*HDO*
rite	ri-te	GRR/*HDO*
ritual	ri-tu-al	GAR/*HOO*/*HDO*
rival	ri-val	GRR/*HDO*
rivalry	ri-val-ry	GRR/*HDO*/GDR
river	ri-ver	GAR/*HDO*
rivet	ri-ve-t	GAR/GAR/GDR
road	roa-d	*HOO*/*HOO*
roam	roa-m	*HOO*/*HDO*
roar	roa-r	*HOO*/*HDO*
roast	roa-st	*HOO*/*HOO*
rob	ro-b	*HAO*/*HOO*
robbed	ro-bbe-d	*HAO*/*HDO*/*HOO*
robber	ro-b-ber	*HAO*/*HDO*/*HDO*
robbery	ro-bbe-ry	*HAO*/*HDO*/GDR
robe	ro-be	*HOO*/*HDO*
robin	ro-bi-n	*HAO*/GAR/GDR
robotic	ro-bo-ti-c	*HOO*/*HAO*/GAR/GDR
robust	ro-bu-st	*HOO*/GAR/*HOO*
rock	ro-ck	*HAO*/*HDO*
rocker	ro-ck-er	*HAO*/*HDO*/*HDO*
rocket	ro-cke-t	*HAO*/GAR/GDR
rod	ro-d	*HAO*/*HOO*

Word	Mouthables	Mouth Movements Notations
rode	ro-de	*HOO/HOO*
rodent	ro-de-nt	*HOO/***GAR/GDR**
roe	roe	*HOO*
rogue	ro-gue	*HOO/HDO*
role	ro-le	*HOO/***GDR**
roll	ro-ll	*HOO/HDO*
roller	ro-l-ler	*HOO/HDO/***GDR**
Roman	Ro-ma-n	*HOO/***GAR/GDR**
romance	ro-ma-nce	*HOO/***GAR/GDR**
Romanesque	Ro-ma-ne-sque	*HOO/***GAR/GAR***/HDO*
romantic	ro-ma-n-ti-c	*HOO/***GAR/GDR/GAR/GDR**
Rome	Ro-me	*HOO/HDO*
romp	ro-mp	*HAO/HDO*
roof	roo-f	*HOO/HDO*
rook	roo-k	*HOO/HDO*
room	roo-m	*HOO/HDO*
roomy	roo-my	*HOO/***GAR**
rooster	roo-ster	*HOO/HDO*
root	roo-t	*HOO/HOO*
rooted	roo-ted	*HOO/***GRR**
rope	ro-pe	*HOO/HDO*
rosary	ro-sa-ry	*HOO/***GAR/GDR**
rose	ro-se	*HOO/HDO*
rosemary	ro-se-ma-ry	*HOO/HDO/***GAR/GDR**
rosy	ro-sy	*HOO/***GAR**
rot	ro-t	*HAO/HOO*
rotate	ro-ta-te	*HOO/HAO/HOO*
rotated	ro-ta-ted	*HOO/HAO/***GRR**
rotation	ro-ta-tion	*HOO/HAO/HOO*
rotten	rot-ten	*HAO/HDO*
rough	rou-gh	**GAR**/*HDO*

Word	Mouthables	Mouth Movements Notations
round	rou-nd	*HAO/HDO*
rounded	rou-n-ded	*HAO/HDO*/**GRR**
rouse	rou-se	**GAR**/*HDO*
rousing	rou-sing	**GAR/GDR**
rout	rou-t	**GAR**/*HOO*
route	rou-te	*HOO/HOO*
row	ro-w	*HOO/HOO*
rowed	ro-we-d	*HOO/HOO/HOO*
row	row	**GAR**
row	rowe-d	**GAR**/*HOO*
rows	ro-ws	**GAR/GDR**
royal	roy-a-l	**GAR/GAR/GDR**
royalty	roy-a-l-ty	**GAR/GAR/GDR/GAR**
rub	ru-b	**GAR**/*HDO*
rubber	ru-bber	**GAR**/*HDO*
rubbery	ru-bbe-ry	**GAR/GAR**/*HDO*
rubbish	ru-bb-i-sh	**GAR**/*HDO*/**GAR**/*HDO*
rubbishy	ru-bb-i-shy	**GAR**/*HDO*/**GAR/GAR**
rubble	ru-bble	**GAR**/*HOO*
ruby	ru-by	*HOO*/**GAR**
rudder	rud-der	**GAR**/*HDO*
ruddy	rud-dy	**GAR/GAR**
rude	ru-de	*HOO/HDO*
ruffle	ru-ffle	**GAR**/*HOO*
ruffled	ru-ffle-d	**GAR**/*HOO/HOO*
rug	ru-g	**GAR**/*HDO*
rugged	ru-g-ged	**GAR**/*HDO*/**GRR**
ruin	ru-i-n	*HOO*/**GAR/GDR**
ruined	ru-i-ne-d	*HOO*/**GAR/GDR**/*HOO*
ruinous	ru-i-n-ous	*HOO*/**GAR/GDR/GAR**
rule	ru-le	*HOO/HDO*

Word	Mouthables	Mouth Movements Notations
ruler	ru-ler	*HOO*/*HDO*
ruling	ru-ling	*HOO*/**GDR**
rumble	ru-m-ble	**GAR**/*HDO*/*HOO*
ruminant	ru-mi-na-nt	*HOO*/**GAR**/**GAR**/**GDR**
ruminate	ru-mi-na-te	*HOO*/**GAR**/*HAO*/*HDO*
rummage	ru-m-ma-ge	**GAR**/*HDO*/*HAO*/*HDO*
rummy	ru-m-my	**GAR**/*HDO*/**GAR**
rumour	ru-mour	*HOO*/*HAO*
rumoured	ru-moure-d	*HOO*/*HAO*/*HOO*
rump	ru-mp	**GAR**/*HDO*
run	ru-n	**GAR**/*HOO*
rung	ru-ng	**GAR**/*HOO*
rung	run-g	*HAO*/*HDO*
runner	ru-nner	**GAR**/*HDO*
running	ru-nning	**GAR**/**GDR**
runny	ru-nny	**GAR**/**GAR**
rural	ru-ral	*HOO*/*HDO*
rush	ru-sh	**GAR**/**GRR**
rushes	ru-she-s	**GAR**/**GAR**/**GDR**
rush	ru-shes	*HAO*/*HDO*
rushed	ru-she-d	**GAR**/*HOO*/*HOO*
Russian	Ru-ssi-a-n	**GAR**/**GDR**/**GAR**/**GDR**
rust	ru-st	**GAR**/*HOO*
rustic	ru-sti-c	**GAR**/**GAR**/**GDR**
rustle	ru-stle	**GAR**/*HOO*
rustled	ru-stle-d	**GAR**/*HOO*/*HOO*
rustler	ru-st-ler	**GAR**/*HDO*/*HDO*
rut	ru-t	**GAR**/*HDO*
ruthless	ru-th-le-ss	*HOO*/**GTR**/**GAR**/**GDR**
rye	rye	**GRR**

Word	Mouthables	Mouth Movements Notations
S		
S	S	**GAR/GDR**
sable	sa-ble	*HAO/HOO*
sabotage	sa-bo-ta-ge	**GAR/***HAO***/GAR/***HDO*
sabre	sa-bre	*HAO/HDO*
saccharine	sa-ccha-ri-ne	**GAR/GAR/GAR/GDR**
sachet	sa-chet	**GAR/***HAO*
sack	sa-ck	**GAR/***HDO*
sacrament	sa-c-ra-me-nt	**GAR/GDR/GAR/GAR/GDR**
sacred	sa-c-re-d	*HAO***/GDR/GAR/***HOO*
sacrifice	sa-c-ri-fi-ce	**GAR/GDR/GAR/GRR/GDR**
sacrilege	sa-c-ri-le-ge	**GAR/GDR/GAR/GAR/***HDO*
sacrilegious	sa-c-ri-le-gi-ous	**GAR/GDR/GAR/GAR/GAR/***HAO*
sacristan	sa-cri-sta-n	**GAR/GAR/GAR/GDR**
sacristy	sa-cri-sty	**GAR/GAR/GAR**
sad	sa-d	**GAR/GDR**
sadden	sad-den	**GAR/***HDO*
saddle	sad-dle	**GAR/***HOO*
sadism	sa-di-sm	*HAO***/GAR/GDR**
sadist	sa-di-st	*HAO***/GAR/***HDO*
sadistic	sa-di-sti-c	**GAR/GAR/GAR/GDR**
safe	sa-fe	*HAO/HDO*
safety	sa-fe-ty	*HAO/HDO***/GAR**
saffron	sa-ff-ro-n	**GAR/***HDO/HAO/HDO*
sag	sa-g	**GAR/***HDO*
sage	sa-ge	*HAO/HDO*
sagged	sa-gge-d	**GAR/***HDO/HOO*
said	sai-d	**GAR/GRR**
sail	sai-l	*HAO/HDO*
sailing	sai-li-ng	*HAO***/GAR/GDR**
sailor	sai-lor	*HAO/HDO*

Word	Mouthables	Mouth Movements Notations
saint	sai-nt	*HAO*/**GDR**
sake	sa-ke	*HAO*/*HDO*
sake	sa-ke	**GAR/GRR**
salad	sa-la-d	**GAR/GAR**/*HDO*
salami	sa-la-mi	**GAR/GAR/GAR**
salary	sa-la-ry	**GAR/GAR**/*HDO*
sale	sa-le	*HAO*/**GDR**
saliva	sa-li-va	**GAR/GRR/GAR**
sallow	sa-llo-w	**GAR**/*HOO*/*HDO*
Sally	sa-lly	**GAR/GAR**
salmon	sa-l-mo-n	**GAR/GDR**/*HAO*/*HDO*
salon	sa-lo-n	**GAR**/*HAO*/*HDO*
saloon	sa-loo-n	**GAR**/*HOO*/*HDO*
salt	sal-t	*HOO*/*HOO*
salty	sal-ty	*HOO*/**GAR**
salutation	sa-lu-ta-tion	**GAR**/*HOO*/*HAO*/*HOO*
salvage	sa-l-vage	**GAR/GDR**/*HDO*
salvation	sa-l-va-tion	**GAR/GDR**/*HAO*/*HOO*
salve	sa-l-ve	**GAR/GDR**/*HDO*
same	sa-me	*HAO*/**GDR**
sample	sam-ple	*HAO*/*HOO*
sanatorium	sa-na-tor-i-um	**GAR/GAR**/*HOO*/**GAR**/*HDO*
sanctify	sa-n-c-ti-fy	**GAR/GDR/GDR/GAR/GRR**
sanctimonious	san-c-ti-mo-ni-ous	**GAR/GDR/GAR**/*HOO*/**GAR/GAR**
sanction	san-c-tion	**GAR/GDR**/*HOO*
sanctuary	san-c-tu-ar-y	**GAR/GDR**/*HOO*/*HAO*/*HDO*
sand	sa-nd	**GAR/GDR**
sandalwood	sa-n-dal-woo-d	**GAR//GDR**/*HDO*/*HOO*/*HDO*
sandel	sa-n-del	**GAR/GDR**/*HOO*
sandy	sa-n-dy	**GAR/GDR/GAR**
sane	sa-ne	*HAO*/**GDR**

Word	Mouthables	Mouth Movements Notations
sang	san-g	**GAR/GRR**
sanitary	sa-ni-tar-y	**GAR/GAR**/*HAO*/*HDO*
sanitation	sa-ni-ta-tion	**GAR/GAR**/*HAO*/*HOO*
sank	san-k	**GAR/GRR**
sap	sa-p	**GAR**/*HDO*
sapphire	sa-pphi-re	**GAR/GRR**/*HDO*
sarcasm	sar-ca-s-m	**GAR/GAR/GDR**/*HDO*
sarcastic	sar-ca-sti-c	**GAR/GAR/GAR/GDR**
sardine	sar-di-ne	*HAO*/**GAR/GDR**
Sardinia	Sar-di-ni-a	*HAO*/**GAR/GAR/GAR**
Sardinian	Sar-di-ni-a-n	*HAO*/**GAR/GAR/GAR/GDR**
sarge	sar-ge	*HAO*/*HDO*
sartorial	sar-to-ri-a-l	*HAO*/*HOO*/**GAR/GAR/GDR**
sash	sa-sh	**GAR**/*HDO*
sat	sa-t	**GAR/GRR**
satanic	sa-ta-ni-c	**GAR/GAR/GAR/GDR**
satchel	sa-t-che-l	**GAR**/*HDO*/**GAR/GDR**
satellite	sa-te-lli-te	**GAR**/*HDO*/**GRR**/*HDO*
satiate	sa-ti-a-te	*HAO*/*HDO*/*HAO*/*HDO*
satin	sa-ti-n	**GAR/GAR/GDR**
satire	sa-ti-re	**GAR/GRR**/*HDO*
satisfaction	sa-ti-s-fa-c-tion	**GAR/GAR/GDR/GAR/GDR**/*HOO*
satisfactory	sa-ti-s-fa-c-to-ry	**GAR/GAR/GDR/GAR**/*HOO*/*HDO*
satisfied	sa-ti-s-fie-d	**GAR/GAR/GDR/GRR**/*HOO*
satisfy	sa-ti-s-fy	**GAR/GAR/GDR/GRR**
saturate	sa-tu-ra-te	**GAR**/*HOO*/*HAO*/*HDO*
Saturday	Sa-tur-day	**GAR**/*HAO*/*HAO*
satyr	sa-tyr	**GAR**/*HAO*
sauce	sau-ce	*HOO*/**GDR**
saucer	sau-cer	*HOO*/*HDO*
saucy	sau-cy	*HOO*/**GAR**

Word	Mouthables	Mouth Movements Notations
Saudi	Sau-di	**GAR/GAR**
sauna	sau-na	*HOO*/**GAR**
saunter	sau-n-ter	*HOO/HDO/HDO*
sausage	sau-sage	*HAO/HDO*
savage	sa-vage	**GAR**/*HDO*
savannah	sa-va-nnah	**GAR/GAR**/*HAO*
save	sa-ve	*HAO*/**GRR**
saver	sa-ver	*HAO/HDO*
saving	sa-vi-ng	*HAO*/**GAR/GDR**
savour	sa-vour	*HAO/HAO*
savoury	sa-vou-ry	*HAO/HOO*/**GDR**
saw	saw	*HOO*
saw	sa-w	*HDO*
sawmill	saw-mi-ll	*HDO*/**GAR/GDR**
sawn	saw-n	*HOO*/**GRR**
sax	sa-x	**GAR/GDR**
Saxon	Sa-xo-n	**GAR**/*HAO/HDO*
say	say	*HAO*
saying	say-i-ng	*HAO*/**GAR/GDR**
scab	sca-b	**GAR**/*HDO*
scabies	sca-bi-es	*HAO*/**GAR/GDR**
scaffold	sca-ffo-ld	**GAR**/*HOO*/**GDR**
scald	sca-l-d	**GAR/GDR/GRR**
scale	sca-le	*HAO/HDO*
scalpel	sca-l-pel	**GAR/GDR**/*HDO*
scamp	sca-mp	**GAR/GDR**
scan	sca-n	**GAR/GDR**
scandal	sca-n-dal	**GAR/GDR**/*HDO*
scandalize	sca-n-da-li-ze	**GAR/GDR/GAR/GRR/GDR**
scandalous	sca-n-da-lou-s	**GAR/GDR/GAR/GAR**/*HDO*
Scandinavia	Sca-n-di-na-vi-a	**GAR/GDR/GAR**/*HAO*/**GAR/GAR**

Word	Mouthables	Mouth Movements Notations
Scandinavian	Sca-n-di-na-vi-a-n	GDR/GDR/GAR/*HAO*/GAR/GAR/GDR
scanty	sca-n-ty	GAR/GDR/GAR
scar	scar	*HAO*
scarce	scar-ce	GAR/GDR
scarcely	scar-ce-ly	GAR/GDR/GDR
scare	sca-re	GAR/*HDO*
scarf	scar-f	*HAO*/*HDO*
scarlet	scar-let	*HAO*/GDR
scarp	scar-p	*HAO*/*HDO*
scary	sca-ry	GAR/GAR
scatched	scra-tche-d	GAR/*HOO*/*HOO*
scathing	sca-th-i-ng	*HAO*/GTR/GAR/GDR
scatter	sca-tter	GAR/*HDO*
scatty	sca-tty	GAR/GAR
scavenge	sca-ve-n-ge	GAR/GAR/GDR/*HDO*
scenario	sce-nar-i-o	GAR/*HAO*/GAR/*HOO*
scene	sce-ne	GRR/GDR
scenery	sce-ner-y	GRR/*HDO*/*HDO*
scenic	sce-ni-c	GRR/GAR/GDR
scent	sce-nt	GAR/GDR
sceptic	sce-p-ti-c	GAR/*HDO*/GAR/GDR
sceptical	sce-p-ti-cal	GAR/*HDO*/GAR/*HDO*
scepticism	sce-p-ti-ci-sm	GRR/*HDO*/GAR/GAR/GDR
schedule	sche-du-le	GAR/*HOO*/*HDO*
scheme	sche-me	GRR/*HDO*
schism	sch-i-sm	GDR/GAR/GDR
schmaltzy	sch-ma-l-tzy	GDR/GAR/GDR/GAR
schnapps	sch-na-pps	*HOO*/GAR/*HDO*
scholar	scho-lar	*HAO*/*HDO*
scholarly	scho-lar-ly	*HAO*/*HAO*/GDR

Word	Mouthables	Mouth Movements Notations
scholarship	scho-lar-shi-p	*HAO*/*HAO*/**GAR**/*HDO*
scholastic	scho-la-sti-c	*HAO*/**GAR**/**GAR**/**GDR**
school	s-choo-l	*HDO*/*HOO*/*HDO*
science	sci-e-nce	**GRR/GAR/GDR**
scientific	sci-e-n-ti-fi-c	**GRR/GAR/GDR/GAR/GAR/GDR**
scientist	sci-e-n-ti-st	**GRR/GAR/GDR/GAR**/*HOO*
scifi	sci-fi	**GRR/GRR**
scissors	sci-ssor-s	**GAR**/*HOO*/*HDO*
scoff	sco-ff	*HAO*/*HDO*
scold	sco-l-d	*HOO*/**GDR**/*HOO*
scolding	sco-l-di-ng	*HOO*/**GDR**/**GAR**/**GDR**
scoot	scoo-t	*HOO*/*HOO*
scooted	scoo-ted	*HOO*/**GRR**
scooter	scoo-ter	*HOO*/*HDO*
scope	sco-pe	*HOO*/*HDO*
scorch	scor-ch	*HOO*/*HDO*
scorcher	scor-cher	*HOO*/**GDR**
score	score	*HOO*
scorn	scor-n	*HOO*/**GDR**
scornful	scor-n-ful	*HOO*/**GDR**/*HDO*
scorpion	scor-pi-o-n	*HOO*/**GAR**/*HAO*/*HDO*
Scot	Sco-t	*HAO*/*HDO*
scotch	sco-tch	*HAO*/*HDO*
Scotch	Sco-t-ch	*HAO*/*HDO*/*HDO*
Scotland	Sco-t-la-nd	*HAO*/*HDO*/**GAR**/**GDR**
Scots	Sco-ts	*HAO*/*HDO*
Scotsman	Sco-ts-ma-n	*HAO*/*HDO*/**GAR**/**GDR**
Scottish	Sco-tti-sh	*HAO*/**GAR**/*HDO*
scour	scou-r	*HAO*/*HDO*
scour	scou-re-d	*HAO*/*HDO*/*HOO*
scourer	scou-rer	*HAO*/*HDO*

Word	Mouthables	Mouth Movements Notations
scourge	scour-ge	**GAR**/*HDO*
scourged	scour-ge-d	**GAR**/*HDO*/*HOO*
scourging	scour-ging	**GAR/GDR**
scout	scou-t	*HAO*/*HOO*
scowl	scow-l	**GAR**/*HDO*
scrabble	scra-bble	**GAR**/*HOO*
scraggy	scra-ggy	**GAR/GAR**
scram	scra-m	**GAR/GDR**
scramble	scra-m-ble	**GAR/GDR**/*HOO*
scrap	scra-p	**GAR/GDR**
scrape	scra-pe	*HAO*/*HDO*
scratch	scra-tch	**GAR**/*HOO*
scratchy	scra-tchy	**GAR/GAR**
scrawl	scraw-l	*HOO*/*HDO*
scrawny	scraw-ny	*HOO*/**GAR**
scream	screa-m	**GRR/GDR**
screech	scree-ch	**GRR**/*HDO*
screen	scree-n	**GRR/GDR**
screw	screw	*HOO*
screwy	scre-wy	*HOO*/**GAR**
scribble	scri-bble	**GAR**/*HOO*
scrimmage	scrim-mage	**GAR**/*HDO*
scrimp	scri-mp	**GAR/GDR**
script	scri-pt	**GAR**/*HDO*
scroll	scro-ll	*HOO*/*HDO*
scrounge	scrou-n-ge	**GAR/GDR**/*HDO*
scrub	scru-b	**GAR**/*HDO*
scruff	scru-ff	**GAR**/*HDO*
scruffy	scru-ffy	**GAR/GAR**
scull	scu-ll	**GAR/GDR**
sculled	scu-lle-d	**GAR/GDR**/*HOO*

Word	Mouthables	Mouth Movements Notations
scrumptious	scru-mp-ti-ous	**GAR**/*HDO*/*HDO*/*HAO*
scrunch	scru-nch	**GAR/GDR**
scruple	scru-ple	*HOO*/*HDO*
scrupulous	scru-pu-lous	*HOO*/**GAR**/*HAO*
scrutinize	scru-ti-ni-ze	*HOO*/**GAR/GRR/GDR**
scrutiny	scru-ti-ny	*HOO*/**GAR/GAR**
scuba	scu-ba	*HOO*/**GAR**
scuff	scu-ff	**GAR**/*HDO*
scuffle	scu-ffle	**GAR**/*HOO*
sculpt	scu-l-p-t	**GAR/GDR**/*HDO*/*HOO*
sculpted	scu-l-p-ted	**GAR/GDR**/*HDO*/**GRR**
sculptor	scu-l-p-tor	**GAR/GDR**/*HDO*/*HDO*
sculpture	scu-l-p-tu-re	**GAR/GDR**/*HDO*/*HOO*/*HDO*
scum	scu-m	**GAR**/*HDO*
scurry	scu-rry	**GAR/GAR**
scuttle	scu-ttle	**GAR**/*HOO*
scythe	scy-the	**GRR/GTR**
sea	sea	**GDR**
seal	se-al	**GRR/GDR**
sealing	sea-ling	**GRR/GDR**
seam	sea-m	**GRR/GDR**
seaman	sea-ma-n	**GRR/GAR/GDR**
seamy	sea-my	**GRR/GAR**
sear	se-ar	**GRR/GAR**
seared	se-are-d	**GRR/GAR**/*HOO*
search	sear-ch	*HOO*/*HDO*
season	sea-so-n	**GRR**/*HAO*/**GDR**
seasonal	sea-so-nal	**GRR**/*HAO*/*HDO*
seasoned	sea-so-ne-d	**GRR**/*HAO*/**GDR**/*HOO*
seasoning	sea-so-ni-ng	**GRR**/*HAO*/**GAR/GDR**
seasweed	sea-wee-d	**GRR/GRR**/*HDO*

Word	Mouthables	Mouth Movements Notations
seat	sea-t	**GRR**/*HDO*
secesssion	se-ces-sion	**GAR/GAR**/*HOO*
secluded	se-clu-ded	**GAR**/*HOO*/**GRR**
seclusion	se-clu-sion	**GAR**/*HOO*/*HOO*
second	se-co-nd	**GAR**/*HAO*/**GDR**
secondary	sec-on-dary	**GAR**/*HAO*/*HDO*
secrecy	se-cre-cy	**GRR/GAR/GAR**
secret	se-cre-t	**GRR/GAR**/*HOO*
secretary	se-cre-ta-ry	**GAR/GAR/GAR**/*HDO*
sect	se-ct	**GAR**/*HDO*
section	se-c-tion	**GAR/GDR**/*HOO*
sector	se-c-tor	**GAR/GDR**/*HDO*
secular	se-c-u-lar	**GAR/GDR**/*HOO*/*HAO*
secure	se-cu-re	**GAR**/*HOO*/*HDO*
security	se-cu-ri-ty	**GAR**/*HOO*/**GAR/GAR**
sedan	se-da-n	**GAR/GAR/GDR**
sedate	se-da-te	**GAR**/*HAO*/*HDO*
sedative	se-da-ti-ve	**GAR/GAR/GAR/GDR**
sedentary	se-de-n-tar-y	**GAR/GAR/GDR/GAR**/*HDO*
seduce	se-du-ce	**GAR**/*HOO*/**GDR**
seductive	se-du-c-ti-ve	**GAR/GAR/GDR/GAR/GDR**
see	see	**GRR**
seed	see-d	**GRR**/*HDO*
seek	see-k	**GRR**/*HDO*
seem	see-m	**GRR**/*HDO*
seen	see-n	**GRR/GRR**
seep	see-p	**GRR**/*HDO*
seethe	see-the	**GRR/GTR**
seer	se-er	**GRR**/*HDO*
segregate	se-gre-ga-te	**GAR/GAR**/*HAO*/*HDO*
seismic	sei-s-mi-c	**GRR/GDR/GAR/GDR**

Word	Mouthables	Mouth Movements Notations
seize	sei-ze	**GRR/GDR**
seizure	sei-zu-re	**GRR**/*HOO*/*HDO*
seldom	se-l-do-m	**GAR/GDR**/*HAO*/*HDO*
select	se-le-ct	**GAR/GAR**/*HOO*
selection	se-le-c-tion	**GAR/GAR/GDR**/*HOO*
selective	se-le-c-ti-ve	**GAR/GAR/GDR/GAR/GDR**
self	se-lf	**GAR/GDR**
sell	sel-l	**GAR/GRR**
seller	se-ller	**GAR**/*HDO*
seltzer	se-l-tzer	**GAR/GDR/GDR**
selves	se-l-ves	**GAR/GDR**/*HDO*
semolina	se-mo-li-na	**GAR/GAR/GAR/GAR**
senate	se-na-te	**GAR/GAR**/*HDO*
senator	se-na-tor	**GAR/GAR**/*HOO*
send	se-nd	**GAR/GRR**
sendor	se-n-dor	**GAR/GDR**/*HDO*
senile	se-ni-le	**GRR/GRR**/*HDO*
senility	se-ni-li-ty	**GRR/GAR/GAR/GAR**
senior	se-ni-or	**GRR/GAR**/*HDO*
sensation	se-n-sa-tion	**GAR/GDR**/*HAO*/*HOO*
sensational	se-n-sa-tion-al	**GAR/GDR**/*HAO*/*HOO*/*HDO*
sensationalize	se-n-sa-tion-a-li-ze	**GAR/GDR**/*HAO*/*HOO*/**GAR/GRR/ GDR**
sense	se-n-se	**GAR/GDR**/*HDO*
sensibility	se-n-si-bi-li-ty	**GAR/GDR/GAR/GAR/GAR/GAR**
sensible	se-n-si-ble	**GAR/GDR/GAR**/*HOO*
sensitive	se-n-si-ti-ve	**GAR/GDR/GAR/GAR**/*HDO*
sensitivity	se-n-si-ti-vi-ty	**GAR/GDR/GAR/GAR/GAR/GAR**
sensitize	se-n-si-ti-ze	**GAR/GDR/GAR/GRR/GDR**
sensor	se-n-sor	**GAR/GDR**/*HDO*
sensual	se-n-su-al	**GAR/GDR**/*HOO*/*HDO*

Word	Mouthables	Mouth Movements Notations
sensuous	se-n-su-ous	GAR/GDR/*HOO*/GAR
sent	se-nt	GAR/GRR
sentence	se-n-te-nce	GAR/GDR/GAR/GDR
sentiment	se-n-ti-me-nt	GAR/GDR/GAR/GAR/GDR
sentry	se-n-try	GAR/GDR/*HDO*
separate	se-pa-ra-te	GAR/GAR/GAR/*HDO*
separate	se-pa-ra-ted	GAR/GAR/*HAO*/GRR
September	Se-p-te-m-ber	GAR/GDR/GAR/*HDO*/*HDO*
sequel	se-quel	GRR/*HDO*
sequence	se-que-nce	GRR/GAR/GDR
sequester	se-que-ster	GAR/GAR/*HDO*
sequestration	se-que-stra-tion	GAR/GAR/*HAO*/*HOO*
sequin	se-qui-n	GRR/GAR/GDR
serenade	se-re-na-de	GAR/GAR/*HAO*/*HDO*
serene	se-re-ne	GAR/GRR/GDR
serenity	se-re-ni-ty	GAR/GAR/GAR/GAR
sergeant	ser-gea-nt	*HAO*/GAR/GDR
serial	se-ri-al	GRR/GAR/GDR
serialize	se-ri-a-li-ze	GRR/GAR/GAR/GRR/GDR
series	se-ri-es	GRR/GAR/GDR
serious	se-ri-ous	GRR/GAR/GAR
sermon	ser-mo-n	*HAO*/*HAO*/*HDO*
serrated	se-rra-ted	GAR/*HAO*/GRR
servant	ser-va-nt	*HAO*/GAR/GDR
serve	ser-ve	*HAO*/*HDO*
service	ser-vi-ce	*HAO*/GAR/GDR
serviceable	ser-vi-ce-a-ble	*HAO*/GAR/GDR/GAR/*HOO*
serviette	ser-vi-e-tte	*HAO*/GAR/GAR/*HDO*
servile	ser-vi-le	*HAO*/GRR/GDR
servility	ser-vi-li-ty	*HAO*/GAR/GAR/GAR
serving	ser-vi-ng	*HAO*/GAR/GDR

Word	Mouthables	Mouth Movements Notations
session	se-ssion	**GAR**/*HOO*
set	se-t	**GAR**/*HOO*
settee	se-ttee	**GAR/GRR**
setting	se-tti-ng	**GAR/GAR/GDR**
settle	se-ttle	**GAR**/*HOO*
settlement	se-ttle-me-nt	**GAR**/*HOO*/**GAR/GDR**
seven	se-ven	**GAR**/*HDO*
seventeen	se-ve-n-tee-n	**GAR/GAR/GDR/GRR/GDR**
seventh	se-ve-nth	**GARGDR/GTR**
seventy	se-ve-n-ty	**GAR/GAR/GDR/GAR**
sever	se-ver	**GAR**/*HDO*
several	se-ve-ral	**GAR**/*HAO/HDO*
severe	se-ve-re	**GAR/GRR**/*HDO*
severity	se-ve-ri-ty	**GAR/GAR/GAR/GAR**
sew	sew	*HOO*
sewage	sew-a-ge	**GAR**/*HAO/HDO*
sewer	sew-er	**GAR**/*HDO*
sewerage	sew-er-a-ge	**GAR**/*HDO/HAO/HDO*
sewn	sew-n	*HOO*/**GDR**
sex	se-x	**GAR/GDR**
sexism	se-xi-sm	**GAR/GAR/GDR**
sexton	sex-to-n	**GAR**/*HAO*/**GDR**
sexual	se-xu-al	**GAR**/*HOO/HDO*
shabby	sha-bby	**GAR/GAR**
shack	sha-ck	**GAR**/*HDO*
shade	sha-de	*HAO/HDO*
shadow	sha-do-w	**GAR**/*HOO/HDO*
shady	sha-dy	*HAO*/**GAR**
shaft	shaf-t	*HAO/HOO*
shake	sha-ke	*HAO*/**GRR**
shaky	sha-ky	*HAO*/**GAR**

Word	Mouthables	Mouth Movements Notations
shall	sha-ll	**GAR/GDR**
shallow	sha-llo-w	**GAR**/*HAO/HDO*
sham	sha-m	**GAR**/*HDO*
shambles	sha-m-ble-s	**GAR**/*HDO/HOO/HDO*
shambolic	sha-m-bo-li-c	**GAR**/*HDO/HAO*/**GAR/GDR**
shame	sha-me	*HAO/HDO*
shampoo	sha-m-poo	**GAR**/*HDO/HOO*
shamrock	sha-m-ro-ck	**GAR**/*HDO/HAO/HDO*
shandy	sha-n-dy	**GAR/GDR/GDR**
shape	sha-pe	*HAO/HDO*
shapeless	sha-pe-le-ss	*HAO/HDO*/**GAR/GDR**
shapely	sha-pe-ly	*HAO/HDO*/**GAR**
share	share	*HAO*
shark	shar-k	*HAO/HDO*
sharp	shar-p	*HAO/HDO*
sharpen	shar-pe-n	*HAO*/**GAR/GDR**
sharper	shar-per	*HAO/HDO*
shatter	sha-tter	**GAR**/*HDO*
shave	sha-ve	*HAO/HDO*
shaven	sha-v-en	*HAO/HDO/HDO*
shaver	sha-ver	*HAO/HDO*
shavings	sha-vi-ngs	*HAO*/**GAR/GDR**
shawl	shaw-l	*HOO/HDO*
she	she	**GDR**
sheaf	shea-f	**GRR**/*HDO*
shear	she-ar	**GRR**/*HAO*
shear	she-are-d	**GRR**/*HAO/HOO*
shears	she-ar-s	**GRR**/*HAO/HDO*
sheath	shea-th	**GRR/GTR**
sheaves	shea-ve-s	**GRR**/*HDO/HDO*
shed	she-d	**GAR**/*HOO*

Word	Mouthables	Mouth Movements Notations
sheen	shee-n	**GRR/GDR**
sheep	shee-p	**GRR**/*HDO*
sheepish	shee-pi-sh	**GRR/GAR**/*HDO*
sheer	she-er	**GRR/GDR**
sheet	shee-t	**GRR/GDR**
sheets	shee-ts	**GRR/GDR**
sheik	shei-k	*HAO/HDO*
shelf	she-lf	**GAR**/*HDO*
shell	she-ll	**GAR/GDR**
shelter	she-l-ter	**GAR/GDR**/*HDO*
shelves	she-l-ves	**GAR/GDR**/*HDO*
shelving	she-l-ving	**GAR/GDR/GDR**
shepherd	she-pher-d	**GAR**/*HAO/HOO*
sherbet	sher-be-t	**GAR/GAR**/*HDO*
sheriff	she-ri-ff	**GAR/GAR**/*HDO*
shield	shie-ld	**GAR/GDR**
shift	shi-ft	**GAR**/*HDO*
shiftless	shi-ft-le-ss	**GAR**/*HDO*/**GAR/GDR**
shifty	shi-f-ty	**GAR/GDR/GAR**
shimmer	shi-mmer	**GAR**/*HDO*
shin	shi-n	**GAR/GDR**
shindy	shi-n-dy	**GAR/GDR/GAR**
shine	shi-ne	**GRR/GDR**
shiner	shi-ner	**GRR**/*HDO*
ship	shi-p	**GAR/GDR**
shipment	shi-p-me-nt	**GAR/GDR/GAR/GDR**
shipping	shi-pp-ing	**GAR/GDR/GDR**
shirk	shir-k	*HAO/HOO*
shirt	shir-t	*HAO/HDO*
shit	sh-i-t	*HOO*/**GAR**/*HOO*
shiver	sh-i-ver	*HOO*/**GAR**/*HDO*

Word	Mouthables	Mouth Movements Notations
shoal	sh-oa-l	*HOO/HOO/HDO*
shock	sh-o-ck	*HOO/HAO/HDO*
shocking	sh-o-cki-ng	*HOO/HAO/***GDR**
shoddy	sh-o-ddy	*HOO/HAO/***GAR**
shoe	shoe	*HOO*
shoes	shoe-s	*HOO/HDO*
shone	sh-o-ne	*HOO/HAO/HDO*
shoo	s-hoo	*HOO/HOO*
shoo-k	shoo-k	*HOO/HDO*
shoot	shoo-t	*HOO/HOO*
shop	sh-o-p	*HOO/HAO/HDO*
shopper	sh-o-pper	*HOO/HAO/HDO*
shopping	sh-o-pping	*HOO/HAO/***GDR**
shore	sh-ore	*HOO/HOO*
shorn	sh-or-n	*HOO/HOO/***GDR**
short	sh-or-t	*HOO/HOO/HOO*
shortage	sh-or-tage	*HOO/HOO/HDO*
shot	sh-o-t	*HOO/HAO/HOO*
should	shoul-d	*HOO/HDO*
shoulder	sh-oul-der	*HOO/HOO/HDO*
shout	sh-ou-t	*HOO/HAO/HOO*
shove	sh-o-ve	*HOO/***GAR***HDO*
shovel	sh-o-ve-l	*HOO/***GAR/GAR***/GDR**
show	show	*HOO*
showed	sho-we-d	*HOO/HOO/HOO*
show	sho-w	*HOO/HDO*
shower	sh-ow-er	*HOO/***GAR***/HDO*
shown	show-n	*HOO/***GDR**
showy	sh-o-wy	*HOO/HOO/***GAR**
shrank	sh-ran-k	**GDR/GAR/GDR**
shred	sh-re-d	**GDR/GAR**/*HOO*

Word	Mouthables	Mouth Movements Notations
shredder	sh-re-dder	**GDR/GAR/***HDO*
shrewd	shrew-d	*HOO/HOO*
shrill	shri-ll	**GAR/GDR**
shrimp	shri-mp	**GAR/***HDO*
shrine	sh-ri-ne	**GDR/GRR/GDR**
shrink	sh-rin-k	**GDR/GAR/GRR**
shrivel	sh-ri-vel	**GDR/GAR/***HDO*
shrub	sh-ru-b	*HOO/***GAR/***HDO*
shrug	sh-ru-g	*HOO/***GAR/***HDO*
shrunk	sh-run-k	*HOO/***GAR/GRR**
shrunken	sh-run-ke-n	*HOO/***GAR/GAR/GDR**
shudder	sh-u-dder	**GDR/GAR/***HDO*
shuffle	sh-u-ffle	**GDR/GAR/***HOO*
shun	sh-u-n	**GDR/GAR/GDR**
shut	sh-u-t	**GDR/GAR/***HOO*
shutter	sh-u-tter	**GDR/GAR/***HDO*
shuttle	sh-u-ttle	**GDR/GAR/***HOO*
shy	shy	**GRR**
Siamese	Si-a-me-se	**GRR/GAR/GRR/GDR**
Sicilian	Si-ci-li-a-n	**GAR/GAR/GAR/GAR/GDR**
Sicily	Si-ci-ly	**GAR/GAR/GDR**
sick	si-ck	**GAR/***HDO*
sicken	si-cke-n	**GAR/GAR/GDR**
sickle	si-ckle	**GAR/***HOO*
sickly	si-ck-ly	**GAR/GDR/GDR**
sickness	si-ck-ne-ss	**GAR/GDR/GAR/***HDO*
side	si-de	**GRR/***HDO*
siege	sie-ge	**GAR/***HDO*
sieve	sie-ve	**GAR/***HDO*
sift	si-ft	**GAR/***HDO*
sigh	si-gh	**GRR/GDR**

Word	Mouthables	Mouth Movements Notations
sighed	si-ghe-d	**GRR/GDR/**_HOO_
sight	si-ght	**GRR/**_HDO_
sign	si-gn	**GRR/GDR**
signal	si-g-nal	**GAR/GDR/**_HDO_
signature	si-g-na-tu-re	**GAR/GDR/GAR/**_HOO/HDO_
significance	si-g-ni-fi-ca-nce	**GAR/GDR/GAR/GAR/GAR/GDR**
significant	si-g-ni-fi-ca-nt	**GAR/GDR/GAR/GAR/GAR/GDR**
signify	si-g-ni-fy	**GAR/GDR/GAR/GRR**
silence	si-le-nce	**GRR/GAR/GDR**
silencer	si-le-n-cer	**GRR/GAR/GDR/**_HDO_
silent	si-le-nt	**GRR/GAR/GDR**
silk	si-l-k	**GAR/GDR/**_HDO_
silken	si-l-ken	**GAR/GDR/**_HDO_
silky	si-l-ky	**GAR/GDR/GAR**
silly	si-l-ly	**GAR/GDR/GAR**
silver	si-l-ver	**GAR/GDR/**_HDO_
silvery	si-l-ver-y	**GAR/GDR/**_HAO_**/GAR**
similar	si-mi-lar	**GAR/GAR/**_HAO_
similes	si-mi-le-s	**GAR/GAR/GRR/GDR**
simmer	si-mmer	**GAR/**_HDO_
simple	si-m-ple	**GAR/GDR/**_HOO_
simplicity	si-m-pli-ci-ty	**GAR/GDR/GAR/GAR/GAR**
simplify	si-m-pli-fy	**GAR/GDR/GAR/GRR**
simplistic	si-m-pli-sti-c	**GAR/GDR/GAR/GAR/GDR**
simulate	si-mu-la-te	**GAR/**_HOO/HAO/HDO_
simultaneous	si-mu-l-ta-ne-ous	**GAR/GAR/GDR/**_HAO_**/GRR/**_HAO_
sin	si-n	**GAR/GDR**
since	si-nce	**GAR/GDR**
sincere	si-n-ce-re	**GAR/GDR/GRR/**_HDO_
sincerity	si-n-ce-ri-ty	**GAR/GDR/GAR/GAR/GAR**
sinew	si-new	**GAR/**_HOO_

Word	Mouthables	Mouth Movements Notations
sinewy	si-new-y	GAR/*HOO*/GAR
sinful	si-n-ful	GAR/GDR/*HDO*
sing	sin-g	GAR/GRR
singe	si-n-ge	GAR/GDR/*HDO*
singer	sin-ger	GAR/*HDO*
single	sin-gle	GAR/*HOO*
singlet	sin-g-le-t	GAR/GDR/GAR/*HDO*
singular	sin-gu-lar	GAR/GDR/*HOO*/*HAO*
sinister	si-ni-ster	GAR/GAR/*HDO*
sink	sin-k	GAR/GRR
sinner	si-nner	GAR/*HDO*
sinuous	si-nu-ous	GAR/*HOO*/*HAO*
sip	si-p	GAR/*HDO*
siphon	si-ph-o-n	GRR/*HDO*/*HAO*/*HDO*
sir	sir	*HAO*
siren	si-re-n	GRR/GAR/GDR
sirlion	sir-lio-n	*HAO*/*HAO*/*HDO*
sissy	si-ssy	GAR/GAR
sister	si-ster	GAR/*HDO*
sit	si-t	GAR/GRR
site	si-te	GRR/*HDO*
sitting	si-tti-ng	GAR/GAR/GDR
situated	si-tu-a-ted	GAR/*HOO*/*HAO*/GRR
situation	si-tu-a-tion	GAR/*HOO*/*HAO*/*HOO*
six	si-x	GAR/GDR
sixteen	si-x-tee-n	GAR/GDR/GRR/GDR
sixth	si-x-th	GAR/GDR/GTR
sixty	si-x-ty	GAR/GDR/GAR
sizable	si-za-ble	GRR/GAR/*HOO*
sizzle	si-zzle	GAR/*HOO*
skate	ska-te	*HAO*/*HDO*

Word	Mouthables	Mouth Movements Notations
skein	skei-n	*HAO/HDO*
skeleton	ske-le-to-n	**GAR/GAR**/*HAO/HDO*
skeptic	ske-p-ti-c	**GAR/GDR/GAR/GDR**
sketch	ske-tch	**GAR**/*HDO*
sketchy	ske-tch-y	**GAR**/*HDO*/**GAR**
skew	ske-w	*HOO/HOO*
skewed	ske-we-d	*HOO/HOO/HOO*
skewer	ske-wer	*HOO/HDO*
skewwhiff	skew-whi-ff	*HOO*/**GAR**/*HDO*
ski	ski	**GAR**
skid	ski-d	**GAR**/*HOO*
skiing	ski-ing	**GAR/GDR**
skilful	ski-l-ful	**GAR/GDR**/*HOO*
skill	ski-ll	**GAR/GDR**
skilled	ski-lle-d	**GAR/GDR**/*HOO*
skim	ski-m	**GAR**/*HDO*
skimpy	ski-m-py	**GAR**/*HDO*/**GAR**
skin	ski-n	**GAR/GDR**
skinny	ski-n-ny	**GAR/GDR/GAR**
skint	ski-n-t	**GAR/GDR**/*HOO*
skip	ski-p	**GAR**/*HDO*
skipper	ski-pper	**GAR**/*HDO*
skirmish	skir-mi-sh	*HAO*/**GAR**/*HDO*
skirt	skir-t	*HAO/HOO*
skittle	ski ttle	**GAR**/*HOO*
skive	ski-ve	**GRR**/*HDO*
skull	sk-u-ll	**GDR/GAR/GDR**
sky	sky	**GRR**
slab	sla-b	**GAR**/*HDO*
slack	sla-ck	**GAR**/*HDO*
slacken	sla-cken	**GAR**/*HDO*

Word	Mouthables	Mouth Movements Notations
slain	slai-n	*HAO*/**GRR**
slam	sla-m	**GAR/GRR**
slander	slan-der	*HAO/HOO*
slang	sla-ng	**GAR/GDR**
slangy	sla-ng-y	**GAR/GDR/GAR**
slant	slan-t	*HAO/HOO*
slanted	slan-ted	*HAO*/**GRR**
slap	sla-p	**GAR**/*HDO*
slash	sla-sh	**GAR**/*HDO*
slate	sla-te	*HAO/HDO*
slaughter	slaugh-ter	*HOO/HOO*
Slav	Slav	*HAO*
slave	sla-ve	*HAO/HDO*
slavery	sla-ve-ry	*HAO*/**GAR**/*HDO*
slay	s-lay	**GRR**/*HAO*
sleazy	slea-zy	**GRR/GAR**
sledge	sle-d-ge	**GAR**/*HDO/HDO*
sleek	slee-k	**GRR**/*HDO*
sleep	slee-p	**GRR**/*HDO*
sleeper	slee-per	**GRR**/*HDO*
sleepless	slee-p-le-ss	**GRR**/*HDO*/**GAR**/*HDO*
sleepy	slee-py	**GRR/GAR**
sleet	slee-t	**GRR**/*HOO*
sleeve	slee-ve	**GRR**/*HDO*
sleigh	slei-gh	*HAO/HDO*
slender	sle-n-der	**GAR/GDR**/*HDO*
slept	sle-pt	**GAR/GRR**
sleuth	sleu-th	*HOO/HTO*
slew	slew	*HOO*
slice	sli-ce	**GRR/GRR**
slick	sli-ck	**GAR**/*HDO*

Word	Mouthables	Mouth Movements Notations
slide	sli-de	**GRR**/*HDO*
slight	sli-ght	**GRR**/*HDO*
slim	sli-m	**GAR**/*HDO*
slime	sli-me	**GRR**/*HDO*
slimy	sli-my	**GRR/GAR**
sling	slin-g	**GAR/GRR**
slink	slin-k	**GAR/GRR**
slinky	slin-ky	**GAR/GAR**
slip	sli-p	**GAR**/*HDO*
slipper	sli-pper	**GAR**/*HDO*
slippery	sli-ppe-ry	**GAR/GAR**/*HDO*
slippy	sli-ppy	**GAR/GAR**
slit	sli-t	**GAR**/*HOO*
slob	slo-b	*HAO/HDO*
sloe	sloe	*HOO*
slog	slo-g	*HAO/HDO*
slop	slo-p	*HAO/HDO*
slope	slo-pe	*HOO/HDO*
sloppy	slo-ppy	*HAO*/**GAR**
sloshed	slo-she-d	*HAO/HOO/HOO*
slot	s-lo-t	*HOO/HAO/HOO*
sloth	s-lo-th	*HOO/HOO/HTO*
slovenly	slo-ve-n-ly	**GAR/GAR/GDR/GAR**
slow	s-lo-w	*HOO/HOO/HDO*
sludge	slu-dge	**GAR**/*HDO*
slug	slu-g	**GAR**/*HDO*
slugard	slu-gar-d	**GAR/GAR**/*HDO*
slugged	slu-gge-d	**GAR**/*HOO/HOO*
sluggish	slu-gg-i-sh	**GAR**/*HDO*/**GAR**/*HDO*
slum	slu-m	**GAR**/*HDO*
slump	slu-mp	**GAR**/*HDO*

Word	Mouthables	Mouth Movements Notations
slung	slu-ng	**GAR/GRR**
slunk	slu-nk	**GAR/GRR**
slush	slu-sh	**GAR**/*HDO*
sly	sly	**GRR**
smack	s-mac-k	**GRR/GAR/GDR**
smack	s-mac-ke-d	**GRR/GAR/GDR**/*HOO*
small	s-mal-l	*HOO/HOO/HDO*
smallish	s-mal-li-sh	*HOO/HOO/***GAR**/*HDO*
smart	s-mar-t	*HOO/HAO/HOO*
smarten	s-mar-ten	*HOO/HAO/HDO*
smash	s-ma-sh	**GRR/GAR**/*HDO*
smashing	s-ma-shi-ng	**GRR/GAR/GDR/GDR**
smatering	s-ma-tter-i-ng	**GRR/GAR**/*HAO/***GAR/GDR**
smear	s-me-ar	**GRR/GRR**/*HAO*
smeared	s-me-are-d	**GRR/GRR**/*HAO/HOO*
smell	s-me-ll	**GRR/GAR/GDR**
smelly	s-me-lly	**GRR/GAR/GAR**
smelt	s-me-lt	**GRR/GAR/GDR**
smile	s-mi-le	**GRR/GRR/GDR**
smiled	s-mi-le-d	**GRR/GRR/GDR**/*HOO*
smirk	s-mir-k	*HOO/HAO/HOO*
smirk	s-mir-k	*HOO/HOO/HDO*
smirked	s-mir-ke-d	*HOO/HOO/HOO*
smith	s-mi-th	**GRR/GAR/GTR**
smoggy	s-mo-ggy	**GRR**/*HAO/***GAR**
smoke	s-mo-ke	**GRR**/*HOO/HDO*
smoked	s-mo-ke-d	**GRR**/*HOO/HOO/HOO*
smoker	s-mo-ker	**GRR**/*HOO/HDO*
smoky	s-mo-ky	**GRR**/*HOO/***GAR**
smooth	s-moo-th	*HOO/HOO/HTO*
smother	s-mo-th-er	**GRR/GAR/GTR**/*HDO*

Word	Mouthables	Mouth Movements Notations
smuggle	s-mu-ggle	GRR/GAR/*HOO*
smugly	s-mu-g-ly	GRR/GAR/GDR/GDR
snack	s-na-ck	GRR/GAR/*HDO*
snail	s-nai-l	GRR/*HAO*/GDR
snake	s-na-ke	GRR/*HAO*/*HDO*
snaky	s-na-ky	GRR/*HAO*/GAR
snap	s-na-p	GRR/GAR/*HDO*
snappy	s-na-ppy	GRR/GAR/GAR
snare	s-nare	GRR/*HAO*
snarl	s-nar-l	GRR/GAR/GDR
snatch	sna-tch	GAR/*HDO*
snatchy	sna-t-chy	GAR/*HDO*/GDR
sneak	s-nea-k	GRR/GRR/GDR
sneakers	s-nea-ker-s	GRR/GRR/*HDO*/*HDO*
sneaking	s-nea-ki-ng	GRR/GRR/GAR/GDR
sneaky	s-nea-ky	GRR/GRR/GAR
snear	s-ne-ar	GRR/GRR/*HAO*
sneeze	s-nee-ze	GRR/GRR/GDR
sniff	s-ni-ff	GRR/GAR/*HDO*
sniffy	s-ni-ffy	GRR/GAR/GAR
sniiger	s-ni-gger	GRR/GAR/*HDO*
snip	sni-p	GAR/*HDO*
sniper	s-ni-per	GRR/GAR/*HDO*
snippet	sni-ppe-t	GAR/GAR/GDR
snivel	s-ni-vel	GRR/GAR/*HDO*
snobbery	s-no-bbe-ry	GRR/*HAO*/*HDO*/GAR
snobbish	s-no-bbi-sh	GRR/*HAO*/GAR/*HDO*
snokel	s-no-kel	*HOO*/*HOO*/*HOO*
snoop	s-noo-p	*HOO*/*HOO*/*HDO*
snooper	s-noo-per	*HOO*/*HOO*/*HDO*
snooty	s-noo-ty	*HOO*/*HOO*/GAR

Word	Mouthables	Mouth Movements Notations
snooze	s-noo-ze	*HOO*/*HOO*/**GDR**
snore	s-no-re	*HOO*/*HOO*/*HDO*
snort	s-nor-t	*HOO*/*HOO*/*HOO*
snout	s-nou-t	**GRR**/**GAR**/*HOO*
snow	s-no-w	*HOO*/*HOO*/*HDO*
snub	s-nu-b	**GRR**/**GAR**/*HDO*
snuff	s-nu-ff	**GRR**/**GAR**/*HDO*
snug	s-nu-g	**GRR**/**GAR**/*HDO*
snuggle	s-nu-ggle	**GRR**/**GAR**/*HOO*
so	s-o	*HOO*/*HOO*
soap	soa-p	*HOO*/*HDO*
soar	s-oar	*HOO*/*HAO*
soared	s-oare-d	*HOO*/*HAO*/*HOO*
sob	s-o-b	*HOO*/*HAO*/*HDO*
sober	s-o-ber	*HOO*/*HOO*/*HDO*
soccer	s-oc-cer	*HOO*/*HAO*/*HDO*
sociable	s-o-ci-a-ble	*HOO*/*HOO*/**GDR**/**GAR**/*HOO*
social	s-o-cial	*HOO*/*HOO*/**GDR**
Socialism	S-o-cia-li-sm	*HOO*/*HOO*/**GDR**/**GAR**/*HDO*
Socialist	S-o-cia-li-st	*HOO*/*HOO*/**GDR**/**GAR**/*HOO*
socialize	s-o-cia-li-ze	*HOO*/*HOO*/**GDR**/**GRR**/**GDR**
society	s-o-ci-e-ty	*HOO*/*HOO*/**GRR**/**GAR**/**GAR**
sock	s-o-ck	*HOO*/*HAO*/*HOO*
sock	s-o-ck	*HOO*/*HAO*/*HDO*
socked	s-o-cke-d	*HOO*/*HAO*/*HOO*/*HOO*
socket	so-cke-t	*HAO*/**GAR**/**GDR**
sod	s-o-d	*HOO*/*HAO*/*HOO*
sodden	so-d-den	*HAO*/*HOO*/*HDO*
sodium	s-o-di-u-m	*HOO*/*HOO*/**GAR**/**GAR**/*HDO*
sofa	s-o-fa	*HOO*/*HOO*/**GAR**
soft	s-o-ft	*HOO*/*HAO*/*HDO*

Word	Mouthables	Mouth Movements Notations
soften	so-f-ten	*HAO/HDO/HDO*
softener	so-f-ten-er	*HAO/HDO/HDO/HDO*
soggy	s-o-ggy	*HOO/HAO/***GAR**
soil	s-oi-l	**GRR/GAR/GDR**
solace	so-la-ce	*HOO/***GAR/GDR**
solar	s-o-lar	*HOO/HOO/HAO*
sold	so-ld	*HOO/HOO*
soldier	so-l-dier	*HOO/***GDR/GAR**
sole	so-le	*HOO/HDO*
solemn	so-le-mn	*HAO/***GAR/***HDO*
solemnity	so-le-m-ni-ty	*HAO/***GAR/***HDO/***GAR/GDR**
solicit	so-li-ci-t	*HOO/***GAR/GAR/***HOO*
solicitor	so-li-ci-tor	*HOO/***GAR/GAR/***HDO*
solicitous	so-li-ci-tous	*HOO/***GAR/GAR/GAR**
solid	so-li-d	*HAO/***GAR/***HDO*
solidarity	so-li-da-ri-ty	*HAO/***GAR/GAR/GAR/GAR**
solidify	so-li-di-fy	*HOO/***GAR/GAR/GRR**
solitaire	so-li-taire	*HAO/***GAR/***HAO*
solitary	so-li-ta-ry	*HAO/***GAR/***HAO/**GDR**
solitude	so-li-tu-de	*HAO/***GAR/***HOO/HDO*
solo	so-lo	*HOO/HOO*
soloist	so-lo-i-st	*HOO/HOO/***GAR/GDR**
soluble	so-lu-ble	*HAO/HOO/HOO*
solution	so-lu-tion	*HOO/HOO/HOO*
solve	so-l-ve	*HAO/***GDR/***HDO*
solvency	so-l-ve-ncy	*HAO/***GDR/GAR/GDR**
solvent	so-l-ve-nt	*HAO/***GDR/GAR/GDR**
Somaili	So-mai-li	*HOO/***GAR/GAR**
sombre	so-m-bre	*HAO/HDO/HDO*
some	so-me	**GAR/***HDO*
somersault	so-mer-sau-lt	*HAO/HDO/HOO/HDO*

Word	Mouthables	Mouth Movements Notations
son	so-n	*HAO/HDO*
song	son-g	*HAO/HDO*
sonny	son-ny	*HAO*/**GAR**
sonorous	so-no-rous	*HAO/HAO/HAO*
soon	soo-n	*HOO/HDO*
soot	soo-t	*HOO/HDO*
soothe	soo-the	*HOO/HTO*
sophisticated	so-phi-sti-ca-ted	*HAO*/**GAR/GAR**/*HAO*/**GRR**
sorbet	sor-bet	*HOO/HAO*
sordid	sor-di-d	*HOO*/**GAR**/*HDO*
sore	so-re	*HOO/HDO*
sorrow	so-rro-w	*HAO/HOO/HDO*
sorry	so-rry	*HAO*/**GDR**
sort	sor-t	*HOO/HOO*
sorted	sor-ted	*HOO*/**GRR**
sought	sough-t	*HOO/HOO*
soul	so-ul	*HOO/HDO*
soulful	so-ul-ful	*HOO/HDO/HDO*
sound	sou-n-d	**GAR/GDR**/*HDO*
soup	sou-p	*HOO/HDO*
sour	so-ur	**GAR/GAR**
source	sour-ce	*HOO/HDO*
south	sou-th	**GAR/GTR**
southerly	so-u-ther-ly	**GRR/GaAR/GTR/GDR**
southern	so-u-ther-n	**GRR/GAR/GTR/GDR**
sovereign	so-ver-eig-n	*HAO/HAO/HAO*/**GDR**
sovereignty	so-ver-eig-nty	*HAO/HAO/HAO*/**GDR**
sow	so-w	*HOO/HOO*
sow	so-we-d	*HOO/HOO/HOO*
sown	so-w-n	*HOO/HOO*/**GDR**
spa	spa	*HAO*

Word	Mouthables	Mouth Movements Notations
space	sp-a-ce	**GDR**/*HAO*/**GDR**
spacing	sp-a-ci-ng	**GDR**/*HAO*/**GAR**/**GDR**
spacious	sp-a-ci-ous	**GDR**/*HAO*/*HDO*/*HAO*
spade	sp-a-de	**GDR**/*HAO*/*HDO*
Spain	Sp-ai-n	**GDR**/*HAO*/**GDR**
span	spa-n	**GAR**/**GDR**
Spaniard	Spa-ni-ar-d	**GAR**/**GAR**/*HAO*/*HOO*
Spanish	Spa-ni-sh	**GAR**/**GAR**/*HDO*
spank	span-k	**GAR**/*HDO*
spanned	spa-nne-d	**GAR**/**GDR**/*HOO*
spanner	spa-nner	**GAR**/*HDO*
spare	spare	**GAR**
sparing	spar-i-ng	**GAR**/**GAR**/**GDR**
spark	spar-k	*HAO*/*HDO*
sparkle	spar-kle	*HAO*/*HOO*
sparkling	spar-k-li-ng	*HAO*/*HDO*/**GAR**/**GDR**
sparse	spar-se	*HAO*/*HDO*
spasm	spa-sm	**GAR**/*HDO*
spat	spa-t	**GAR**/**GRR**
spate	spa-te	*HAO*/*HOO*
spatter	spa-tter	**GAR**/*HDO*
spattered	spa-ttere-d	**GAR**/*HOO*/*HOO*
spay	spay	*HAO*
spayed	spaye-d	*HAO*/*HOO*
speak	spea-k	**GRR**/**GRR**
speaker	spea-ker	**GRR**/*HDO*
spear	spe-ar	**GRR**/*HAO*
spearmint	spe-ar-mi-nt	**GRR**/*HAO*/**GAR**/**GDR**
special	spe-cial	**GAR**/*HDO*
specialist	spe-ci-a-li-st	**GAR**/**GDR**/**GAR**/*HOO*
speciality	spe-ci-a-li-ty	**GAR**/**GDR**/**GAR**/**GAR**/**GAR**

Word	Mouthables	Mouth Movements Notations
specialize	spe-cia-li-ze	**GAR/GDR/GRR**/*HDO*
specific	spe-ci-fi-c	**GAR/GAR/GAR/GDR**
specify	spe-ci-fy	**GAR/GAR/GRR**
specimen	spe-ci-me-n	**GAR/GAR/GAR/GDR**
speckle	spe-ckle	**GAR**/*HOO*
specs	spe-cs	**GAR**/*HDO*
spectacle	spe-c-ta-cle	**GAR/GDR/GAR**/*HOO*
spectacular	spe-c-ta-cu-lar	**GAR/GDR/GAR**/*HOO*/*HAO*
spectator	spe-c-ta-tor	**GAR/GDR**/*HAO*/*HDO*
sped	spe-d	**GAR/GRR**
speech	spee-ch	**GRR**/*HDO*
speed	spee-d	**GRR/GRR**
speeding	spee-ding	**GRR/GDR**
speedy	spee-dy	**GRR/GAR**
spell	spe-ll	**GAR/GRR**
spelling	spe-lli-ng	**GAR/GAR/GDR**
spelt	spe-lt	**GAR/GDR**
spend	spe-nd	**GAR/GRR**
spent	spe-nt	**GAR/GRR**
sphere	s-phe-re	**GAR/GRR**/*HDO*
spherical	s-phe-ri-cal	**GAR/GAR/GAR**/*HDO*
sphinx	s-phi-nx	**GRR/GAR/GDR**
spice	spi-ce	**GRR/GDR**
spicy	spi-cy	**GRR/GAR**
spider	spi-der	**GRR**/*HDO*
spike	spi-ke	**GRR**/*HDO*
spikey	spi-key	**GRR/GAR**
spill	spi-ll	**GAR/GRR**
spin	spi-n	**GAR/GRR**
spinach	spi-nach	**GAR**/*HDO*
spine	spi-ne	**GRR/GDR**

Word	Mouthables	Mouth Movements Notations
spiny	spi-ny	**GRR/GAR**
spiral	spi-ral	**GRR/**_HDO_
spire	spi-re	**GRR/**_HDO_
spirit	spi-ri-t	**GAR/GAR/**_HOO_
spirited	spi-ri-ted	**GAR/GAR/GRR**
spiritual	spi-ri-tu-al	**GAR/GAR/**_HOO_**/GDR**
spit	spi-t	**GAR/GRR**
spite	spi-te	**GRR/**_HDO_
spiteful	spi-te-ful	**GRR/**_HDO_**/**_HOO_
spits	sp-i-ts	**GDR/GAR/**_HDO_
spittle	spi-ttle	**GAR/**_HOO_
splash	sp-la-sh	**GDR/GAR/**_HDO_
spleen	sp-lee-n	**GDR/GRR/GDR**
splendid	sp-le-n-di-d	**GDR/GAR/GDR/GAR/**_HDO_
splendour	sp-le-n-do-ur	**GDR/GAR/GDR/**_HAO_**/**_HDO_
splint	sp-li-nt	**GDR/GAR/GRR**
splinter	sp-li-n-ter	**GDR/GAR/GDR/**_HDO_
split	sp-li-t	**GDR/GAR/**_HOO_
splutter	sp-lu-tter	**GDR/GAR/**_HDO_
spoil	sp-oi-l	**GDR/GAR/GDR**
spoils	spoi-ls	**GAR/GDR**
spoke	spo-ke	_HOO_**/**_HDO_
spoken	spo-ken	_HOO_**/**_HDO_
spokesman	spo-kes-ma-n	_HOO_**/**_HDO_**/GAR/GDR**
sponge	spo-nge	**GAR/GDR**
sponger	spo-n-ger	**GAR/GDR/**_HDO_
spongy	spo-n-gy	**GAR/GDR/GAR**
sponsor	spo-n-sor	_HAO_**/**_HDO_**/**_HOO_
sponsorship	spo-n-sor-shi-p	_HAO_**/**_HDO_**/**_HOO_**/GAR/GDR**
spontaneous	spo-n-ta-ne-ous	_HAO_**/GDR/**_HAO_**/GAR/**_HAO_
spool	spoo-l	_HOO_**/**_HDO_

Word	Mouthables	Mouth Movements Notations
spoon	spoo-n	*HOO*/**GDR**
sport	spor-t	*HOO*/*HDO*
sporty	spor-ty	*HOO*/**GAR**
spot	sp-o-t	*HDO*/*HAO*/*HDO*
spotty	sp-o-tty	*HDO*/*HAO*/**GAR**
spout	sp-ou-t	*HDO*/*HAO*/*HDO*
sprain	sp-rai-n	**GDR**/*HAO*/**GDR**
sprang	sp-ra-ng	**GDR/GAR/GDR**
sprawl	sp-raw-l	*HDO*/*HOO*/*HDO*
spread	sp-rea-d	**GDR/GAR**/*HDO*
sprightly	sp-righ-t-ly	**GDR/GRR**/*HDO*/**GDR**
spring	sp-ri-ng	**GDR/GAR/GDR**
springy	sp-ri-ng-y	**GDR/GRR/GDR/GAR**
sprinkle	sp-ri-n-kle	**GDR/GAR/GDR**/*HOO*
sprinkler	sp-ri-n-kler	**GDR/GAR/GDR**/*HDO*
sprinkling	sp-ri-n-k-ling	**GDR/GAR/GDR**/*HOO*/**GDR**
sprint	sp-ri-n-t	**GDR/GAR/GDR**/*HDO*
sprout	sp-rou-t	*HDO*/*HAO*/*HOO*
spruce	sp-ru-ce	*HOO*/*HOO*/*HDO*
spun	sp-u-n	*HDO*/**GAR**/*HOO*
spur	sp-ur	*HDO*/*HAO*
spurt	sp-ur-t	**GDR/GAR**/*HOO*
sputter	sp-u-tter	**GDR/GAR**/*HDO*
spy	spy	**GRR**
squabble	squa-bble	**GAR**/*HOO*
squad	squa-d	*HAO*/*HOO*
squander	squa-n-der	**GAR/GDR**/*HDO*
square	squa-re	*HAO*/*HDO*
squash	squa-sh	**GAR**/*HDO*
squat	squa-t	**GAR**/*HOO*
squeak	squea-k	**GRR**/*HDO*

Word	Mouthables	Mouth Movements Notations
squeal	squea-l	**GRR/GDR**
squeamish	squea-m-i-sh	**GRR/GDR/GAR**/*HDO*
squeaze	squee-ze	**GRR/GDR**
squid	squi-d	**GAR**/*HOO*
squint	squi-nt	**GAR/GDR**
squire	squi-re	**GRR**/*HDO*
squirm	squir-m	*HOO/HDO*
squirrel	squi-rrel	**GAR**/*HOO*
squirt	squir-t	*HOO/HOO*
stab	sta-b	**GAR**/*HOO*
stability	sta-bi-li-ty	**GAR/GAR/GAR/GAR**
stable	sta-ble	*HAO/HOO*
stack	sta-ck	**GAR**/*HDO*
stadium	sta-di-um	*HAO*/**GAR**/*HDO*
staff	staf-f	*HAO/HDO*
stag	sta-g	**GAR**/*HDO*
stage	sta-ge	*HAO/HDO*
stagger	sta-gger	**GAR**/*HDO*
staging	sta-gi-ng	*HAO*/**GAR/GDR**
stagnant	sta-g-na-nt	**GAR/GDR/GAR/GDR**
stain	st-ai-n	**GRR**/*HAO*/**GDR**
stair	stair	**GAR**
stairs	sta-irs	**GAR**/*HDO*
stake	st-a-ke	**GDR**/*HAO/HDO*
stale	st a le	**GDR**/*HAO*/**GDR**
stalk	stal-k	*HOO/HDO*
stall	stal-l	*HOO/HOO*
stall	stal-l	*HOO/HDO*
stamina	sta-mi-na	**GAR/GAR/GAR**
stammer	sta-mm-er	**GAR/GDR**/*HDO*
stamp	sta-mp	**GAR/GDR**

Word	Mouthables	Mouth Movements Notations
stampede	sta-m-pe-de	**GAR/GDR/GRR/GDR**
stand	sta-nd	**GAR/GRR**
standard	sta-n-dar-d	**GAR/GDR**/*HAO*/*HOO*
standing	sta-n-di-ng	**GAR/GDR/GAR/GDR**
stank	sta-nk	**GAR/GRR**
staple	st-a-ple	**GRR**/*HAO*/*HOO*
stapler	st-a-p-ler	**GRR**/*HAO*/*HDO*/*HDO*
star	star	*HAO*
starch	star-ch	*HAO*/*HDO*
stare	sta-re	**GAR**/*HDO*
start	star-t	*HAO*/*HOO*
starter	star-ter	*HAO*/*HDO*
startle	star-tle	*HAO*/*HOO*
starve	star-ve	*HAO*/*HDO*
state	sta-te	*HAO*/*HDO*
stately	sta-te-ly	*HAO*/*HDO*/**GDR**
statement	sta-te-men-t	*HAO*/*HDO*/**GAR**/*HDO*
statesman	sta-tes-ma-n	*HAO*/*HDO*/**GAR/GDR**
station	sta-tion	*HAO*/*HOO*
stationer	sta-tion-er	*HAO*/*HOO*/*HDO*
stationery	sta-tion-er-y	*HAO*/*HOO*/*HOO*/*HDO*
statistics	sta-ti-sti-cs	**GAR/GAR/GAR/GDR**
statue	sta-tue	**GAR**/*HOO*
status	sta-tu-s	*HAO*/**GAR**/*HDO*
statute	sta-tu-te	**GAR**/*HOO*/*HDO*
stay	stay	*HAO*
steadfast	st-ea-d-fas-t	**GRR/GAR/GDR**/*HAO*/*HOO*
steady	st-ea-dy	**GRR/GAR/GAR**
steak	stea-k	*HAO*/*HDO*
steal	stea-l	**GRR/GDR**
stealthy	stea-l-th-y	**GAR/GDR/GTR/GAR**

Word	Mouthables	Mouth Movements Notations
steam	stea-m	**GRR**/*HDO*
steep	stee-p	**GRR**/*HDO*
steeple	stee-ple	**GRR**/*HOO*
steer	stee-r	**GRR**/*HDO*
stem	st-e-m	**GRR/GAR**/*HDO*
stench	st-e-n-ch	**GRR/GAR/GDR**/*HDO*
step	st-e-p	**GRR/GAR**/*HDO*
Stephen	Ste-phen	**GRR**/*HDO*
stereo	ste-re-o	**GAR/GRR**/*HOO*
sterile	ste-ri-le	**GAR/GRR/GDR**
sterility	ste-ri-li-ty	**GAR/GAR/GAR/GAR**
sterilize	ste-ri-li-ze	**GAR/GAR/GRR**/*HDO*
sterling	ster-li-ng	*HAO*/**GAR/GDR**
stern	ster-n	*HAO*/*HDO*
stetson	ste-t-so-n	**GAR**/*HOO*/*HAO*/*HDO*
stew	stew	*HOO*
steward	stew-ar-d	*HOO*/*HAO*/*HDO*
stick	sti-ck	**GAR/GRR**
stick	st-i-ck	**GRR/GAR**/*HDO*
sticker	sti-cker	**GAR**/*HDO*
stickler	st-i-ck-ler	**GRR/GAR**/*HDO*/*HDO*
sticky	sti-cky	**GRR/GAR**
stiff	sti-ff	**GAR**/*HDO*
stiffen	sti-ffen	**GAR**/*HDO*
stifle	sti-fle	**GRR**/*HOO*
still	sti-ll	**GAR/GDR**
stimulate	sti-mu-la-te	**GAR**/*HOO*/*HAO*/*HDO*
sting	sti-ng	**GAR/GRR**
stingy	sti-n-gy	**GAR/GDR/GAR**
stink	stin-k	**GAR/GRR**
stinking	stin-king	**GAR/GDR**

Word	Mouthables	Mouth Movements Notations
stir	stir	*HOO*
stitch	sti-tch	**GAR**/*HDO*
stock	stoc-k	*HAO*/*HDO*
Stockholm	Stoc-k-ho-lm	*HAO*/*HDO*/*HOO*/*HDO*
stocking	stoc-king	*HAO*/**GDR**
stodgy	sto-d-gy	*HAO*/**GDR**/**GAR**
stoke	sto-ke	*HOO*/*HDO*
stole	sto-le	*HOO*/*HOO*
stole	sto-le	*HOO*/*HDO*
stolen	sto-len	*HOO*/*HDO*
stolid	sto-li-d	*HAO*/**GAR**/*HDO*
stomach	sto-ma-ch	**GAR**/**GAR**/*HDO*
stone	sto-ne	*HOO*/**GDR**
stone	sto-nes	*HOO*/**GDR**
stony	sto-ny	*HOO*/**GAR**
stood	stoo-d	*HOO*/*HOO*
stool	stoo-l	*HOO*/*HDO*
stoop	stoo-p	*HOO*/*HDO*
stop	sto-p	*HAO*/*HDO*
store	sto-re	*HOO*/*HOO*
store	sto-re	*HAO*/*HDO*
stored	sto-re-d	*HOO*/*HOO*/*HOO*
storey	sto-rey	*HAO*/**GAR**
stork	stor-k	*HOO*/*HDO*
storm	stor-m	*HOO*/**GDR**
stormy	stor-my	*HOO*/**GAR**
story	sto-ry	*HOO*/**GAR**
story	sto-ry	*HAO*/**GDR**
stout	stou-t	**GAR**/*HOO*
stove	sto-ve	*HOO*/*HDO*
stow	sto-w	*HOO*/*HDO*

Word	Mouthables	Mouth Movements Notations
stowed	sto-we-d	*HOO/HOO/HOO*
straight	st-raigh-t	**GDR**/*HAO*/*HOO*
strain	st-rai-n	**GDR**/*HAO*/**GDR**
strange	st-ran-ge	**GDR**/*HAO*/*HDO*
stranger	st-ra-n-ger	**GDR**/*HAO*/**GDR**/*HDO*
strangle	st-ran-gle	**GDR**/**GAR**/*HOO*
strap	st-ra-p	**GDR**/**GAR**/*HDO*
strapping	st-ra-pping	**GDR**/**GAR**/**GDR**
Strasbourg	St-ra-s-bour-g	**GDR**/**GAR**/**GDR**/*HOO*/*HDO*
stratagem	st-ra-ta-ge-m	**GDR**/**GAR**/**GAR**/**GDR**
strategic	st-ra-te-gi-c	**GDR**/**GAR**/**GRR**/**GAR**/**GDR**
strategy	st-ra-te-gy	**GDR**/**GAR**/*HAO*/**GAR**
straw	s-traw	**GRR**/*HOO*
strawberry	s-traw-ber-ry	**GRR**/*HOO*/*HAO*/**GAR**
stray	s-tray	**GRR**/*HAO*
streak	strea-k	**GRR**/*HDO*
stream	s-trea-m	**GRR**/**GRR**/*HDO*
streamer	s-trea-mer	**GRR**/**GRR**/*HDO*
street	stree-t	**GRR**/*HOO*
strength	st-re-ng-th	**GDR**/**GAR**/**GDR**/**GTR**
strengthen	st-re-ng-then	**GDR**/**GAR**/**GDR**/*HTO*
stress	s-tre-ss	**GRR**/**GAR**/*HDO*
stretch	s-tre-tch	**GRR**/**GAR**/*HDO*
stretcher	s-tre-tcher	**GRR**/**GAR**/*HDO*
stretchy	s-tre-tchy	**GRR**/**GAR**/**GAR**
strew	strew	*HOO*
strew	strewe-d	*HOO/HOO*
strewn	strew-n	*HOO*/**GDR**
strict	s-tri-ct	**GRR**/**GAR**/**GDR**
stridden	s-tri-dden	**GRR**/**GAR**/*HDO*
stride	s-tri-de	**GRR**/**GRR**/**GRR**

Word	Mouthables	Mouth Movements Notations
strike	stri-ke	**GRR/GRR**
strike	stri-ke	**GRR**/*HDO*
string	s-tri-ng	**GRR/GAR/GRR**
string	str-i-ng	**GRR/GAR/GDR**
stringent	s-tri-n-ge-nt	**GRR/GAR/GDR/GAR/GDR**
strip	s-tri-p	**GRR/GAR**/*HDO*
stripe	stri-pe	**GRR**/*HDO*
stripper	s-tri-pper	**GRR/GAR**/*HDO*
stripy	s-tri-py	**GRR/GRR/GAR**
strive	s-tri-ve	**GRR/GRR/GRR**
strode	stro-de	*HOO/HOO*
stroke	stro-ke	*HOO/HDO*
stroll	stro-ll	*HOO*/**GRR**
stroller	stro-ller	*HOO/HDO*
strong	stro-ng	*HAO*/**GDR**
strove	str-o-ve	*HOO/HOO/HOO*
struck	stru-ck	**GAR**/*HOO*
structure	s-tru-c-tu-re	**GRR/GAR/GDR**/*HOO/HDO*
struggle	s-tru-ggle	**GRR/GAR**/*HOO*
strung	s-tru-ng	**GRR/GAR/GRR**
strut	s-tru-t	**GRR/GAR**/*HOO*
stub	s-tu-b	**GRR/GAR**/*HDO*
stubborn	s-tu-bbor-n	**GRR/GAR**/*HOO*/**GDR**
stuck	s-tu-ck	**GRR/GAR**/*HOO*
stud	s-tu-d	**GRR/GAR**/*HOO*
student	stu-de-nt	*HOO*/**GAR/GDR**
studio	stu-di-o	*HOO*/**GAR**/*HOO*
study	s-tu-dy	**GRR/GAR/GAR**
stuff	s-tu-ff	**GRR/GAR**/*HDO*
stuffing	s-tu-ffing	**GRR/GAR/GDR**
stuffy	s-tu-ffy	**GRR/GAR/GAR**

Word	Mouthables	Mouth Movements Notations
stumble	s-tu-m-ble	GRR/GAR/*HDO*/*HOO*
stump	s-tu-mp	GRR/GAR/*HDO*
stun	s-tu-n	GRR/GAR/GRR
stung	s-tu-ng	GRR/GAR/GRR
stunk	s-tu-nk	GRR/GAR/GRR
stupefy	stu-pe-fy	*HOO*/GRR/GRR
stupid	stu-pi-d	*HOO*/GAR/GDR
stupidity	stu-pi-di-ty	*HOO*/GAR/GAR/GAR
stupor	stu-por	*HOO*/*HDO*
sturdy	stur-dy	*HAO*/GAR
stutter	s-tu-tter	GRR/GAR/*HDO*
sty	s-ty	GRR/GRR
style	s-ty-le	GRR/GRR/GDR
stylish	s-ty-li-sh	GRR/GRR/GAR/*HDO*
stylized	s-ty-li-ze-d	GRR/GRR/GDR/*HOO*
subdue	su-b-due	GAR/*HDO*/*HOO*
subject	su-b-je-ct	GAR/*HDO*/GAR/*HOO*
subjective	su-b-jec-ti-ve	GAR/*HDO*/GAR/GAR/GDR
sublime	su-bli-me	GAR/GRR/*HDO*
subliminal	su-bli-mi-nal	GAR/GAR/GAR/*HDO*
submarine	su-b-ma-ri-ne	GAR/*HDO*/GAR/GAR/GDR
subpoena	su-b-p(o)e-na	GAR/*HDO*/GRR/GAR
subscribe	su-b-scri-be	GAR/*HDO*/GRR/*HDO*
subscription	su-b-scri-p-tion	GAR/*HOO*/GAR/*HDO*/*HOO*
subsequent	su-b-se-que-nt	GAR/*HDO*/GAR/GAR/GDR
subside	su-b-si-de	GAR/*HDO*/GRR/*HDO*
subsidy	su-b-si-dy	GAR/*HDO*/GAR/GAR
subsistence	su-b-si-ste-nce	GAR/*HDO*/GAR/GAR/GDR
subsoil	su-b-soi-l	GAR/*HDO*/GAR/GDR
substance	su-b-sta-nce	GAR/*HDO*/GAR/GDR
substantial	su-b-sta-n-tial	GAR/*HDO*/GAR/GDR/*HDO*

Word	Mouthables	Mouth Movements Notations
substitional	su-b-sti-tu-tion-al	GAR/*HDO*/GAR/*HOO*/*HOO*/*HDO*
substitute	su-b-sti-tu-te	GAR/*HDO*/GAR/*HOO*/*HDO*
subterfuge	su-b-ter-fu-ge	GAR/*HDO*/*HAO*/*HOO*/*HDO*
subtitle	su-b-ti-tle	GAR/*HDO*/GRR/*HOO*
subtle	sub-tle	GAR/*HOO*
subtraction	su-b-tra-c-tion	GAR/*HDO*/GAR/GDR/*HOO*
suburb	su-bur-b	GAR/GAR/*HDO*
suburban	su-bur-ba-n	GAR/GAR/GAR/GDR
suburbia	su-bur-bi-a	GAR/GAR/GAR/GAR
subversive	su-b-ver-si-ve	GAR/*HDO*/*HOO*/GAR/GDR
subvert	su-b-ver-t	GAR/*HDO*/*HOO*/*HOO*
subway	su-b-way	GAR/*HDO*/*HAO*
succeed	su-c-cee-d	GAR/GDR/GRR/GRR
success	su-c-ce-ss	GAR/GDR/GAR/GDR
successor	su-c-ce-ssor	GAR/GDR/GAR/*HDO*
succint	su-c-ci-nct	GAR/GDR/GAR/GDR
succour	su-c-cour	GAR/GDR/*HAO*
succulent	su-c-cu-le-nt	GAR/GDR/*HOO*/GAR/GDR
such	su-ch	GAR/*HDO*
suck	su-ck	GAR/*HDO*
sucker	su-cker	GAR/*HDO*
sudden	su-dden	GAR/*HDO*
sue	sue	*HOO*
suede	s-ue-de	GRR/*HAO*/*HDO*
suet	su-et	*HOO*/GDR
suffer	su-ffer	GAR/*HDO*
suffering	su-ffe-ring	GAR/*HDO*/GDR
sufficient	su-ffi-ci-e-nt	GAR/GAR/GAR/GAR/GDR
suffix	su-ff-i-x	GAR/*HDO*/GAR/GDR
suffocate	su-ffo-ca-te	GAR/*HOO*/*HAO*/*HDO*
suffrage	su-ff-ra-ge	GAR/*HDO*/*HAO*/*HDO*

Word	Mouthables	Mouth Movements Notations
sugar	su-gar	*HOO/HDO*
suggest	su-gge-st	**GAR/GAR**/*HOO*
suggestible	su-gge-sti-ble	**GAR/GAR/GAR**/*HOO*
suggestion	su-gge-stion	**GAR/GAR**/*HOO*
suggestive	su-gge-sti-ve	**GAR/GAR/GAR**/*HDO*
suicidal	su-i-ci-dal	*HOO*/**GAR/GRR**/*HOO*
suicide	su-i-ci-de	*HOO*/**GAR/GRR**/*HDO*
suit	sui-t	*HOO/HOO*
suit	sui-t	*HOO/HDO*
suitable	sui-ta-ble	*HOO*/**GAR**/*HOO*
suitcase	sui-t-ca-se	*HOO/HDO/HAO/HDO*
suite	s-(u)i-te	**GRR/GAR**/*HDO*
suited	sui-ted	*HOO*/**GRR**
sulfur	su-l-fur	**GAR/GDR**/*HDO*
sulky	su-l-ky	**GAR/GDR/GAR**
sully	su-lly	**GAR/GDR**
sulphur	su-l-phur	**GAR/GDR**/*HDO*
sultana	su-l-tan-a	**GAR/GDR**/*HAO*/**GAR**
sultry	su-l-try	**GAR/GDR/GDR**
sum	su-m	**GAR/GDR**
summarize	su-mma-ri-ze	**GAR/GAR/GRR/GDR**
summary	su-mma-ry	**GAR/GAR**/*HDO*
summer	su-mmer	**GAR**/*HDO*
summit	su-mmi-t	**GAR/GAR**/*HOO*
summon	su-mmo-n	**GAR/GAR/GDR**
summoned	su-m-mo-ne-d	**GAR/GDR**/*HAO*/**GDR**/*HOO*
sumptuous	su-mp-tu-ous	**GAR**/*HDO/HOO*/**GAR**
sun	su-n	**GAR/GDR**
sunburn	su-n-bur-n	**GAR/GDR**/*HDO*/**GDR**
sundae	sun-dae	**GAR**/*HAO*
Sunday	Su-n-day	**GAR/GDR**/*HAO*

Word	Mouthables	Mouth Movements Notations
sundial	su-n-di-a-l	**GAR/GDR/GRR/GAR/GDR**
sung	su-ng	**GAR/GDR**
sunglasses	su-n-glas-se-s	**GAR/GDR**/*HAO*/**GAR/GDR**
sunny	su-nny	**GAR/GAR**
sunrise	su-n-ri-se	**GAR/GDR/GRR**/*HDO*
sunset	su-n-se-t	**GAR/GDR/GAR**/*HOO*
sunshine	su-n-shi-ne	**GAR/GDR/GRR/GDR**
sunstroke	su-n-stro-ke	**GAR/GDR**/*HOO*/*HDO*
suntan	su-n-ta-n	**GAR/GDR/GAR/GDR**
super	su-per	*HOO*/*HDO*
superb	su-per-b	*HOO*/*HAO*/*HDO*
supercilious	su-per-ci-li-ous	**GAR/GAR/GAR/GAR/GAR**
superficial	su-per-fi-ci-al	*HOO*/*HAO*/**GAR/GDR**/*HDO*
superfluous	su-per-flu-ous	**GAR**/*HAO*/*HOO*/*HAO*
superior	su-pe-ri-or	*HOO*/**GRR/GAR**/*HDO*
superlative	su-per-la-ti-ve	*HOO*/*HAO*/**GAR/GAR/GDR**
supersede	su-per-se-de	*HOO*/*HAO*/**GRR**/*HDO*
superstitious	su-per-sti-ti-ous	*HOO*/*HAO*/**GAR**/*HDO*/*HAO*
supervise	su-per-vi-se	*HOO*/*HAO*/**GRR**/*HDO*
supervision	su-per-vi-sion	*HOO*/*HAO*/**GAR**/*HOO*
supper	su-pper	**GAR**/*HDO*
supple	su-pple	**GAR**/*HOO*
supplement	su-pp-le-me-nt	**GAR/GDR/GAR/GAR/GDR**
supply	su-pp-ly	**GAR/GDR/GRR**
support	su-ppor-t	**GAR**/*HOO*/*HOO*
suppose	su-ppo-se	**GAR**/*HOO*/*HDO*
suppository	su-ppo-si-to-ry	**GAR**/*HAO*/**GAR**/*HOO*/**GDR**
suppress	su-ppre-ss	**GAR/GAR**/*HDO*
supremacy	su-pre-ma-cy	*HOO*/**GAR/GAR/GAR**
supreme	su-pre-me	*HOO*/**GRR**/*HDO*
surcharge	sur-char-ge	**GAR**/*HAO*/*HDO*

Word	Mouthables	Mouth Movements Notations
sure	su-re	*HOO/HDO*
surety	su-re-ty	*HOO*/GAR/GAR
surface	sur-fa-ce	*HAO/HAO*/GDR
surfing	sur-fi-ng	*HAO*/GAR/GDR
surge	sur-ge	*HAO/HDO*
surgeon	sur-ge-o-n	*HAO/HDO/HAO/HDO*
surgery	sur-ge-ry	*HAO/HDO*/GDR
surly	sur-ly	GAR/GDR
surname	sur-na-me	*HAO/HAO/HDO*
surplus	sur-plu-s	*HAO*/GAR/*HDO*
surprise	sur-pri-se	*HAO*/GRR/*HDO*
surrender	sur-re-n-der	*HAO*/GAR/GDR/*HDO*
surreptitious	su-rre-p-ti-ti-ous	GAR/GAR/GDR/GAR/GDR/*HAO*
surrogate	su-rro-ga-te	GAR/*HOO/HAO/HDO*
surround	su-rrou-nd	GAR/GAR/GDR
surroundings	su-rrou-n-dings	GAR/GAR/GDR/GDR
surtax	sur-ta-x	*HAO*/GAR/GDR
survey	sur-vey	*HAO/HAO*
surveyor	sur-vey-or	*HAO/HAO/HDO*
survival	sur-vi-val	GAR/GRR/*HDO*
survive	sur-vi-ve	GAR/GRR/*HDO*
survivor	sur-vi-vor	GAR/GRR/*HDO*
susceptible	su-s-ce-pti-ble	GAR/GDR/GAR/GAR/*HOO*
suspect	su-s-pe-ct	GAR/GDR/GAR/*HOO*
suspend	su-s-pe-nd	GAR/GDR/GARGDR
suspenders	su-s-pe-n-der-s	GAR/GDR/GAR/GDR/*HDO/HDO*
suspense	su-s-pe-n-se	GAR/GDR/GAR/GDR/*HDO*
suspension	su-s-pe-n-sion	GAR/GDR/GAR/GDR/*HOO*
suspicion	su-s-pi-cion	GAR/GDR/GAR/*HDO*
suspicious	su-s-pi-ci-ous	GAR/GDR/GAR/*HDO/HAO*
sustain	su-stai-n	GAR/*HAO*/GDR

Word	Mouthables	Mouth Movements Notations
Suzy	Su-zy	*HOO*/**GAR**
swallow	swa-llow	**GAR**/*HOO*
swallow	swa-llo-we-d	**GAR**/*HOO*/*HOO*/*HOO*
swallow	swal-lo-w	*HAO*/*HOO*/*HDO*
swam	swa-m	**GAR/GRR**
swamp	swam-p	*HOO*/*HDO*
swampy	swam-py	*HOO*/**GAR**
swan	swa-n	*HOO*/**GDR**
swap	sw-a-p	*HOO*/*HAO*/*HDO*
swarm	swar-m	*HOO*/**GDR**
sway	s-way	**GRR**/*HAO*
swear	swea-r	**GAR/GRR**
sweat	swea-t	**GAR/GRR**
sweater	swea-ter	**GAR**/*HDO*
Swede	S-we-de	**GRR/GRR**/*HDO*
Sweden	S-we-den	**GRR/GRR**/*HDO*
Swedish	S-we-di-sh	**GRR/GRR/GAR**/*HDO*
sweep	s-wee-p	**GRR/GRR/GRR**
sweeper	s-wee-per	**GRR/GRR**/*HDO*
sweet	s-wee-t	**GRR/GRR/GRR**
sweeten	s-wee-ten	**GRR/GRR**/*HDO*
sweetener	s-wee-ten-er	**GRR/GRR**/*HDO*/*HDO*
swell	s-we-ll	**GRR/GAR/GDR**
swelling	s-we-lli-ng	**GRR/GAR/GAR/GDR**
sweltering	s-we-l-ter-ing	**GRR/GAR/GDR**/*HDO*/**GDR**
swept	s-we-pt	**GRR/GAR/GRR**
swerve	s-wer-ve	**GRR**/*HAO*/*HOO*
swerved	s-wer-ve-d	**GRR**/*HAO*/*HOO*/*HOO*
swerve	s-wer-ve	**GRR**/*HAO*/*HDO*
swift	s-wi-ft	**GRR/GAR**/*HDO*
swim	s-wi-m	**GRR/GAR/GDR**

Word	Mouthables	Mouth Movements Notations
swimming	s-wi-m-mi-ng	GRR/GAR/GDR/GAR/GDR
swindle	s-wi-n-dle	GRR/GAR/GDR/*HOO*
swine	s-wi-ne	GRR/GRR/GDR
swing	s-wi-ng	GRR/GAR/GRR
swingeing	s-wi-n-geing	GRR/GAR/GDR/GDR
swinging	s-win-ging	GRR/GAR/GDR
swipe	sw-i-pe	GRR/GRR/GDR
swirl	swir-l	*HOO/HDO*
Swiss	S-wi-ss	GRR/GAR/GDR
switch	s-wi-tch	GRR/GAR/*HDO*
Switzerland	Swi-t-zer-lan-d	GAR/*HOO*/GAR/GAR/*HOO*
swollen	swo-lle-n	*HOO*/GAR/GDR
swoop	swoo-p	*HOO/HDO*
sword	swor-d	*HOO/HDO*
swore	swore	*HAO*
sworn	swor-n	*HOO*/GDR
swot	swo-t	*HAO/HOO*
swum	s-wu-m	GRR/GAR/*HDO*
swung	s-wu-ng	GRR/GAR/GRR
syllable	sy-lla-ble	GAR/GAR/*HOO*
syllabus	sy-lla-bu-s	GAR/GAR/GAR/*HDO*
symbol	sy-m-bo-l	GAR/*HDO/HAO/HDO*
symbolic	sy-m-bo-li-c	GAR/*HDO/HAO*/GAR/GDR
symbolize	sy-m-bo-li-ze	GAR/*HDO/HAO*/GRR/GDR
symmetrical	sy-mme-tri-cal	GAR/GAR/GAR/*HDO*
symmetry	sy-m-me-try	GAR/GDR/GAR/*HDO*
sympathetic	sy-m-pa-the-ti-c	GAR/GDR/GAR/GTR/GAR/GDR
sympathize	sy-m-pa-thi-ze	GAR/GDR/GAR/GTR/*HDO*
sympathizer	sy-m-pa-thi-zer	GAR/GDR/GAR/GTR/*HDO*
sympathy	sy-m-pa-th-y	GAR/GDR/GTR/GAR
symphonic	sy-m-pho-ni-c	GAR/GDR/*HAO*/GAR/GDR

Word	Mouthables	Mouth Movements Notations
symphony	sy-m-pho-ny	GAR/GDR/*HOO*/GAR
symptom	sy-mp-to-m	GAR/GDR/*HAO*/*HDO*
synagogue	sy-na-go-gue	GAR/GAR/*HAO*/*HDO*
synchronize	sy-n-chro-ni-ze	GAR/GDR/*HOO*/GRR/*HDO*
syncopate	sy-n-co-pa-te	GAR/GDR/*HOO*/*HAO*/*HDO*
syndicate	sy-n-di-ca-te	GAR/GDR/GAR/*HAO*/*HDO*
synonym	sy-no-ny-m	GAR/*HOO*/GAR/*HDO*
syntax	sy-n-ta-x	GAR/GDR/GAR/GDR
synthesis	sy-n-th-e-si-s	GAR/GDR/GTR/GAR/GAR/GDR
synthesize	sy-n-th-e-si-ze	GAR/GDR/GTR/GAR/GRR/GDR
synthetic	sy-n-th-e-ti-c	GAR/GDR/GTR/GAR/GAR/GDR
syphon	sy-pho-n	GRR/*HAO*/*HDO*
Syria	Sy-ri-a	GAR/GAR/GAR
syringe	sy-ri-nge	GAR/GAR/GDR
syrup	sy-ru-p	GAR/GAR/*HDO*
system	sy-ste-m	GAR/GAR/*HDO*

Word	Mouthables	Mouth Movements Notations
T		
T	T	**GRR**
tab	ta-b	**GAR**/*HDO*
table	ta-ble	*HAO/HOO*
tablet	ta-b-le-t	**GAR**/*HDO*/**GAR**/*HOO*
tabloid	ta-b-loi-d	**GAR/GDR/GAR**/*HOO*
taboo	ta-boo	**GAR**/*HOO*
tachometer	ta-c-ho-me-ter	**GAR/GDR**/*HOO*/**GAR**/*HDO*
tack	tac-k	**GAR**/*HDO*
tackle	tac-kle	**GAR**/*HOO*
tacky	ta-c-ky	**GAR/GDR/GAR**
tact	ta-c-t	**GAR/GDR**/*HOO*
tactics	ta-c-ti-cs	**GAR/GDR/GAR/GDR**
tag	ta-g	**GAR**/*HDO*
tail	tai-l	*HAO*/**GDR**
tailor	tai-lor	*HAO/HDO*
taint	tai-nt	*HAO*/**GRR**
take	ta-ke	*HAO*/**GRR**
taken	ta-ke-n	*HAO*/**GAR/GRR**
takings	ta-ki-ng-s	*HAO*/**GAR/GDR**/*HDO*
talc	ta-lc	**GAR/GDR**
tale	ta-le	*HAO*/**GDR**
talent	ta-le-nt	**GAR/GAR/GDR**
talisman	ta-li-s-ma-n	**GAR/GAR/GDR/GAR/GDR**
talk	tal-k	*HOO/HOO*
talkative	tal-ka-ti-ve	*HOO*/**GAR/GAR**/*HDO*
tall	tal-l	*HOO/HDO*
tallow	ta-llo-w	**GAR**/*HOO/HDO*
tally	ta-lly	**GAR/GAR**
talon	ta-lo-n	**GAR**/*HAO/HDO*
tame	ta-me	*HAO/HDO*

Word	Mouthables	Mouth Movements Notations
tamer	ta-mer	*HAO/HDO*
tampon	ta-m-po-n	**GAR**/*HDO/HAO/HDO*
tan	ta-n	**GAR/GDR**
tang	ta-ng	**GAR/GDR**
tangent	ta-n-ge-nt	**GAR/GDR/GAR/GDR**
tangerine	ta-n-ge-ri-ne	**GAR/GDR**/*HDO*/**GAR/GDR**
tangle	tan-gle	**GAR**/*HOO*
tank	tan-k	**GAR**/*HDO*
tankard	tan-kar-d	**GAR**/*HAO/HDO*
tanker	tan-ker	**GAR**/*HDO*
tannery	ta-nne-ry	**GAR/GAR**/*/HDO*
tantalize	ta-n-ta-li-ze	**GAR/GDR/GAR/GRR/GDR**
tap	ta-p	**GAR**/*HDO*
tape	ta-pe	*HAO/HDO*
taper	ta-per	*HAO/HDO*
tapestry	ta-pe-stry	**GAR/GAR**/*HDO*
tar	tar	*HAO*
target	tar-ge-t	*HAO*/**GAR**/*HOO*
tariff	ta-ri-ff	**GAR/GAR**/*HDO*
tarnish	tar-ni-sh	**GAR/GAR**/*HDO*
tart	tar-t	*HAO/HOO*
tartar	tar-tar	*HAO/HAO*
task	tas-k	*HAO/HDO*
taste	ta-ste	*HAO/HDO*
tasteful	ta-ste-ful	*HAO/HDO/HOO*
tasteless	ta-ste-le-ss	*HAO/HDO*/**GAR/GDR**
taster	ta-ster	*HAO/HDO*
taters	ta-tter-s	**GAR**/*HDO/HDO*
tattered	ta-ttere-d	**GAR**/*HOO/HOO*
tattoo	ta-ttoo	**GAR**/*HOO*
taught	taugh-t	*HOO/HOO*

Word	Mouthables	Mouth Movements Notations
taunt	tau-n-t	GAR/GDR/GRR
taut	tau-t	*HOO/HDO*
tawny	taw-ny	*HOO*/GAR
tax	ta-x	GAR/GRR
taxed	ta-xe-d	GAR/*HOO/HOO*
taxable	ta-xa-ble	GAR/GAR/*HOO*
taxi	ta-xi	GAR/GAR
taxicab	ta-xi-ca-b	GAR/GAR/GAR/*HDO*
tea	tea	GRR
teach	tea-ch	GRR/GRR
teacher	tea-cher	GRR/*HDO*
teaching	tea-chi-ng	GAR/GAR/GDR
team	tea-m	GRR/*HDO*
tear	tear	GAR
tear	te-ar	GRR/*HAO*
tease	tea-se	GRR/*HDO*
teaser	tea-ser	GRR/*HDO*
teat	tea-t	GRR/*HOO*
technical	te-ch-ni-cal	GAR/*HDO*/GAR/*HDO*
technicality	te-ch-ni-ca-li-ty	GAR/*HDO*/GAR/GAR/GAR/GAR
technology	te-ch-no-lo-gy	GAR/*HDO/HAO/HOO*/GAR
teenager	tee-na-ger	GRR/*HAO/HDO*
teens	tee-ns	GRR/GDR
teeth	tee-th	GRR/GTR
teetotal	tee-to-tal	GRR/*HOO/HDO*
telegram	te-le-gra-m	GAR/GAR/GAR/*HDO*
telegraphe	te-le-graphe	GAR/GAR/*HDO*
telephone	te-le-pho-ne	GAR/GAR/*HOO*/GDR
telephonist	te-le-pho-ni-st	GAR/GAR/*HOO*/GAR/*HOO*
telescope	te-le-sco-pe	GAR/GAR/*HOO/HDO*
televise	te-le-vi-se	GAR/GAR/GRR/*HDO*

Word	Mouthables	Mouth Movements Notations
television	te-le-vi-sion	GAR/GAR/GAR/*HOO*
telex	te-le-x	GAR/GAR/GDR
tell	te-ll	GAR/GRR
teller	tel-ler	GAR/*HDO*
telling	te-lling	GAR/GDR
telly	te-lly	GAR/GAR
temp	te-mp	GAR/*HDO*
temper	te-m-per	GAR/*HDO*/*HDO*
temperamental	te-m-pe-ra-men-tal	GAR/*HDO*/*HAO*/GAR/GAR/*HDO*
temperate	te-m-pe-ra-te	GAR/*HDO*/*HAO*/*HAO*/*HDO*
temperature	te-m-pe-ra-tu-re	GAR/*HDO*/*HAO*/GAR/*HOO*/*HDO*
temple	te-m-ple	GAR/*HDO*/*HOO*
temporary	te-m-por-a-ry	GAR/*HDO*/*HOO*/GAR/*HDO*
tempt	tem-p-t	GAR/*HDO*/*HOO*
temptation	tem-p-ta-tion	GAR/*HDO*/*HAO*/*HOO*
tempting	tem-p-ti-ng	GAR/*HDO*/GAR/GDR
ten	te-n	GAR/GDR
tenacious	te-na-ci-ous	GAR/*HAO*/*HDO*/*HAO*
tenancy	te-nan-cy	GAR/GAR/GDR
tenant	te-nan-t	GAR/GAR/*HOO*
tend	te-nd	GAR/GDR
tendency	te-n-de-n-cy	GAR/GDR/GAR/GDR/GAR
tender	te-n-der	GAR/GDR/*HDO*
tendon	te-n-do-n	GAR/GDR/*HAO*/*HDO*
tenement	te-ne-me-nt	GAR/GAR/GAR/GDR
tenner	ten-ner	GAR/*HDO*
tennis	ten-ni-s	GAR/GAR/GDR
tenor	te-nor	GAR/*HOO*
tense	ten-se	GAR/*HDO*
tense	te-n-se	GAR/GDR/GRR
tension	te-n-sion	GAR/GDR/*HOO*

Word	Mouthables	Mouth Movements Notations
tent	ten-t	**GAR**/*HDO*
tentative	te-n-ta-ti-ve	**GAR/GDR/GAR/GAR/GDR**
tenth	te-n-th	**GAR/GDR/GTR**
tenure	te-nu-re	**GAR**/*HOO/HDO*
tepid	te-pi-d	**GAR/GAR**/*HDO*
term	ter-m	*HOO/HDO*
terminal	ter-mi-nal	*HOO*/**GAR**/*HDO*
terminally	ter-mi-na-lly	*HOO*/**GAR/GAR/GDR**
terminus	ter-mi-nus	*HOO*/**GAR/GAR**
termite	ter-mi-te	*HOO*/**GRR**/*HDO*
terrace	te-rra-ce	**GAR/GAR/GDR**
terracotta	te-rra-co-tta	**GAR/GAR**/*HAO*/**GAR**
terrestrial	te-rre-stri-a-l	**GAR/GAR/GAR/GAR/GDR**
terrible	te-rri-ble	**GAR/GAR**/*HOO*
terribly	te-rri-bly	**GAR/GAR/GDR**
terrific	te-rri-fi-c	**GAR/GAR/GAR/GDR**
terrified	te-rri-fie-d	**GAR/GAR/GRR**/*HOO*
terrify	te-rri-fy	**GAR/GAR/GRR**
territory	te-rri-to-ry	**GAR/GAR**/*HAO/HDO*
terror	te-rror	**GAR**/*HDO*
terrorism	te-rror-i-sm	**GAR**/*HDO*/**GAR/GDR**
terrorist	te-rror-i-st	**GAR**/*HDO*/**GAR**/*HOO*
terrorize	te-rro-ri-ze	**GAR**/*HOO*/**GRR/GDR**
terse	ter-se	**GAR**/*HDO*
tertiary	ter-tia-ry	**GAR**/*IIDO*/**GDR**
test	te-st	**GAR/GRR**
testament	te-sta-me-nt	**GAR/GAR/GAR/GDR**
testicle	te-sti-cle	**GAR/GAR**/*HOO*
testify	te-sti-fy	**GAR/GAR/GRR**
testimonial	te-sti-mo-ni-a-l	**GAR/GAR**/*HOO*/**GAR/GAR/GDR**
testimony	te-sti-mo-ny	**GAR/GAR**/*HOO*/**GAR**

Word	Mouthables	Mouth Movements Notations
testing	te-sti-ng	**GAR/GAR/GDR**
text	te-xt	**GAR/GDR**
textile	te-x-ti-le	**GAR/GDR/GRR/GDR**
texture	te-x-tu-re	**GAR/GDR**/*HOO/HDO*
Thames	Tha-me-s	*HAO/HDO/HDO*
than	th-a-n	**GTR/GAR/GDR**
thank	th-an-k	**GTR/GAR**/*HDO*
thankful	th-an-k-ful	**GTR/GAR**/*HDO/HOO*
thankless	th-an-k-le-ss	**GTR/GAR**/*HDO*/**GAR/GDR**
thanks	th-an-k-s	**GTR/GAR**/*HDO/HDO*
that	th-a-t	**GTR/GAR**/*HOO*
thatch	th-a-tch	**GTR/GAR**/*HDO*
thaw	th-aw	*HTO/HOO*
the	th-e	**GTR/GAR**
the	th-e	**GTR/GRR**
theatre	th-ea-tre	**GTR/GRR**/*HDO*
theatrical	th-e-a-tri-cal	**GTR/GRR/GAR/GAR**/*HDO*
theft	th-e-ft	**GTR/GAR**/*HDO*
their	th-eir	**GTR/GAR**
theirs	th-eir-s	**GTR/GAR**/*HDO*
them	th-e-m	**GTR/GAR**/*HDO*
theme	th-e-me	**GTR/GRR**/*HDO*
themselves	th-e-m-se-lves	**GTR/GAR**/*HDO*/**GAR/GDR**
then	th-e-n	**GTR/GAR/GDR**
theologian	th-e-o-lo-gi-a-n	**GTR/GRR**/*HOO/HAO*/**GAR/GAR/GDR**
theorem	th-e-o-re-m	**GTR/GRR**/*HOO*/**GAR**/*HDO*
theoretical	th-e-o-re-ti-cal	**GTR/GRR**/*HOO*/**GAR/GAR**/*HDO*
theoretician	th-e-o-re-ti-cian	**GTR/GRR**/*HOO*/**GAR/GAR/GDR**
theorist	th-e-o-ri-st	**GTR/GRR**/*HOO*/**GAR**/*HDO*
theorize	th-e-o-ri-ze	**GTR/GRR**/*HOO*/**GRR/GDR**

Word	Mouthables	Mouth Movements Notations
theory	th-e-o-ry	**GTR/GRR/**_HOO/HDO_
therapeutic	th-e-ra-peu-ti-c	**GTR/GAR/GAR/**_HOO/_**GAR/GDR**
therapy	th-e-ra-py	**GTR/GAR/GAR/GAR**
there	th-ere	_HTO/HDO_
thermal	th-er-mal	_HTO/HAO/HDO_
thermometer	th-er-mo-me-ter	_HTO/HAO/HAO/_**GAR/**_HDO_
thermonuclear	th-er-mo-nu-cle-ar	_HTO/HAO/HOO/HOO/_**GRR/**_HAO_
thermos	th-er-mo-s	_HTO/HAO/HAO/HDO_
these	th-e-se	**GTR/GRR/GDR**
thesis	th-e-si-s	**GTR/GRR/GAR/GDR**
they	th-ey	**GTR/**_HAO_
thick	th-i-ck	**GTR/GAR/**_HDO_
thicken	th-i-cken	**GTR/GAR/**_HDO_
thicket	th-i-cke-t	**GTR/GAR/GAR/**_HDO_
thief	th-ie-f	**GTR/GAR/**_HDO_
thigh	th-i-gh	**GTR/GRR/**_HDO_
thimble	th-i-m-ble	**GTR/GAR/**_HDO/HOO_
thin	th-i-n	**GTR/GAR/GDR**
thing	th-in-g	**GTR/GAR/GDR**
think	th-in-k	**GTR/GAR/GDR**
thinker	th-in-ker	**GTR/GAR/**_HDO_
thinking	th-in-ki-ng	**GTR/GAR/GAR/GDR**
thinner	th-i-nner	**GTR/GAR/**_HDO_
third	th-ir-d	_HTO/HAO/HOO_
thirdly	th-ir-d-ly	_HTO/HAO/HOO/_**GDR**
thirst	th-ir-st	_HTO/HAO/HOO_
thirsty	th-ir-sty	_HTO/HAO/_**GAR**
thirteen	th-ir-tee-n	_HTO/HAO/_**GRR/GDR**
thirty	th-ir-ty	_HTO/HAO/_**GAR**
this	th-i-s	**GTR/GAR/GDR**
thistle	th-i-stle	**GTR/GAR/**_HOO_

Word	Mouthables	Mouth Movements Notations
thorn	th-or-n	*HTO*/*HOO*/**GDR**
thorough	th-o-rough	**GTR/GAR**/*HDO*
those	tho-se	*HTO*/*HDO*
though	th-o-ugh	*HTO*/*HOO*/*HDO*
thought	th-ough-t	*HTO*/*HOO*/*HOO*
thousand	th-ou-sa-nd	**GTR/GAR/GAR/GDR**
thousandth	th-ou-sa-ndth	**GTR/GAR/GAR/GTR**
thrash	th-ra-sh	**GTR/GAR**/*HDO*
thrashing	th-ra-shi-ng	**GTR/GAR/GAR/GDR**
thread	th-rea-d	**GTR/GAR**/*HOO*
threat	th-rea-t	**GTR/GAR**/*HOO*
threaten	th-rea-ten	**GTR/GAR**/*HDO*
three	th-ree	**GTR/GRR**
thresh	th-re-sh	**GTR/GAR**/*HDO*
threw	th-rew	*HTO*/*HOO*
thrift	th-ri-ft	**GTR/GAR**/*HDO*
thrill	th-ri-ll	**GTR/GAR/GDR**
thrive	th-ri-ve	**GTR/GRR/GRR**
thriving	th-ri-ving	**GTR/GRR/GDR**
throat	th-roa-t	*HTO*/*HOO*/*HOO*
throb	th-ro-b	*HTO*/*HAO*/*HDO*
throe	th-roe	*HTO*/*HOO*
throes	th-roe-s	*HTO*/*HOO*/*HDO*
throne	th-ro-ne	*HTO*/*HOO*/**GDR**
through	th-rou-gh	*HTO*/*HOO*/*HDO*
throve	th-ro-ve	*HTO*/*HOO*/*HDO*
throw	th-ro-w	*HTO*/*HOO*/*HDO*
thrown	th-ro-w-n	*HTO*/*HOO*/*HDO*/**GDR**
thrush	th-ru-sh	*HTO*/**GAR**/*HDO*
thrust	th-ru-st	*HTO*/**GAR**/*HOO*
thud	th-u-d	**GTR/GAR**/*HOO*

Word	Mouthables	Mouth Movements Notations
thug	th-u-g	GTR/GAR/*HDO*
thuggery	th-u-gge-ry	GTR/GAR/*HDO*/*HDO*
thumb	th-u-mb	GTR/GAR/*HDO*
thump	th-u-mp	GTR/GAR/*HDO*
thunder	th-u-n-der	GTR/GAR/GDR/*HDO*
thunderous	th-u-n-der-ous	GTR/GAR/GDR/*HDO*/*HAO*
Thursday	Thur-s-day	*HTO*/*HDO*/*HAO*
thus	th-u-s	GTR/GAR/*HDO*
thyme	thy-me	GRR/*HDO*
thyroid	th-y-roi-d	GTR/GRR/*HAO*/*HOO*
tick	ti-ck	GAR/GRR
ticked	ti-cke-d	GAR/GDR/*HOO*
tick	tic-k	GAR/*HDO*
ticket	tic-ke-t	GAR/GAR/GDR
tickle	ti-ckle	GAR/*HOO*
ticklish	ti-ck-li-sh	GAR/*HDO*/GAR/*HDO*
tidal	ti-dal	GRR/*HDO*
tide	ti-de	GRR/*HDO*
tidy	ti-dy	GRR/GAR
tie	tie	GRR
tier	ti-er	GAR/*HDO*
tiger	ti-ger	GRR/*HDO*
tight	tigh-t	GRR/GRR
tighten	tigh-ten	GRR/GAR/GDR
tightness	tigh-t-ne-ss	GRR/*HOO*/GAR/GDR
tights	tigh-ts	GRR/*HDO*
tigress	ti-g-re-ss	GRR/*HDO*/GAR/*HDO*
tile	ti-le	GRR/GDR
till	til-l	GAR/*HDO*
tilt	ti-l-t	GAR/GDR/*HOO*
timber	ti-m-ber	GAR/*HDO*/*HDO*

Word	Mouthables	Mouth Movements Notations
time	ti-me	**GRR**/*HDO*
timeless	ti-me-le-ss	**GRR**/*HDO*/**GAR**/*HDO*
timely	ti-me-ly	**GRR**/*HDO*/**GDR**
timer	ti-mer	**GRR**/*HDO*
timid	ti-mi-d	**GAR**/**GAR**/*HOO*
timing	ti-mi-ng	**GRR**/**GAR**/**GDR**
tin	ti-n	**GAR**/**GDR**
tinge	ti-n-ge	**GAR**/**GDR**/*HDO*
tingle	ti-n-gle	**GAR**/**GDR**/*HOO*
tinker	ti-n-ker	**GAR**/**GDR**/*HDO*
tinkle	ti-n-kle	**GAR**/**GDR**/*HOO*
tinned	ti-nne-d	**GAR**/**GDR**/*HOO*
tint	ti-nt	**GAR**/**GDR**
tiny	ti-ny	**GRR**/**GAR**
tip	ti-p	**GAR**/**GRR**
tipped	ti-ppe-d	**GAR**/**GDR**/*HOO*
tip	ti-p	**GAR**/*HDO*
tipple	ti-pple	**GAR**/*HOO*
tipsy	ti-p-sy	**GAR**/**GDR**/**GAR**
tire	ti-re	**GRR**/**GDR**
tire	ti-re	**GRR**/*HDO*
tired	ti-re-d	**GRR**/**GDR**/*HOO*
tireless	ti-re-le-ss	**GRR**/**GDR**/**GAR**/**GDR**
tiresome	ti-re-so-me	**GRR**/**GDR**/*HAO*/*HDO*
tissue	ti-ssue	**GAR**/*HOO*
tit	ti-t	**GAR**/**GDR**
title	ti-tle	**GRR**/*HOO*
titled	ti-tle-d	**GRR**/*HOO*/*HOO*
tits	ti-ts	**GAR**/**GDR**
titter	ti-tter	**GAR**/*HDO*
toad	toa-d	*HOO*/*HOO*

Word	Mouthables	Mouth Movements Notations
toast	toa-st	*HOO/HOO*
toaster	toa-ster	*HOO/HDO*
tobacco	to-bac-co	*HAO/***GAR***/HOO*
tobacconist	to-bac-co-ni-st	*HAO/***GAR***/HAO/***GAR***/GDR*
today	to-day	*HOO/HAO*
toe	toe	*HOO*
toffee	tof-fee	*HAO/***GRR**
together	to-ge-th-er	*HOO/***GAR***/HTO/HDO*
togetherness	to-ge-ther-ne-ss	*HOO/***GAR***/HTO/***GAR***/GDR*
toil	toi-l	**GAR/GDR**
toilet	toi-le-t	**GAR/GAR/GDR**
toiletries	toi-le-tri-es	**GAR/GAR/GAR/GDR**
token	to-ke-n	*HOO/***GAR***/GDR*
told	to-ld	*HOO/HOO*
tolerable	to-ler-a-ble	*HAO/HAO/***GAR***/HOO*
tolerant	to-le-ra-nt	*HAO/***GAR***/GAR***/GDR*
toll	to-ll	*HOO/HDO*
toll	to-lle-d	*HOO/HOO/HOO*
tomato	to-ma-to	*HOO/***GAR***/HOO*
tomb	to-mb	*HOO/HDO*
tomboy	to-m-boy	*HAO/HDO/HAO*
tomorrow	to-mo-rro-w	*HOO/HAO/HOO/HDO*
ton	to-n	**GAR/GDR**
tone	to-ne	*HOO/***GDR**
tongs	to-ngs	*HAO/***GDR**
tongue	to-n-gue	**GAR/GDR***/HDO*
tonic	to-ni-c	*HAO/***GAR***/GDR*
tonight	to-nigh-t	*HOO/***GRR***/HOO*
tonnage	to-n-nage	**GAR/GDR***/HDO*
too	too	*HOO*
took	too-k	*HOO/HDO*

Word	Mouthables	Mouth Movements Notations
tool	too-l	*HOO*/HDO
tooth	too-th	*HOO*/**GTR**
toothless	too-th-le-ss	*HOO*/**GTR/GAR/GDR**
top	to-p	*HAO*/HDO
topaz	to-pa-z	*HOO*/**GAR/GDR**
topic	to-pi-c	*HAO*/**GAR/GDR**
topical	to-pi-cal	*HAO*/**GAR**/HDO
topless	to-p-le-ss	*HAO*/**GDR/GAR/GDR**
topple	to-pple	*HAO*/HOO
topsails	to-p-sai-ls	*HAO*/HDO/*HAO*/**GDR**
torch	tor-ch	*HOO*/HDO
tore	tore	*HOO*
toreador	to-re-a-dor	*HAO*/**GRR/GAR**/*HOO*
torment	tor-me-nt	*HOO*/**GAR/GRR**
torn	tor-n	*HOO*/**GRR**
torpedo	tor-pe-do	*HOO*/**GRR**/*HOO*
torpor	tor-por	*HOO*/HAO
torrent	tor-re-nt	*HAO*/**GAR/GDR**
torrid	tor-ri-d	*HAO*/**GAR/GRR**
torsion	tor-sion	*HOO*/HOO
tortoise	tor-toi-se	*HOO*/**GAR**/HDO
tortuous	tor-tu-ous	*HOO*/HOO/HAO
torture	tor-tu-re	*HOO*/HOO/HDO
Tory	To-ry	*HOO*/HDO
toss	to-ss	*HAO*/HDO
tot	to-t	*HAO*/HOO
total	to-tal	*HOO*/HDO
totalitarian	to-ta-li-tar-i-an	*HOO*/**GAR/GAR/GAR/GAR/GDR**
totter	tot-ter	*HAO*/HDO
touch	tou-ch	**GAR**/HDO
touched	tou-che-d	**GAR**/HDO/*HOO*

Word	Mouthables	Mouth Movements Notations
touching	tou-ching	**GAR/GDR**
touchy	tou-chy	**GAR/GAR**
tough	tou-gh	**GAR**/*HDO*
toughen	tou-gh-en	**GAR**/*HDO/HDO*
tour	tou-r	*HOO/HDO*
tourism	tou-ri-sm	*HOO/***GAR***/HDO*
tourist	tou-ri-st	*HOO/***GAR/GDR**
tournament	tour-na-me-nt	*HOO/***GAR/GAR/GDR**
tourniquet	tour-ni-quet	*HOO/***GAR**/*HAO*
tousle	tou-sle	**GAR**/*HOO*
tout	tou-t	**GAR**/*HOO*
tow	tow	*HOO*
toward	to-war-d	*HOO/HAO/HOO*
towards	to-war-ds	*HOO/HAO/HDO*
towed	towe-d	*HOO/HOO*
towel	tow-e-l	**GAR/GAR/GDR**
tower	tow-er	**GAR**/*HDO*
towering	tow-er-ing	**GAR**/*HAO*/**GDR**
town	tow-n	**GAR/GDR**
toxic	to-xi-c	*HAO*/**GAR/GDR**
toy	toy	**GAR**
trace	tra-ce	*HAO*/**GDR**
tracing	tra-ci-ng	*HAO*/**GAR/GDR**
track	tra-ck	**GAR**/*HDO*
tracker	tra-cker	**GAR**/*HDO*
tract	tra-ct	**GAR**/*HOO*
traction	tra-c-tion	**GAR/GDR**/*HOO*
tractor	tra-c-tor	**GAR/GDR**/*HDO*
trade	tra-de	*HAO/HDO*
trader	tra-der	*HAO/HDO*
trading	tra-ding	*HAO*/**GDR**

Word	Mouthables	Mouth Movements Notations
traditional	tra-di-tion-al	**GAR/GAR/**_HOO_/_HDO_
traffic	tra-ffi-c	**GAR/GAR/**_HDO_
trafficker	tra-ffi-cker	**GAR/GAR/**_HDO_
tragedy	tra-ge-dy	**GAR/GAR/GAR**
tragic	tra-gi-c	**GAR/GAR/GDR**
trail	trai-l	_HAO/HDO_
trailer	trai-ler	_HAO/HDO_
train	trai-n	_HAO/_**GDR**
trained	trai-ne-d	_HAO/_**GDR/**_HOO_
trainee	trai-nee	_HAO/_**GRR**
trainer	trai-ner	_HAO/HDO_
trait	trai-t	_HAO/HOO_
tram	tra-m	**GAR/**_HDO_
tramp	tra-mp	**GAR/**_HDO_
trample	tra-m-ple	**GAR/**_HOO/HOO_
tranquillity	tra-n-qui-lli-ty	**GAR/GDR/GAR/GAR/GAR**
tranquillizer	tra-n-qui-lli-zer	**GAR/GDR/GAR/GRR/**_HDO_
transaction	tra-n-sa-c-tion	**GAR/GDR/GAR/GDR/**_HOO_
transfer	tra-ns-fer	**GAR/GDR/**_HDO_
transform	tra-ns-for-m	**GAR/GDR/**_HOO/HDO_
transformer	tra-ns-for-mer	**GAR/GDR/**_HOO/HDO_
transfusion	tra-ns-fu-sion	**GAR/GDR/**_HOO/HOO_
transient	tra-n-si-e-nt	**GAR/GDR/GAR/GAR/GDR**
transit	tra-n-si-t	**GAR/GDR/GAR/**_HDO_
transitory	tra-n-si-to-ry	**GAR/GDR/GAR/**_HOO/HDO_
translatable	tra-ns-la-ta-ble	**GAR/GDR/**_HAO/_**GAR/**_HOO_
translate	tra-ns-la-te	**GAR/GDR/**_HAO/HDO_
translation	tra-ns-la-tion	**GAR/GDR/**_HAO/HOO_
transmission	tra-ns-mi-ssion	**GAR/GDR/GAR/**_HOO_
transmitter	tra-ns-mi-tter	**GAR/GDR/GAR/**_HDO_
transparent	tra-ns-pa-re-nt	**GAR/GDR/GAR/GAR/GDR**

Word	Mouthables	Mouth Movements Notations
transport	tra-ns-por-t	**GAR/GDR**/*HOO*/*HOO*
transverse	tra-ns-ver-se	**GAR/GDR**/*HOO*/*HDO*
trap	tra-p	**GAR/GDR**
trash	tra-sh	**GAR**/*HDO*
trashy	tra-shy	**GAR/GAR**
trauma	trau-ma	*HOO*/**GAR**
travel	tra-vel	**GAR**/*HDO*
traveler	tra-vel-ler	**GAR**/*HDO*/*HDO*
trawl	traw-l	*HOO*/*HDO*
trawler	traw-ler	*HOO*/*HDO*
tray	tray	*HAO*
treacherous	trea-che-rous	**GAR/GAR/GAR**
treachery	trea-che-ry	**GAR/GAR/GAR**
tread	trea-d	**GAR/GRR**
treadle	trea-dle	**GAR**/*HOO*
treason	trea-son	**GRR**/*HDO*
treasury	trea-su-ry	**GAR**/*HOO*/*HDO*
treat	trea-t	**GRR/GRR**
treatise	trea-ti-se	**GRR/GAR/GDR**
treatment	trea-t-men-t	**GRR/GRR/GAR**/*HOO*
treaty	trea-ty	**GRR/GAR**
treble	tre-ble	**GAR**/*HOO*
tree	tree	**GRR**
trek	tre-k	**GAR**/*HDO*
trellis	tre-lli-s	**GAR/GAR/GDR**
tremble	tre-m-ble	**GAR/GDR**/*HOO*
tremendous	tre-men-dous	**GAR/GAR**/*HAO*
tremour	tre-mour	**GAR/GAR**
trench	tre-n-ch	**GAR/GDR**/*HDO*
trend	tre-n-d	**GAR/GDR**/*HOO*
trendy	tre-n-dy	**GAR/GDR/GAR**

Word	Mouthables	Mouth Movements Notations
trespass	tre-s-pas-s	**GAR/GDR/***HAO/HDO*
trespasser	tre-s-pas-ser	**GAR/GDR/***HAO/HDO*
tressure	tre-ssu-re	**GAR/***HOO/HDO*
tressurer	tre-ssu-rer	**GAR/***HOO/HDO*
trestle	tre-stle	**GAR/***HOO*
triangle	tri-an-gle	**GRR/GAR/***HOO*
triangular	tri-an-gu-lar	**GRR/GAR/***HOO/HAO*
tribe	tri-be	**GRR/***HDO*
tribunal	tri-bu-nal	**GRR/***HOO/HDO*
tribute	tri-bu-te	**GAR/***HOO/HDO*
trice	tri-ce	**GRR/GDR**
trick	tri-ck	**GAR/***HDO*
trickery	tri-cke-ry	**GAR/GAR/GDR**
tricky	tri-cky	**GAR/GAR**
trident	tri-de-nt	**GRR/GAR/GDR**
tried	trie-d	**GRR/GRR**
trifle	tri-fle	**GRR/***HOO*
trifling	tri-fli-ng	**GRR/GAR/GDR**
trigger	tri-gger	**GAR/***HDO*
trillion	tri-lli-o-n	**GAR/GAR/GAR/GDR**
trim	tri-m	**GAR/***HDO*
trimming	tri-m-mi-ng	**GAR/GDR/GAR/GDR**
trinket	tri-n-ke-t	**GAR/GDR/GAR/GDR**
trip	tri-p	**GAR/***HDO*
triple	tri-ple	**GAR/***HOO*
triplicate	tri-pli-ca-te	**GAR/GAR/***HAO/HDO*
tripper	tri-pper	**GAR/***HDO*
triumph	tri-u-mph	**GRR/GAR/***HDO*
trivial	tri-vi-al	**GAR/GAR/GDR**
trod	tro-d	*HAO/HOO*
trodden	tro-d-den	*HAO/HDO/HDO*

Word	Mouthables	Mouth Movements Notations
trolley	tro-lley	*HAO*/**GAR**
troop	troo-p	*HOO*/*HDO*
trooper	troo-per	*HOO*/*HDO*
trophy	tro-phy	*HOO*/**GAR**
tropic	tro-pi-c	*HAO*/**GAR/GDR**
tropical	tro-pi-cal	*HAO*/**GAR**/*HDO*
trot	tro-t	*HAO*/*HOO*
trouble	tro-u-ble	**GAR/GAR**/*HOO*
troubled	tro-u-ble-d	**GAR/GAR**/*HOO*/*HOO*
troupe	trou-pe	*HOO*/*HDO*
trousers	trou-ser-s	*HAO*/*HDO*/*HDO*
trousseau	trou-ss-eau	*HOO*/*HDO*/*HOO*
trout	trou-t	**GAR**/*HOO*
trowel	tro-we-l	*HAO*/**GAR/GDR**
truant	tru-a-nt	*HOO*/**GAR/GDR**
truce	tru-ce	*HOO*/**GDR**
truck	tr-u-ck	**GRR/GAR**/*HDO*
trucker	tr-u-cker	**GRR/GAR**/*HDO*
truculent	tru-cu-le-nt	**GAR**/*HOO*/**GAR/GDR**
trudge	tru-dge	**GAR**/*HDO*
truffle	tru-ffle	**GAR**/*HOO*
truly	tru-ly	*HOO*/**GDR**
trump	tru-mp	**GAR**/*HDO*
trumpet	tru-m-pe-t	**GAR**/*HDO*/**GAR**/*HDO*
trumpeter	tru-m-pe-ter	**GAR**/*HDO*/**GAR**/*HDO*
truncheon	tru-n-che-o-n	**GAR/GDR/GAR**/*HAO*/*HDO*
trundle	tru-n-dle	**GAR/GDR**/*HOO*
trunk	tru-nk	**GAR/GDR**
trust	tru-st	**GAR**/*HOO*
trustee	tru-stee	**GAR/GRR**
trustful	tru-st-ful	**GAR**/*HOO*/*HOO*

Word	Mouthables	Mouth Movements Notations
truth	tru-th	*HOO*/**GTR**
truthful	tru-th-ful	*HOO*/**GTR**/*HOO*
try	try	**GRR**
trying	try-i-ng	**GRR/GAR/GDR**
tub	tu-b	**GAR**/*HDO*
tube	tu-be	*HOO*/*HDO*
tuber	tu-ber	*HOO*/*HDO*
tubing	tu-bi-ng	*HOO*/**GAR/GDR**
tubular	tu-bu-lar	*HOO*/*HOO*/*HAO*
tuck	tuc-k	**GAR**/*HDO*
Tuesday	Tue-s-day	*HOO*/*HDO*/*HAO*
tuft	tu-ft	**GAR**/*HDO*
tug	tu-g	**GAR**/*HDO*
tulip	tu-li-p	*HOO*/**GAR**/*HDO*
tumble	tu-m-ble	**GAR**/*HDO*/*HOO*
tumbler	tu-m-bler	**GAR**/*HDO*/*HDO*
tummy	tu-mmy	**GAR/GAR**
tumour	tu-mour	*HOO*/**GAR**
tumult	tu-mu-lt	*HOO*/**GAR/GDR**
tuna	tu-na	*HOO*/**GAR**
tune	tu-ne	*HOO*/**GDR**
tuner	tu-ner	*HOO*/*HDO*
Tunisian	Tu-ni-si-a-n	*HOO*/**GAR/GAR/GAR/GDR**
tunnel	tu-nnel	**GAR**/*HOO*
turban	tur-ba-n	*HAO*/**GAR/GDR**
turbid	tur-bi-d	*HAO*/**GAR/GDR**
turbojet	tur-bo-je-t	*HAO*/*HOO*/**GAR/GDR**
turbulent	tur-bu-le-nt	*HAO*/*HOO*/**GAR/GDR**
tureen	tu-ree-n	*HOO*/**GRR/GDR**
turf	tur-f	*HAO*/*HDO*
Turin	Tu-ri-n	*HOO*/**GAR/GDR**

Word	Mouthables	Mouth Movements Notations
Turk	Tur-k	*HAO*/HDO
turkey	tur-key	*HAO*/**GRR**
Turkey	Tur-key	*HAO*/*HDO*
Turkish	Tur-ki-sh	*HAO*/**GAR**/*HDO*
turmoil	tur-moi-l	*HAO*/**GAR**/*HDO*
turn	tur-n	*HAO*/*HDO*
turning	tur-ning	*HAO*/**GDR**
turnip	tur-ni-p	*HAO*/**GAR/GDR**
turnover	tur-no-ver	*HAO*/*HOO*/*HDO*
turpentine	tur-pe-n-ti-ne	*HAO*/**GAR/GDR/GRR/GDR**
turquoise	tur-quoi-se	*HAO*/**GAR**/*HDO*
turtle	tur-tle	*HAO*/*HOO*
tusk	tu-sk	**GAR**/*HDO*
tussle	tu-ssle	**GAR**/*HOO*
tussock	tu-sso-ck	**GAR**/*HAO*/*HDO*
tutor	tu-tor	*HOO*/*HDO*
tutorial	tu-to-ri-al	*HOO*/*HOO*/**GAR**/*HDO*
tuxedo	tu-xe-do	**GAR/GRR**/*HOO*
twaddle	twad-dle	**GAR**/*HOO*
twang	twa-ng	**GAR/GDR**
tweak	twea-k	**GRR**/*HDO*
twee	twee	**GRR**
tweed	twee-d	**GRR**/*HDO*
tweet	twee-t	**GRR**/*HOO*
tweezers	twee-zer-s	**GRR**/*HDO*/*HDO*
twelfth	twe-l-fth	**GAR/GDR/GTR**
twelve	twe-l-ve	**GAR/GDR**/*HDO*
twenty	twe-n-ty	**GAR/GDR/GAR**
twerp	twer-p	**GAR**/*HDO*
twice	twi-ce	**GRR/GDR**
twiddle	twi-ddle	**GAR**/*HOO*

Word	Mouthables	Mouth Movements Notations
twig	twi-g	**GAR/GDR**
twilight	twi-ligh-t	**GRR/GRR/***HOO*
twin	twi-n	**GAR/GDR**
twine	twi-ne	**GRR/GDR**
twinge	twi-n-ge	**GAR/GDR/***HDO*
twinkle	twi-n-kle	**GAR/GDR/***HOO*
twinkling	twi-n-kli-ng	**GAR/GDR/GAR/GDR**
twirl	twir-l	*HOO/HDO*
twist	twi-st	**GAR/GRR**
twisted	twi-sted	**GAR/GRR**
twister	twi-ster	**GAR/***HDO*
twit	twi-t	**GAR/***HOO*
twitch	twi-tch	**GAR/***HDO*
twitter	twi-tter	**GAR/***HDO*
two	two	*HOO*
twofold	two-fo-ld	*HOO/HOO/***GDR**
tycoon	ty-coo-n	**GRR/***HOO***/GDR**
tyke	ty-ke	**GRR/***HDO*
type	ty-pe	**GRR/***HDO*
typhoid	ty-phoi-d	**GRR/GAR/***HOO*
typhoon	ty-phoo-n	**GRR/***HOO***/GDR**
typhus	ty-phu-s	**GRR/GAR/***HDO*
typical	ty-pi-cal	**GAR/GAR/***HDO*
typist	ty-pi-st	**GRR/GAR/***HOO*
tyrannize	ty-ra-nni-ze	**GAR/GAR/GRR/***HDO*
tyranny	ty-ra-nny	**GAR/GAR/GAR**
tyrant	ty-ra-nt	**GRR/GAR/GDR**
tyre	ty-re	**GRR/***HDO*

Word	Mouthables	Mouth Movements Notations
U		
U	U	*HOO*
u	u	**GAR**
udder	u-dder	**GAR**/*HDO*
ugly	u-g-ly	**GAR**/*HDO*/**GAR**
ulcer	u-l-cer	**GAR/GDR**/*HDO*
ulterior	u-l-te-ri-or	**GAR/GDR/GRR/GAR**/*HDO*
ultimate	u-l-ti-ma-te	**GAR/GDR/GAR**/*HAO*/*HDO*
ultimatum	u-l-ti-ma-tu-m	**GAR/GDR/GAR**/*HAO*/**GAR/GDR**
umbrella	u-m-bre-lla	**GAR/GDR/GAR/GAR**
umpire	u-m-pi-re	**GAR/GDR/GRR**/*HDO*
umpteen	um-p-tee-n	**GAR/GDR/GRR/GDR**
umpteenth	um-p-tee-n-th	**GAR/GDR/GRR/GDR/GTR**
unabiased	u-n-bi-a-se-d	**GAR/GDR/GRR/GAR**/*HDO*/*HOO*
unable	u-na-ble	**GAR**/*HAO*/*HOO*
unaccountable	u-na-ccou-n-ta-ble	**GAR/GAR/GAR/GDR/GAR**/*HOO*
unaffected	u-na-ffe-c-ted	**GAR/GAR/GAR/GDR/GRR**
unanimous	u-na-ni-mou-s	*HOO*/**GAR/GAR/GAR**/*HDO*
unannounced	u-na-nnou-ce-d	**GAR/GAR/GAR/GDR**/*HOO*
unassuming	u-na-ssu-mi-ng	**GAR/GAR**/*HOO*/**GAR/GDR**
unattached	u-na-tta-che-d	**GAR/GAR/GAR**/*HOO*/*HOO*
unattended	u-na-tte-n-ded	**GAR/GAR/GAR/GDR/GRR**
unavailing	u-na-vai-ling	**GAR/GAR**/*HAO*/**GDR**
unawares	u-na-ware-s	**GAR/GAR/GAR**/*HDO*
unbecoming	u-n-be-co-mi-ng	**GAR/GDR/GRR**/*HAO*/**GAR/GDR**
unbelievable	u-n-be-lie-va-ble	**GAR/GDR/GRR/GAR/GAR**/*HOO*
unbiased	u-n-bi-a-se-d	**GAR/GDR/GRR/GAR**/*HOO*/*HOO*
unbind	u-n-bi-n-d	**GAR/GDR/GRR/GDR**/*HOO*
uncertain	u-n-cer-tai-n	**GAR/GDR**/*HAO*/*HAO*/**GDR**
uncle	u-n-cle	**GAR/GDR**/*HOO*

Word	Mouthables	Mouth Movements Notations
underestimate	u-n-der-e-sti-ma-te	**GAR/GDR**/*HAO*/**GAR/GAR**/*HAO/ HDO*
underground	u-n-der-grou-nd	**GAR/GDR**/*HAO*/**GAR/GDR**
understate	u-n-der-sta-te	**GAR/GDR**/*HAO/HAOHDO*
undies	u-n-die-s	**GAR/GDR/GAR/GDR**
undo	u-n-do	**GAR/GDR**/*HOO*
uniform	u-ni-for-m	*HOO*/**GAR**/*HOO/HDO*
unify	u-ni-fy	*HOO*/**GAR/GRR**
unilateral	u-ni-la-ter-al	*HOO*/**GAR**/*HAO/HDO*
unimpeachable	u-n-i-m-pea-cha-ble	**GAR/GDR/GAR/GDR/GRR/GAR**/*HOO*
uninhibited	u-n-i-n-hi-bi-ted	**GAR/GDR/GAR/GDR/GAR/GAR/GRR**
union	u-ni-o-n	*HOO*/**GAR**/*HAO/HDO*
unionist	u-ni-o-ni-st	*HOO*/**GAR**/*HAO*/**GAR/GDR**
unique	u-ni-que	*HOO*/**GAR**/*HDO*
unit	u-ni-t	*HOO*/**GAR**/*HOO*
unite	u-ni-te	*HOO*/**GRR**/*HDO*
united	u-ni-ted	*HOO*/**GRR/GRR**
unity	u-ni-ty	*HOO*/**GAR/GAR**
universal	u-ni-ver-sal	*HOO*/**GAR**/*HAO/HDO*
universe	u-ni-ver-se	*HOO*/**GAR**/*HAO/HDO*
university	u-ni-ver-si-ty	*HOO*/**GAR**/*HAO*/**GAR/GAR**
unmigated	u-n-mi-ti-ga-ted	**GAR/GDR/GAR/GAR**/*HAO*/**GRR**
unmistakable	u-n-mi-sta-ka-ble	**GAR/GDR/GAR**/*HAO*/**GAR**/*HOO*
unnerving	u-n-ner-ving	**GAR/GDR**/*HAO*/**GDR**
unparallel	u-n-pa-ra-lle-l	**GAR/GDR/GAR/GAR/GAR/GDR**
unprecedented	u-n-pre-ce-de-n-ted	**GAR/GDR/GAR/GRR/GAR/GDR/ GRR**
unpretentious	u-n-pre-te-n-ti-ous	**GAR/GDR/GRR/GAR/GDR**/*HDO/ HAO*
unprofitable	u-n-pro-fi-ta-ble	**GAR/GDR**/*HAO*/**GAR/GAR**/*HOO*

Word	Mouthables	Mouth Movements Notations
unreliable	u-n-re-li-a-ble	**GAR/GDR/GRR/GRR/GAR/***HOO*
unsatisfactory	u-n-sa-ti-s-fa-c-tory	**GAR/GDR/GAR/GAR/GDR/GAR/** **GDR/***HDO*
unsavoury	u-n-sa-vou-ry	**GAR/GDR/***HAO/HAO/***GDR**
unscheduled	u-n-sche-du-le-d	**GAR/GDR/GAR/***HOO/HOO/HOO*
unsolicited	u-n-so-li-ci-ted	**GAR/GDR/***HOO/***GAR/GAR/GRR**
unstable	u-n-sta-ble	**GAR/GDR/***HAO/HOO*
unsuccessful	u-n-su-cce-ss-ful	**GAR/GDR/GAR/GAR/***HDO/HOO*
until	u-n-ti-l	**GAR/GDR/GAR/GDR**
untrue	u-n-true	**GAR/GDR/***HOO*
untrustworthy	u-n-tru-st-wor-th-y	**GAR/GDR/GAR/***HOO/HAO/***GTR/** **GAR**
unusual	u-n-u-su-al	**GAR/GDR/***HOO/HOO/HDO*
unwelcome	u-n-we-l-co-me	**GAR/GDR/GAR/GDR/GAR/***HDO*
unwillingly	u-n-wi-lli-ng-ly	**GAR/GDR/GAR/GAR/GDR/GDR**
unwitting	u-n-wi-tti-ng	**GAR/GDR/GAR/GAR/GDR**
up	u-p	**GAR/***HDO*
update	u-p-da-te	**GAR/GDR/***HAO/HDO*
upfront	u-p-fro-nt	**GAR/***HDO/***GAR/GDR**
uphill	u-p-hi-ll	**GAR/GDR/GAR/GDR**
uphold	u-p-ho-ld	**GAR/GDR/***HOO/HDO*
uplift	u-p-li-ft	**GAR/GDR/GAR/***HDO*
upmarket	u-p-mar-ke-t	**GAR/GDR/***HAO/***GAR/GDR**
upon	u-po-n	**GAR/***HAO/HDO*
upper	u-pper	**GAR/***HDO*
upright	u-p-righ-t	**GAR/***HDO/***GRR/***HOO*
uprising	u-p-ri-si-ng	**GAR/***HDO/***GRR/GAR/GDR**
uproot	u-p-roo-t	**GAR/***HDO/HOO/HOO*
upset	u-p-se-t	**GAR/***HDO/***GAR/***HOO*
upshot	u-p-sho-t	**GAR/***HDO/HAO/HOO*
upstairs	u-p-stair-s	**GAR/***HDO/***GAR/***HDO*
upstream	u-p-strea-m	**GAR/***HDO/***GRR/***HDO*

Word	Mouthables	Mouth Movements Notations
upturn	u-p-tur-n	**GAR**/*HDO*/*HAO*/**GDR**
urban	ur-ban	*HAO*/*HDO*
urchin	ur-chi-n	*HAO*/**GAR**/**GDR**
urge	ur-ge	*HOO*/*HDO*
urgency	ur-ge-n-cy	*HOO*/**GAR**/**GDR**/**GAR**
urgent	ur-ge-nt	*HOO*/**GAR**/**GDR**
urinate	u-ri-na-te	*HOO*/**GAR**/*HAO*/*HDO*
urine	u-ri-ne	*HOO*/**GAR**/**GDR**
urn	ur-n	**GAR**/**GDR**
us	u-s	**GAR**/**GDR**
usable	u-sa-ble	*HOO*/**GAR**/*HOO*
usage	u-sage	*HOO*/*HDO*
use	u-se	*HOO*/*HDO*
useful	u-se-ful	*HOO*/*HDO*/*HOO*
usher	u-sher	**GAR**/*HDO*
usherette	u-sher-e-tte	**GAR**/*HDO*/**GAR**/*HDO*
usual	u-su-al	*HOO*/*HOO*/**GDR**
utensil	u-te-n-si-l	*HOO*/**GAR**/**GDR**/**GAR**/**GDR**
utility	u-ti-li-ty	*HOO*/**GAR**/**GAR**/**GAR**
utmost	u-t-mo-st	**GAR**/*HOO*/*HOO*/*HOO*
utter	u-tter	**GAR**/*HDO*
uxurious	u-xu-ri-ous	**GAR**/*HOO*/**GAR**/*HAO*

Word	Mouthables	Mouth Movements Notations
V		
V	V	**GRR**
vacancy	va-ca-n-cy	*HAO*/**GAR/GDR/GDR**
vacant	va-ca-nt	*HAO*/**GAR/GDR**
vacation	va-ca-tion	*HAO/HAO/HOO*
vaccinate	va-cci-na-te	**GAR/GAR**/*HAO/HDO*
vaccine	va-cci-ne	**GAR/GAR/GDR**
vacuous	va-cu-ous	**GAR**/*HOO/HAO*
vacuum	va-cuu-m	**GAR**/*HOO/HDO*
vagabond	va-ga-bo-nd	**GAR/GAR**/*HAO*/**GDR**
vagrancy	va-g-ra-n-cy	*HAO*/**GDR/GAR/GDR/GAR**
vagrant	va-g-ra-nt	*HAO*/**GDR/GAR/GDR**
vague	va-gue	*HAO/HDO*
vain	vai-n	*HAO*/**GDR**
valediction	va-le-di-c-tion	**GAR/GAR/GAR/GDR**/*HOO*
valentine	va-le-n-ti-ne	**GAR/GAR/GRR/GDR**
valiant	va-li-a-nt	**GAR/GAR/GAR/GDR**
valid	va-li-d	**GAR/GAR**/*HDO*
validation	va-li-da-tion	**GAR/GAR**/*HAO/HOO*
valley	va-lley	**GAR/GRR**
valuable	va-lu-a-ble	**GAR**/*HOO*/**GAR**/*HOO*
valuation	va-lu-a-tion	**GAR**/*HOO/HAO/HOO*
value	va-lue	**GAR**/*HOO*
valuer	va-lu-er	**GAR**/*HOO/HDO*
valve	va-l-ve	**GAR/GDR**/*HDO*
vamp	va-mp	**GAR**/*HDO*
vampire	va-m-pi-re	**GAR/GDR/GRR/GDR**
van	va-n	**GAR/GDR**
vandal	va-n-dal	**GAR/GDR**/*HOO*
vane	va-ne	*HAO*/**GDR**
vanguard	va-n-guar-d	**GAR/GDR/GAR**/*HOO*

Word	Mouthables	Mouth Movements Notations
vanilla	va-ni-lla	**GAR/GAR/GAR**
vanish	va-ni-sh	**GAR/GAR/**_HDO_
vanity	va-ni-ty	**GAR/GAR/GAR**
vantage	van-ta-ge	_HAO/HAO/HDO_
vaporize	va-po-ri-ze	_HAO/HOO/_**GRR/GDR**
vaporizer	va-po-ri-zer	_HAO/HOO/_**GRR/GDR**
vapour	va-pour	_HAO/HAO_
variable	va-ri-a-ble	**GAR/GAR/GAR/**_HOO_
variance	va-ri-a-nce	**GAR/GAR/GAR/GDR**
variant	va-ri-a-nt	**GAR/GAR/GAR/GDR**
variation	va-ri-a-tion	**GAR/GAR/**_HAO/HOO_
variegated	va-rie-ga-ted	**GAR/GAR/**_HAO/_**GRR**
varierty	va-ri-e-ty	**GAR/GRR/GAR/GAR**
varnish	var-ni-sh	_HAO/_**GAR/**_HDO_
vary	var-y	**GAR/**_HDO_
varying	var-y-i-ng	**GAR/GAR/GAR/GDR**
vase	vase	_HAO_
vaseline	va-se-li-ne	**GAR/GRR/GAR/GDR**
vast	vas-t	_HAO/HOO_
vat	va-t	**GAR/**_HOO_
vatican	va-ti-ca-n	**GAR/GAR/GAR/GDR**
vault	vau-lt	_HOO/_**GRR**
vault	vau-lt	_HOO/HOO_
vaulted	vau-l-ted	_HOO/_**GDR/GRR**
veal	vea-l	**GRR/GDR**
veer	ve-er	**GRR/**_HDO_
veg	ve-g	**GAR/**_HDO_
veg	ve-ge-ta-bles	**GAR/GAR/GAR/**_HOO_
vegetarian	ve-ge-tar-i-an	**GAR/GAR/GAR/GAR/GDR**
vegetation	ve-ge-ta-tion	**GAR/GAR/**_HAO/HOO_
vehemence	ve-he-me-nce	**GRR/GAR/GAR/GDR**

Word	Mouthables	Mouth Movements Notations
vehement	ve-he-me-nt	GRR/GAR/GAR/GDR
vehicle	ve-hi-cle	GRR/GAR/*HOO*
veil	vei-l	*HAO*/GDR
veiled	vei-le-d	*HAO*/*HOO*/*HOO*
vein	vei-n	*HAO*/GDR
velvet	ve-l-ve-t	GAR/GDR/GAR/*HOO*
venal	ve-nal	GRR/*HOO*
vendetta	ve-n-de-tta	GAR/GDR/GAR/GAR
vendor	ve-n-dor	GAR/GDR/*HOO*
venerate	ve-ner-a-te	GAR/*HAO*/*HAO*/*HDO*
venereal	ve-ne-re-al	GAR/GRR/GRR/GDR
Venetian	Ve-ne-ti-an	GAR/GRR/*HDO*/*HDO*
vengeance	ve-n-ge-a-nce	GAR/GDR/GAR/GAR/GDR
Venice	Ve-ni-ce	GAR/GAR/GDR
venison	ve-ni-son	GAR/GAR/*HDO*
venom	ve-no-m	GAR/GAR//*HDO*
venous	ve-no-us	GRR/GAR/*HAO*
vent	ve-nt	GAR/GDR
ventilate	ve-n-ti-la-te	GAR/GDR/GAR/*HAO*/*HDO*
ventilator	ve-n-ti-la-tor	GAR/GDR/GAR/*HAO*/*HOO*
ventriloquist	ve-n-tri-lo-qui-st	GAR/GDR/GAR/*HOO*/GAR/*HOO*
venture	ve-n-tu-re	GAR/GDR/*HOO*/*HDO*
venue	ve-n-ue	GAR/GDR/*HOO*
verandah	ver-a-n-dah	*HAO*/GAR/GDR/GAR
verb	ver-b	*HOO*/*HDO*
verbal	ver-bal	*HOO*/*HOO*
verbalize	ver-bal-i-ze	*HOO*/*HDO*/GRR/GDR
verbose	ver-bo-se	*HAO*/*HOO*/*HDO*
verdict	ver-di-ct	*HAO*/GAR/GDR
verdigris	ver-di-gri-s	*HAO*/GAR/GAR/GDR
verge	ver-ge	*HAO*/*HDO*

Word	Mouthables	Mouth Movements Notations
verger	ver-ger	*HOO/HDO*
verging	ver-gi-ng	*HAO*/**GAR/GDR**
verify	ve-ri-fy	**GAR/GAR/GRR**
vermin	ver-mi-n	*HAO*/**GAR/GDR**
verrification	ve-ri-fi-ca-tion	**GAR/GAR/GAR**/*HAO/HOO*
versatile	ver-sa-ti-le	*HOO*/**GAR/GRR/GDR**
verse	ver-se	*HAO/HDO*
versed	ver-se-d	*HAO/HOO/HOO*
version	ver-sion	*HOO/HOO*
versus	ver-su-s	*HAO*/**GAR/GDR**
vertebrate	ver-te-bra-te	*HAO*/**GAR**/*HAO/HDO*
vertical	ver-ti-cal	*HAO*/**GAR**/*HDO*
very	ve-ry	**GAR**/*HDO*
vessel	ve-ssel	**GAR**/*HDO*
vest	ve-st	**GAR**/*HOO*
vestige	ve-sti-ge	**GAR/GAR**/*HDO*
vestment	ve-st-me-nt	**GAR**/*HOO*/**GAR/GDR**
vestry	ve-st-ry	**GAR**/*HOO/HDO*
vet	ve-t	**GAR**/*HOO*
veteran	ve-te-ra-n	**GAR/GAR/GAR/GDR**
veterinary	ve-te-ri-na-ry	**GAR/GAR/GAR/GAR**/*HDO*
vex	ve-x	**GAR/GRR**
vexed	ve-xe-d	**GAR/GDR**/*HOO*
via	vi-a	**GRR/GAR**
viable	vi-a-ble	**GRR/GAR**/*HOO*
viaduct	vi-a-du-ct	**GRR/GAR/GAR**/*HOO*
vicar	vi-car	**GAR**/*HAO*
vicarage	vi-ca-rage	**GAR/GAR**/*HDO*
viscount	vi-scou-nt	**GRR/GAR/GDR**
viscous	vi-scou-s	**GAR/GAR**/*HDO*
vow	vow	*HAO*
vowed	vowe-d	*HAO/HOO*

Word	Mouthables	Mouth Movements Notations
W		
W	W	*HOO/HOO*
wad	wa-d	*HOO/HDO*
wadding	wa-dding	*HOO*/**GDR**
waddle	wa-ddle	*HOO/HOO*
wade	wa-de	*HAO/HDO*
waffle	waf-fle	*HAO/HOO*
wag	wa-g	**GAR**/*HDO*
wage	wa-ge	*HAO/HDO*
wagon	wa-go-n	**GAR**/*HAO/HDO*
wail	wai-l	*HAO*/**GDR**
waist	wai-st	*HAO/HOO*
waisted	wai-sted	*HAO*/**GRR**
wait	wai-t	*HAO*/**GRR**
waited	wai-ted	*HAO*/**GRR**
waiter	wai-ter	*HAO/HDO*
waitress	wai-tre-ss	*HAO*/**GAR**/*HDO*
wake	wa-ke	*HAO*/**GRR**
waken	wa-ke-n	*HAO*/**GAR/GDR**
Wales	Wa-les	*HAO/HDO*
walk	wal-k	*HOO/HDO*
wall	wal-l	*HOO/HDO*
wallet	wal-le-t	*HAO*/**GAR**/*HOO*
wallop	wal-lo-p	*HAO/HAO/HDO*
wallow	wal-lo-w	*HAO/HOO/IIDO*
walnut	wal-nu-t	*HOO*/**GAR**/*HOO*
walrus	wal-ru-s	*HOO*/**GAR**/*HDO*
waltz	wal-tz	*HOO*/**GDR**
wand	wan-d	*IIAO/HDO*
wander	wan-der	*HAO/HDO*
Wandered	Wan-dere-d	*HAO/HDO/HOO*

Word	Mouthables	Mouth Movements Notations
wanderer	wa-n-der-er	*HAO*/**GDR**/*HDO*/*HDO*
wane	wa-ne	*HAO*/**GDR**
wangle	wan-gle	**GAR**/*HOO*
want	wan-t	*HAO*/*HOO*
wanted	wan-ted	*HAO*/**GRR**
war	war	*HOO*
warble	war-ble	*HAO*/*HOO*
ward	war-d	*HAO*/*HOO*
warden	war-den	*HOO*/*HDO*
warder	war-der	*HOO*/*HDO*
wardrobe	war-dro-be	*HAO*/*HOO*/*HDO*
ware	ware	**GAR**
warehouse	ware-hou-se	**GAR**/*HAO*/*HDO*
warfare	war-fa-re	*HOO*/*HAO*/*HDO*
warm	war-m	*HOO*/*HDO*
warmonger	war-mon-ger	*HOO*/**GAR**/*HDO*
warmth	war-m-th	*HOO*/*HDO*/**GTR**
warn	war-n	*HOO*/**GRR**
warning	war-ni-ng	*HOO*/**GAR**/**GDR**
warp	war-p	*HAO*/*HDO*
warrant	wa-rra-nt	**GAR**/**GAR**/**GDR**
warrior	war-ri-or	**GAR**/**GAR**/*HOO*
wary	war-y	**GAR**/**GAR**
wash	wa-sh	*HAO*/*HDO*
washable	wa-sha-ble	*HAO*/**GAR**/*HOO*
washer	wa-sher	*HAO*/*HDO*
washing	wa-shi-ng	*HAO*/**GAR**/**GDR**
wasp	wa-sp	*HAO*/**GDR**
wastage	wa-stage	*HAO*/*HDO*
waste	wa-ste	*HAO*/**GRR**
wasteful	wa-ste-ful	*HAO*/**GRR**/*HOO*
watch	wat-ch	*HAO*/*HDO*

Word	Mouthables	Mouth Movements Notations
watchful	wat-ch-ful	*HAO/HDO/HOO*
water	wa-ter	*HOO/HDO*
waterfall	wa-ter-fall	*HOO/HDO/HOO*
watery	wa-te-ry	*HOO/HAO/***GDR**
wave	wa-ve	*HAO/HDO*
waver	wa-ver	*HAO/HDO*
wax	wa-x	**GAR/GRR**
way	way	*HAO*
we	we	**GRR**
weak	wea-k	**GRR/GDR**
weaken	wea-ke-n	**GRR/GAR/GDR**
wealth	wea-lth	**GAR/GTR**
wealthy	wea-l-th-y	**GAR/GDR/GTR/GAR**
wean	wea-n	**GRR/GDR**
weapon	wea-po-n	**GAR/***HAO/HDO*
wear	wear	**GAR**
wearable	wea-ra-ble	**GAR/GAR/***HOO*
weary	wea-ry	**GRR/GDR**
weather	wea-ther	**GAR/***HDO*
weave	wea-ve	**GRR/GRR**
web	we-b	**GAR/***HDO*
webbed	we-bbe-d	**GAR/***HOO/HOO*
wedding	we-ddi-ng	**GAR/GAR/GDR**
wedge	we-(d)ge	**GAR/***HDO*
Wednesday	We(dne)-s-day	**GAR/GDR/***HAO*
weed	wee-d	**GRR/GDR**
week	wee-k	**GRR/***HDO*
weekly	wee-kly	**GRR/GDR**
weep	wee-p	**GRR/GRR**
weigh	weigh	*HAO*
weight	weigh-t	*HAO/HOO*

Word	Mouthables	Mouth Movements Notations
welcome	we-l-co-me	**GAR/GDR/***HAO/HDO*
weld	we-ld	**GRR/GRR**
welfare	we-l-fare	**GAR/GDR/***HAO*
well	wel-l	**GAR/GDR**
well	wel-l	*HAO/HDO*
wellingtons	we-lli-ng-to-ns	**GAR/GAR/GDR/***HAO/HDO*
Welsh	We-l-sh	**GAR/GDR/***HDO*
Welshman	We-l-sh-ma-n	**GAR/GDR/***HDO***/GAR/GDR**
went	we-nt	**GAR/GRR**
wept	we-pt	**GAR/GRR**
west	we-st	**GAR/***HDO*
westerly	we-ster-ly	**GAR/***HAO***/GDR**
western	we-ster-n	**GAR/***HAO***/GDR**
westerner	we-ster-ner	**GAR/***HAO***/GDR**
westwards	we-st-war-ds	**GAR/***HOO/HAO/HDO*
wet	we-t	**GAR/***HOO*
whack	wha-ck	**GAR/***HDO*
whacked	wha-cke-d	**GAR/***HOO/HOO*
whale	wha-le	*HAO/HDO*
wharf	whar-f	*HAO/HDO*
what	wha-t	*HAO/HOO*
whatever	wha-t-e-ver	*HAO/HOO/***GAR/***HDO*
wheat	whea-t	**GRR/***HOO*
wheedle	whee-dle	**GRR/***HOO*
wheel	whee-l	**GRR/GDR**
wheeze	whee-ze	**GRR/GDR**
when	whe-n	**GAR/GDR**
whenever	whe-n-e-ver	**GAR/GDR/GAR/***HDO*
where	whe-re	*HAO/HDO*
wherever	wher-e-ver	*HAO/***GAR/***HDO*
whether	whe-ther	**GAR/GDR**

Word	Mouthables	Mouth Movements Notations
which	whi-ch	**GAR**/*HDO*
whichever	whi-ch-e-ver	**GAR**/*HDO*/**GAR**/*HDO*
whiff	whi-ff	**GAR**/*HDO*
while	whi-le	**GRR/GDR**
whim	whi-m	**GAR**/*HDO*
whimsical	whi-m-si-cal	**GAR**/*HDO*/**GAR**/*HDO*
whine	whi-ne	**GRR/GDR**
whinny	whi-nny	**GAR/GAR**
whip	whi-p	**GAR**/*HDO*
whirl	whir-l	*HOO*/*HDO*
whirr	whir-r	*HOO*/*HDO*
whisk	whi-sk	**GAR**/*HDO*
whiskers	whi-s-ker-s	**GAR/GDR**/*HOO*/*HDO*
whisky	whi-s-ky	**GAR/GDR/GAR**
whisper	whi-s-per	**GAR/GDR**/*HDO*
whistle	whi-stle	**GAR**/*HOO*
white	whi-te	**GRR**/*HDO*
whiz	whi-z	**GAR/GDR**
who	who	*HOO*
whoever	who-e-ver	*HOO*/**GAR**/*HDO*
whole	who-le	*HOO*/*HDO*
whom	who-m	*HOO*/*HDO*
whore	who-re	*HOO*/*HDO*
whose	who-se	*HOO*/*HDO*
why	why	**GRR**
wicked	wi-cked	**GAR/GRR**
wicker	wi-cker	**GAR**/*HDO*
wide	wi-de	**GRR/GDR**
widen	wi-den	**GRR**/*HDO*
widow	wi-do-w	**GAR**/*HOO*/*HDO*
widower	wi-do-wer	**GRR**/*HOO*/*HDO*

Word	Mouthables	Mouth Movements Notations
width	wi-dth	**GAR/GTR**
wife	wi-fe	**GRR**/*HDO*
wiful	wi-l-ful	**GAR/GDR**/*HOO*
wig	wi-g	**GAR**/*HDO*
wild	wi-ld	**GRR/GDR**
wilderness	wi-l-der-ne-ss	**GAR/GDR**/*HDO*/**GAR***HDO*
will	wi-ll	**GAR/GDR**
willies	wi-llie-s	**GAR/GAR/GDR**
willing	wi-lli-ng	**GAR/GAR/GDR**
willingly	wi-lli-ng-ly	**GAR/GAR/GDR/GDR**
willow	wi-llo-w	**GAR**/*HOO*/*HDO*
win	wi-n	**GAR/GRR**
winch	wi-n-ch	**GAR/GDR**/*HDO*
wind	wi-nd	**GAR/GRR**
winded	wi-n-ded	**GAR/GDR/GRR**
wind	wi-n-d	**GRR/GDR**/*HOO*
windfall	wi-n-d-fall	**GAR/GDR**/*HDO*/*HDO*
windy	wi-n-dy	**GAR/GDR/GAR**
wine	wi-ne	**GRR/GDR**
wing	win-g	**GAR/GDR**
wink	win-k	**GAR/GDR**
winning	wi-n-ning	**GAR/GDR/GDR**
winter	wi-n-ter	**GAR/GDR**/*HDO*
wintry	wi-n-try	**GAR/GDR**/*HDO*
wipe	wi-pe	**GRR**/*HDO*
wire	wi-re	**GRR**/*HDO*
wiring	wi-ring	**GRR/GDR**
wiry	wi-ry	**GRR/GAR**
wisdom	wi-s-do-m	**GAR/GDR**/*HAO*/*HDO*
wise	wi-se	**GRR**/*HDO*
wish	wi-sh	**GAR**/*HDO*

Word	Mouthables	Mouth Movements Notations
wishful	wi-sh-ful	GAR/*HOO*/*HDO*
wisp	wi-sp	GAR/*HDO*
wisteria	wi-ste-ri-a	GAR/GRR/GAR/GAR
wistful	wi-st-ful	GAR/*HOO*/*HOO*
wit	wi-t	GAR/*HDO*
witch	wi-tch	GAR/*HDO*
with	wi-th	GAR/GTR
withdraw	wi-th-dra-w	GAR/GTR/*HOO*/*HDO*
withdrawal	wi-th-dra-wal	GAR/GTR/*HOO*/*HDO*
wither	wi-th-er	GAR/GTR/*HDO*
withering	wi-th-er-i-ng	GAR/GTR/*HDO*/GAR/GDR
withhold	wi-th-ho-ld	GAR/GTR/*HOO*/*HDO*
without	wi-th-ou-t	GAR/GTR/GAR/*HOO*
withstand	wi-th-sta-nd	GAR/GTR/GAR/GDR
witness	wi-t-ne-ss	GAR/*HOO*/GAR/*HDO*
wits	wi-ts	GAR/*HDO*
witticism	wi-tti-ci-sm	GAR/GAR/GAR/*HDO*
witty	wi-tty	GAR/GAR
wives	wi-ves	GRR/*HDO*
wizard	wi-zar-d	GAR/*HAO*/*HOO*
wizened	wi-ze-ne-d	GAR/GAR/GDR/*HOO*
wobble	wob-ble	*HAO*/*HOO*
woe	woe	*HOO*
woke	wo-ke	*HOO*/*HDO*
woken	wo ken	*HOO*/*HDO*
wolf	wo-l-f	*HOO*/*HDO*/*HDO*
woman	wo-ma-n	*HOO*/GAR/GDR
womanize	wo-ma-ni-ze	*HOO*/GAR/GRR/GDR
womanly	wo-ma-n-ly	*HOO*/GAR/GDR/GDR
womb	wo-mb	*HOO*/*HDO*
women	wo-me-n	*HOO*/GAR/GDR

Word	Mouthables	Mouth Movements Notations
won	wo-n	*HAO*/**GDR**
wonder	wo-n-der	**GAR/GDR**/*HDO*
wondered	wo-n-dere-d	**GAR/GDR**/*HDO/HOO*
wonderful	wo-n-der-ful	**GAR/GDR**/*HDO/HOO*
wonky	won-ky	*HAO*/**GAR**
wont	wo-nt	*HOO*/**GDR**
woo	woo	*HOO*
wood	woo-d	*HOO/HOO*
woodcock	woo-d-coc-k	*HOO/HDO/HAO/HDO*
wooded	woo-ded	*HOO*/**GRR**
wooden	woo-den	*HOO/HDO*
wool	woo-l	*HOO*/**GDR**
woollen	woo-lle-n	*HOO*/**GAR/GDR**
woolly	woo-lly	*HOO*/**GAR**
word	wor-d	**GAR**/*HOO*
wordy	wor-dy	**GAR/GAR**
wore	wo-re	*HOO/HDO*
work	wor-k	**GAR**/*HDO*
workable	wor-ka-ble	**GAR/GAR**/*HOO*
workaholic	wor-ka-ho-li-c	**GAR/GAR**/*HAO*/**GAR/GDR**
worker	wor-ker	**GAR**/*HDO*
works	wor-ks	**GAR**/*HDO*
world	wor-ld	*HOO/HDO*
worldly	wor-ld-ly	*HOO/HDO*/**GDR**
worldwide	wor-ld-wi-de	*HOO/HDO*/**GRR**/*HDO*
worm	wor-m	*HAO/HDO*
worn	worn	*HOO*
worry	wor-ry	**GAR/GAR**
worse	wor-se	**GAR**/*HDO*
worsen	wor-sen	**GAR**/*HDO*
worship	wor-shi-p	*HOO*/**GAR/GDR**

Word	Mouthables	Mouth Movements Notations
worst	wor-st	**GAR**/*HOO*
worth	wor-th	*HAO/HTO*
worthwhile	wor-th-whi-le	*HAO/HTO*/**GRR/GDR**
worthy	wor-thy	*HAO*/**GTR**
would	would	*HOO*
wound	wou-nd	*HAO*/**GDR**
wound	wou-n-ded	*HOO*/**GDR/GRR**
wove	wo-ve	*HOO/HDO*
woven	wo-ve-n	*HOO*/**GAR/GDR**
wrangle	wra-n-gle	**GAR/GDR**/*HOO*
wrap	wra-p	**GAR**/*HDO*
wrapper	wra-pper	**GAR**/*HDO*
wrapping	wra-ppi-ng	**GAR/GAR/GDR**
wreath	wrea-th	**GRR/GTR**
wreck	wre-ck	**GAR**/*HDO*
wreckage	wre-c-kage	**GAR/GDR**/*HDO*
wrecker	wre-cker	**GAR**/*HDO*
wrench	wre-n-ch	**GAR/GDR**/*HDO*
wrestle	wre-stle	**GAR**/*HOO*
wrestling	wre-st-ling	**GAR**/*HOO*/**GDR**
wretched	wre-tched	**GAR/GRR**
wriggle	wri-ggle	**GAR**/*HOO*
wring	wri-ng	**GAR/GRR**
wrinkle	wri-n-kle	**GAR/GDR**/*HOO*
wrist	wri-st	**GAR**/*HOO*
writ	wri-t	**GAR**/*HOO*
write	wri-te	**GRR/GRR**
writer	wri-ter	**GRR**/*HDO*
writhe	wri-the	**GRR/GTR**
writing	wri-ting	**GRR/GDR**
written	wri-tten	**GAR**/*HDO*

Word	Mouthables	Mouth Movements Notations
wrong	wron-g	*HAO/HDO*
wrongful	wron-g-ful	*HAO/HDO/HOO*
wrongly	wron-g-ly	*HAO/HDO/***GDR**
wrote	wro-te	*HOO/HOO*
wrought	wrough-t	*HOO/HOO*
wrung	wrun-g	**GAR/***HOO*
wry	wr-y	**GRR/GRR**

Word	Mouthables	Mouth Movements Notations
X		
X	X	**GAR/GDR**
xenophobe	xe-no-pho-be	**GAR**/*HOO*/*HOO*/*HDO*
xenophobic	xe-no-pho-bi-c	**GAR**/*HOO*/*HOO*/**GAR/GDR**
Xmas	X-ma-s	**GAR/GDR/GAR/GDR**
Xray	X-ray	**GAR/GDR**/*HAO*
xylophone	xy-lo-pho-ne	**GRR**/*HOO*/*HOO*/**GDR**

Word	Mouthables	Mouth Movements Notations
Y		
Y	Y	**GRR**
yacht	yach-t	*HAO/HOO*
yachting	yach-ti-ng	*HAO*/**GAR/GDR**
yank	ya-nk	**GAR/GRR**
Yank	Yan-k	**GAR**/*HDO*
yanked	ya-nke-d	**GAR/GDR**/*HOO*
Yankee	Yan-kee	**GAR/GRR**
yap	ya-p	**GAR**/*HDO*
yard	yar-d	*HAO/HOO*
yarn	yar-n	*HAO*/**GDR**
yawn	yaw-n	*HOO*/**GDR**
year	ye-ar	**GRR**/*HAO*
yearly	ye-ar-ly	**GRR**/*HDO*/**GDR**
yearn	year-n	**GAR/GDR**
yeast	yea-st	**GRR**/*HOO*
yell	ye-ll	**GAR/GRR**
yellow	ye-llo-w	**GAR**/*HOO/HDO*
yelp	ye-lp	**GAR/GDR**
yen	ye-n	**GAR/GDR**
yeomanry	yeo-ma-n-ry	*HOO*/**GAR/GDR/GDR**
yes	ye-s	**GAR/GDR**
yesterday	ye-s-ter-day	**GAR/GDR**/*HDO/HAO*
yet	ye-t	**GAR**/*HOO*
yew	yew	*HDO*
yield	yie-l-d	**GAR/GDR**/*HOO*
yielding	yie-l-ding	**GAR/GDR/GDR**
yob	yo-b	*HAO/HDO*
yoke	yo-ke	*HOO/HDO*
yonks	yon-ks	*HAO/HDO*
you	you	*HOO*

Word	Mouthables	Mouth Movements Notations
young	youn-g	**GAR**/*HDO*
youngster	youn-g-ster	**GAR**/*HDO*/*HDO*
your	yo-ur	*HOO*/*HDO*
yours	yo-ur-s	*HOO*/*HOO*/*HDO*
yourself	yo-ur-se-l-f	*HOO*/*HDO*/**GAR**/**GDR**/*HDO*
yourselves	yo-ur-se-l-ves	*HOO*/*HDO*/**GAR**/**GDR**/*HDO*
youth	you-th	*HOO*/**GTR**
yowl	yow-l	**GAR/GRR**
yowl	yow-l	**GAR/GDR**
yowled	yow-le-d	**GAR/GDR**/*HOO*
Yugoslav	Yu-go-sla-v	*HOO*/*HOO*/**GAR**/*HDO*
yuky	yu-ky	**GAR/GAR**
yummy	yu-mmy	**GAR/GAR**

Word	Mouthables	Mouth Movements Notations
Z		
z	z	**GAR/GRR**
zany	za-ny	*HAO*/**GAR**
zap	za-p	**GAR/GDR**
zeal	zea-l	**GRR/GDR**
zealot	zea-lo-t	**GAR**/*HAO*/*HDO*
zealous	zea-lou-s	**GAR/GAR**/*HDO*
zebra	ze-bra	**GRR/GAR**
zenith	ze-ni-th	**GAR/GAR/GTR**
zephyr	ze-ph-yr	**GAR**/*HDO*/*HAO*
zero	ze-ro	**GRR**/*HOO*
zest	ze-st	**GAR/GDR**
zilch	zi-l-ch	**GAR/GDR**/*HDO*
zing	zi-ng	**GAR/GDR**
Zionist	Zi-o-ni-st	**GRR**/*HAO*/**GAR/GDR**
zip	zi-p	**GAR/GDR**
zippy	zi-p-py	**GRR/GDR/GAR**
zircon	zir-co-n	**GAR**/*HAO*/*HDO*
zodiac	zo-di-a-c	*HOO*/**GAR/GAR/GDR**
zologist	zo-o-lo-gi-st	*HOO/HAO/HOO*/**GAR/GDR**
zombie	zo-m-bie	*HAO/HDO*/**GAR**
zone	zo-ne	*HOO*/**GDR**
zoo	zoo	*HOO*
zoom	zoo-m	*HOO/HDO*
zucchini	zu-cchi-ni	*HOO*/**GAR/GAR**
Zulu	Zu-lu	*HOO/HOO*

Further Notes and Comments

Note 1

The English alphabet must be one of the greatest mysteries of the English language in that it seems to have little obvious connection to the English language and is very confusing, as it does not seem, in many cases, to be pronounced as we are taught to say it at school.

This is not helped by the fact that such important information is not taught by parents or via parents' voices, but often by an English teacher whose voice patterns have no comparison to our parents, and therefore the connection with language is often missed. We recommend and encourage parents to teach their children the alphabet so that their children can make the connection with the spoken language more quickly.

Note 2

Breathing

Though there is a debate about whether we should breathe through the nose or the mouth, humans and primates should and can do both, particularly when they are communicating through the mouth, which is very natural. Doing one should not exclude the other. When dogs howl or woof and other primates make communication noises, they are doing exactly this.

Breathing through the mouth while talking is not to be confused with the problems associated with mouth breathing at other times, such as when thinking, relaxing, or sleeping. However, there is no doubt that the intake of breath through the mouth when speaking is very important for correct pronunciation, as is breathing out almost as quickly. In this particular case, you are not trying to absorb oxygen, but you are using the mouth as a musical instrument. It is not always practical to do this quickly and effectively through the nose, and it would be very unwise to do so in some situations. Breathing through the nose is often done before we dive into a pool. This is quite normal because when swimming underwater, we need to retain air, but when we are speaking in English, the opposite is true.

Note 3

People to thank and remember:

I owe my main thanks to my parents, whose system of speaking I absorbed effortlessly. It was always very clear, easy to understand, and very neutral and unaffected English because they predominantly used vertical mouth movements. Why they spoke in the way they did, I am not sure, but my grandfather was a textile industrialist and a fairly well-known choral singer. I never met him, but he may have helped my father. My grandmother, who I did meet, also spoke very clearly. My mother, who came from Lancashire, was interested in acting, but as far as I am aware, never had any elocution lessons. It is surprising that all these close parents and relatives spoke in a similar way. I believe that the rhythm and the consistent regulated breathing of parents, particularly the mother, have an important part in transferring language to children, especially in terms of regulating mouth movements.

Bearing in mind that most of my early life was spent in the heart of Yorkshire, not an area known for speaking the very best of English, though certainly far from the worst, it is amazing that I speak comprehensible English. With two parents from different sides of the Pennines, there is no question that it is completely by luck and good fortune and not due to my skill or efforts!

Future Educational Publications

The Lost Secret of Speaking Perfect English—Part One will be a much more detailed book that will go into teaching methods, exercises, and concepts related to *The Moving Mouth Dictionary*.

The Lost Secret of Speaking Perfect English—Part Two will explore the moving mouth patterns that have come out of the dictionary, which will enable the reader to search words of similar patterns. It will explain the meaning of the patterns, why they occur, why they are helpful, and the possible connections with our animal and emotional past.

Other dictionaries are planned that will be specifically aimed at professional people who require specific terminology, such as pilots, doctors, and commercial and business people.

The end of the beginning is often only the beginning of the end!

The Moving Mouth Dictionary is the personal copyright of Peter Francis Bulmer produced in association with the Breathing English Organisation www.breathingenglish.org, started on 11/07/2007 and most recently updated on 11/12/2013.

CPSIA information can be obtained at www.ICGtesting.com
Printed in the USA
BVOW05*1025140714

359105BV00016B/807/P